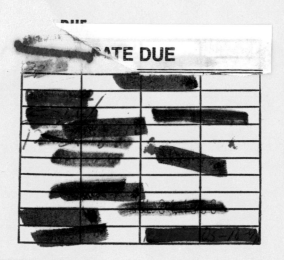

LONGMAN LINGUISTICS LIBRARY
Title no 21

TEXT AND CONTEXT
EXPLORATIONS IN THE SEMANTICS AND PRAGMATICS
OF DISCOURSE

LONGMAN LINGUISTICS LIBRARY

General Editors
R. H. Robins, University of London
G. N. Leech, University of Lancaster

Text and Context

Explorations in the semantics and pragmatics of discourse

Teun A. van Dijk
University of Amsterdam

LONGMAN
LONDON AND NEW YORK

LONGMAN GROUP LIMITED LONDON

Associated companies, branches and representatives throughout the world

Published in the United States of America by Longman Inc, New York
© Longman Group Ltd 1977

First published 1977
ISBN 0 582 55085 8

Library of Congress Cataloging in Publication Data
Dijk, T. A. van.
Text and context

(Longman linguistics library)
Bibliography: p.
Includes index
1. Discourse analysis. 2. Semantics (Philosophy)
3. Pragmatics. I. Title
P302.D5   415   76-44866
ISBN 0-582-55085-8

Printed in Great Britain by Whitstable Litho Ltd., Whitstable, Kent *for* Doro

Preface

One of the major recent developments in linguistics and its neighbouring disciplines is the increasing attention being paid to the relevance of various kinds of CONTEXT. Renewed attempts are made in sociolinguistics and the social sciences to define the systematic relationships between social and cultural contexts and the structures and functions of language. In particular, philosophy of language has shown the linguist how pragmatic context constitutes the conditions determining the appropriateness of natural language utterances taken as speech acts.

Similarly, more emphasis is being given to the fact that utterances of natural language may be theoretically reconstructed as sequences of sentences, in which morpho-phonological, syntactic and semantic properties of a sentence are accounted for in relation to those of other sentences of the sequence. Besides this recognition of its role of 'verbal context', *eg* in the explication of such notions as coherence, the sequence is also being studied in its own right, viz as DISCOURSE. Some of the properties of discourse have received attention from a proper linguistic point of view, *eg* in the framework of so-called TEXT GRAMMARS, whereas other specific structures of discourse and discourse processing are now being investigated in cognitive psychology, anthropology, sociology, philosophy and poetics.

This book is intended as a contribution to the more specific linguistic study of discourse. It summarizes and further elaborates part of the investigations I have been undertaking since the publication of my dissertation *Some Aspects of Text Grammars* in 1972. I am acutely aware of the weaknesses of that book. The present study therefore aims at providing some corrections by establishing a more explicit and more systematic approach to the linguistic study of discourse. Yet, the nature of this book is more modest. Instead of devising a large programmatic framework, I have preferred to do exploratory research on some more specific, but fundamental, topics of a theory of discourse, viz on such notions as CONNECTION, COHERENCE, TOPIC OF DISCOURSE, and THE RELATIONS BETWEEN THE SEMANTICS AND PRAGMATICS OF DISCOURSE, which have received too little attention in recent (text) grammatical research. Furthermore, no particular claims are made for the format of a possible grammar of discourse; nor do I attempt a critique of other proposals made on the issues treated in this book. Topics such as quantification, pronominalization, presupposition, etc, which have been extensively studied both in sentence grammars and text grammars in the last few years, have been ignored in this book in favour of an inquiry into other basic problems of semantics and pragmatics. One of these problems for instance is that regarding the relationship between COMPOSITE SENTENCES on the one hand and SEQUENCES OF SENTENCES on the other hand.

It turns out that such an investigation cannot be made without appeal to a sound PRAGMATIC THEORY, because a characterization of discourse in terms of sequences of sentences simultaneously requires an account of conditions on sequences of speech acts.

Although it will be claimed that, both at the semantic and the pragmatic levels, MACRO-STRUCTURES of discourse and conversation should be postulated, especially in order to account for the notion of TOPIC OF DISCOURSE used to define linear connection and coherence in composite sentences and sequences, this book will pay only limited attention to macro-structures, for which separate treatment in terms of cognitive processes and of other theories, eg of narrative structures, is necessary.

As already mentioned, my observations are not being made within the framework of a specific type of grammar: rather, my theoretical tools are borrowed from certain domains of philosophy, philosophical logic, cognitive psychology and artificial intelligence. This is not without methodological problems, but these have had to be passed over without thorough discussion here. One of these problems concerns the nature of the notion of interpretation as defined respectively by a FORMAL SEMANTICS and COGNITIVE SEMANTICS. Thus, the assignment of semantic structures to discourse is based both on abstract 'logical' conditions and on conditions defined in terms of conventional world knowledge, and it is not easy to determine a priori which of these should be made explicit in a more specific linguistic semantics of discourse.

Similar remarks should be made on the precise status of a pragmatic theory with respect to a grammar, in a strict sense, on the one hand, and the philosophy and logic of action and the theory of social interaction on the other hand. More than ever, the linguist finds himself at the crossroads of several disciplines, and a more or less arbitrary restriction on the domain and problems of linguistic theory would not be fruitful at the moment for the development of new approaches to the study of natural language.

The organization of this book is straightforward and will be explained in the introductory chapter, in which some basic problems of the study of discourse are raised. The inquiry is in two parts, one semantic and the other pragmatic, which means that all aspects of the surface structure properties of discourse are neglected. In the semantics we proceed from a study of the conditions of connection between propositions, as expressed by natural connectives, to other coherence conditions of discourse, first at the level of sequences and then at the level of global semantic macro-structures. In the second or pragmatic part, some of these phenomena are taken up again in terms of speech acts and speech act sequences.

Since the theoretical foundations of these respective parts, viz FORMAL SEMANTICS and the PHILOSOPHY OF ACTION, are not yet generally familiar to the student of linguistics, I have added two introductory chapters about these important domains instead of referring the reader to other introductory surveys (if any), which are short, simple and relevant enough for our purposes. For further details, however, we have referred to more specialized studies in these respective fields.

Not only is the aim to explore the linguistic theory of discourse and the relations between semantics and pragmatics in general, but to provide an introduction to the subject and offer some insights into a number of basic issues in (text) grammatical theory. Some elementary knowledge of modern linguistics and the theory of speech acts, however, is presupposed, as well as some notions from rudimentary set theory. Although notions from formal semantics are explained and applied, our mode of exposition will on the whole be informal. Finally, it should be emphasized that on many points our observations are tentative and/or incomplete, many issues deserving book-length treatment. It seemed more appropriate at the moment, however, to raise a number of issues and show how they are interrelated rather than to go into the full intricacies of one single phenomenon.

For critical comments on the preliminary draft of this book and for discussions concerning some of the topics treated in it I am indebted to Lubomír Doležel, Alois Eder, Uwe Mönnich, Petr Sgall, Helmut Schnelle, and in particular to David Harrah, Cees van Rees, Hugo Verdaasdonk, Jeroen Groenendijk and Martin Stokhof who have pointed out my worst errors (some of which require correction in our future work). To Robert de Beaugrande I am indebted for many helpful suggestions on style, and I also would like to acknowledge the helpful comments of the editors of the *Linguistics Library* in which this book appears, as well as the assistance and suggestions of Peggy Drinkwater of Longman.

Finally, special thanks for many discussions and suggestions are due to my wife Dorothea Franck, who has also been the essential 'happiness condition' in the production context of this text, and to whom, therefore, this book is dedicated.

University of Amsterdam   TAVD
June 1976

Contents

Acknowledgements

We are grateful to the following for permission to reproduce copyright material:

Executors of James Joyce Estate, Jonathan Cape Limited, and the Society of Authors for an excerpt from 'Ivy Day in the Committee Room' from *Dubliners* by James Joyce; Robert Hale & Co, and James Hadley Chase for extracts from his book *Just The Way It Is*.

Symbols and technical conventions

CONNECTIVES

&, ∨, ⊃, ≡	logical connectives of conjunction, disjunction, material implication/conditional, material equivalence
~	logical negation
*	meta-variable for connectives
⊢	derivability (provability, theoremhood) in logical syntax
⊩	semantic entailment
=	identity; strict material equivalence
⥽	strict material implication
⟩	relevant implication/conditional
⇒	strict relevant implication (expressing entailment)
→, ←, ↔	causal relations of necessitation, conditioning, together with □, ⬭, ◊
⟶	semantic mapping (macro-rule) (based on entailment)

OPERATORS

□, ⬭, ◊	modal (alethic) operators of necessity, probability and possibility
P, F, N	tense operators of past, future and now
K, B, W	epistemic, doxastic and boulomaeic operators of knowledge, belief and want
I, DO	action operators of intention and bringing about
T	change operator over states of affairs

SET-THEORETICAL SYMBOLS

∈, ∉, ⊰	is an element of, is not an element of, is part of
{., .}	set indicators
⟨., .⟩	ordered set (*n*-tuple) indicators

$\cup$	set-union
$\phi(.\,,\,.\,,\,.)$	functions (where ϕ may be any letter)

EXPRESSIONS

$p, q, r, \ldots$	proposition letters
$\alpha\,\beta, \gamma, \ldots$	meta-variables for propositions
$x, y, z, \ldots$	individual variables
$a, b, c, \ldots$	individual constants
$u, v, \ldots$	action variables
$A, B, C, \ldots$	event variables/constants; person variables/constants
$f, g, h, \ldots$	predicate letters
$\phi, \psi, \ldots$	predicate (meta-)variables
$S_i, S_j, \ldots$	sentence variables
$\Sigma_i, \Sigma_j, \ldots$	sequence (of sentences) variables
$f_i, f_j, \ldots$	fact variables

QUANTIFIERS

$\forall$	universal quantifier: for all ...
$\exists$	existential quantifier: for at least one ...

SEMANTIC SYMBOLS

V	valuation function
V^+	valuation function for truth and connection values
$1, 0$	truth and falsity; connectedness and disconnectedness; topic and comment
$D;\ d_i, d_j, \ldots$	set of individuals and its members
$W;\ w_i, w_j, \ldots$	set of possible worlds and its members
$T;\ t_i, t_j, \ldots$	set of time points and its members
$Z;\ z_i, z_j, \ldots$	set of possible topics of discourse/conversation and its members
$\langle D, W, \ldots, V \rangle$	model of modal predicate logics
Δ_k	union of the sets of individuals referred to by expressions of sentences satisfied in the first $k-1$ models of a discourse model (*ie* the set of previously mentioned referents).
$*\phi(= V(\phi))$	the denotatum of ϕ
L, l_i, l_j	the set of locations and its members
$w_0, t_0, z_0, \ldots$	the *actual* possible world, time point, topic of conversation, ...
R	binary relation over W: accessibility, alternativity (sometimes with epistemic index)
$<$	binary relation over T: precedence
$\mid$	binary relation over Z: initiatability
F, f_i, f_j	set of conceptual frames and its members
$T(\ )$	topicalization function

PRAGMATIC SYMBOLS

$C, c_i, c_j, \ldots$	set of possible contexts and its members
c_0	the actual context
$S(\ )$	speaker function
$H(\ )$	hearer function
$U, u_i, u_j, \ldots$	set of utterance types and its members
u_0	the actual utterance type
$|u_0|$	the actual utterance token
$\langle t_0, l_0, c_0 \ldots \rangle$	here-now in actual context

OTHER CONVENTIONS

1 Cited expressions and sentences are always in *italics* when occurring in the text (but not when shown on separate example lines).
2 Propositions are enclosed between bold 'single quotes'.
3 Utterances are in italics and between "*double quotes*".
4 Concepts are between 'single quotes'.
5 Important and theoretical terms are in SMALL CAPITALS.
6 Frame-names are in SPACED SMALL CAPITALS.

INTRODUCTION

Chapter 1

The linguistic study of discourse

1 Aims and problems

1.1

In this introductory chapter we will first sketch the place of our investigation within the domain of the linguistic study of discourse. Next, we will explain how the chapters are related to a unifying theoretical framework; and finally, we will touch briefly on some other areas of a more general interdisciplinary study of discourse and their relation to the more specific linguistic account provided in this book.

1.2

The linguistic study of discourse, being part of the more general study of natural language, must share its basic aims with linguistic theories in general and with grammars in particular. Therefore, it should be determined what the empirical object of such a study is, which properties of that object should be accounted for, and what the nature of such an account should be. More particularly it must be made clear in which respect both object and account are SPECIFIC to the domain of linguistic theory.

Linguistic theory deals with SYSTEMS of natural language, ie with their actual or possible structures, their historical development, cultural differentiation, social function, and cognitive basis. Such systems are usually made explicit as systems of conventional RULES determining language behaviour as it manifests itself in the use of verbal utterances in communicative situations. The rules are CONVENTIONAL[1] in the sense of being shared by most members of a linguistic community: they KNOW these rules implicitly and are able to *use* them such that verbal utterances may count as being determined by the particular language system of the community as it is cognitively acquired by the individual language user. It is the aim of a GRAMMAR to give a theoretical reconstruction of such a particular rule system. Such a reconstruction, which involves the usual abstractions, generalizations and idealizations, requires the formulation of the levels, categories, units, types of rule and constraints necessary to describe the abstract structure of the UTTERANCES[2] of language users. One of the empirical aims of grammars is to be able to codetermine which types of utterance are conventionally ACCEPTABLE[3] (and which are not) for the language users of a speech community. The part of acceptability accounted for by the grammar, viz GRAMMATICALNESS, pertains to certain properties of the abstract structure of utterances: phonological, morphological and syntactical. Apart from these properties of 'form' a grammar is also required to specify the meaning structure related to these forms, although in the strict sense the meaning of utterances is not 'part of' the structure of the utterance, but assigned to the utterance by the language user. In this sense, a grammar is usually roughly characterized as a THEORETICAL FORM-MEANING RULE SYSTEM: it must also specify how morpho-syntactic structures are related to semantic structures.

1.3

These few general remarks about linguistic theory and grammar ignore a great number of methodological problems, which have given rise to several controversies about the necessary levels of description, the units of analysis, the empirical basis of grammar, etc.

The explorations we want to undertake here are based on two assumptions regarding linguistic theory in general and the scope and domain of grammars in particular which are closely related to these problems. The first assumption is that the theoretical reconstruction of utterances at the levels of form and meaning should be complemented by a third level, viz that of ACTION. That is, an utterance should not only be characterized in terms of its internal structure and the meaning assigned to it, but also in terms of the act accomplished by producing such an utterance. This PRAGMATIC level of description provides crucial conditions for reconstructing part of the conventions that make utterances acceptable, viz their APPROPRIATENESS with respect to the communicative context. In other words, pragmatic rules, which are also conventional and hence known by the language users of a speech community, determine the systematic use of utterances. Whether this pragmatic level of analysis should be incorporated into the grammar – taken in a broad sense – or constitute an autonomous linguistic subtheory to be systematically related to the grammar is one of the methodological problems which cannot be solved in this book. There is no a priori reason why a grammar should not be a FORM-MEANING-ACTION RULE SYSTEM, in which abstract forms of utterances are related to both meaning and function of these forms in theoretically reconstructed contexts of communication.[4]

The second major assumption on which our inquiry is based pertains to the nature of ABSTRACT UNITS in terms of which utterances are theoretically reconstructed. It has been usual in most linguistic theories to consider the SENTENCE as the maximum unit of description both at the morphosyntactic and the semantic levels of description.[5] This does not mean it was not recognized that utterances may be viewed as manifesting possibly several sentences, but that this could be accounted for by describing each sentence separately, or by taking SEQUENCES OF SENTENCES to be equivalent with COMPOUND SENTENCES. We hope to show in this book that these approaches are inadequate: there are systematic differences between compound sentences and sequences of sentences, especially at a pragmatic level of description, and the meaning of sentences may depend on the meaning of other sentences of the same utterance although not always in the same way as the meanings of clauses in compound or complex sentences. These are reasons which have led us to assume that utterances should be reconstructed in terms of a larger unit, viz that of TEXT. This term will here be used to denote the abstract theoretical construct underlying what is usually called a DISCOURSE. Those utterances which can be assigned textual structure are thus acceptable discourses of the language – at this level of the account of acceptability, *ie* are well-formed and interpretable. In this way we disregard the possibility of dialogue-discourse, *ie* a sequence of utterances by different speakers, but it may be assumed that such a sequence also may have textual structure similar to that of (monologue-) discourse as it is discussed here.

An important corollary of these two assumptions is the further assumption that discourse is systematically related to communicative action. In other words, the pragmatic component should not merely specify appropriateness conditions for sentences, but also for discourses. It is one of the major aims of this book, then, to make explicit the systematic relations between TEXT and PRAGMATIC CONTEXT.

1.4

The general assumptions formulated above are not without methodological problems and require further specification. Many of the problems involved pertain to the SCOPE of linguistic theory in general and of grammars in particular.

First of all, it should be specified what kind of SEMANTICS is needed, both for the description of sentences and for that of texts. Although a grammar was roughly characterized as a form-meaning rule mechanism, it is obvious in the description of such phenomena as pronouns, determiners and topic-comment articulation, that besides meaning we also need an explication of REFERENCE.[6] The notion of INTERPRETATION becomes ambiguous in this respect, denoting both the assignment of meaning to certain 'forms' (expressions) and the assignment of referents to certain expressions. Since a theory of reference has been elaborated, mainly in philosophy and in logical semantics, but is not yet integrated into elementary linguistics, we will explain some major concepts of a formal semantics in the next chapter in order to be able to describe a number of crucial properties of composite sentences and discourses.

A second problem for an adequate linguistic theory of discourse also pertains to semantics, this time taken in a perhaps still wider sense involving KNOWLEDGE and COGNITIVE STRUCTURES in general. In linguistic grammars, the meaning of sentences is assigned on the basis of the meanings of expressions (words or morphemes, and phrases) as specified by a LEXICON. Now, it is far from easy to make a clear distinction between lexical meanings of words on the one hand, and conventional knowledge about the 'world' on the other hand. If a sentence like *The table is laughing* is in some sense unacceptable, it is not so much because of our language but rather because of the POSSIBLE FACTS of our actual world and those worlds similar to it. Similarly, whether clauses or sentences can be meaningfully combined into one sentence or one discourse, respectively, depends on an interpretation in which conventional knowledge of the world is involved, of which the knowledge represented by a grammatical lexicon is only a subset. Although it cannot possibly be a relevant task of linguistics to specify this knowledge of the world itself, we may expect a semantics to indicate how this knowledge is used in the interpretation of sentences and discourse, viz by formulating the CONDITIONS which make expressions meaningful.[7]

By thus specifying the semantics as a theory which explicates both meaning and reference, and both lexical meaning and general meaningfulness conditions determined by world knowledge, we will be able to make explicit one of the central notions of a semantic analysis of discourse, viz COHERENCE.

It should be emphasized that these methodological problems of a linguistic theory of semantics and its delimitation with respect to a theory of reference, formal semantics and cognitive semantics, are of a more general nature. They become relevant in a serious analysis of notions such as MEANING-FULNESS, INTERPRETATION, and ENTAILMENT both for sentences and for discourse.

1.5

A third problem also touches upon questions of the scope of linguistic theories. Discourse may have certain structures which while based on conventional rules cannot properly be called linguistic or which at least cannot be made explicit by a linguistic grammar.

A well-known example are those structures defining a certain TYPE or sort of discourse, *eg* NARRATIVE STRUCTURES underlying a story. Another example are those structures which are traditionally called RHETORICAL: when the sentences in a sequence have the same syntactic structures, for instance, such parallelism has no grammatical function, but it may have a rhetorical function related to the EFFECT of the utterance on the hearer. We do not want to treat such structures within a linguistic theory of discourse because they are restricted to certain types of discourse or certain STYLISTIC USES of language, and because they cannot be accounted for in terms of a grammatical form-meaning-action rule system: a parallel syntactic structure is not assigned a conventional meaning or a conventional speech act. Hence, in a LINGUISTIC THEORY OF DISCOURSE we are only concerned with the general conditions, morpho-syntactic, semantic and pragmatic, determining the well-formedness, interpretability and appropriateness, respectively, of any discourse of a particular language. Other discourse structures are to be specified by other theories of the more general STUDY OF DISCOURSE, to which we will briefly return below.

What may be required of a linguistic theory of discourse, however, is that it takes a form such that it can be related to other theories of discourse. In order to be able to describe parallelism we need a syntax specifying the appropriate categories, and in order to define narrative categories or functions we need a discourse semantics with units or levels of analysis which can be assigned such narrative functions.

1.6

The latter requirement raises a fourth major problem for the linguistic description of discourse. Even if it should be linguistically interesting to postulate a THEORETICAL UNIT of TEXT in order to explicate the structure of discourse, it does not follow that the set of levels, categories, rules and constraints necessary to account adequately for discourse structure is different from that used in the account of sentence structure. And, indeed, many of the relations holding between clauses in compound sentences also hold between sentences in a sequence, and conversely.

As such, this fact would not make a linguistic study of discourse trivial: it would show that certain rules and constraints can be GENERALIZED for sequences of sentences, and that composite sentences and sequences – whatever their other differences – are equivalent at some level of description.

Moreover, it may also be the case that with the same set of categories, levels, units, types of rule and constraints important systematic differences between composite sentences and sequences of sentences can be described. For instance, although the basic rules for pronominalization and connectives are identical within or between sentences, there are other constraints which differentiate the APPLICATION of the rules. These constraints are mainly semantic and pragmatic, and explain the fact that not all composite sentences can be transformed into a sequence of sentences, especially the complex sentences in which some clause is hierarchically subordinate to the main clause, or conversely, that not all sequences can be reduced to a composite sentence, especially those sequences in which there is a change of speech act or a change of topic of discourse – a notion to be explained in this book. These differences are grammatically relevant owing to the criterion that different morpho-syntactic structures may be related to different semantic and pragmatic structures. In other words: if different forms systematically have different meanings or different functions, this should be accounted for by the grammar (taken in the large sense, ie including a pragmatic component). We will investigate this point in detail throughout this book on the example of the various natural connectives as used between clauses in composite sentences on the one hand and between sentences in discourse on the other hand.

1.7

We have just indicated that if discourse is simply taken as a sequence, ie as a linearly ordered n-tuple of sentences, the difference between this and a description of composite sentences would be reduced to a presumably small set of mainly semantic and pragmatic constraints. In this book we will ignore possible differences at the morpho-phonological and syntactic levels.

Besides these differences in constraints it should be asked whether an adequate linguistic characterization of discourse also requires other UNITS and LEVELS of description. We have already assumed that the unit of TEXT should be postulated, and that the description of discourse should also take place at a pragmatic level.

The assumption of extra units and levels for a linguistic description of discourse does not mean that they would be EXCLUSIVE to multiple-sentence discourses. It may, however, be the case that certain phenomena appear more clearly in a longer discourse than in one, even composite, sentence, *ie* in a one-sentence discourse. One of the characteristic examples is the notion of TOPIC OF DISCOURSE, briefly mentioned above, or more generally the notion TOPIC OF CONVERSATION, denoting what a discourse or part of it 'is about'. Thus, it may intuitively be said that several sentences in a sequence belong to the 'same' topic of discourse. However, as we shall show, it may not be possible to determine the relevant topic of discourse to which an individual sentence on its own belongs but only in conjunction with the other sentences of that particular part of the discourse.

It seems to follow that a notion such as topic of discourse cannot simply be explained in terms of semantic relations between successive sentences. Rather, each of the sentences may contribute one 'element' such that a certain STRUCTURE of these elements defines the topic of that sequence in much the same way as, at the syntactic level, words can be assigned a syntactic function only with respect to a structure 'covering' the whole clause or sentence.

These and other observations have led to the assumption that we should postulate an additional level of semantic description, viz that of SEMANTIC MACRO-STRUCTURES. In this book we will not attempt to provide a full theory of textual macro-structures, but we will try to show that certain semantic constraints on both composite sentences and discourse sequences are to be accounted for in terms of notions such as topic of discourse or THEME, and that these can only be made explicit at a level of macro-structural semantic description. Note that macro-structures are not specific units: they are normal semantic structures, *eg* of the usual propositional form, but they are not expressed by one clause or sentence but by a sequence of sentences. In other words, macro-structures are a more GLOBAL LEVEL of semantic description; they define the meaning of parts of a discourse and of the whole discourse on the basis of the meanings of the individual sentences. This is in line with a crucial characteristic of an explicit semantics. Thus, as for any serious linguistic theory, RULES must be formulated systematically relating the semantic representation of sentences to that, at the macro-level, of the sequence.

This notion of macro-structure is RELATIVE with respect to underlying semantic levels. The rules should be such that they operate on a sequence of macro-structures to yield still more global macro-structures, until the most general macro-structure of a discourse is reached. We see that the semantic structure of a discourse may be hierarchically organized at several levels of analysis.

It will be shown that assuming this additional level of semantic analysis not only has important COGNITIVE IMPLICATIONS, explaining the processes of comprehension and retention of discourse, but that these cognitive implications are also GRAMMATICALLY relevant to the adequate description of the use of certain connectives, PRO-forms, determiners, adverbs, and the distinction of paragraphs in written language or paragraph markers in oral speech of some natural languages.[8] Similarly, they are also necessary for the description of speech acts which are not based on individual sentences but which require a macro-structural propositional basis.

One of the problems arising with the assumption of macro-structures is again the delimitation of grammatical versus cognitive semantics. It may be argued that macro-structures are only the result of COGNITIVE PROCESSES of comprehension, involving generalization and abstraction as a condition for necessary information organization and reduction in memory. Clearly, in a semantics in which a distinction is no longer made between 'grammatical' and 'cognitive', this would no longer be a problem, because any kind of meaning would be described in terms of conventionally based cognitive processes of interpretation. In the sense in which a linguistic theory is an abstraction from actual cognitive processes and representations, we will however assume that an account of the meaning of sequences of sentences in a discourse in terms of some kind of semantic macro-structures is a proper task of linguistic theory.[9] In other words, we assume that the rules of macro-interpretation belong to the semantic competence of language users and that they are conventional, allowing members of a speech community to convey meanings at several levels of interpretation.

1.8

In the previous sections we have argued that at least certain properties of discourse can and should be accounted for in linguistics. We used the rather neutral and vague term 'linguistic theory', thus provisionally avoiding the need to speak of a GRAMMAR of discourse. Obviously, if we take this notion in a very restricted sense, only a few properties of discourse can be accounted for. If, however, we are prepared to take the notion of a grammar in a, still methodologically sound, wider sense, including a pragmatic component, a reference semantics, a semantics with world-knowledge interpretation conditions, and a macro-semantics, we shall be able to account for many general properties of discourse within the grammar itself. Although the discussion about this matter, ie one 'large' grammar or a 'strict' grammar associated with several other (semantic and pragmatic) theories, may in some sense be rather spurious, we are in principle inclined to propose the 'large' conception of a grammar. The main reason for preferring this option is to be able to account, within the same grammatical framework, for a number of

GENERALIZATIONS (both for sentences and discourse) within the same grammatical framework, and to show how at all levels the various rules and constraints are interrelated: syntactic structures or morphemes may only have a specific pragmatic function; certain meanings are systematically related to certain speech acts; interpretability, even of isolated sentences and clauses, requires reference and world knowledge conditions, and clauses in composite sentences may be connected only by a topic of discourse, which may go beyond the sentence boundary, requiring a specific macro-semantics of sequences.

It is the main task of this book to show how these interrelations between composite sentences and sequences and between semantics and pragmatics operate. Although we would like to propose our investigation as belonging to a 'grammar' in a wide sense as characterized above, we do not want to specify the precise structure of such a grammar but only to give some of its possible FRAGMENTS, and some relationships between the semantic and pragmatic fragments of such a grammar.

2 The organization of this study
2.1
In the previous section we have outlined some of the aims and problems of a linguistic study of discourse. Our investigation takes place against that background, and we now have to indicate how the inquiry is organized and how the subsequent chapters are interrelated.
2.2
First of all it should be emphasized that only some properties of discourse – including those of sentences – will be treated. As was mentioned earlier we will pay no attention to possible morpho-phonological and syntactic rules characterizing discourse, but focus attention on SEMANTIC and PRAGMATIC phenomena. The only observations which may in some sense be called syntactic are those relating to differences between compound and complex sentences, and between compound sentences and sequences of sentences, but the conditions underlying these differences will be shown to be semantic and pragmatic.

Secondly, we will ignore those phenomena which have been extensively studied in earlier work on discourse, especially pronominalization, articles and definitivization, and presupposition, phenomena which have also received much attention in sentence grammars.[10]

Thirdly, we will mainly focus attention on what may be called MONO-LOGICAL DISCOURSE, even if it may be argued that dialogues and conversation in general would constitute an empirically better warranted approach to discourse. Although we have provisionally assumed that natural language utterances are to be reconstructed as discourses in terms of texts, it may well be that a discourse – having textual structure – is constituted by

several utterances of several speakers. The structural unity of such a
CONVERSATION is at least in part determined by the constraints determining
monological discourse, including pragmatic rules of speech act sequencing.[11]

Finally, little attention will be paid to METHODOLOGICAL and EMPIRICAL
problems. Some of the methodological issues have been touched upon above,
especially with regard to the types of semantics required. This means that at
some points we will not hesitate to combine conditions formulated in terms of
formal semantics with those given in terms of a cognitive semantics. This
does not imply, however, that a formal semantics can be used as a model of
cognitive semantic processing. Similarly, apart from some remarks about the
cognitive role of macro-structures and the social implications of pragmatic
rules, hardly any empirical base for our investigation will be established,
although the proposed analyses may contain suggestions for relevant experiments.

2.3

Our inquiry consists of two main parts: viz a SEMANTIC and a PRAGMATIC
investigation, which are SYSTEMATICALLY RELATED to each other in the
sense that the same phenomena which are described at the semantic level will
also be studied at the pragmatic level. Each part will be introduced by a
chapter of FOUNDATIONS in which the analytical terms will be explained.
Thus, the semantic part will be preceded by an introduction to formal,
LOGICAL SEMANTICS, and the pragmatics by an introduction to the THEORY
OF ACTION.

These are theories which do not themselves belong to linguistics but to the
philosophical and logical foundations of linguistic theory, much in the same
way as some branches of mathematics and the theory of automata were used
in setting up generative syntax. We do not, however, have the ambition to
provide a formalization of the analysis: the relevant notions from formal
semantics and the theory of action will be used in a more 'qualitative' way,
serving heuristic theory formation with the help of more or less non-
ambiguous technical terms defined in the foundational disciplines. Note that
even the two introductory chapters are related: in order to define action we
will be using notions from formal semantics, whereas the semantics of action
sentences and action discourse requires analytical insight into the 'ontology'
of action. Moreover, in both cases, ie those of meaning-reference and action,
we are concerned with a description of what will be called INTENSIONAL
OBJECTS, and in both cases we may speak of the INTERPRETATION of objects
(utterances, doings).

2.4

A first phenomenon which will receive extensive attention is that of
CONNECTION, the CONDITIONS OF CONNECTION and the natural CON-
NECTIVES expressing connection relations. Both in sentence grammars
and in the study of discourse connectives have hardly been studied in a
systematic way, and most relevant studies have been provided in philosophy
and logic, mostly about logical connectives and their relations with natural

connectives. The idea of this study was to investigate the semantic 'roots' determining the COMBINATION OF PROPOSITIONS IN PAIRS, to be expressed either by composite sentences or sequences of sentences. Given the semantic rules for the interpretation of clauses, very little was known about the conditions which determine the meaningfulness of any type of COMPOSITE EXPRESSIONS in natural language. In other words, we did not have explicit insight into the meaning of natural language connectives, including the regular conjunctions and adverbs. It was found that such phenomena as REFERENTIAL IDENTITY, determining pronominalization and definitivization, although often paid attention to in discourse studies, are NEITHER NECESSARY NOR SUFFICIENT to determine the meaningfulness of composite expressions (sentences or sequences) if the related propositions are not CONNECTED. The connection conditions are important because they decide whether a sequence of propositions can be expressed in one sentence at all. The notion of connection will be studied in terms of a formal semantics and hinges upon RELATIONS BETWEEN FACTS in possible worlds, RELATIVE TO a certain TOPIC OF DISCOURSE.

Connection, however, is a specific phenomenon of a set of other COHERENCE phenomena in natural language. That is, sequences of propositions underlying a discourse are not only pairwise connected, but also satisfy other coherence conditions, in which the notion of topic of conversation also plays an important role, together with phenomena such as REFERENTIAL IDENTITY AND DIFFERENCE, the DISTRIBUTION OF SEMANTIC INFORMATION, TOPIC AND COMMENT, PRESUPPOSITION and 'assertion' (INTRODUCTION). These other coherence phenomena will be studied in a later chapter and several discourse fragments analysed.

Finally, it becomes essential to explicate the primitive notion of a TOPIC OF DISCOURSE, viz in terms of MACRO-STRUCTURES, in the last semantic chapter. It will be shown that macro-structures define what may be called the meaning of a whole passage or discourse, and thus at the same time determine the connection and other coherence constraints operating in sentences and sequences.

In the second part of the book it should first be made clear in what respect SPEECH ACTS can be described in terms of a THEORY OF ACTION, and how the basic concept of pragmatics, viz that of CONTEXT, should be defined, with respect to which discourses are to be evaluated as APPROPRIATE or not, depending on the systematic relations between text structure and context structure.

The inquiry then runs parallel with that in the semantic part of the book. It examines which pragmatic conditions are involved in connection and in the use of connectives and concludes that we should speak both of SEMANTIC AND PRAGMATIC CONNECTIVES, the first relating propositions, the second relating speech acts. It will then be shown which pragmatic constraints determine whether a sequence of propositions is to be expressed in one sentence or several sentences, although it should be admitted that some of the evidence is based on rather fine differences about which our reflective judgements – outside natural contexts of communication – may be rather weak.

Similarly, pragmatic rules are sought which codetermine the distribution of semantic information in discourse. This means that a systematic study is required of the links between sequences of sentences, sequences of propositions and sequences of speech acts. Just as propositions are to be connected, so we require sequences of speech acts to be 'connected' in one PRAGMATICALLY COHERENT discourse.

Finally, the systematics of the theoretical framework lead us to assume, in the last chapter, that we should also speak of macro-structures at the pragmatic level, and postulate MACRO-SPEECH ACTS. Just as we have meanings for a whole sequence, so a sequence of speech acts may at a higher level of analysis constitute another speech act, which may not be implied by the individual speech acts in isolation. Since macro-speech acts also require a 'content', *ie* a propositional base, it is possible to relate them to the semantic macro-structures.

Thus, in both parts we move from relatively 'local' phenomena, also manifested in composite sentences, to phenomena of a larger scope of sequence and discourse description. Instead of studying various semantic and pragmatic properties of discourse in isolation, we have followed one of the basic methodological criteria of a theory of grammar, viz that the levels studied be systematically related: thus, at one level, it was found that the more global constraints of macro-structures are based on operations on the 'local' meanings of the respective sentences of the discourse, but that conversely the meaningfulness of composite sentences and pairs of sentences depends on the macro-structure. This means that the semantics of sentences and that of sequences and discourses cannot be dissociated from each other. The same holds for the integration at the pragmatic level of description and for the semantic-pragmatic links.

3 The study of discourse[12]
3.1

Although we have not been very restrictive in the delimitation of the linguistic part of a more general study of discourse, it is obvious that not all systematic properties of discourse belong to the domain of linguistic theory and grammar. The conventional rules and conditions of meaning- and reference-interpretation, and those of world-knowledge use, and pragmatic action and functions have been liberally integrated into the task of linguistic discourse analysis, but this is less obviously so for other conventional rules and conditions, such as those mentioned earlier of NARRATIVE THEORY and RHETORIC. The categories, units, levels and rules involved here are different from those used in syntax, semantics and pragmatics of natural language, although a similar SEMIOTIC distinction may be made in the neighbouring disciplines.

3.2

The primary interdisciplinary studies are, of course, the PSYCHOLINGUISTIC and SOCIOLINGUISTIC studies of discourse which are undertaken in order to be able to provide an empirical basis for a linguistic study of discourse. Theoretical and experimental studies are being carried out at the moment regarding the cognitive PROCESSES of discourse production, comprehension, storage, and reproduction.[13] Besides the more general conventional rules, these processes require STRATEGIES of comprehension of a more probabilistic nature, during which hypotheses are formed with respect to referent identification, connection, coherence and macro-structures. Questions about the selection, combination and abstraction of INFORMATION from discourse and the formation and transformation of KNOWLEDGE AND BELIEFS are relevant here, and are important for linguistics if it is further shown that these processes depend on the structure of the discourse. In the chapter on macro-structures we will briefly consider these cognitive implications of the theory.

At the moment, there are few insights into the ACQUISITION of specific discourse rules, but experiments now being carried out with story-telling of children may shed light on that problem soon.

Much of current work in sociolinguistics has been focused on properties of morpho-phonological and syntactic structure: hence the specific semantic and pragmatic constraints holding in discourse have not yet been demonstrated to depend systematically on differences of social context, apart from the well-known STYLISTIC differences (lexicon, sentence length and sentence complexity).[14] Whether there are social differences in connection and coherence rules, the distribution of information, and the construction of topics of discourse and conversation is an empirical question still to be investigated.

3.3

Much of the most interesting work on discourse has been done outside linguistics in such disciplines as ANTHROPOLOGY, SOCIOLOGY, RHETORIC and LITERARY SCHOLARSHIP. Recently, ANTHROPOLOGY has paid extensive attention, within the 'ethnography of speaking' paradigm, to the various types of discourse used in different cultures (narratives, riddles, word-games, invectives, etc),[15] and to the theory of narrative in the analysis of myth.[16]

SOCIOLOGY, under the label of 'ethnomethodology', has focused on the analysis of everyday conversation, rules of sequencing and the micro-social constraints on discourse and speech acts in interaction.[17]

SOCIAL PSYCHOLOGY has less paid attention to a systematic analysis of discourse than to the systematic EFFECTS of discourse and its 'content' on the beliefs and behaviour of individuals in society, especially in the framework of analysing mass media messages.[18] The interesting problems here are to be solved with the help of the results of a cognitive approach to discourse, in which it is determined which semantic structures expressed by which surface structures and stylistic structures are stored in memory and affect existing knowledge and beliefs. At the moment some behaviouristic evidence exists about the relations between discourse structure and the change of beliefs and attitudes, but there is little explanatory insight into the underlying cognitive and social processes.

Finally, the disciplines of RHETORIC, STYLISTICS and LITERARY SCHOLARSHIP[19] should be mentioned as those which have been most concerned with the study of certain properties of discourse and certain types of discourse. It has been argued above that the specific structures described by these disciplines should be viewed as 'additional' to the basic linguistic structure of the discourse. These structures differentiate discourse types and determine specific effects of discourse communication, eg aesthetic emotional, epistemic effects. Our linguistic theory of discourse will have to function as an appropriate basis for the study of the more specific structures and functions. For instance, narrative units and categories may now be more explicitly related to discourse at the level of macro-semantics. Similarly, certain stylistic and literary operations consist precisely in changing the more general rules and conditions of connection and coherence.

It is in this sense that a linguistic theory of discourse is intended not only as a contribution to linguistics but also as a basis for the study of discourse in other disciplines, thus further advancing the integration of discourse analysis into the general study of language and communication.[20]

Notes

1 Whereas the emphasis in the generative-transformational paradigm in linguistic theory has been mainly on the cognitive basis of language, we would like to stress also the social basis of language and language use, in which the central notion of 'convention' is to be defined. For a general discussion of this notion, see Lewis (1968).

2 The notion of 'utterance' is not without problems. First of all it is ambiguous in the sense of denoting both an object and an act, viz the act of producing that object. We use the term only in the first sense, viz as the product of an act of speech or writing. Secondly, we should distinguish between utterance TYPES and utterance TOKENS, the latter being the unique, physical speech product of a speaker during a specific period of speaking. When we use the term we use it to mean an utterance type. For further discussion, see Chapter 7 and the attempts at definition in Kasher (1972).

3 'Acceptability', mostly used in linguistics as a term belonging to the theory of 'performance' – ie the actual use of language – is a concept which is far from clear. For extensive discussion of the term, see the contributions in Greenbaum, ed (1977), eg van Dijk (1977).

4 Formulating pragmatic rules in the grammar means that such a grammar must account not only for the ability to construct 'correct' utterances but for the ability to use such utterances adequately in some communicative situation. The latter ability has been called 'communicative competence' (see Hymes, 1972). In several linguistic schools, eg in tagmemics (see Pike, 1967) and functional grammar (eg Firth, 1957, 1968; Halliday, 1973), this idea was already present in some form before arising in the present context of pragmatics and the study of language use.

5 Again with the exception of those linguists associated with the 'schools' mentioned in note 4, who have often stressed the relevance of a linguistic study of discourse. The same holds for one of the 'founders' of structuralist linguistics, Zellig Harris, although his 'discourse analysis' has little to do with the analysis of discourse but is rather a theory of syntactic structure of sentences. See Harris (1963) and comments by *eg* Bierwisch (1965a). For a brief survey of the 'history' of discourse linguistics and text grammar, see van Dijk (1972a, Ch 1). For readers on the topic, see van Dijk and Petöfi, eds (1977) and Dressler, ed (1977).

6 There is much work in philosophy on the notion of reference. For introductory reading and further references, see Linsky (1967) and Linsky, ed (1971). See also Geach (1962) and Strawson (1971). For references to logical semantics, see the notes to the next chapter.

7 In cognitive psychology and artificial intelligence these parts of knowledge are called 'frames', a notion which will be used to establish the coherence of a discourse. Attempts have been made in computer simulation of language comprehension to make explicit at least some fragment of our conventional knowledge of the world. See Charniak (1972) and Bobrow and Collins, eds (1975), and the notes to the succeeding chapters for further references to cognitive semantics.

8 See Longacre (1970). Examples of the other surface manifestations of macro-structures are given in Chapter 5.

9 In this respect we find ourselves in disagreement with certain critics of our earlier work in text grammar (*eg* Dascal and Margalit, 1974), whatever the further justification of their criticism. In this book we hope to make the macro-structures and especially the macro-rules more explicit, relating the macro-structures to the semantic representations of the sentences of the discourse. In Chapter 5 it will also be shown that macro-structures have been empirically assessed by experiments.

10 See the references in van Dijk (1972a, 1973a) and those given in the bibliography of text linguistics by Dressler and Schmidt (1973). For the major portion of current work on these phenomena, both in sentence grammar and text grammar, the reader is referred to the linguistic journals, and to the monograph series on text linguistics from Buske Verlag (Hamburg) and De Gruyter Verlag (Berlin–New York). See also Halliday and Hasan (1976). Dressler (1972) gives a first introduction.

11 See the references given in note 17 below regarding the analysis of conversation.

12 Since the study of discourse involves research in various disciplines of the humanities and the social sciences, it is impossible to give a complete set of references to various approaches to discourse. For each domain we mention a few works which are either representative, introductory or contain many further references. We have mentioned the various disciplines in order to pay tribute to the important insights into discourse obtained by various scholars outside linguistics, and to show, however briefly, where and how our own linguistic research in this book could be applied.

13 See the references for the psychology of discourse in Chapter 5.

14 See however Labov (1972a, Part III, 1972b, Ch. 3, and 8), and comments by him on Bernstein's code distinction (restricted versus elaborated) (Bernstein, 1971) which also pertains to discourse properties.

15 See Baumann and Scherzer, eds (1974) and Gumperz and Hymes, eds (1972).

16 This work has become theoretically interesting since the (re-)discovery of the work of Propp (1968[1928]), and has been carried out mainly in the Soviet Union, France, the USA, Canada and Finland. See Maranda, ed (1972), issues 4 and 8 of *Communications* (Paris), and the further references given in van Dijk (1972a, 1975a).

17 See the contributions in Sudnow, ed (1972), especially the work by Sacks and Schegloff.

18 See *eg* Himmelfarb and Hendrickson Eagly, eds (1974) for readings on attitude change, and Holsti (1969) and Gerbner, *et al*, eds (1969), in particular for the

content analysis of discourse or 'messages'. Well-known studies on the effect of discourse structure in persuasive contexts have been carried out by Hovland and associates, see *eg* Hovland, *et al* (1957). Thus, several studies have been made on propaganda, political discourse, and advertising which belong to the larger field of discourse studies.

19 For these disciplines and their relevance to linguistics and the study of discourse, see van Dijk (1972*a*) and references given there. See also Plett (1975).

20 For surveys or introductions to this more general study of discourse, see Schmidt (1973), Rommetveit (1974) and Dressler, ed (1977).

PART I
SEMANTICS

Chapter 2

A brief introduction to formal semantics

1 Formal languages

1.1

In the following chapters we will use some concepts from FORMAL or LOGICAL SEMANTICS. Since this kind of semantics is not yet a standard component of elementary linguistics, we will give a fragmentary introduction to the basic notions in this field. For more complete introductions we refer to the various handbooks of logic, in which also the syntactic and axiomatic properties of logical systems and their relations to semantics are treated.[1] At the end of this chapter we also pay attention briefly to the relations between formal semantics and the study of natural language.

1.2

Formal semantics is part of the study of FORMAL LANGUAGES. Unlike natural languages, formal languages are artificial; they are constructed by logicians and mathematicians. Yet, formal languages and natural languages have certain abstract structures in common, which allows the application of logic in grammar. Furthermore, besides the study of the specific properties of various formal systems per se, logic and mathematics may support the FORMALIZATION of theories in the natural and social sciences.

A language, whether natural or artificial, may be defined as a set of symbolic EXPRESSIONS. In a formal language this set is strictly defined: RULES stipulate what is an expression of a particular formal language and what is not. Just as in grammar, we here speak of rules of SYNTAX, in particular, of rules that define which expressions are WELL-FORMED and are called FORMATION RULES. Such rules operate on symbols: they specify which sequences of symbols are well-formed. The set of different symbols used in a particular formal language will be called the LEXICON of that language. Symbols belong to various CATEGORIES, just as words in natural language are of various syntactic categories (nouns, verbs, etc). The categories determine whether a sequence of symbols is well-formed or not.

One basic and elementary formal language is that of PROPOSITIONAL LOGIC. The language of a standard propositional logic has expressions from the following four CATEGORIES:

(i) proposition letters: $p, q, r, \ldots$
(ii) binary connectives: &, $\vee$, $\supset$, $\equiv$
(iii) a symbol of negation: $\sim$
(iv) structure symbols: (,), [,] (parentheses)

The FORMATION RULES then define which sequences of these symbols are WELL-FORMED FORMULAE (wff's) of that language. If α and β denote wff's,[2] we may formulate the following rules: (i) each proposition letter is a wff; (ii) $\alpha * \beta$ is a wff, where '$*$' denotes a binary connective; (iii) $\sim \alpha$ is a wff. Note that the rules are recursive: α and β may stand also for compound wff's. The parentheses or structural symbols indicate the scope of the connectives and negation.[3] According to these rules the following sequences of symbols are wff's: $p, p \vee q, (p \& q) \vee r, (q \& r) \supset (p \vee r), \sim [p \vee \sim (r \& \sim s)]$; and $pq, p \vee \& r, p \sim \vee s, (\ )p \sim \& \sim \vee)$ are not. Some of the well-formed formulae are equivalent, ie may be mutually substituted for each other. Thus $p \& q$ is equivalent to $q \& p, p \vee q$ to $q \vee p$.

A characteristic subset of syntactic rules of a formal system are the DEFINITIONS of this system, eg definitions of the connectives in terms of each other: $p \& q$ may be defined as $\sim (\sim p \vee \sim q), p \vee q$ as $\sim (\sim p \& \sim q), \sim \sim p$ as p, $p \equiv q$ as $(p \supset q) \& (q \supset p)$, and $p \supset q$ as $\sim (p \& \sim q)$.

Typical of formal systems are the DERIVATION RULES. These rules allow us to derive one formula from a sequence of one or more other formulae. A formula thus derived is called a THEOREM if it is derived from a primitive formula, ie an AXIOM, or from another formula derived from an axiom, ie from another theorem. The set of axioms is characteristic of a particular logical system. Thus, a theorem can be derived (or PROVED) from axioms and other theorems with rules of definition and rules of derivation (also called RULES OF INFERENCE). Characteristic axioms of a propositional logic are, for example: $(p \vee p) \supset p$, $q \supset (p \vee q)$, $(p \vee q) \supset (q \vee p)$ and $(q \supset r) \supset ((p \vee q) \supset (p \vee r))$. Well-known theorems include $p \equiv p, p \supset (p \vee q), (p \& q) \supset p, p \supset (q \supset p)$.

Derivation rules are the following: (i) detachment: if $p \supset q$ and p are given, derive: q; (ii) substitution: any proposition letter may be uniformly substituted for another proposition letter in a formula.

Given these derivation rules and the axioms it may be proved that the theorems given are indeed derivable and that the equivalences in the definitions are also theorems. It is possible to choose other axioms and other derivation rules in order to characterize the same set of theorems of this logical system.

2 Truth-functional semantics

2.1

A logical system not only consists of a set of formulae as specified in the syntax: formulae are also assigned an INTERPRETATION. Such an interpretation is given by the SEMANTICS of the system. A system without rules of interpretation is often called a CALCULUS. The rationale for the syntactic rules, however, is often semantic. That is, the categories, axioms and derivation rules are already chosen with an eye to their semantic roles. In a propositional system like the one briefly referred to above, the propositional letters are interpreted as expressions of PROPOSITIONS. There are various conceptions of this notion of a proposition. In linguistics, the meaning of a declarative sentence is often called a proposition. Sometimes the term STATEMENT is also used. In the semantics of (propositional) logical systems, a proposition is simply defined as an object which is assigned a TRUTH-VALUE. In classical systems this means that a proposition is either assigned the value TRUE or the value FALSE (but not both). Some systems also use a third truth-value, viz NEITHER TRUE NOR FALSE or INDETERMINATE. We see that the content or meaning of a proposition is disregarded in such a semantics: what is relevant here is only whether a proposition is true or false.

Compound formulae, *ie* expressions containing several propositional variables, are interpreted as expressing COMPOUND PROPOSITIONS. These are also either true or false, and their truth-value is determined by (i) the truth-value of the propositional variables, (ii) the values of the connectives. In other words: THE INTERPRETATION OF AN EXPRESSION IS DETERMINED BY THE INTERPRETATION OF EACH PART OF THE EXPRESSION. This is an important principle in formal semantics. Since the value of a compound proposition is either 'true' or 'false', and since this value depends on the truth-values of the component propositions (also either 'true' or 'false'), we say that this semantics is TRUTH-FUNCTIONAL. The only thing we need to know is how the connectives operate on the values of the component propositions. These connectives are usually interpreted as follows: &: 'and', ∨ : 'or', ⊃ : 'if ... then', ≡ : 'if and only if' (or 'is equivalent to'). These interpretations do not run parallel with those of the connectives *and, or, if ... then, if and only if* in natural language. This will be one of the major topics to be discussed in the next chapter. The 'meaning' of the logical connectives is much more restricted. Moreover, it will be given only in TRUTH-FUNCTIONAL terms: *ie* for each connective it is specified how it determines the truth-value of a compound expression, given the values of the component propositions. Thus, the semantic role of the connective '&' is the following: it makes the compound proposition 'true' if both conjuncts are 'true', and it makes the compound formula 'false' if one or both of the conjuncts is 'false'. Such semantic interpretations of the connectives are usually given in TRUTH TABLES. The values 'true' and 'false' are usually abbreviated as 't' and 'f', or as '1' and '0', respectively.[4] A truth table for the connectives used in the system introduced above is as follows:

and *or* *if...then* *if and only if* *not*

p q	$p \& q$	$p \lor q$	$p \supset q$	$p \equiv q$	$\sim p$
1 1	1	1	1	1	0
1 0	0	1	0	0	0
0 1	0	1	1	0	1
0 0	0	0	1	1	1

Since negation behaves like the connectives, in that the truth-value of the whole formula depends on the value of the proposition, it is also included in the truth table.

It should be noted again that the interpretation of the various connectives, especially of '$\supset$', does not always follow our (natural) language intuitions. Thus, the compound proposition 'If Peter is ill, he has called a doctor' is true also if 'Peter is ill' is false. There are logical systems which would assign the value 'neither true nor false' in such a case. Such proposals, and their importance for the analysis of the connectives in natural language, will be discussed in the next chapter.

Note also that the truth table allows us to determine the truth-value of any well-formed formula of the system: instead of p or q we may have more complex formulae (of which each elementary part is assigned a truth-value as in the table), eg $(p \& q) \lor (p \supset r)$, of which we only need to know the 'total' truth-value in order to compute the value of a still more complex formula of which it forms a part.

2.2

It was said above that much of the syntax of formal languages is worked out within a semantic perspective. One of the central properties of the derivation rules is that they are being formulated such that they 'preserve truth'. That is, given a formula α and a formula β, if β is derivable from α, then if α is true β is also true. This means that if we choose formulae as axioms which are ASSUMED to be true, all theorems which are derivable from these axioms will also be true. This is precisely the way a calculus is set up: we are interested not only in well-formed formulae but also in true formulae. In particular, we are interested in the set of VALID formulae of a system: a valid formula is a formula which is true under any interpretation of its component (atomic) propositions. Thus, a formula like $p \lor \sim p$ is true whatever p means (in truth-functional terms: whether p is true or p is false). The same holds for $(p \lor q) \equiv (q \lor p)$: whether $p \lor q$ is true or false (throughout the whole formula), the formula will remain true under any interpretation. We may say that in such valid formulae truth is 'structural': it only depends on the form of the expression and the connectives used.

A formal system is usually required to be CONSISTENT. This means that if

consistent

the formula α can be derived in it, the formula $\sim\alpha$ cannot possibly be derivable. According to our definition of validity the formula $\sim\alpha$ would then be false under any interpretation (of the component propositions of α).

complete

Another typical logical property of the propositional system discussed above is its COMPLETENESS, which establishes a clear connection between the syntax and the semantics: a system is complete if and only if every valid wff is also derivable as a theorem. This is the case if the axioms are valid and the derivation rules validity-preserving. One of the central tasks of logicians is to PROVE that some constructed system is really consistent and complete (or incomplete).

Although the notions of truth and validity are closely intertwined with syntactic notions, we should make a clear distinction between SYNTACTIC DERIVABILITY as a relation between wff's and the truth-preserving relation between interpreted wff's, viz propositions. The latter relation (which will also be discussed below) is that of SEMANTIC ENTAILMENT. If β is derivable from α, then it is said that α ENTAILS β, or rather that the proposition expressed by α entails the proposition expressed by β, and conversely if the system is complete.

The syntactic relation of derivability between formulae may itself also be expressed by a symbol, viz by '$\vdash$', where $\alpha \vdash \beta$ is read: 'β is derivable from α'. When we just write $\vdash\alpha$, this means 'α is derivable' (in a system), or simply 'α is a theorem' (of a system). Similarly we use the symbol '$\Vdash$' to denote semantic entailment, where $\alpha \Vdash \beta$ reads 'α entails β', and $\Vdash\alpha$ reads 'α is valid' (in some interpreted system).

3 Predicate logic and its semantics
3.1
The propositional system briefly introduced above is, so to speak, a 'basic' system. It may express simple or compound propositions as 'wholes', *ie* it does not give a further analysis of the logical INTERNAL structure of the propositions. Sentences like *Peter is ill* and *Peter didn't know whether Mary would sell him her jewels for the ridiculous price of £100* are both treated alike. It is natural, however, to say that the truth-value of the propositions themselves is also determined by the various parts of their internal structure.

A language with categories of expressions for such parts of sentences is that of a PREDICATE LOGIC. Its typical categories are:

   (i) individual variables: $x, y, z, \ldots$
  (ii) individual constants: $a, b, c, \ldots$
 (iii) n-place predicate letters: $f(..), g(..,..), \ldots$
 (iv) quantifiers: $\exists, \forall$

Further it has negation, connectives and auxiliary symbols (plus a comma) as in a propositional logic. The intended interpretations of these symbols are as follows. Individual expressions are interpreted as (stand for, or denote) individual things or objects: a variable as an arbitrary object, and a constant as some specific or particular object, like the expressions *someone* and *Peter* (or *the boy*) in natural language. *N*-place predicate letters are interpreted as expressing properties of, or relations between such things or objects, like *is ill*, *walks* and *loves* or *sells*, respectively. The quantifiers are interpreted as follows: '∃*x*' is read as 'For at least one *x*', and '∀*x*' as 'For all *x*'. In natural language we have more quantifiers, *eg many*, *some*, *most*, etc. Again, the logical system only uses some of the elements of natural language, and this use is moreover restricted in specific ways. The reasons for these particular uses in logic are partly to be sought in its role as a foundation of mathematics.

Although some basic elements of the sentence structure of natural languages appear also in the categories and syntax of predicate logics, it must be borne in mind that predicate logics were not primarily developed as a means for linguistic analysis. We shall return below to the possible applications of logic in linguistics.

The FORMATION RULES of a predicate logic are the following: (i) if *f* is an *n*-place predicate letter and $a_1, \ldots, a_n$ are TERMS (*ie* individual variables or constants), then $f(a_1, \ldots a_n)$ is a wff; (ii) if α and β are wff's so are ∼α, (∀*x*)(α), (∃*x*)(α), and α ∗ β. Usually we put parentheses before and after the sequence of terms, and commas between the terms. According to these rules the following sequences of symbols are wff's of a predicate language: $f(a)$, $f(x)$, $g(b, y)$, (∀*x*)($f(x, a)$), (∀*y*)(∃*z*)($g(y, z)$), whereas bg, a(∀*x*) and (∃*x*)(∃*y*) are not.

Variables are said to be BOUND by the corresponding quantifiers, as in (∃*x*)($g(x, a)$) and (∀*y*)($h(x, y, z)$), and called FREE if this is not the case, as *x* in $g(a, x)$ and (∃*y*)($g(x, y)$). A wff containing free variables is called a PROPOSITIONAL FUNCTION, a wff without propositional variables is called a SENTENCE. Thus, a propositional function such as $f(x)$ may be turned into a sentence if we substitute *a* for *x*. If we take expressions from natural language, *is ill* (*x*) would be a propositional function and *is ill* (*Peter*) would be a sentence.

We usually put parentheses around that part of the formula which is the SCOPE of a quantifier. Thus in (∃*x*)($f(x, a)$) & $g(b)$ only the part $f(x, a)$ is under the scope of the quantifier. The same holds for the use of the sign of negation.

A formula such as ∼(∀*x*)(∃*y*)[$f(x, y) ⊃ g(y, x)$] would *eg* be read as: It is not the case that for all *x* there is at least one *y* such that: if *x* has a relation *f* to *y*, then *y* has a relation *g* to *x*.

Many predicate logics have an additional specific category, viz a binary relation (between individuals) of IDENTITY (=), usually written not before the variables but between them: $a = b$ and (∃*x*)(∃*y*)($x = y$) are well-formed. Just as logical connectives may be defined in terms of each other (and negation), logical quantifiers may be defined in terms of each other. Thus, 'all *x* have a property *g*' could also be read as '*no x* does *not* have *g*', and conversely 'some *x* (at least one) have *h*' may be read as '*not* all *x* do *not* have *h*'. Again, this equivalence does not always hold for the corresponding natural language quantifiers.

The AXIOMATIZATION of this predicate calculus is based on the propositional calculus; theorems in the latter become theorems in the former by substitution: if $p \supset p$ is valid then $fa \supset fa$, $(\exists x)[h(x)] \supset (\exists x)[h(x)]$ are theorems of the predicate calculus. Further axioms are of course necessary, *eg* for the properties of the quantifiers. Thus it will be assumed that under some further conditions formulae of the type $(\forall x)[f(x)] \supset fa$ are theorems. Indeed, if f is a property of all objects, then it is also a property of some (any) object a (or b, or c, etc). Further we have the equivalence of $(\forall x)[f(x)]$ with $f(x)$: if any arbitrary x has f, then all x have f, and conversely. Formulae of the structure $(\forall x)[f(x) \supset g(x)] \supset (\forall x)[f(x)] \supset (\forall x)[g(x)]$ are also theorems.

As rules of derivation we may have (i) the predicate logical version of the detachment rule (also called MODUS PONENS): if $\alpha \supset \beta$ and α are theorems then β is a theorem, (ii) and the rule of universal generalization which allows us to go from formulae like (fx) to formulae like $(\forall x)[f(x)]$. Similar axioms and rules may be given for the existential quantifier $\exists$; if a formula like fa is a theorem we may infer $(\exists x)[f(x)]$: indeed, if some specific particular individual has f, then we may safely conclude that there is at least one individual with this property (whereas the converse does not hold, of course). Several combinations of axioms and derivation rules are possible in order to define the same set of theorems.

3.2

The SEMANTICS for a predicate logical system such as the one very roughly sketched above requires also a number of specific properties. As in a propositional system wff's are either true or false, where compound wff's again are interpreted according to the truth tables for the connectives (including negation). The truth-value of an atomic proposition, however, now depends on the VALUES of its internal parts: we must INTERPRET the predicate letters, the individual constants and variables, and the quantifiers.

Above, it was said that individual expressions are intended to be interpreted as (denoting, referring to) INDIVIDUAL THINGS or objects. Hence, we need a set of such things as possible values for the individual expressions. This set is usually called a DOMAIN and denoted by the symbol D, where the members of D are $d_1, d_2, \ldots$ In interpreting an individual expression we take some member d_i from D as the VALUE of that expression. The assignment of values is operated by a function, viz a VALUATION FUNCTION, which takes expressions of some formal language as arguments. Such a function will be denoted by the letter V. Thus, wff's from the propositional and predicate calculi are assigned a value from the sets {true, false} or $\{0, 1\}$, as follows: $V(\alpha) = 1$, $V(\beta) = 0$, or $V(\alpha \& \beta) = 0$, for example. Similarly, the function V will assign some member d_i of D to some expression like a: $V(a) = d_i$ or $V(b) = d_j$. Predicate letters are classically interpreted as SETS of objects, viz the set of objects having a certain property or the set of pairs (triples, $\ldots n$-tuples) of objects standing in a certain relation to each other. A

predicate like the natural language expression *is ill* would thus be interpreted
as the set of ill things (people), and the predicate *loves* as the set of pairs $\langle x, y \rangle$
such that x loves y. The sets which are the values of predicate letters are the
subsets $D_1, D_2, \ldots$ of D, or of the cartesian product $D \times D$. The valuation of a
predicate letter is thus written as $V(f) = D_i$, where D_i is the set of things
having the property f. From these interpretations of the parts of a proposition, the interpretation of the whole proposition is simply given as follows
(iff = if and only if): $V(f(a)) = 1$ iff $V(a) \in V(f)$, $V(f(a)) = 0$ iff $V(a) \notin V(f)$.[5]
In words: a proposition is true if the object denoted by a is a member of the
set denoted by f. Thus a proposition like 'John is ill' is true, if there is some
object John, if there is a set of ill people, and if the object John belongs to this
set, viz has the property of illness which characterizes this set. Similarly, for
the interpretation of an expression like $g(a, b)$, where a pair of objects $\langle d_i, d_j \rangle$
must be an element of the set D_i denoted by g, where D_i is a subset of $D \times D$.

The formal semantics of quantifiers has a number of complications which
cannot be discussed here. A formula like $(\exists x)[f(x)]$ is true iff there is a d in D
such that, for some individual constant a, the value of a is d, and the formula
$f(a)$ is true. That is, an existentially quantified formula is true if one arbitrary
individual satisfies the predicate. A universally quantified formula is true if
for every $d \in D$ such that d is a value of a constant $a, b \ldots$ the formulae $f(a)$,
$f(b), \ldots$ are true. We see that an existential quantifier is related to an (infinite)
disjunction of formulae, and a universal quantifier to an (infinite) conjunction of formulae.

The conditions given above, in terms of valuation functions and a domain
(and its elements and subsets) are TRUTH CONDITIONS. In all cases where
these conditions are not satisfied the formula will be assigned the value 0
(falsity). These truth conditions are RECURSIVE. If we know the interpretation rules for the various types of expressions (categories) and of their
structural combinations, we can interpret any formula of the language, which
is an aim of a semantics.

3.3

It has been shown that formulae of a formal language are interpreted with
respect to a domain of individuals, also called the UNIVERSE OF DISCOURSE,
and under a certain valuation. An ordered pair of such a domain and a
valuation function, viz $\langle D, V \rangle$, is called a MODEL. A formula is said to be true
(or false) IN a model. If a formula is true in at least one model (*ie* for some
universe of discourse under some valuation) it is called SATISFIABLE. A valid
formula is a formula which is true in all models. Since formal semantics
interprets formal language in terms of models, it is sometimes also called
MODEL THEORETICAL semantics.

This semantics, as we have seen, is formulated in a SET-THEORETICAL
language: the universe of discourse with respect to which formulae are
assigned truth-values is characterized in terms of sets, operations on or
relations between sets, members of sets, and functions. It is possible to give a
semantics also in terms of other mathematical systems (*eg* of algebra or
topology).

Below, it will be shown that a semantics for natural language must be 'richer' than the elementary semantics outlined above. If it could intuitively be said that semantics specifies the relations between (language) expressions and the 'things' these expressions are 'about', it should be emphasized that a formal system not only gives the formal (or logical) structure of these expressions but also a formal reconstruction of those structures of the universe of discourse needed to interpret these expressions.

4 Modal logics and their semantics
4.1
The propositional and predicate logical systems are the basic and standard systems of logic, even if there are many variants of each system, *ie* with different sets of axioms, rules, categories in their syntax and with different types of semantics.

These basic systems may however be enriched with additional categories of expressions for a certain number of reasons, *eg* in order to be able to express certain structures of formal or natural languages. One of these categories is that of MODAL expressions, *eg It is necessary (that), It is possible (that), It is known (that), It is obligatory (that), It is wished (that)*, etc. To these various kinds of *modalities*, viz alethic (necessary, possible), epistemic (knowledge), doxastic (belief), deontic (obligation, permission), boulomaeic (want, wish, preference), etc we may add expressions of TIME, like *It is (now) the case (that), It was (has been) the case (that), It will be the case (that)*, which are also expressed by TENSES in natural language.

Whereas a predicate logic such as the one discussed above makes explicit the logical structure of such sentences as *Peter is ill* or *Peter hit Mary and John went to Paris*, it does not account for the tenses in these simple sentences (among other things), nor can it account for such modifications of these sentences as *Perhaps Peter is ill* or *Peter wants to hit Mary and John must go to Paris*. The addition of a special category of modal and tense expressions to propositional and predicate logical systems therefore considerably enhances their *expressive power* with respect to the structure of sentences in natural language.
4.2
Formally speaking, modal expressions are *operators:* they combine with non-modal sentences to make more complex sentences. Given a sentence *Peter is ill*, we obtain another sentence by prefixing *It is possible that.*

Most thoroughly studied are the alethic modalities *It is necessary that* and *It is possible that*, which are usually symbolized by '$\square$' and '$\lozenge$', respectively, and prefixed to any wff. Thus $\square p, \square(p \,\&\, q), \lozenge(p \supset q)$ are wff's of a MODAL PROPOSITIONAL CALCULUS, and $\square(\forall x)[f(x)]$, $\lozenge g(a, b)$, $\square(\forall x)(\exists y)[h(x, y)] \,\&\, \lozenge fa$, are wff's of a MODAL PREDICATE CALCULUS.[6] Modal expressions may also modify modal sentences, hence expressions of the type $\Box\Box p$, $\Box\Diamond q$, $\Diamond\Box\Diamond r$ are also well-formed where each modal operator may be preceded by a sign of negation.

As is usual in setting up a new (or extended) logical system, appropriate axioms and derivation rules must be formulated for the new category of expressions. Differences in this respect define different modal systems.

Necessity and possibility are related notions and may, just like the quantifiers, be defined in terms of each other, such that $\Box p \equiv \sim\Diamond\sim p$ and $\Diamond p \equiv \sim\Box\sim p$ are valid wff's. Indeed, if something is necessarily the case then it is impossible that it is not the case, and something is possibly the case, if it is not necessarily not the case.

We may have various types of necessity or possibility: something may be physically, biologically, psychologically or sociologically necessary or possible. The modalities treated in modal logics are LOGICAL MODALITIES, which are an abstraction and generalization from the other modalities. Thus, we say that valid formulae of a logical system (tautologies) are logically true or LOGICALLY NECESSARY. Similarly, a wff which follows logically from other wff's follows necessarily. A wff which is not logically or necessarily true is called CONTINGENT or contingently true. Its truth does not depend on purely logical properties of a formula, but on the facts of the universe of discourse.

Another specific element of modal systems are the connectives of LOGICAL or STRICT IMPLICATION and EQUIVALENCE, written as '$\dashv$' and '$=$' respectively. The first formalizes the relation of logical derivability between sentences, and is usually taken to have the relation of ENTAILMENT between a proposition as its semantic counterpart. Its relation to the notions of necessity and possibility, mentioned above, is given in the definition of '$\dashv$': $p \dashv q \equiv \Box(p \supset q)$. Two sentences are logically equivalent if they mutually imply each other logically (strictly).

Note that the modal operators and the modal connectives are not truth-functional: by simply knowing the truth-value of α we do not know yet whether $\Box\alpha$ is true or false.

The intuitively sound principles which normally are taken as axioms for modal systems are: $\Box p \supset p$, (or $p \supset \Diamond p$), $\Box(p \supset q) \supset (\Box p \supset \Box q)$.

Derivation rules are the usual rule of substitution and modus ponens. A specific modal derivation rule specifies that if a wff α is a theorem or axiom, $\Box\alpha$ is also (rule of necessitation). Indeed, a tautology is NECESSARILY true.

4.3

The most interesting feature of modal languages is perhaps their SEMANTICS: how do we interpret sentences with modal expressions? It has been indicated that modal operators are not truth-functional, so what kind of models do we need in order to satisfy wff's with such operators?

In order to explain the specific elements of modal semantics, we take another modal system as an illustrative example, viz TENSE LOGIC. Operators of tense logic are for example P for *It was the case (that)*, F for *It will be the case (that)*, where Pp, $F(p \lor q)$, $PF(p \& q)$, $FP(\exists x)[f(x) \supset g(x)]$ are wff's, for example. Formulae without P or F are to be read in the present tense. Now what will be the semantic rule for interpreting sentences like *Peter was ill* or *If Peter is ill, he will call a doctor?* In non-modal predicate logic no tense differentiation can be interpreted, or rather we merely have present tense (or even tenseless) sentences. Intuitively, then, a sentence like *Peter was ill* is true (now) if *Peter is ill* is true 'somewhere' in the past. This past, as well as the future, for that matter, is determined by the present 'now', viz the moment at which the sentence is uttered. Call this moment N, standing for 'now'. N is a point (or period) of TIME. The past will now be constructed as the (linearly ordered) set of time points which PRECEDE N, the future as the sequence of time points which FOLLOW N (or, equivalently, which N precedes). Thus, the truth of the sentence *John is ill* somewhere in the past, is simply truth WITH RESPECT TO or AT some point (or period) of time preceding N. In a model satisfying tense-logical sentences we thus seem to need as specific additional elements: (i) a set T of time points (ii) a binary relation '$<$' for PRECEDENCE, defined over members of T, such that $t_i < t_j$ reads: 't_i precedes t_j'. That we interpret sentences with respect to a point or period of time, or in general with respect to a certain SITUATION, seems very natural: *I have a headache* is true now, *I went to the movies* is true NOW if the sentence *I go to the movies* is true at some point(s) preceding now. Hence, the interpretations of formulae like $P\alpha$ and $F\alpha$ go stepwise: $P\alpha$ is true (now) iff α is true at some $t_i < N$, and $F\alpha$ is true iff α is true at some point t_j, such that $N < t_j$.

4.4

The interpretation of necessity and possibility is very similar. If we take the notion of a SITUATION introduced above, we may say that p is necessarily true if p is true in ANY SITUATION WE CAN IMAGINE. Similarly, we say that p is possible, if there is AT LEAST ONE IMAGINABLE SITUATION in which p is true. Modal semantics has introduced a technical notion for such an imaginable situation, viz the notion of a POSSIBLE WORLD.

Although the notion of a possible world should be seen as a formal primitive, it may be intuitively characterized by such terms as 'situation', mentioned above, or 'state of affairs'. More specifically, a possible world is 'something' AT which a set of propositions are satisfied. Conversely, a proposition is therefore often defined as a set of possible worlds, viz the set of possible worlds at which this proposition is satisfied. Note that the notion of a possible world should not be identified with our intuitive ideas of (our) 'world', 'reality', etc, but as an abstract construct of semantic theory (model theory). Thus, our actual world is just one element of a set of possible worlds. A possible world, as the term 'possible' suggests, is also any state of affairs which is not the case but which MIGHT have been the case. This possibility may be of various types: we may imagine a situation where the facts are different from the real or actual facts, but compatible with the postulates (laws, principles, etc) of the actual world. On the other hand we may imagine worlds with partly or fully different laws of nature, *ie* worlds which are increasingly DISSIMILAR to our 'own' world, or rather to the set of worlds which could have been the real world, *ie* those worlds satisfying the same set of basic postulates.

When we think of our actual world, we do not have a mere static conception of this world: things are going on, events happen, actions are performed. Instead of possible situations or states of affairs we may therefore also take possible worlds as COURSES OF EVENTS. Since such courses of events are determined also by the course of time, a STATE of such a course of events may be defined as a pair consisting of a possible world and a time point from the set T introduced above. If W denotes the set of possible worlds, with w_1, w_2, ... as elements, a state of a possible world at one moment, *ie* a SITUATION, would be denoted by pairs like $\langle w_i, t_i \rangle$.

If we just speak of a possible world we may mean such a time point or period or a possible course of events, but often a possible world is intuitively conceived of in a larger sense, such that many compatible courses of events may occur 'in' a possible world. Further interpretations of the term are possible, each with philosophical advantages and problems.

Since the notion of a possible world and that of a proposition are so closely related, we may also valuate expressions not with respect to possible worlds but with respect to sets of propositions, viz DESCRIPTIONS of such worlds. The advantage is, among other things, that such descriptions may be partial, incomplete or even inconsistent. This may be especially relevant in the semantics for epistemic and doxastic logics: it may be that we neither know whether p nor whether $\sim p$ is the case in a certain world (description).

If we take some possible world w_i from the set W, we say that the worlds of the set are the ALTERNATIVE possible worlds of w_i. Just as we took some specific time point ('now') as a distinguished element from the set of time points T, in order to define the ordering of moments of time with respect to this particular time point, we also take a specific world as a 'point of view' with respect to the set of possible worlds, viz the ACTUAL WORLD (w_0). Similarly, whereas we had a binary relation over T, viz precedence, in the semantics of tense logic, we here need a binary relation over possible worlds, denoting the alternativity or rather the ACCESSIBILITY of worlds to/from each other. This notion of accessibility is often explained by comparing it to the intuitive notion of imaginability of a world, or more particularly to the knowledge we have about other possible worlds. Accessibility is also a primitive however, formally speaking. It is usually denoted by R. This relation may have different formal properties, according to which the various modal systems are differentiated. If somebody in a world w_i knows what is the case in w_i itself (which is normal) the relation is REFLEXIVE, that is we have access to our own world (in this epistemic modal system). If somebody in w_i has access to (knows about, say) a world w_j, and conversely somebody in w_j has access to w_i, the relation R is SYMMETRIC. Finally, if somebody in w_i knows everything somebody else in w_j knows about a third world w_k, which means that we have access to w_k, via w_j, from w_i, R is TRANSITIVE. These various properties of R, which may correspond to various actual relationships between situations or persons (knowledge, belief, etc), are dependent upon specific axioms and derivation rules in the different modal systems.

4.5

To interpret modal sentences we must know more about 'what there may be' than we need to interpret non-modal sentences. To be more specific, we are forced to design an abstract ontological picture by the use of possible worlds, relations between them, and by letting valuations of expressions be given 'at' such worlds. A modal semantics thus requires MODELS including at least the triple $\langle W, w_0, R \rangle$, and if we want to include the temporal aspect, we would need $\langle W, w_0, R, T, \langle, t_0 \rangle$ where W is a set of possible worlds, w_0 a specific element of W (the actual world), R a relation of accessibility defined over members of W, and the temporal notions as defined above, where t_0 indicates 'Now'. For modal predicate calculi we further need a set D of individuals, as for non-modal predicate systems.

There are a number of philosophical problems with such a set of individuals. First of all, what belongs to this set and what not: what is a 'thing'? Should we include properties, abstract notions, facts like events and actions, or only discrete concrete objects, like chairs, pipes, pigs, and persons? What about water, tobacco, skin, and other mass objects or continuous objects? We will not decide such questions here, but include any abstract or concrete individual thing with the practical criterion that we must be able to refer to it (*eg* by the pronoun *it*). A more specific problem for modal logic: do we assume that the set of individuals is identical for all possible worlds? Intuitively, we know that objects come into existence, are destroyed and that certain objects are imaginable but do not occur in our actual world. For reasons of simplicity, therefore, we briefly assume one set D of individuals of which each world selects its own subset. Below, we will briefly touch upon this issue again.

The sequence of abstract notions reconstructing purely formally the notion of (possible) 'reality' with which the semantic rules relate the sentences of a formal language is called a MODEL STRUCTURE. Valuations of expressions, thus, are given with respect to such model structures. The combination of a model structure and a valuation function is a MODEL, as discussed above. Sentences thus are true or false in a model structure under a given interpretation. Since possible worlds are a central element of model structures we often simply say that a sentence is true at (or in) a (possible) world.

The interpretation of $\square p$, would now run as follows: $V(\square p, w_i) = 1$ iff for all worlds w_j, such that $w_i R w_j$, $V(p, w_j) = 1$. If not, $V(\square p, w_i) = 0$. And for possibility: $V(\lozenge p, w_i) = 1$ iff for at least one w_j, such that $w_i R w_j$, $V(p, w_i) = 1$. If not, $V(\lozenge p, w_i) = 0$.

We see that the valuation function now has pairs of arguments, viz from the set of wff's, and from the set of possible worlds. In our example w_i is the world at which the modal sentence is interpreted; it is the point of view for the 'inspection' of the alternative worlds: if in all those worlds p holds, then $\Box p$ holds in w_i; if there is at least one (eg w_i itself if R is reflexive), $\Diamond p$ holds in w_i. We immediately see that the axiom $p \supset \Diamond p$ is indeed valid. A (modal) wff is valid if it is true in all (modal) models.

The 'stepwise' interpretation of modal wff's with one operator also characterizes the interpretation of wff's with several modal operators, eg $\Box\Box p, \Diamond\Diamond p,$ or $\Box\Diamond p$. We just have to make one step more, and see whether for all w_j-worlds in which $\Box p$ is true it is the case that p is true in all the worlds accessible from w_j-worlds. If the relation R is transitive (and reflexive) we would 'see' these worlds anyway, and $\Box\Box p$ would be equivalent with $\Box p$: necessity, then, is always necessary. We see that iteration of modal operators also leads to philosophically problematic issues.

4.6

Modalities in quantified formulae raise a number of problems. We have already indicated that the domain of individuals or universe of discourse, which is the core of predicate logical models, may be taken to be really 'universal' in the sense that each world has the same individuals (though there may well be different properties and relations between them), or each world has its own set of individuals, or we have a general set of POSSIBLE INDIVIDUALS of which each world selects, by some selection function to be added to the model structure, its own set of ACTUAL individuals.

The differences involved appear from such formulae as $(\forall x)[\Box f(x)]$ and $\Box(\forall x)[f(x)]$; in the first formula it is the case for all individuals of a set that in each world these individuals have the property f necessarily; in the second formula, all objects of each world (which may hence be different sets of things) have a certain property. Modalities prefixed to predicates (or propositional functions) are usually called MODALITIES DE RE, modalities prefixed to a whole sentence are called MODALITIES DE DICTO. In the latter it is the whole proposition which is necessarily true, in the former the whole proposition is contingent, but an object's having a certain property is necessary. This means that the 'same' object in all other worlds also has this property. Yet, two objects from different worlds can hardly be said to be IDENTICAL in the strict sense.

Ignoring again important philosophical intricacies we speak of identical individuals in different worlds only as COUNTERPARTS,[7] which are SIMILAR to a given individual, eg possess the same set of NECESSARY (ESSENTIAL) or relevant properties. If we say *Peter would buy a yacht if he had the money*, we refer to a counterpart of Peter in some alternative, counterfactual, world. This counterpart Peter is probably very much like the actual Peter (in particular, he would also buy, and even does buy, a yacht) with the ACCIDENTAL difference that he has money, whereas the actual Peter has not.

The same does not hold only for objects but for states of affairs or facts in general: in order to interpret COUNTERFACTUAL SENTENCES, like the one given here, we must assume that the world in which Peter will buy a yacht if he has the money is very similar to ours: at least it must be a world where yachts can be bought, and where a considerable amount of money is needed for buying a yacht, where yachts exist, and also where people may have the wish to acquire things like yachts.[8]

5 Extension and intension
5.1

The problems of counterparts, transworld identity of individuals, and similarities between possible worlds, bring us to a more general issue in current formal, and especially modal, semantics. It has been shown that formal semantics is not strictly about MEANING, but rather about REFERENCE: it specifies the objects denoted by sentences and parts of sentences, and thus provides CONDITIONS under which sentences are true or false. Such objects are variously called REFERENTS, DENOTATA or EXTENSIONS. Depending on the semantics, languages are extensional if their expressions have such extensions as values. This is less obviously the case for the extensions 'truth' and 'falsity' themselves; at least they are not identifiable objects of a possible world. In order to have a more coherent semantics, we shall therefore assume that the extensions of sentences are FACTS in some possible world,[9] and reserve notions like 'true' and 'false' for properties of sentences, propositions or even utterances of these; a sentence is 'true', then, if the fact it denotes 'exists' in some possible world. Such a fact is a composite 'thing', and exists if an individual has a certain property (belongs to a set) as specified in the truth conditions.

Modal languages are not truth-functional; similarly, a modal operator does not refer to objects of the extensional type, but rather indicates 'where' some fact exists, and should therefore be interpreted rather as an operation or function. There are other objects of reference of (parts of) sentences which do not have a straightforward extensional character. When I say *A lion has four legs*, the phrase *A lion* is a GENERIC expression, and neither denotes some particular object in some particular world, nor a set of such objects (the extensional value of a predicate). Similarly, in a sentence *The man who wins the match will receive a thousand pounds*, the expression *the man who wins the match* may not refer to a particular man, but to the (only) individual who satisfies some property (winning the race) in some future world. Such objects, which are characterized by some property, will be called INTENSIONAL objects.[10] They have a CONCEPTUAL or POSSIBLE nature, rather than an ACTUAL nature. In the strict sense, extensional objects are specific spatio-temporally defined properties of a particular possible world, and as such are 'unique'. When I talk about Peter, I do not usually refer to this momentarily physical existence of Peter here and now, but to something which remains more or less 'identical' or similar in a series of situations (a 'life'). Formally speaking, an individual is a FUNCTION defining a set of counterparts for a set of possible worlds, or for a set of moments of time, or combinations of these (situations).

We should, however, go a step higher when talking about concepts. The concept 'man' defines a set of DIFFERENT individuals (*ie* different constant individual functions, *eg* Peter, Lord Byron, Sherlock Holmes, etc) in different (sets of) possible worlds. Similarly, complex terms like *the man who will win the race* or *the girl next door* may thus refer to an individual concept or else to an actual individual satisfying this conceptual function in the actual world. In this respect the noun phrase *the girl next door* is ambiguous, for it may refer to an individual concept (anyone who lives next door and of whom I know it is a girl) or to some particular, identified individual, say Sally, whom I know. The first use of terms or noun phrases is often called QUALIFYING, the second REFERENTIAL.[11]

Characteristic of intensional expressions is their behaviour under substitution and identity. In principle, expressions referring to the same object may be mutually substituted, which makes *Amsterdam is beautiful* and *The capital of the Netherlands is beautiful* equivalent. Not, however, in modal contexts, because it may well be that the expression *the capital of the Netherlands* picks out another individual in some worlds than the expression *Amsterdam:* the Netherlands in some imaginable time or world COULD have had another town as its capital, whereas *Amsterdam* always refers to the 'same' town. This is particularly true in epistemic/doxastic sentences: if we prefix the phrase *John believes that* to the sentences above, it may well be that they are not equivalent, viz if John (erroneously) believes that The Hague is the capital of the Netherlands. This means that the equivalence does not hold in the worlds which are epistemically or doxastically accessible with respect to what John knows or believes.

Interpretation apparently must not only be given with respect to some world(s), and from the point of view of some (actual) world, but also from the point of view of persons in these worlds, viz with respect to their wants, wishes, knowledge, beliefs and intentions, also called PROPOSITIONAL ATTITUDES. The semantics for sentences with such expressions (*John knows, wants, hopes,* etc *that,* or simply *hopefully, must, perhaps,* etc) requires a specific relation of accessibility depending on the type of attitude and further specified with respect to a given individual person.[12] An expression like $B_a p$, for *a believes that p* is thus true if p is true in a world compatible with *a*'s beliefs, *ie* in a world in which the set $B(a)$ of *a*'s beliefs is satisfied.

A sentence like *John believes that the capital of the Netherlands is beautiful* is ambiguous in another sense, now with respect to the speaker. In fact, this speaker may just refer to John's belief (some proposition in John's Belief-set), but the speaker may also refer to the capital of the Netherlands (correctly thinking of Amsterdam or not) and predicate of it that John believes it to be beautiful. In the latter case John may have said *Amsterdam is beautiful*. The first sort of reference is called OPAQUE, the second TRANSPARENT, because in the first case the hearer does not know whether the speaker 'shares' the reference with a person he talks about, whereas in the transparent context a speaker himself refers to the (same) objects.

The use of such terms as speaker, hearer and what they know or believe brings us close to the domain of PRAGMATICS, to be discussed in the second part of this book. This shows that notions like truth and reference, although belonging to the domain of (formal and linguistic) semantics, may have pragmatic constraints.

5.2

With an account of intensions we seem to be a step closer to what is usually understood as the MEANING of an expression. In the use of natural language expressions we first must know what an expression means before we are able to establish its referent. In other words, reference 'depends on' meaning. The meaning of an expression seems indeed to be a conceptual construct which, for some possible world, may take an individual object as a value or extension. Intensions have the same formal structure. They are functions from the set of possible worlds (or moments of time) to the set of individuals (*ie* individual constant functions). In intuitive terms: they enable us to say: 'This thing, here and now, is a table', *ie* 'this is (an instance of) an actualization of the table-concept'.

It is a well-known assumption in linguistics, psychology and philosophy that meanings are COMPLEX objects: meanings have components, features, semantic markers, etc, specifying the PROPERTIES a 'thing' essentially or conventionally possesses. Such properties may be expressed in a set of SEMANTIC POSTULATES, of the form: $(\forall x)[f(x) \supset (g(x) \& h(x) \ldots)]$, or rather of this form with necessity prefixed before the formula as a whole, or before the propositional function, thus applying to the connective which then from a material implication ($\supset$) turns into a logical implication ($\dashv$) (see the formulae in 4.6 above). Below in 6.3. and in the next chapter we argue that even the logical implication does not seem the correct formal basis for the expression of entailment relations between propositions, but that we need a 'relevant' conditional expressing some kind of semantic interdependence of sentences or propositions.

Now, if we say that any object which has the property of being a horse necessarily also has the properties of being a mammal and an animal, we thereby mean that any horse in any possible world would have these properties. In other words: the three concepts are inherently related if each instantiation of the 'horse'-concept in each possible world would also instantiate the 'mammal'- and 'animal'-concept. We might also say that we cannot even imagine a horse which is not an animate mammal, or else we would no longer call 'it' a horse. However, there are important philosophical problems: we might consider the property 'does not fly' as essential for horses. Yet, we can easily imagine a world with at least one flying horse (Pegasus). This seems possible only if we assume some additional essential property which is roughly compatible with the other essential properties, or if some property is dropped which is 'marginal' enough (to neigh, for instance) to keep the rest of the concept intact. We see that the notion of SIMILARITY of worlds and of concepts plays an important role in a formal semantics of conceptual meaning.

Note that these remarks not only hold for individual concepts but also for what may be called PROPERTY CONCEPTS: the yellow of this particular lemon is also an instantiation (more or less constant under slight differences of light or perception) of the property concept 'yellow' which is necessarily linked with the property concept 'having colour'.

Thus, both for individual concepts and property concepts we might assume that they consist of some specific SELECTION of concepts (basic concepts?) of semantic space, in the sense that in any instantiation (as individual or property) in some possible world these concepts would be instantiated together. This would be a condition determined by the basic cognitive mechanisms of perception, which allow us to discriminate different things, to compare things, and to see a thing under various conditions (of time and place) as the 'same' thing. We here arrive at some fundamental philosophical problems of formal semantics (ontology) and cognition, in which very little insight exists at the moment. Our intention is only to show that the problem of meaning is related to modality and to the kind of semantics we propose to use.[13]

Note finally that what has been said about individual concepts and property concepts may also be said about FACT CONCEPTS (*eg* 'a boy being ill') taking facts as values in possible worlds. Fact concepts could be identified with the notion of a ('possible') PROPOSITION.[14]

5.3

The discussion of intensional objects and the structure of semantic space has been independent of a specific formal language, because the languages introduced were essentially extensional, with the possible exception of modal operators. We may however also design an INTENSIONAL LANGUAGE and a corresponding INTENSIONAL LOGIC. Such a language would have special expressions with intensions as values. For example, besides the propositional letter p, interpreted as a truth value or as a fact (in some possible world) we might have an expression $\acute{p}$ interpreted as the proposition or fact concept taking actual values (truth values or facts) depending on moments of time or in general on possible worlds. Similarly, in an intensional predicate logic we would have expressions for intensional objects (individual concepts) and for concepts of properties or relations. The intensional two-place predicate ⟨love⟩ would denote the concept of loving, *ie* the characteristic function which for each possible world or moment of time would assign the set of those individuals (pairs) satisfying this property. Futhermore, specific connectives might be needed to connect intensional formulae, because we would not only have simple truth-functional operations, but also operations on propositions (*ie* fact concepts). The intensional nature of natural language connectives will be studied in the next chapter. Finally, specific formation and derivation rules are necessary. For instance, as in modal contexts, substitution in intensional contexts, like *I believe that* . . . , of referentially identical expressions is not always possible, so that rules for identity and substitution of extensional versus intensional expressions should be formulated. The semantics for such systems, as informally discussed above, would not only have domains of 'real' individuals and real facts (space-time events and states) but a whole array of different types of concepts. As soon as such a semantics further takes into account properties of speech contexts we are halfway to a FORMAL PRAGMATICS. The meaning and reference of expressions would in that case further be determined by moment, place, speaker/hearer of the UTTERED expression. That is, the model structures would not only have a particular possible world from a set of such worlds, but a whole series of INDICES codetermining the interpretation. Such a semantics, therefore, is called an INDEXICAL or CONTEXTUAL SEMANTICS.[15] One of the elements in such a complex index is what may be called 'previous discourse'. Another, related to it, could be 'topic of conversation'. It is the aim of this book to provide more insight into the way sentences are interpreted RELATIVE TO other sentences in the same discourse, and relative to the discourse as a whole.

6 Formal semantics and natural language
6.1
At various points in the previous sections it has been emphasized that certain logical expressions or categories do not have exact counterparts in natural language.

Conversely, the structure of natural language sentences is so complex that not even the most sophisticated non-standard logic adequately reconstructs it. The tendency to add various modal and other operators, different connectives, various sorts of individual variables, other types of quantifiers, etc – all with their specific semantic interpretation – is also a consequence of a wish to analyse the logical structure of natural language.

There have been many attempts in recent years to apply formal semantics to natural language, *eg* in order to determine more precisely meaning and truth differences between expressions or sentences, to provide a basis for the interpretation of pronouns and quantifiers, to define notions such as presupposition, and so on.

These investigations will not be further referred to here, but we will try to give an example of this application of the tools of formal semantics to the characterization of connectives, connection and coherence in natural discourse.[16]
6.2
Of the great number of problems and proposed solutions in the domain of formal semantics of natural language we will briefly mention only two.

First of all, there does not exist a straightforward and more or less explicit relation between natural language sentences and logical sentences. The so-called LOGICAL STRUCTURE of a natural language sentence like *Peter is ill* was 'translated' rather intuitively in logical sentences like *ill(a)*, but hardly any formula would be adequate to represent such sentences as *The little boy who had stolen the orange wanted to eat it before he was seen*. Moreover, the semantics of formal languages is tightly interwoven with the syntactic structure of the expressions of the language: expressions of a specific CATEGORY receive different interpretations from those of other categories.

In order to make the semantics of natural language explicit we therefore need a syntax in which the categories are very explicit and at the same time have an intended semantic function. Thus, in such a syntax, a category would be needed for expressions like *he, the man* or *the man who stole a thousand pounds from my neighbour last week*, because in all cases these expressions may be interpreted as a specific individual. One of the systems now being worked out that aims at such a semantically oriented explicit syntax is called CATEGORIAL GRAMMAR (or CATEGORIAL SYNTAX).[17] The basic idea of such a categorial syntax is that only a few basic categories are needed in order to derive definitions of many other categories. If for example we had the categories 'sentence' and 'name' (or 'noun phrase') we could derive a category like 'verb phrase' by saying that it is the category which when following a 'name' yields a 'sentence'.

Once a categorial syntax for natural language sentences (which is by no means a simple enterprise) is defined, we would expect a formal semantics to interpret such syntactic structures. However, a categorial syntax is not usually formulated in the form of a proper logical language. What is needed, then, is a system of translation, which translates the sentences of natural language as they are categorially analysed into sentences of a specific logic, *eg* an INTENSIONAL LOGIC, as described earlier, because of the fact that natural language may refer to intensional objects; *ie* it not only denotes things, but its expressions have sense or meaning. Finally, the expressions of the intensional logic may be given a formal, model theoretical, semantics as described above. The crucial point in such a semantics is that the interpretation takes place according to the respective categories of the expressions as specified by the syntax. That is, corresponding to the syntactic categories we need semantic categories or TYPES (*eg* the type of entities, truth values, etc) to which the assigned values must belong. The same holds for the interpretation of operations.

In this system the complexity of the analysis of very simple sentences is such that it would be ill-advised to use such a formal grammar for the description of discourse structures and very complex sentences here. It is not our aim to elaborate the formal basis of a grammar, but to make systematic observations of linguistic phenomena in more intuitive and semi-formal ways.

6.3

The second major problem of a formal semantics of natural language is how to obtain a proper analysis not of syntactic but now of SEMANTIC

CATEGORIES. In current linguistic semantics we would qualify sentences like *The table was laughing* as semantically deviant or weird or strange, due to the fact that so-called SELECTION RESTRICTIONS in the combination of certain categories are violated: the use of the verb 'laughing' requires that the subject of the sentence (or in general: the expression it 'applies to') denotes a human or at least higher animate object. In other words, the concepts of table and of laughing are incompatible, at least in our actual possible world and in those worlds having similar physical and biological laws.

Classical logics do not have such constraints on the combination of categories; they do not differentiate between different SORTS of objects at all: any predicate may apply to any object. Hence, in order to give a sound account of our natural language use and intuitions with respect to the compatibility of semantic or ontological categories, our formal semantics must be SORTAL or CATEGORIAL.[18] In such a semantics we would not be obliged to say that a sentence like *The table is laughing* is simply false, in the same way as *Peter is laughing* may now be false, but that such a sentence is SORTALLY INCORRECT. It is characteristic of sortally incorrect sentences that they cannot properly be interpreted: we do not know under what conditions they should be true or false (in w_0). Hence, we will only interpret the set of sortally correct sentences of the language (and perhaps those sortally incorrect sentences which may have, ad hoc, a specific, *eg* metaphorical meaning).[19] A sentence may be said to be sortally correct if the intension of its individual or referring expression(s) belongs to the characteristic RANGE of a predicate. The range of the predicate 'laughing' would be, for instance, the set of individual concepts in semantic space defined by the concept 'human'. The individual concept ('possible object') 'table' does not belong to this set, so that the sentence is sortally incorrect.

Further details of this kind of sortal semantics will not be given here: only very few scattered approaches have been undertaken to provide a philosophical and formal base for such a semantics. One of the many problems is of course a sensible delimitation of such a sortal (intensional) semantics against a representation of the actual possible world. If the CONCEPTS, *ie* the intensions, of 'table' and 'laughing' are INCOMPATIBLE, this would mean that there is no possible world in which tables may be laughing. Although it may be questionable whether we should CALL such objects tables, we may very well imagine possible worlds (in fairy tales) where living objects (who can laugh) at least have forms and functions of (our) tables. Hence, compatibility and therefore sortal correctness is to be defined relative to sets of 'normal' worlds. In other words: a sentence is sortally incorrect RELATIVE TO a (sub)set of worlds W_i, if in no element $w \in W_i$ there is an actual fact satisfying the proposition expressed by that sentence.[20] The distinction between the CONVENTIONS of natural language meanings or concepts on the one hand, and our actual knowledge of what is possible in our world(s) is therefore not always very clear. Hence meanings may change, as well as the range of the objects which a predicate may apply to.

In this book we will not be concerned with this compatibility of concepts within the sentence, but with the compatibility of sentences in sequences, viz with the conditions imposed upon combinations of propositions. But it must be borne in mind that these conditions presuppose insight into the semantic structure of sentences as they are made explicit in current logical grammars.

Notes

1 For a general introduction to logic, see Thomason (1970) and Massey (1970) who are also concerned with semantics. For an introduction to modal logics, the semantics of which will be the basis of our semantic analysis of certain discourse phenomena, see Hughes and Cresswell (1968). For another elementary introduction to formal semantics, see especially Thomason (1973a). Other references will be given below.

2 The symbols α and β are so-called META-VARIABLES. They are expressions of the META-LANGUAGE, *ie* the language in which we speak about a (here logical) language. They denote well-formed formulae of a language, both elementary and compound. Although we may sometimes use such meta-symbols, the language used to speak ABOUT the logical language is itself mostly a natural language, here English.

3 Such parentheses are important in the structure of the formula. Without them a formula would be often ambiguous: $p \& q \lor r$ may be read either as $(p \& q) \lor r$, or as $p \& (q \lor r)$, *ie* either as a disjunction or as a conjunction.

4 We prefer to use the more neutral value symbols 1 and 0, which might also be interpreted as 'satisfied' or 'non-satisfied', *eg* in those formulae (in other types of logic) where we would not like to give truth-values, or as 'correct', 'incorrect', as we will do in the next chapter.

5 As with many points in our elementary introduction we conceal important philosophical and logical problems at this point. Thus, some would take a formula such as $f(a)$, *eg The girl is pretty*, to be false not only if the individual girl denoted by the phrase *the girl* does not belong to the set of pretty people, as denoted by the predicate expression *is pretty*, but also if there is no girl at all, or if there are not any pretty people (*ie* if the set were empty), as intended referentially. Others would prefer to call the formula 'unhappy', 'incorrect' or assign it a third truth value, *eg* 'neither true nor false', on the argument that only those formulae can seriously be called true or false which have expressions with corresponding referents. This problem was one of those dividing Russell and Strawson and their respective followers, and has been the origin of the discussion of the notion of presupposition: in the sentence above it would be presupposed, not asserted, that there is a (particular) girl, and asserted that she is pretty, where only the asserted 'part' of the sentence would be true or false. For the relevant original papers, see Copi and Gould, eds (1967), and also Strawson (1971) for further discussion. A recent study – among many – on this topic is Kempson (1975), to which we refer the reader for an introduction and for further references. Some aspects of this problem will be discussed in Chapter 4.

6 A recommended standard introduction to modal logic and its semantics is Hughes and Cresswell (1968), to which we refer the reader for details concerning our introductory remarks.

7 For an extensive discussion of these and similar problems, see Kripke (1972), Lewis (1973, 39 *ff*). For a discussion of counterparts in linguistics, see Lakoff (1968). For criticism of counterpart-theory, see Rescher (1975).

8 For a general discussion about similarity relations between possible worlds, and in particular their role in the interpretation of counterfactual sentences, see Lewis (1973) and Rescher (1975).

9 Introducing FACTS as a primitive type in the semantics is not without problems, whatever the intuitive advantages of such a strategy may be. Just as we would like to have as many individuals as we need for the reference of referring expressions, we would like to have as much denotata for sentences as we have true propositions expressed by these sentences, and not just the two values 'truth' and 'falsity'. One of the problems is whether we would admit also 'negative' facts as values for negative sentences, or only 'positive' facts, whereby a negative sentence would be true if the (possible) fact denoted by it were not an element of the intended world. Below, we will explain this notion of a 'possible object' and a 'possible fact'. We will see in Chapter 4 that we also need facts in an account of presuppositions (eg of gerunds, see J. Martin, 1975). See also R. M. Martin (1967).

10 For a discussion of possible individuals and individual concepts, see Montague (1974, especially Chapter 5), Hintikka (1973), and Rescher (1975).

11 For a discussion of this distinction between 'qualifying' and 'referential' terms and related problems, see Donellan (1970). For the more general problem of reference in modal contexts, see the important collection of papers edited by Linsky (1971).

12 See Hintikka (1971) for a first attempt to provide a semantics for sentences with propositional attitudes.

13 The most extensive discussion of these intricate problems has been given by Kripke (1972) the founder of model theoretical, possible world semantics for modal logics. For the notion of 'individual concept', see Montague (1974) and Cresswell (1973). For the formal semantic approach to the interpretation of 'sortal' correctness of sentences (ie sentences satisfying some kind of selection restrictions on the combination of predicates and arguments), see 6.3 below and the references given there. An important source is Carnap (1956).

14 This touches upon the general philosophical discussion concerning the nature of propositions. We here do not identify propositions with statements or assertions. Sentences may express a proposition (which is the sense or meaning of the clause or sentence) even if we do not use the sentence to refer to a particular fact, thereby making a statement ABOUT that fact, thus making an assertion (with the intention that the hearer get some information about that fact). See Part II for the pragmatic aspects of information transmission and the nature of assertion. If we say, then, that sentences or propositions are true or false, we thereby mean those which are USED to denote some fact. This does not mean that such a sentence should be ACTUALLY used (any more than a proposition is ACTUALLY expressed when we say that a sentence expresses a proposition). The PARTICULAR meaning of a particular sentence, then, derives from a particular use in order to refer to a particular fact.

   For an extensive discussion of these and related issues concerning propositions/sentences/statements/assertions, see among others: Strawson (1952, 1971, 1974), Kearns (1975), Carnap (1956). The latter also emphasizes a further distinction between the sense and the intension of a sentence, the latter being constant, the first dependent on certain oblique contexts as discussed in 5.1 above (eg John thinks (that), John claims (that), etc). These additional problems of formal semantics will be ignored here.

15 A semantics with indices representing properties of the pragmatic context has mainly been initiated (under the term 'formal pragmatics') by Montague (see Montague, 1974). See also Thomason (1973b), Cresswell (1973) and Lewis (1970). Since the central notion is still that of 'truth condition' (viz with respect not only to possible worlds, but to other indices as well), this study belongs to semantics and not to pragmatics (which has another central concept, viz that of appropriateness. See Part II).

16 For recent work more specifically focusing on the application of formal semantics

in the analysis of natural language, see Davidson and Harman, eds (1972), Hintikka, Moravcsik and Suppes, eds (1973), Keenan, ed (1975), Cresswell (1973).

17 Categorial grammar of which the first ideas were worked out some twenty years ago has received renewed interest in the last few years, especially under the impact of Montague's work (see Montague, 1974, and especially Thomason's introduction in that collection of Montague's articles). For an introduction, see Cresswell (1973).

   One of the important differences with the semantics of other types of grammar is that in a categorial approach not only expressions are receiving an explicit interpretation, but also the operations or structures relating the expressions.

18 Although the problem of semantic (conceptual) categories has a long history in philosophy, little current work has been devoted to the foundations and elaboration of a formal sortal semantics in which there are constraints on predication. See Sommers (1963), van Fraassen (1967, 1969) and Thomason (1972). See also Goddard and Routley (1973).

19 See Guenthner (1975) and van Dijk (1975b) for a formal semantic analysis of metaphorical sentences in terms of sortal semantics.

20 Hence such sentences express what may be called 'impossible propositions' relative to a set of worlds: no fact of this type can ever become actualized in any of these worlds.

Chapter 3

Connection and connectives

1 Connection

1.1 *Aims and problems of discourse semantics*

1.1.1

In Chapter 2 it has been briefly explained that the task of a semantics in a formal system consists in the formulation of rules of interpretation for the well-formed formulae of that system. Such interpretations recursively specify under what conditions a formula is true or false with respect to some model, where the truth-value of a formula depends on the values assigned to its different parts according to the syntactic categories of those parts. Instead of assigning extensions such as truth-values, individuals, and sets of individuals, we may assign intensions of various kinds to the parts of a formula of an intensional language, viz propositions, concepts, operations, etc.

In many respects the semantics of natural languages follows this schema. We have expressions (sentences) which are morpho-syntactically well-formed and which must be interpreted, such that the interpretation of the whole sentence should be a function of the interpretation of its parts. Such interpretations are usually of the INTENSIONAL type: what is specified is the MEANING of a sentence, together with the meanings of morphemes and phrases constituting this sentence meaning.

Such a semantics can be explicit in the sense of a formal semantics only if a certain number of requirements are satisfied. One of these requirements is that the syntactic structures as defined by syntactic rules and categories run parallel with structures at the semantic level: expressions belonging to one category must be assigned the same type of value and the syntactic relations between them must be reflected in semantic structures. Until very recently the syntactic models for natural language did not fully meet these conditions:

syntactic structures, although satisfying the important criterion of non-ambiguity, were not normally specified such that explicit semantic rules of interpretation could be given in terms of their rules and categories.

There is another, systematic, difference between formal and linguistic semantics. A formal semantics can only give an interpretation of the logical properties of expressions and does not account for non-logical, conventional content or meanings of expressions. Nor will it specifiy non-logical relations between the meanings of parts of a sentence.[1]

These and other problems in current grammar and logic cannot possibly be solved in this book. We will focus attention on one particular problem (or cluster of problems) of linguistic semantics, viz the SEMANTIC RELATIONS BETWEEN PROPOSITIONS IN SENTENCES AND DISCOURSES.

1.1.2
According to the aims of semantics the study of the relations between sentences in a discourse will have first of all to show how the meaning and reference of sequences of sentences depends on the meaning and reference of their component sentences. At this point a difference from logical semantics is already apparent. A formal semantics only interprets simple or compound sentences, not SEQUENCES of sentences. Sequences of sentences, in logic, appear only in DERIVATIONS. Whereas within compound sentences the interpretation is determined by connectives, sequences of formulae are related by operations of transformation and inference of which the semantic function is their truth- or validity-preserving nature. Within such a perspective it should be considered whether sequences of sentences in natural language have the properties of compound sentences or those of derivational sequences in formal languages, or perhaps both. In the first case we must specify a category of CONNECTIVES of natural language sentences/sequences and their semantic role in interpretation. In the second case, it must be shown what notion of derivation could be involved in natural language discourse, what the derivational rules are, and what semantic (or other) role they play. More generally the investigation pertains to the (semantic) CONDITIONS under which sentences are CONNECTED, either by connectives or by rules (or by both).

Note that in truth-functional logic the formulae in a compound formula are not directly connected, but only via their respective contribution to the truth-value of the whole formula. Given the rule of substitution, formulae may even be replaced by other formulae. This is not normally the case for sentences and sequences in natural language. It will be shown in this chapter that the connectives and connections involved are INTENSIONAL.

1.1.3
Connectives typically range over sentences or propositions as 'wholes'. In sentences and sequences of natural language, however, we also have semantic 'connections' between parts of different sentences. The use of PRO-FORMS and ARTICLES is a well-known example, where identity of reference is involved. This indicates that interclausal and intersentential relations are not

only based on (intensional) meanings, but also on reference, of which a model-theoretic account can be given. Although we will not be primarily concerned in this book with problems of pronominalization, which have had extensive discussion in current grammars already, one of the tasks of a semantics of discourse is to investigate how reference is 'organized' in a sequence of sentences. Reference may be 'identical', *ie* terms may denote the 'same' individual, but only under some further conditions. Similarly, reference also changes and these changes must follow certain constraints. This is not only the case for reference to individuals, but typically holds for 'reference' to properties of and relations between individuals. In the reference to individuals and to properties and relations, the interpretation of a sentence will depend on the interpretation of preceding sentences. That is, we not only interpret relative to a model but also with respect to a set or sequence of previous sentences, viz RELATIVE TO SETS OR SEQUENCES OF MODELS. Hence, a discourse semantics essentially formulates CONDITIONS OF RELATIVE INTERPRETATION. We may assume provisionally that connection is to be defined in terms of this semantic interdependence: A sentence α is CONNECTED with a sentence (or sequence of sentences) β, if α is interpreted relative to β.

1.1.4
In our introductory chapter it has been suggested that sequences may be connected without being COHERENT. That is, connection may be a necessary but not a sufficient condition for the acceptability of discourse.

Connectedness seems to be a condition imposed upon PAIRS OF SENTENCES, but it may be the case that the whole sequence of connections must satisfy specific conditions of coherence. It will be assumed that these conditions are of two types, viz LINEAR and GLOBAL. It is the task of a discourse semantics to make explicit our language intuitions about these conditions and types of coherence. It is at this level that we should explain the specific properties of relations of presupposition, topic-comment, focus, and of INFORMATION DISTRIBUTION in general in natural language discourse. This will be the aim of the next chapter.

1.2 *Conditions of semantic connection*
1.2.1
Above we have used the term 'connection' in order to refer to a specific relation between sentences. Strictly speaking, however, sentences are syntactical objects, and if connection is a semantic notion, as we assumed, we should rather speak of connected PROPOSITIONS. Sentences and sequences of sentences may EXPRESS such a relation between propositions, *eg* by CONNECTIVES of various syntactic categories (conjunctions, adverbs, particles). If we speak of connected sentences (or clauses) we mean sentences of which the 'underlying' propositions are connected. The property of n-tuples of propositions such that they are connected will be called CONNECTEDNESS or CONNECTION. Another term which is also used in recent logics is

RELEVANCE. The latter term, however, will be reserved to denote certain pragmatic properties of sentences or propositions, viz a certain aspect of their appropriateness in a communicative context.

1.2.2

In order to illustrate the notion of connection, let us give a number of examples:

[1]*a:* John is a bachelor, so he is not married.
   b: John is a bachelor, so he buys too many records.
   c: John is a bachelor, so Amsterdam is the capital of the Netherlands.

[2]*a:* Because Harry did not work hard enough, he flunked his exam.
   b: Because Harry did not work hard enough, Mary kissed him on the cheek.
   c: Because Harry did not work hard enough, the moon is turning around the earth.

[3]*a:* Amsterdam is the capital of the Netherlands. It has 800,000 inhabitants.
   b: Amsterdam is the capital of the Netherlands. Do you like Amsterdam?
   c: Amsterdam is the capital of the Netherlands. I hereby declare this meeting opened.

[4]*a:* A. Where are you going for your holidays this summer?
       B. I'll probably go to Portugal.
   b: A. Where are you going for your holidays this summer?
       B. This summer my brother will go to Portugal.
   c: A. Where are you going for your holidays this summer?
       B. Could you please tell me the time?

We have taken various groups of examples, compound sentences [1], complex sentences [2], sequences of sentences [3] and dialogue sequences [4]. In each group the (*a*) examples seem perfectly acceptable, the (*b*) examples are less acceptable or only acceptable in very specific situations, whereas the (*c*) examples seem definitely unacceptable. What sorts of constraints determine these intuitions about the semantic acceptability of these sentences and discourses?

First of all it should be observed that these constraints are indeed SEMANTIC and not syntactic: the sentences in the (*c*) examples are, as such, perfectly well-formed.

Secondly, connection is not dependent on the presence of connectives. In [3] and [4] the sentences are connected or not connected without the (explicit) presence of connectives. Conversely, the presence of connectives does not make sentences connected, as can be seen in [1]*c* and [2]*c*: rather the use of connectives presupposes that sentences are connected. In that case, the connective, as will be shown in detail in the next section, indicates various sorts of connection, viz implication in [1], cause or reason in [2] and perhaps conjunction in [3]. It should be explained also why the use of different connectives determines the acceptability of a pair of connected sentences: in [2]*b* the use of *although* instead of *because* seems more appropriate.

A first condition on connection, as in [1]*a*, could be a relation between MEANINGS or SENSES of words in sentences. The concept 'bachelor' CONTAINS the concept of 'not-married' according to a meaning postulate of natural language. As such, a meaning relation of this type is not a sufficient condition for two sentences to be connected. The sentence

[5] John is a bachelor, so Peter is not married.

is normally unacceptable. The connectedness of [1]*a*, therefore, also depends on the arguments of the predicates *is a bachelor* and *is not married*, viz on the values of the referring phrases *John* and *he*. More particularly, these values must be identical in order for the first proposition to ENTAIL the second proposition, as required by the meaning postulate $(\forall x)[bachelor\ (x) \rightarrow \sim married\ (x)]$. In other words, a meaning relation may be a condition of connection only 'via' the propositional structure, and 'via' reference to identical individuals having the related properties.

The presence of identical referents, as in the (*b*) examples, however, does not as such guarantee that two sentences are acceptable as a pair. Intuitively, a sentence like [1]*b* seems 'strange' although we are talking about the same individual, viz John. We do not (immediately) see in what respect the FACT that John is a bachelor could be related to the FACT that he buys too many records, at least not in the sense that the second proposition is a consequence of the first proposition. The use of another connective, *eg: and*, does not seem to enhance the acceptability of [1]*b* very much. Similarly, in [3]*b*, the fact that Amsterdam is the capital of the Netherlands does not seem directly related to the fact that you may like it (or not).

Nevertheless, reference to identical referents seems to make sentences/ sequences more acceptable even if the predicates or propositions are not related. In the (*c*) examples, there is neither identity (or other relation) between individuals nor between their properties: the 'whole' facts do not seem related. Ultimately, the connection between propositions is determined by the RELATEDNESS OF THE FACTS denoted by them, it seems.

Note that referential identity of individuals is not a NECESSARY condition of fact relatedness either:

[6] Yesterday it was very hot, so we went to the beach.

The fact denoted by the antecedent of this sentence is causally or rationally related to the fact denoted by the consequent. Such a relation between facts requires further specification, as may be seen in such examples as

[7] Yesterday it was very hot, so we went to the beach last week.

Facts are (at least, causally) related only if they satisfy certain conditions of TEMPORAL ORDERING. Similarly, we would not normally consider sequences like [8] to be acceptable:

[8] I dreamt that it was very hot. So I went to the beach.

The fact that it is hot in some dream-world is not a normal reason for going to the beach in the actual world. At least in these examples, the relatedness of facts seems to require also RELATEDNESS OF POSSIBLE WORLDS, *eg* temporal consecution of time points in the actual world and IDENTITY OF WORLDS or world types. A sentence like [8] would only be acceptable if the event of dreaming were related to the event of going to the beach, which would make [9] acceptable:

[9] It was so hot today, that I dreamt that I was on the beach.

The temperature may, in the actual world, influence my dreaming as such, but also its contents, *ie* facts in worlds ACCESSIBLE from the actual world.

1.2.3

The provisional conclusion from the discussion of the given examples is that clauses and sentences are connected if the facts denoted by their propositions are related in related worlds. The question then arises under what conditions we may say that facts are related. Although it is often the case that individuals 'involved' in these facts are identical, this is neither a sufficient nor a necessary condition.

One of the clear types of fact relatedness is that of CAUSE or REASON. According to our definition of cause in Chapter 6, given for EVENTS, an event A causes an event B if A is a SUFFICIENT CONDITION for the occurrence of B, *ie* in at least one possible world the occurrence of A is incompatible with the non-occurrence of B.[2] A similar definition could be given for a reason relation, where A means 'knowledge of A' and B denotes an action or a consequence of an action. These relations would account for the connection in [2]*a* and [6]. Similarly, in [1]*a*, the consequent denotes a NECESSARY CONSEQUENCE of the fact denoted by the antecedent.

The relations of condition and consequence characterizing connection, do not seem to hold in general, however. In [3]*a* we could hardly say that Amsterdam's being a capital 'determines' the fact that it has a certain number of inhabitants. The same is true in such sentences as

[10] We went to the beach and played football.
[11] We went to the beach, but Peter went to the swimming pool.
[12] We went to Rome and so did the Johnsons.

In these examples the consequent does not express a proposition denoting a fact which somehow is a consequence of the fact denoted by the antecedent. Yet, the facts seem somehow related. In [10] we would normally interpret that we played football on the beach, at least in one reading. In that case 'going to the beach' is a condition for 'playing football on the beach'. Conversely, within a situation of being on the beach, playing football is a POSSIBLE event. No such interpretation seems likely in [11] and [12] unless our going to the beach is sufficient reason for Peter to go to the swimming pool, and our going to Rome a sufficient condition for the Johnsons to go there too. Whereas in the cause and reason examples the first fact was incompatible with the non-occurrence of the second fact (at least in a given situation), the minimal condition in sentences like [3]a and in [10–12] seems to be that the two facts are simply COMPATIBLE. Two facts are compatible if the occurrence of the one does not exclude the occurrence of the other in a given situation. In terms of propositions: $\lozenge(p\&q)$ or $\sim\square(p \supset \sim q)$.

The notion of compatibility needs further qualification, however. Take for example the following sentence:

[13] We went to the beach and Peter was born in Manchester.

Logically speaking, the facts denoted by the conjuncts are compatible; they do not mutually exclude each other, yet we do not feel that the sentence is connected, because we fail to discover a relation between the facts denoted by its clauses.

The difference with sentences like [11] and [12] seems to involve a difference between TYPES of fact referred to. A sentence like [11] is acceptable because both clauses denote a SIMILAR activity, occurring at roughly the same time, whereas in [12] the action TYPES, possibly occurring at different times, are identical. Moreover, in both cases it is implied that there is a relation (of friendship, family membership or acquaintance) between the individuals of which these activities are predicated. In [13] the particular activity of our going to the beach cannot thus directly be compared with the more general property of Peter's being born in Manchester. The fact concepts involved, we might say, are too DISTANT in logical space; they come from different RANGES.

Similarity of worlds and facts must be specified from a certain POINT OF VIEW. Going to the beach and going to the swimming pool may be similar from the point of view of 'pleasant human activities' for example, and from the point of view of an intended time or possible world, *eg* 'yesterday'. Typically, a sentence like [11] could be appropriately uttered after a question like "What did you do yesterday?" After such a question, however, we may not appropriately answer with [13] or the second clause of [13]. It follows that we interpret relations between facts with respect to some COMMON BASIS.

1.2.4

The notion of POINT OF VIEW with respect to which the similarity of worlds and facts is to be determined not only has semantic but also PRAGMATIC properties. Sentences are connected (or not) FOR some speaker and hearer in a particular context of communication. What is connected for certain speech participants in some context may well be disconnected for other participants. (We use *connected* and *disconnected* (instead of the more normal *unconnected*) as technical terms.) Nevertheless, the CONDITIONS making discourse connected are not ad hoc. They are conventional and hence are general, in the sense that we should be able to formulate something like 'If speaker and hearer knew such and such, and if they already have said so and so, then some sentence or sequence S is connected if it expresses the propositions $\langle p, \ldots \rangle$'.

Similarly, conditions for the appropriateness of speech acts are involved if sentences like those given above are used in order to make an assertion. In that case we want the hearer to acquire some information, but there are some principles determining the amount and the sort of information which may be given by uttering a sentence or a discourse. Thus, after a question like "*What did you do yesterday?*", or its equivalent, reference must be made in the answer to yesterday's activities, such that reference to Peter's place of birth is inappropriate. We shall come back to these and similar pragmatic conditions for speech acts and information transmission later.

1.2.5

Instead of using terms like 'point of view', a more semantic characterization of the conditions involved could be formulated with a notion like TOPIC OF CONVERSATION.[3] For our example [13] this would mean that both conjuncts could not simultaneously 'belong to' the same topic of conversation. For reasons of simplicity, a topic of conversation will be (semantically) defined as a set of propositions. Further specification may then be given in the pragmatics, viz that speakers and hearers 'know' this set, etc. Sometimes this set may be empty: there is no topic of conversation specified, at least not semantically. The set may simply consist of the propositions expressed by previous sentences of the discourse, or by contextual knowledge of other sorts (interaction, perception of the same things, etc). When a conversation starts with a compound sentence, and if no further topic of conversation is specified, then the first conjunct often serves as the topic of conversation for the second conjunct.

It will be shown later that a topic of conversation is not simply identical with the set of available information, but some specific proposition (or set of propositions) entailed by it, viz the MACRO-STRUCTURE.

If we want to give CONDITIONS OF CONNECTION in a formal semantics, we would have to add a set Z of POSSIBLE TOPICS OF CONVERSATION, and a specific element from Z, viz z_0, for the ACTUAL TOPIC OF CONVERSATION. The interpretation of sentences would then be given with respect to elements of Z (and with respect to possible other indices like possible worlds, time point, place, etc). A function like $V(\alpha, w_i, z_i)$ could then be treated in different ways. Depending on the topic of conversation z_i it could have truth or falsity as values or remain undefined (which makes it a partial function) for certain values of z_i. On the other hand, a sentence like [13] may well be true (if both conjuncts are) even if its conjuncts are not connected.[4] In that case we would need a function V^+ which may assign four values:[5]

[14]*a:* true and connected

   b: true but disconnected

   c: false and connected

   d: false and disconnected

where a sentence is said to be connected if it is connected with the topic of conversation. As a short notation for these values we may write (a) 11 (b) 10 (c) 01 (d) 00. For composite sentences $\alpha * \beta$ to be connected to z_i, α must be connected to z_i, and β must be connected to the 'combination' of the first conjunct with the topic of conversation, viz $\{\alpha\} \cup z_i$. Here the symbol '$*$' is used to denote any binary connective of natural language. It will be assumed that only those sentences with the value 'connected', *ie* (a) or (c), may be acceptable in natural conversation.

We may think of topics of conversation from Z as abstract constructs delimiting certain areas or RANGES OF SEMANTIC SPACE from which individual and property concepts may be taken to form propositions (fact concepts). Since connection is to be further determined with respect to CONTEXTS of conversation, a notion to be discussed in Part II, the function V^+ would become a four-place function $V^+(\alpha, w_i, z_i, c_i)$, where c_i is an element of C, the set of possible contexts of communication (or conversation). In our example [13] these conditions would mean in more concrete terms that the first proposition 'our going to the beach' determines a conceptual range allowing reference to us, viz to human individuals, to properties we have, and things or persons we are related to, further to properties (conditions, consequences, modes) of going or travelling (which makes a following sentence *We went by car* or *The train was very crowded* possible), and finally properties of the beach (sand, dunes, water, waves, rocks, activities on the beach and events occurring on beaches). This range is ordered: not any property we have may be selected, only those compatible with travelling/going and beaches. Thus, 'playing football' is a property compatible with the property of being on the beach, whereas 'selling sellotape' is much less so. Clearly, besides systematic semantic relations (between concepts), KNOWLEDGE OF THE WORLD is involved here. This factor must be accounted for by other theories, at least formally, because a full representation of our (changing) knowledge of the world cannot be the aim of logic or linguistics.[6]

Finally, it should be made possible to CHANGE a topic of conversation. We therefore introduce a binary operation '|' of TOPIC CHANGE over members of Z, where $z_0|z_i$ would read: 'the topic of conversation changes from z_0 to z_i', or more restrictedly, 'z_i is an admissible alternative topic of conversation with respect to the actual topic of conversation z_0'. Much as worlds are said to be accessible to one another, topics of conversation can be said to be INITIATABLE from another topic of conversation in some context. The further condition should be added to the connection or relevance conditions mentioned above. Admissible changes of topic of conversation are a problem for an empirical investigation. At the formal level it may be assumed that such a change is possible only if there is at least one concept[7] (individual-, property- or even proposition-concept) belonging to both ranges determined by two topics of conversation, *eg* 'water' in:

[15] We were at the beach, but the water in the swimming pool is much cleaner.

From this discussion it will provisionally be concluded that the minimal condition for the connectedness of propositions expressed by a sentence or sequence is their connection with the same (or related) topic(s) of conversation as defined above. This connection, however, need not be merely conceptual, but may also be factual in the sense that situations (world-time-place units) are specified in which individuals, properties or facts are related (identity, precedence, consecution).

We are aware of the fact that the discussion above only deals with some properties of connection, but these will have to do for a treatment of connectives. Other aspects of coherence will be discussed in Chapters 4 and 5.

2 Connectives

2.1 *Connectives in natural language*
2.1.1
Relations between propositions or facts are typically expressed by a set of expressions from various syntactic categories, which will here be called CONNECTIVES. To this set first of all belong the connectives from the syntactic category of CONJUNCTIONS, both coordinating and subordinating, *eg: and*, *or*, *because*, *for*, *so*, etc. Their function is to make (composite) sentences from (simple) sentences, so they are binary operators. A second subset of connectives comes from the category of SENTENTIAL ADVERBS, such as *yet*, *nevertheless*, *consequently*, etc. They are also operators because they also make sentences out of sentences. Although they normally express a certain relation between propositions, it should be considered whether these adverbs are also binary operators, which would require, for example, that they cannot occur in a single, non-composite sentence. Sentential adverbs themselves may in turn be formed by nominalized propositions preceded by PREPOSITIONS with a 'connective' character, like *due to*, *in spite of* and *as a result of*. A fourth group of connectives, close to or developed from the category of adverbs, is that of various INTERJECTIONS and PARTICLES, which are frequent in such languages as German, Dutch and Greek and which in English are expressed either by intonation or by phrases like *you know*, *isn't it*, etc. Finally, connection may be expressed by predicates of various categories, *eg* nouns, verbs, adjectives, and by full phrases and clauses: *conclusion*, *alternative*, *consequence*, *to conclude*, *to concede*, *to add*, *it follows that*, *it may be concluded that*, etc.

Attention will be focused on the connectives from the conjunction and adverb categories, whereby only examples from English will be given. No further syntactic analysis will be given of sentence- (and sequence-) forming connectives. Sentential conjunctions typically occur at the beginning of clauses and sentences, whereas sentential adverbs may have various positions. Conjunctive connectives may combine with adverbial connectives (*and yet, but nevertheless*) but not with expressions of the same category (*and but, because although*).[8] Systematic differences between the use of interclausal and intersentential connectives will be treated in Part II, because these differences mainly depend on pragmatic factors.

2.1.2

Since it is our aim primarily to describe connections between clauses and sentences, we shall ignore the so-called PHRASAL CONNECTIVES,[9] *ie* connectives making (noun or verb) phrases from phrases, as in *John and Mary, lemons or oranges, walked and talked, strong but gentle, quickly but cautiously*. Some of these composite phrases may be derived from, or are equivalent with, sentential constructions (*eg John went to Rome and Mary went to Rome*), others from group relations between individuals or properties (*John and Mary met in Rome*).

2.1.3

Natural language connectives, in particular the conjunctions, are classified by traditional grammar in various groups, viz:

[16]*a:* conjunction
  b: disjunction, alternation
  c: contrast
  d: concession
  e: condition
  f: causality, reason
  g: finality
  h: circumstantial (time, place, manner)

One of the tasks of a semantics of natural connectives is to make explicit these intuitive distinctions based on the 'meanings' of the various connectives. Similarly, it should be clarified how these different classes are related to each other. It may well be the case that there are a restricted number of abstract BASIC CONNECTIVES of which the various classes are specific variants owing to syntactic and stylistic determinants, *eg* differences between subordinative and coordinative clauses, or between occurrence as interclausal and intersentential connectives.

2.2 *Natural and logical connectives*
2.2.1

Although the LOGICAL CONNECTIVES as discussed in Chapter 2 share certain properties with connectives of natural language, a formal semantics of what has been called the NATURAL CONNECTIVES will have to deal with a certain number of essential differences with respect to logical connectives.

Logical connectives of the classical sort (&, ∨, ⊃) are, first of all, interpreted in TRUTH-FUNCTIONAL terms. Their role is to yield a truth-value of composite formulae given the truth-values of atomic formulae, irrespective of the meaning or sense of the connected formulae. Since one of the acceptability conditions of sentences and sequences in natural language is that the propositions they express be connected, and given the assumption that this connection is based on meaning and reference interdependencies, natural connectives, expressing various types of this connection, must have an INTENSIONAL character. Truth-values are involved only via the operations on propositions or the relations between facts expressed by intensional connectives.

2.2.2

Truth-functional connectives have a certain number of properties as specified by the axioms, definitions, transformation and derivation rules of the propositional calculus: they are interdefinable (with the aid of negation), and some of them are commutative ($p * q \equiv q * p$), associative ($[p * q] * r \equiv p * [q * r]$), distributive ($p * [q * r] \equiv [p * q] * [p * r]$), or transitive ($[[p * q] * [q * r]] * [p * r]$). It will be discussed below in which respect these properties also hold for the various natural connectives. There is no a priori reason why these properties would not also characterize certain intensional relations between propositions.

There is a set of valid formulae, involving material and strict implication, which have a more counterintuitive nature also from a logical point of view, viz:

[17]*a*: $p \supset (q \supset p)$
  b: $\sim p \supset (p \supset q)$
  c: $(p \& \sim p) \supset q$
  d: $q \supset (p \vee \sim p)$
  e: $p \supset (p \vee q)$
  f: $((p \vee q) \& \sim p) \supset q$

The 'paradoxical' nature of these formulae consists in the fact that the consequent contains propositional 'information' not contained in the antecedent: knowledge about truth and/or falsity of p would imply knowledge about truth or falsity of, or a relation to, q. Thus, (*c*) states the validity of the well-known principle that a contradiction implies anything, and (*d*) that a tautology is implied by any formula. Given the antecedents as (true) premises, the consequents may be derived logically. As long as we are merely concerned with truth-values and relations of truth-preservation, as in the valuation of the material conditional and in logical derivation, there is hardly any reason to dispute the validity of the formulae in [17]. More problematic however are the strict ($\dashv$) analogues of [17] where the implication involves a modal notion, viz necessity. It may be argued that for the implication (conditional) to be true in all possible worlds, something more than simple truth-functional dependence of the conjuncts must be involved, viz a relation between their content, especially if '$\dashv$' is interpreted as semantic ENTAILMENT. Formally speaking, the sentence *I am going to the movies* materially and strictly implies *I am going to the movies or I am going to the races*, but we would hardly say that the latter sentence is entailed by the former, because 'going to the races' is not contained in the meaning or content of 'going to the movies'. As soon as the logical connective thus involves meaning relations, it becomes intensional. The same holds for the relations between premises and conclusion in a derivation, where we may require that the conclusion is somehow 'contained' in the joint sequence of premises.

2.2.3

These and other reasons have led to attempts to establish so-called RELEVANCE or CONNEXIVE LOGICS,[10] particularly to account for entailment. In such logics, which have different forms, certain of the intuitively less acceptable principles holding in classical logics are dropped and additional axioms are introduced in order to meet some conditions of relevance or connectedness as discussed in the first part of this chapter for natural language sentences. Indeed, the intuitions about the connectedness of sentences as they are formulated informally by relevance logicians partially correspond to our linguistic intuitions about the relations between sentences of natural language, eg as they appear in argumentative discourse. One of the ways to define a RELEVANT IMPLICATION, $p > q$, is for instance given in terms of the inconsistency of $p \& \sim q$. Similarly, in a RELEVANT DERIVATION we may require that any proposition occurring in the conclusion must also occur in the premises.

The specific axiomatic structure of the various relevance logics will not be discussed here. It should however be emphasized that they only follow part of our linguistic intuitions: they have many valid formulae which in natural language would not hold at all or only in specific situations, eg [17]e.

2.2.4

The interest of relevance logics for our treatment of natural language connectives lies in their SEMANTICS. In order to account for relevant implications, the notion of connection should be formally accounted for in the interpretation of languages with such connectives or derivation rules. This requires specific modifications in the structure of models used for this interpretation.

In the first section of this chapter we have provisionally used a simple version of such a RELEVANCE SEMANTICS: a compound formula $\alpha * \beta$ has a value (or is assigned a third value, eg '(dis-)connected') only if both α and β are interpreted with respect to the same topic of conversation z_i.

Given the definitional relations between propositions and worlds (a proposition is a set of worlds, viz the set of those worlds where it is true, or is the function characterizing this set) connection between propositions may also be given in terms of operations on worlds. Instead of a binary relation (R) of accessibility between worlds, we thus may define COMPATIBILITY between worlds w_j and w_k RELATIVE TO a world w_i, that is, as a ternary relation over the set of possible worlds W. Thus, if w_j and w_k are compatible relative to w_i, and if α holds in w_j, and β in w_k, then α is said to be CONSISTENT with β, $(\alpha \circ \beta)$, in w_i. The relevant implication $\alpha > \beta$ would then be true in w_i iff for all compatible worlds w_j, w_k (ie $Rw_iw_jw_k$) the truth of α in w_j entails the truth of β in w_k.[11] Note, however, that although compatibility and consistency are involved in connection, these notions are necessary but not sufficient elements in a definition of connectedness between propositions in natural language sentences.

Another possibility for singling out the worlds 'relevant' for the interpretation of connected sentences is to use a SELECTION FUNCTION[12] which, given a certain interpretation of α in w_i, selects the worlds w_j in which β can have a value. In other words, the world w_j can only be 'reached' via the interpretation of α in w_i. It is in this sense that the connectedness of a formula $\alpha * \beta$ is specified in terms of the RELATIVE INTERPRETATION of β with respect to (the interpretation of) α. A selection function, just like the notion of topic of conversation, specifies the set of worlds which have a certain SIMILARITY with a given world, viz the world in which the antecedent is true, or in general the world(s) where a topic of conversation is satisfied. Whereas the material condition is also true if α is false, a relevant conditional $\alpha > \beta$, formalizing *if... then* in natural language, would come out true only if β is true in α-worlds, *ie* if α is true. A further restriction in such truth conditions could be formulated by letting the world where a compound $\alpha * \beta$ is to be interpreted be accessible (or be selected) not only with respect to the interpretation of α, but also with respect to the interpretation of β in some possible world. This would be necessary for those cases where a compound sentence makes sense only if the topics of conversation associated with both α and β are taken into account.[13]

Other elements may appear to be necessary components in model structures for connected sentence interpretation. Models and model structures determining the relative interpretations of sentences with respect to other sentence interpretations will be called CONNECTED MODELS and CONNECTED MODEL STRUCTURES.

Finally, it should be noticed that relevance logics and their semantics contain important suggestions for a more explicit treatment of connectives in natural language (unlike other logics in which connectives are only truth-functional and where no connectedness between related sentences or propositions is required) but that they only account for some connectives (especially of the conditional type) and some aspects of connection.

2.2.5

In a treatment of the various natural connectives it should be made more explicit HOW the meaning or reference of sentences depends on that of other sentences and how they are connected, directly or via a common topic of conversation. In other words, the special accessibility relations between or selection functions of possible worlds as discussed above must be specified in more detail in a linguistic semantics.

One of the issues which will be neglected is a specific treatment of NEGATION. Since negation is also a truth-functional operator in classical logics and since it is used in the interdefinition of the binary connectives, the introduction of specific intensional and relevant connectives will also affect the nature of negation. The usual requirements of maximally consistent sets of propositions (or possible worlds) may for instance be dropped, viz that the falsity of p entails the truth of $\sim p$ (or if $p \notin A$ then $\sim p \in A$), and conversely. Moreover, in a grammatical description the difference between EXTERNAL (sentential) and INTERNAL (predicate) negation would become important. Finally, negation in natural language may also be described at the level of speech acts, viz as DENIAL (of a proposition), which would presuppose the explicit or implicit assertion of that proposition in the context. These and other specific problems of negation require separate discussion, so we will concentrate on the binary connectives.

2.2.6

One of the important properties in logical systems is the systematic relationships between connectives and DERIVATIONS. For the material conditional this relationship has been formulated in the so-called DEDUCTION THEOREM, which states that if a formula β is derivable from a sequence $\langle \alpha_1, \alpha_2, \ldots, \alpha_n \rangle$ then $\alpha_n \supset \beta$ is derivable from the sequence $\langle \alpha_1, \alpha_2, \ldots, \alpha_{n-1} \rangle$. In shorter and simpler form: If $\alpha \vdash \beta$, then $\vdash \alpha \supset \beta$. The introduction of relevant or connected conditionals may similarly be accompanied by a relevant deduction theorem: If $\alpha \vdash \beta$ then $\vdash \alpha > \beta$, where '$>$' denotes a relevant conditional. Given the properties of relevant conditionals this would mean that the DERIVATIONAL RELATION (indicating theorem status) would also be relevant. Not only truth or validity is preserved then but also aspects of meaning or intension, a feature which might be indispensable if '$>$' is strengthened with necessity to the STRICT RELEVANT IMPLICATION ($\Rightarrow$) as the syntactic connective representing semantic entailment. Thus, if the sentence *John is a bachelor* implies the sentence *John is not married* necessarily and relevantly in a derivation, then *John is a bachelor* $\Rightarrow$ *John is not married* is a (necessary) theorem. What is involved here is not only logical necessity but also CONCEPTUAL NECESSITY. In a sense the connectives (or relations) discussed here represent in the OBJECT LANGUAGE certain properties of logical systems formulated in the META-LANGUAGE: viz that conclusions in derivations follow necessarily from their premises and that the truth of a conclusion follows from the truth of the premises.

The specific logical problems involved in the further axiomatization of relevant conditionals, relevant strict implications, and their relation to semantics (entailment), the principles of deduction and the relations between meta-language and object-language linked with these connectives, cannot be discussed further here. It is sufficient to point out that there are formal relationships between connectives making compound SENTENCES, and derivational operations on SEQUENCES, relationships which also should be studied for sentences and sequences in discourse, *eg* for such cases as *If John is a bachelor, he is not married* and *John is a bachelor. So, he is not married*.

To summarize: we now have four logical connectives expressing condition or implication, viz the classical material implication ($\alpha \supset \beta$), its modal counterpart, viz strict implication ($\alpha \dashv \beta$), the relevant conditional ($\alpha > \beta$), and its modal counterpart $(\alpha \Rightarrow \beta)$. One of the characteristics of the relevant conditionals, then, is that they are not true when their antecedent is false (as is the case for the material conditionals). They require that the antecedent be true, asserted or presupposed in some world, such that the truth of the whole formula depends on the interpretation of the consequent, relative to the interpretation of the antecedent.

2.3 *Conjunction*
2.3.1

One of the problems in the semantics of natural connectives is their possible ambiguity: the same connective may express different types of connection, and one type of connection may be expressed by various connectives. Typical in this respect is the conjunctive connective *and*, eg in the following examples:

[18] John smoked a cigar and Peter smoked a pipe.
[19] John went to the library and checked his references.
[20] Please go to the store and buy me some beer.
[21] John smoked a cigar and Mary left the room.
[22] I took a sleeping pill and fell asleep.
[23] Give me some more time, and I'll show you how it can be done.
[24] Laugh and the world laughs with you, love and you love alone.
        (Thurber)

Intuitively, the uses of *and* in these sentences may be paraphrased by *eg:* (*and*) *at the same time* [18], (*and*) *there* [19, 20], (*and*) *therefore* [21], (*and*) *then* or (*and*) *so* [22], *if . . . then* [23, 24]. Apparently, therefore, *and* may be used to express not only a conjunction, but also conditionals, causals, temporal and local connectives. On the other hand it may be the case that these various readings of *and* are determined by the connected propositions, such that *and* would merely express a (relevant) conjunction of two propositions, with the following provisional truth-connection conditions (see [14]):

[25]*a:* $V^+((\alpha \text{ and } \beta), w_i, z_i) = 11$ iff $V^+(\alpha, w_i, z_i) = 11$ and
          $V^+(\beta, w_i, z_i) = 11$;
    b: $V^+((\alpha \text{ and } \beta), w_i, z_i) = 01$ iff $V^+(\alpha, w_i, z_i) = 01$
          or $V^+(\beta, w_i, z_i) = 01$;
    c: $V^+((\alpha \text{ and } \beta), w_i, z_i) = 10$ iff $V^+(\alpha, w_i, z_i) = 10$
          or $V^+(\beta, w_i, z_i) = 10$ and $(V(\alpha, w_i) = 1$ and $V(\beta, w_i) = 1)$;
    d: $V^+((\alpha \text{ and } \beta), w_i, z_i) = 00$ iff $V^+(\alpha, w_i, z_i) = 10$ or
          $V^+(\beta, w_i, z_i) = 10$ and $(V(\alpha, w_i) = 0$ or $V(\beta, w_i) = 0)$.

We see that a simple conjunction can have four values, viz true/false and connected/disconnected, where truth depends on the truth of both conjuncts, and connectedness on the connectedness of both conjuncts with respect to the topic of conversation z_i. Thus, a sentence like [18] is true if both conjuncts are true, and connected if both conjuncts are connected with the same topic of conversation z_i. This topic of conversation could consist of propositions like 'After dinner John and Peter were smoking' or 'After dinner our guests were doing something'. In order to account for further aspects, additional constraints may be formulated. First of all, we have assumed the conjunction to be true in the same world as the conjuncts, viz in an unspecified world w_i. In general, however, we may assume that $w_i = w_0$ (where w_0 is the ACTUAL WORLD) if no modal expressions occur in the conjuncts. This means that the past sentences (clauses) are both true at w_0, and hence their present tense variants are true at some point of time preceding $\langle w_0, t_0 \rangle$. If we assume that in sentences like [18] it is normally presumed that John and Peter are smoking during roughly the same period, we must add the condition that the world-time periods at which α, β and α *and* β are interpreted are identical given the truth of $P\alpha$, $P\beta$ and $P\alpha$ *and* $P\beta$ at $\langle w_0, t_0 \rangle$, where P is a past (tense) operator. Such an introduction of TIME RELATIONS would become imperative for the relevant interpretation of the other examples. Thus, in [19], it is usually assumed that checking references takes place at the library and hence immediately follows going to the library. The same holds for the events denoted by the antecedents and consequents of the other examples, which are linearly ordered in time. Thus if α is true at t_i, β true at t_j, the conjunction is true at a period $\langle t_i, t_j \rangle$, with the condition that t_i precedes t_j, *ie* $t_i \leqslant t_j$, where identity represents co-occurrence of events, as in sentence [18]. Besides these time relations, examples like [19–21] are most naturally interpreted as involving LOCAL IDENTITY: checking references takes place at the library, buying beer at the store, and smoking in the room that Mary left. Local identity, just like temporal identity, must be interpreted in a rather broad sense: going to the store is of course not true 'at' the store-location, where buying takes place, etc. In a stricter model structure for the interpretation of location, we thus would need trajectories, directions and similar relations between locations in order to interpret event, action and process sentences.

2.3.2
It may be argued that the temporal and local conditions of identity, consecution or direction are not general conditions for conjunction, because they may differ for particular sentences. Although we were speaking of NATURAL interpretations, a sentence like [20] may in some context also be interpreted such that going to the store and buying beer are independent facts, *eg* two actions to be accomplished by the hearer during the afternoon, where the store may be some previously mentioned book-store. We may also have a sentence like

[26] John went to the library and visited his friend in the hospital.

satisfying such an interpretation. In [26], however, a different location (and time) are expressed (and implied). For sentences like [19] and [20] it must be assumed therefore that the natural interpretation is based on a rule stating that the consequent of a connected sentence is to be interpreted relative to the time and place points at which the antecedent is interpreted if the consequent does not explicitly change the spatio-temporal situation. The same holds for possible worlds in general. This condition may be formulated such that the consequent β is interpreted relative to the topic of conversation z_i together with the antecedent $(z_i \cup \{\alpha\})$. If z_i is empty, it is the antecedent which establishes (provisionally) the topic of conversation. Interpretation with respect to this antecedent seems to imply that, if possible, the fact denoted by the consequent must be directly related to the fact denoted by the antecedent, eg as a whole/part or preparatory act/main act relation. As a general principle for the interpretation of connected sentences it may be postulated that denoted facts are to be related by THE MOST DIRECT RELATIONSHIPS POSSIBLE.

If there is no topic of conversation, and if the antecedent does not establish an unambiguous topic, the consequent may be further added in order to interpret the whole conjunction. Thus, in [20] the hearer only knows to what kind of store he is requested to go if he has interpreted the consequent. In that case 'buying beer' is the more general topic of conversation, viz some action of the hearer desired by the speaker, of which the antecedent expresses a possible condition of success. Hence, if $V(\alpha)$ is part of $V(\beta)$, β is the topic of conversation with respect to which the conjunction is interpreted. This is plausible if we further assume that, as for worlds, the topic of conversation z_i is identical with the ACTUAL TOPIC OF CONVERSATION z_0. This actual topic z_0 is then established by the actual utterance of α and β.

2.3.3

Whereas in sentences [19] and [20] the facts denoted by the antecedents of the conjunctions constitute POSSIBLE CONDITIONS for the facts denoted by the consequents, these conditions have an even stronger character in examples [21–24]. There, a relation of cause/reason and consequence is expressed, whereby the antecedent denotes a SUFFICIENT CONDITION for the occurrence of the consequence. Again the conjunction allows for a possible interpretation, eg of [21], where two facts (actions) co-occur without direct relationships other than temporal and perhaps local identity. That in a natural interpretation a cause or reason relation is assigned should again be explained by the 'closest-possible-link' principle discussed above. For [19] and [20] this link was a kind of part/whole relationship, here two actions or events are most clearly related by a causal connection. This connection is not expressed by the conjunction *and* itself, but follows from the principle that *and* establishes the closest possible link (temporal, local, causal) between facts. Should two possible interpretations conflict in such a case, the connection would be made more explicit by the use of other connectives. Apparently, *and* has both a GENERAL and a NEUTRAL character with respect to other connectives.

The last two examples, [23] and [24], by the use of an imperative clause, are also conditionals. The difference from the previous examples, however, is that we cannot simply speak of the actual truth of the conjuncts, because commands or requests are not commonly said to be true or false, nor the sentences used to perform such speech acts. Indeed, the notion of truth is closely linked with the speech act of assertion, typically expressed by indicative sentences. In commands or requests the speaker does not want the hearer to know that some proposition is true (that some fact exists in some world), but wants the hearer TO MAKE the proposition true in some (future) world. Instead of truth we will therefore use the general term SATISFACTION as the relation between propositions and worlds (facts), where different illocutionary intentions determine the relations of speaker and hearer with respect to this satisfaction relation. These are problems of pragmatics to be discussed in Part II. Important for the truth conditions (which should now be called satisfaction conditions) of natural *and* is that in [23] and [24] the conjuncts are satisfied at w_0 only if their present tense versions are satisfied in worlds which are not epistemically accessible to the speaker (as would be the case for a sentence like *You'll give me some more time, therefore I'll show you how it can be done*), but which are only accessible via his wishes [23]. In the general statement made by [24] it is required that in all possible worlds where the first conjunct is true, the second is also true, owing to the (psychological) necessity of the consequence. We return to these conditions for conditionals below. The use of *and* in such cases is acceptable because the relation of reason and consequence may be the closest link to be established between two facts.

2.3.4

Note that except for examples like [18] natural conjunction is NON-COMMUTATIVE: if antecedent and consequent change place the whole sentence becomes unacceptable even if it remains true. In this respect the ordering of the conjuncts is again similar to that in conditionals. Obviously there are certain principles determining NORMAL ORDERING of sentences denoting related facts. This ordering follows the normal ordering of the facts themselves, viz temporal, conditional and causal ordering of facts. This can be seen in sentence [21] where there is no 'internal' (essential) relation of cause and consequence as in [22]: if we had the sentence *Mary left the room and John smoked a cigar*, we would naturally interpret 'John smokes a cigar' as being true at a time point following the time point at which 'Mary leaves the room' is true.

In addition to normal orderings of facts, the ordering of clauses and sentences is determined by the requirements of relative interpretation themselves, viz in order to specify the model in which the following clause/sentence must be interpreted (identification of place, time, individuals and properties). If in a sentence like [20] it is intended that beer should be bought at the store, this information must be given first. Dependencies of facts and propositions are thus normally ordered linearly (left-right). If this normal ordering is changed this must be indicated by specific grammatical structures (subordination, tense, intonation, etc). The relations between the structure of facts (and hence of model structures), propositions and sentences will be discussed below.

Thus, given these specific constraints on the ordering of sentences, the antecedent either establishes the topic of conversation itself or is added to the topic of conversation and hence specifies the possible worlds in which the consequent can have a value. According to our connection conditions, the commuted versions of conjunctions satisfying this constraint are disconnected. If the antecedent and the consequent are not in this way conditionally related, *ie* if they denote independent facts, and if these facts are SIMILAR from a certain point of view (as specified by the topic of conversation) they are interpreted with respect to the same z_i, the same w_i and the same t_i, so that their ordering is FREE.

Since compound sentences may have different topics of conversation as their conjuncts, natural conjunction is NON-ASSOCIATIVE, *ie* (α *and* (β *and* γ)) $\equiv$ ((α *and* β) *and* γ) is not truth-connection valid. Compare, for instance, the following sentences:

[27] John went to the store and bought some beer, and we had a nice party.
[28] I was so tired and I took a sleeping pill and fell asleep.

In [27] it is the compound action of buying beer at the store which is a condition for having the party, whereas in [28] the fact that I am tired is a condition for a compound consequence. Now, buying beer can be connected with having a party, viz as a possible condition, but going to some store is not a direct condition for having a party. Similarly, being tired and taking a sleeping pill are not directly connected. Thus, those conjuncts (simple or compound) are first taken together which have the closest topical link (preparatory act-main act, cause-consequence). In [28] the first *and* may be substituted by *so*, having the whole following conjunction as its scope, but the second *and* cannot easily be replaced by *so*. Similarly, sentences [27] and [28] may most acceptably be split up into sequences of two sentences after the second and first conjunct respectively.

For similar reasons natural conjunction is NON-DISTRIBUTIVE, *ie* (α *and* (β *and* γ)) $\equiv$ ((α *and* β) *and* (α *and* γ)) is not truth-connection valid because the compound may have different topical conditions as simple α and β and because the compound α *and* β itself may establish a different topic of conversation in the consequent of the equivalence. Moreover, there are other constraints, viz non-repetition of full propositions in the same sentence, which would make the consequent unacceptable. The same arguments make conjunction NON-TRANSITIVE. Since antecedents may determine the worlds in which the consequent is to be interpreted, the relations are not only not valid with respect to connection, but also with respect to truth.

2.3.5

Let us now summarize the conditions involved in the interpretation of natural *and*. A sentence of the form α *and* β is true-connected iff:

(i) both conjuncts are true (or in general: satisfied) in the actual world-situation $\langle w_0, t_0 \rangle$; where *a:* the tensed conjuncts are true (satisfied) if their present tense versions are true in some world $\langle w_i, t_i \rangle$ related to $\langle w_0, t_0 \rangle$;

    b: the (present tense version of the) consequent only has a truth value either in the same world where the antecedent is interpreted or in those worlds selected by the antecedent proposition;

(ii) both conjuncts are connected with the same topic of conversation, identical with or initiatable from the actual topic of conversation, where

    a: the consequent is connected with respect to the topic of conversation and with respect to the antecedent;

    b: the topic of conversation for the conjunct is initiatable from both α and β.

We may add the more general, although still vague, principle

(iii) the facts denoted by the conjuncts are chosen such that they have the closest possible relation, *eg* part-whole, cause-consequence, possible condition-possible consequence.

2.3.6

In the truth-connection conditions the four values 11, 10, 01 and 00 have been assigned. It should be emphasized, however, that since natural conjunctions are intensional we should have assigned intensions to the conjuncts, viz propositions, which are functions with facts as values, for some possible world time point (and other indices). A conjunction, then, is interpreted as a compound proposition resulting from applying an operation to the component propositions, under the connectedness conditions (with the set of propositions taken as the topic of conversation), and such that the consequent proposition depends on the antecedent proposition in the sense that the worlds where it may have values are determined, as well as the kind of facts it may have as values. It will not be attempted here to give a formal account of these conditions.

2.4 *Disjunction*
2.4.1

The logical truth condition of disjunction is that at least one of the disjuncts must be true. Natural language *or* is generally EXCLUSIVE in the sense that at least and at most one disjunct must be true:

[29] I am going to the movies or I am going to visit my aunt.

This sentence is acceptable only if the speaker intends to accomplish either the first or the second act at some (future) time point. If he intended to do both, his (use of the) sentence would be INCORRECT, which is a pragmatic notion, not to be discussed here.[14] If he intends to accomplish one of the acts but in fact later accomplishes both (or neither), his (use of the) sentence is correct, but the sentence itself false. It follows that the world in which the disjuncts are satisfied must not be epistemically accessible. On the other hand it is required that the speaker believes that the facts (*eg* actions) are POSSIBLE in that world. This means that if one of the facts becomes true in that world, the other fact must be true in an ALTERNATIVE POSSIBLE WORLD, where accessibility is RELATIVE to the actual world (of the utterance), because the course of events may be such that at the intended time only one of the facts may become actualized.

Exclusion may be ACCIDENTAL or NECESSARY. Necessary exclusion is based on conceptual or logical inconsistency: I cannot be both married and a bachelor at the same time, nor can I be in London and in Paris (not in London) at the same time. The same applies to contradictory properties. Accidental exclusions are for instance those based on compatible intentions with respect to actions during a certain period, as in [29]. During the evening I may both go to the movies and visit my aunt, at least at different moments of time. Therefore, exclusion is mostly to be viewed with respect to the same time point or time period. If an inclusive interpretation is possible but not desired by the speaker, the explicit exclusive disjunction *either . . . or* must be used.

2.4.2

INCLUSIVE DISJUNCTION is used in those cases where the facts are compatible and where the assertion is made that at least one item of a series has been or can be realized, as in:

[30] Harry went to school in Cambridge or he studied in Oxford.
[31] You may have an orange or you may take a pear.

In such cases each of the disjuncts are possible conditions or consequences of known facts (*eg* Harry's particular accent or my desire for a juicy fruit), where the satisfaction of both alternatives does not contradict these facts.

Since in disjunction the facts themselves are unknown, the disjunction must be INFERRED from other information, as in [30] and in:

[32] John must have had his radio on, or he must have played records.

Both conclusions may be drawn from the information 'that John was listening to music'.

We here again meet the notion of shared background information, *ie* the notion of topic of conversation required for connected sentences. It follows that whereas only one of the disjuncts must be true (in some actual or intended world), both disjuncts must be connected with the SAME TOPIC OF INFORMATION. As in [32] this topic may be a logical (common) consequence of both disjuncts, *eg* 'John was listening to music'. This topic of information must be satisfied in the alternative worlds of which one is actualized. Thus a sentence like

[33] John must have had his radio on, or you may have a pear.

is unacceptable in most contexts because there is no obvious topic of conversation with respect to which both disjuncts could be connected, so that an inductive conclusion for each disjunct is impossible. The inference involved may, as in [32], be expressed by modal auxiliaries and adverbs like *must*, *likely* or *probably*.

2.4.3

Whereas in conjunctions the conjuncts are not only connected with the topic of conversation but may also be directly connected with each other, the very nature of disjunctions does not allow that the disjuncts denote related facts. Since the facts must exist, in exclusive disjunction, in different worlds, they may only be SIMILAR, in the sense that they are alternatives with respect to the same topic of conversation. If only one fact can become true, then the facts cannot be dependent on each other. In the examples of disjunction given so far, therefore, the ordering of clauses is free, so that this sort of natural disjunction is COMMUTATIVE, just like the form of conjunction where the two conjoined facts are mutually independent though connected via the same topic of information.

There is a type of natural disjunction, however, which also has the asymmetric structure of CONDITIONALS:

[34]*a:* Love me or leave me!
  b: This must be the road, or I'm lost.

Such examples may indeed be paraphrased with a conditional and negation 'If you do not love me, leave me', 'If this is not the road, I'm lost'. There may however be differences in PRESUPPOSITION (see following chapter) which seem to prevent the validity of $(p \vee q) \equiv (\sim p \supset q)$ in natural language. In particular, subordinated *if*-clauses may be presupposed, whereas the first disjunct of (coordinated) disjunctions is not. The asymmetric nature of this *or* already appears in the fact that the commuted versions of [34]*a* and especially [34]*b* are not acceptable. The interpretation of asymmetric *or* runs parallel with that of asymmetric *and* with the only difference that the consequent is dependent on the negation of the antecedent. Symmetric *or* as discussed above is also (logically) equivalent with a conditional with negated antecedent. If I visit my aunt or go to the movies, not visiting my aunt implies that I go to the movies, and not going to the movies implies that I'll visit my aunt. For exclusive disjunction, where the disjuncts may not both be true in the same world, it should for this example also be required that visiting my aunt implies that I am not going to the movies, and that going to the movies implies that I am not visiting my aunt, *ie* $p \equiv \sim q$ and $q \equiv \sim p$. If we merely have $\sim p \supset q$, then this conditional could be true also if $\sim p$ is false, *ie* if p is true, and q is true; but p and q may not both be true in exclusive disjunction.

2.4.4

Summarizing the main semantic properties of (exclusive) *or* we may formulate the following conditions for truth/connection:

  (i) at least one and at most one proposition must be true in an epistemically non-accessible world; more specifically, the truth of one of the propositions implies the falsity of the other, and conversely, in the same possible world;

(ii) from the point of view of the actual possible world, then (*ie* the context) the worlds in which the propositions are true and false, respectively, are proper alternatives;

(iii) both propositions must be related to the same topic of conversation, such that none of the propositions is itself the topic of conversation;

(iv) since in asserted disjunctions a statement is made about epistemically non-accessible worlds, the disjunction is inferred from premises with more general knowledge about similar facts, or about intended actions (of the speaker of the utterance);

(v) the propositions denote facts (in different, alternative) worlds which are similar from the point of view of the topic of conversation.

(vi) non-commutative *or* (*or else*) expresses a conditional (of which the conditions are given in the next section), although with different presuppositions from *if . . . then*.

2.4.5

The satisfaction and connectedness conditions given informally above may be made more exact as follows:

[35] $a: V^+((\alpha \text{ or } \beta), w_i, z_i) = 11$ iff

$\quad (V^+(\alpha, w_j, z_i) = 11$ iff $V^+(\beta, w_j, z_i) = 01$, or

$\quad V^+(\beta, w_k, z_i) = 11$ iff $V^+(\alpha, w_k, z_i) = 01$), and

$\quad w_j \neq w_k, w_i \sim R_K w_j, w_i \sim R_K w_k, w_j R w_k;$

$b: V^+((\alpha \text{ or } \beta), w_i, z_i) = 01$ iff

$\quad (V^+(\alpha, w_j, z_i) = 11$ iff $V^+(\beta, w_j, z_i) = 11$ or

$\quad V^+(\beta, w_k, z_i) = 01$ iff $V^+(\alpha, w_k, z_i) = 01$), and

$\quad w_j \neq w_k, w_i \sim R_K w_j, w_i \sim R_K w_k, w_j R w_k;$

$c: V^+((\alpha \text{ or } \beta), w_i, z_i) = 10$ iff

$\quad V^+(\alpha, w_j, z_i) = 10$ iff $V^+(\beta, w_j, z_i) = 00$, or

$\quad V^+(\beta, w_k, z_i) = 10$ iff $V^+(\alpha, w_k, z_i) = 00$), or

$\quad (V^+(\alpha, w_j, z_i) = 11$ iff $V^+(\beta, w_j, z_i) = 00$, or

$\quad V^+(\beta, w_j, z_i) = 11$ iff $V^+(\alpha, w_j, z_i) = 00$), and

$\quad w_j \neq w_k, w_i \sim R_K w_j, w_i \sim R_{KS} w_k, w_j R w_k;$

$d: V^+((\alpha \text{ or } \beta), w_i, z_i) = 00$ if

$\quad (V^+(\alpha, w_j, z_i) = 10$ iff $V^+(\beta, w_j, z_i) = 10$, or

$\quad V^+(\beta, w_k, z_i) = 00$ iff $V^+(\beta, w_k, z_i) = 00$) or

$\quad (V^+(\alpha, w_j, z_i) = 11$ iff $V^+(\beta, w_j, z_i) = 10$, or

$\quad V^+(\beta, w_k, z_i) = 01$ iff $V^+(\alpha, w_k, z_i) = 00$), and

$\quad w_j \neq w_k, w_i \sim R_K w_j, w_i \sim R_K w_k, w_j R w_k.$

Since these are only part of the truth/connection/correctness conditions we will in future omit fully explicit formulations, in order to avoid over-complicating this chapter.

2.5 *Conditionals*
2.5.1

The typical task of connectives is to express relations between facts. These relations may be very loose, as in conjunction and disjunction, or they may have a stronger character, in the sense that facts may somehow DETERMINE or CONDITION each other. The large class of different types of connectives expressing these DEPENDENCY relations between propositions or facts, will be called CONDITIONALS.

There are several ways to classify the conditionals. One obvious criterion is the type of STRENGTH or STRICTNESS of the conditional relation. Secondly, the DIRECTION of the dependency may be expressed, in the sense that A may be said to depend on, or to be determined by, B, or conversely, or A and B may be mutually dependent. Thirdly, the kind(s) of POSSIBLE WORLD in which the facts are related may be considered, *eg* the actual world or a hypothetically actual or non-actual world. This last criterion will be used as our basic distinction for the classification of the conditionals, especially because it is most apparent in linguistic structure. A fourth and last dimension is the one which runs parallel to a distinction made earlier, viz that between modalities DE RE and modalities DE DICTO. That is, connectives may express relations between the (represented) facts themselves, or between our representations of the facts, viz between propositions or sentences. Although the distinction will not always be easy to make, because our knowledge of the facts is intimately related to the ways in which we speak about them, some connectives will be taken to organize the universe of discourse, others as typically organizing the discourse itself. In part, this distinction will allow us to speak of SEMANTIC CONNECTIVES on the one hand and PRAGMATIC CONNECTIVES on the other hand.

2.5.2

Natural conditionals characteristically require the propositions they operate on to be CONNECTED. If propositional connection is based on conceptual and factual relations, such a relation is most clearly exemplified in relations of dependency, and much less so in relations of spatio-temporal co-occurrence and compatibility (conjunction) or non-co-occurrence and incompatibility (disjunction). Although co-occurrence and compatibility are necessary conditions of dependency, we have seen that they are not sufficient to establish connection, for which similarity and a common topic of conversation are required. *And* may be called a NEUTRAL connective because it merely indicates that facts are related, whereas the other connectives more specifically denote the sort of connection. Given a certain topic of conversation, even merely conjoined facts may be viewed from a 'conditional' point of view, because given a certain proposition it selects the class of possible propositions with which it can be conjoined. Instead of fully separating the different classes of natural connectives, we may therefore also consider them to range over a scale running from (connected) compatibility to mutual implication of propositions, *ie* from POSSIBILITY to NECESSITY.

2.5.3 *Actual conditionals*

Under ACTUAL CONDITIONALS we will range connectives such as *because, for, therefore, so, since, due to, hence, thus, while, whilst, as, consequently,* etc. Syntactic and stylistic constraints on their use will be ignored, whereas pragmatic differences will be treated in Part II. Our main concern is to give a semantic characterization. Such a semantic analysis cannot be given in straightforward logical terms, and certainly not in terms of truth dependencies alone. Moreover, there is no logical connective corresponding to this class of actual conditionals. The material and strict conditionals rather correspond to what will be called 'hypothetical' conditionals below.

Characteristic of actual conditionals is, first of all, that both antecedent and consequent are (assumed or asserted to be) SATISFIED in some situation of the ACTUAL WORLD. This actual world will often be identical with that of which the actual context is a part, or else any other world taken as 'point of view'.[15] More problematic are the conditions where the antecedent and/or the consequent are false (non-satisfied). Similarly, it should be indicated what other conditions should be added in order to make an actual conditional true and connected.

Let us discuss these further conditions on several examples:

[36]*a:* Because it did not rain this summer, the soil has dried out.
    b: The soil has dried out, because it did not rain this summer.

The type of example as illustrated by [36] is standard for an actual conditional in which CAUSALITY is involved. For both sentences it seems to hold indeed that they are true (satisfied) if both antecedent and consequent are true (satisfied). They are false (non-satisfied) if the antecedents are true but the consequents false, just as for the classical material conditional. But what value should be assigned to the whole sentences if their antecedents are false? Should we assign the value 'true', as for the material conditional or should we rather follow the analysis given of the so-called RELEVANT CONDITIONALS, which may be true only if the antecedent is true? In that case we may either assign the value 'false' or a third value, viz 'indeterminate' or 'undefined' to the whole sentence. An answer to this problem would require a discussion of the notion of 'truth' and 'truth values' themselves. In this perspective we may restrict the notion of truth to sentences or propositions which are ASSERTED. Now, in [36] we may have readings where the first clause is not asserted but PRESUPPOSED, a notion to be discussed in the next chapter. Provisionally we take a presupposition of a proposition (or sentence) α to be a proposition of which the truth in some context is assumed or taken for granted, and of which the truth is not affected by the denial of α. In more semantic terms we could say that α *presupposes* β if α *entails* β, and $\sim\alpha$ also *entails* β. This is not fully correct, and in particular depends on the properties of entailment used here, but it will provisionally do for our discussion of actual conditionals.[16] Thus, if in [36] the propositions expressed by the first clauses are presupposed, the interpretation of the whole sentence must be based on the fact that the truth of the antecedents is already GIVEN. In that case, when we deny the sentences of [36] we often merely deny their consequents.[17] This would mean that the truth conditions of the whole sentence only depend on the truth or falsity of the consequents. Although in a sense this is correct, we clearly would expect the first sentence also to play a certain role, beyond that of providing a fixed truth value, viz truth.

It is at this point where connectedness and causality come in. First of all, not any true sentence used as antecedent would make the sentence appropriate, but only those denoting a fact which is related to the fact denoted by the consequent, according to the connection conditions given earlier. Secondly, we should account for the first fact being causally related to the second fact. In our brief analysis of causation in Chapter 6, it is assumed that A is a cause of B, if A is a SUFFICIENT CONDITION of B. Thus, the absence of rain is sufficient for the drying out of the soil. Similarly, B is then said to be a POSSIBLE (or probable) CONSEQUENCE of A.

In order to give a semantic account of these highly intricate notions, we again take the possible world road, because causality is intimately linked with modality. It is not sufficient simply to require that both A and B are the case in some (eg actual) world, or that it is not the case that A is the case, but not B. The basic connection, as for all connectives, is that the values of both antecedent and consequent must be sought in those worlds selected by the topic of conversation.

Now, if B is to be dependent on A, and not only accidentally co-occurring, B must be related to A in several possible worlds. More particularly, as was indicated earlier, we assign values to β only in those worlds SELECTED by α. A further constraint is that causes and consequences are linearly ordered in TIME. Thus, if α is true in a situation $\langle w_i, t_i \rangle$, and β in a situation $\langle w_i, t_j \rangle$, then the fact denoted by β cannot be a consequence of the fact denoted by α if t_j precedes t_i. Causal sentences therefore are to be interpreted in COURSES OF EVENTS or COURSES OF ACTION, developing in a given possible world.

Such courses of events may be represented graphically by left-right tree-like structures, where the nodes denote possible world-time situations, characterized by a set of facts, ie by a set of propositions true or satisfied in these situations.[18] Among the possible courses of events there is again the ACTUAL COURSE OF EVENTS. At each node a possible alternative course of events may be taken. It will provisionally be assumed that we may not come back to a branch which has been left: once taken a course of events w_j its events may be similar but not identical to those of w_i. As is explained in the theory of events in Chapter 6, the links between nodes are to be interpreted as CHANGES, including a ZERO-CHANGE, where a situation remains 'identical' but for its temporal characterization. An example of how such a tree would look is shown overleaf on p 70:

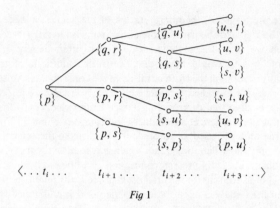

$$\langle \ldots t_i \ldots \qquad t_{i+1} \ldots \qquad t_{i+2} \ldots \qquad t_{i+3} \ldots \rangle$$

Fig 1

The notions of condition and consequence will now be defined in terms of such SEMANTIC TREES (which are simply representations of model structures). Instead of facts A, B,..., we will therefore speak of propositions $p, q, \ldots$ Now, a consequence q of p in some possible course of events w_i, will first of all have to FOLLOW p in that course of events, *ie* occur at a node to the right of the node where p occurs, such that these nodes are connected by a path. Similarly, an IMMEDIATE consequence will have to follow immediately, *ie:* at t_{i+1}, when p occurs at t_i.

In order to express the fact that the occurrence of q following p somewhere in the tree is not accidental when q is a consequence of p, it will be required that at at least one point (node) of the tree where p occurs, q will occur at ALL following nodes:

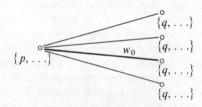

Fig 2

That is, from the point of view of p, q is NECESSARY (*eg* physically), because it is true in all possible courses of events which may be taken from node $\{p, \ldots\}$, not only in the actual course of events w_0. For our particular example this would mean that it is not only true in the actual world that 'the soil has dried out' follows 'it did not rain this summer', but also that GIVEN THE FACTS AS THEY ARE THIS COULD NOT HAVE BEEN OTHERWISE. That is, in this situation at least, the drying out of the soil was INEVITABLE.

On the other hand, a situation may arise where it does not rain, but where the soil does not dry out because of OTHER FACTS, *eg* irrigation. This means that q does not necessarily follow p everywhere in the tree, but AT LEAST IN ONE SUBTREE. This is why q is only a POSSIBLE consequence of p, *ie* possible with respect to all other possible courses of events (subtrees, trees), although in a particular situation, with particular initial facts, this consequence is necessary. Note that this is a form of RELATIVE NECESSITY. It is the RELATION to p which is necessary, not q itself, because the drying out of soil remains of course a contingent fact.

Whereas in our example we had possible consequence, we may also have a relation of NECESSARY CONSEQUENCE. In that case q is not only true at all nodes following a particular node where p is true, but anywhere in the tree (or in all possible trees) after a node where p is true. This necessity may be of different kinds, *eg* physical or biological necessity. Thus, in all possible courses of events where butter is heated in certain circumstances (pressure, etc), this event is followed by the event or process of melting of the butter Similarly, if one's heart stops beating this will, in all possible situations where no other heart is supplied, result in death. These necessities exemplify the BASIC POSTULATES of 'our' world, holding anywhere in the tree of possible courses of events compatible with the actual course of events. Many of the 'everyday' causal relations we are talking about hold in MOST subtrees: they define our expectations about NORMAL courses of events. INCIDENTAL consequences hold in at least one or FEW subtrees, as in:

[37] Because he fell off his chair John died.

Now, we say that p is a SUFFICIENT CONDITION or CAUSE of q iff q is a (possible or necessary) consequence of p.[19] POSSIBLE and NECESSARY CONDITIONS may now be defined in a similar way, viz as the converse of consequence. A proposition p is a POSSIBLE CONDITION of q if, in at least one subtree, q at $\langle w_i, t_{i+j} \rangle$ is preceded by p at $\langle w_i, t_i \rangle$, and for any $\langle w_k, t_{i+j} \rangle$ where q is true it is also preceded by p at $\langle w_i, t_i \rangle$. Similarly, a condition is NECESSARY if anywhere in the tree (or in all trees) q is preceded by p. In other words, p is a necessary/possible condition of q, if anywhere/somewhere q may be reached only by going 'via' a p-node, and q is a necessary/possible consequence of p if from everywhere/somewhere where p is true we reach only q-nodes.[20]

It is precisely this difference of PERSPECTIVE or POINT OF VIEW which differentiates [36]a and [36]b. In [36]a a consequence is asserted from the point of view of a p-node. In [36]b a cause is asserted from the point of view of a q-node. Later, other semantic and pragmatic differences involved here will be discussed.

It goes without saying that this account is a considerable simplification, and no precise formal definition has been given of the tree-model-structures used to interpret actual (causal) connectives. Furthermore, the cause-consequence relations used in natural language are usually INDIRECT, characterizing CAUSAL CHAINS of which two states may be mentioned but also subchains causing subsequent subchains. The drying out of soil, for instance, is a process taking place gradually through a whole period of time. Similarly, SETS OF CAUSES and SETS OF CONSEQUENCES, some possible, others necessary, may be involved.

What has been proposed for the analysis of causal relations between events may be generalized to *reasons for actions*, as in the following sentences:

[38]*a:* Because it did not rain this summer, we irrigated our fields.
    b: We irrigated our fields, because it did not rain this summer.

As will be explained in the theory of actions in Chapter 6, it cannot properly be said that the absence of rain CAUSES our irrigation of the fields, at least not in those worlds which are not fully deterministic. Rather, the absence of rain, or our knowledge of the absence of rain, constitutes a SUFFICIENT REASON in a process of decision-making resulting in the act of irrigation. This means that at least in one situation the decision to irrigate is a NECESSARY CONCLUSION from a set of premises of which our knowledge about the absence of rain is a specific member. Norms, rules, laws and conventions in general may require that in some situation (red light) we always carry out a specific action (stopping). In such cases we may therefore speak of NECESSARY REASONS, but it should be noted that necessity is not physical or biological here but DEONTIC, *ie* they are OBLIGATIONS.

Again, in [38]*a* focus is on the consequent action and in [38]*b* on the reasons for a certain action. Those discourses where causes/reasons of a certain event/action are asserted will be called EXPLANATIONS. There are a number of pragmatic reasons why such explanations must be PLAUSIBLE, which means that causes/reasons must be indicated which are such in most possible situations. Thus, in cases where causes are incidental, as in [37], an acceptable explanation would further require an indication of additional circumstances (John's age, the way he fell, etc) as codeterminants of the consequence. So, not any causal sentence may serve as an explanation. Explanatory sentences (or sequences) typically use the connective *for*,[21] such that for the sentence schema α, *for* β, $V(\beta)$ is assumed to be the cause of or reason for $V(\alpha)$. When we want to focus on the consequences of a certain number of facts, and if these consequences are plausible, we use the connective *so*, as in the schema α, *so* β. Whereas *for* typically marks a set of premises, *so* typically marks a set of conclusions. The conditions for the use of the connectives *for* and *so*, therefore, do not directly pertain to facts but to the discourse about those facts, and need further description in pragmatic terms later. There it should also be made clear why certain causal connectives are sentence-forming (*because, for, since, while*) and why others are sequence-forming (*therefore, so, hence, thus*), and how these differences can be made functional in communicative interaction.

Actual conditionals may be used to interrelate not only events and actions, but also states of affairs, and thus express dependencies of properties or relations:

[39] He has fever because he is ill.
[40] She has been in France because she has been in Paris.

Here, *because* expresses IMPLICATION rather than cause or reason. The relations between the facts are CONCEPTUAL in these cases: fever and illness are necessarily related in most situations, and being in Paris is inconsistent with not being in France in all possible normal worlds (where Paris is in France). In terms of the tree-model structures introduced above, the truth conditions of this type of implication would be given in terms of truth of propositions at the same node. The sentence α *implies* β would be true if at any node where the proposition expressed by α occurs the proposition expressed by β also occurs. The converse, of course, need not be the case: in not every situation where we are in France do we need also to be in Paris. Implicational connectives are specific in the sense that they are based on general conceptual or factual knowledge, and therefore may indicate INFERENTIAL RELATIONS between propositions, as are usually denoted by *so*, *therefore*, *thus* and *hence* in sentence initial position, marking a conclusion drawn from premises. The inference thus expressed by an implication may go from a 'larger' fact to a 'smaller' fact, or conversely, *eg* from whole to part, set to element, etc. The element of necessity playing a role here is not, of course, logical necessity and need not even be conceptual necessity (involving essential properties), but may also be based on ACCIDENTAL GENERALITY, *eg* habit, norm or rule, as in the following well-known example:

[41] John is at home because his lights are burning.

The antecedent in this sentence denotes a known fact and indicates a conclusion, of which the consequent indicates a premise. The general fact 'behind' the implication would then be 'Whenever John's lights are burning, John is at home', which together with the asserted premise yields the (presupposed) conclusion by MODUS PONENS:

[42]a: $p > q$
$\quad b$: p

$\quad$ ———

$\quad c$: q

In this inference (a) is the general fact (known at least to the speaker), (b) is asserted and (c) is presupposed in the context of conversation (by observation or a previous utterance). If we put the second clause of [42] first, we assert the conclusion, whereas the premise is given. It will be assumed that the use of implicational *because*, however, rather focuses attention on the inter-dependencies of facts, whereas the use of sentence-initial *so* and *therefore* is typically used to denote the inferential relations. We will come back to this point in Chapter 8.

The various interpretations of the causal connectives and their ambiguity with respect to their connective or their inferential function, raises the problem of an unambiguous FORMAL REPRESENTATION for this class of connectives. We have possible and necessary conditions and possible and necessary consequences, or causes, whereas the interdependency itself has been identified with a form of NECESSITATION. We shall use the simple arrow ($\rightarrow$) for necessitation, under the interpretation given above in terms of possible worlds (situations) or courses of events. This connection operates in two directions, backwards to denote (possible and necessary) condition, and forwards to denote (possible and necessary) consequence or sufficient condition (cause). Thus $\alpha \leftarrow \beta$ is read as 'α is a condition for β', and $\alpha \rightarrow \beta$ as 'β is a consequence of α', or 'α causes β'. Since this kind of necessity may hold in all possible situations (trees or subtrees), in most situations or in at least one situation, we prefix the corresponding modalities to the whole sentence: $\square(\alpha \rightarrow \beta)$ or $\square(\alpha \leftarrow \beta)$, $\boxdot(\alpha \rightarrow \beta)$ or $\boxdot(\alpha \leftarrow \beta)$, and $\lozenge(\alpha \rightarrow \beta)$ or $\lozenge(\alpha \leftarrow \beta)$, where the non-standard modality '$\boxdot$' is read as 'it is probable that' or 'it is likely that', being related to the quantifier *for most* . . .[22] In order to emphasize the fact that the modalities attach to the relation (connection), they will be written as: $\square\!\rightarrow$, $\boxdot\!\rightarrow$, $\lozenge\!\rightarrow$, $\leftarrow\!\square$, $\leftarrow\!\boxdot$, $\leftarrow\!\lozenge$. Since in a sentence a possible condition may have a necessary consequence, DOUBLE CONNECTIVES may be used, *eg* $\leftarrow\!\square\lozenge\!\rightarrow$, $\leftarrow\!\boxdot\square\!\rightarrow$, $\leftarrow\!\lozenge\lozenge\!\rightarrow$, $\leftarrow\!\lozenge\boxdot\!\rightarrow$.

The sentences:

[43] Because he jumped from the Empire State building, he is dead.
[44] Because he fell off his chair, he is dead.
[45] Because his brain functions have stopped, he is dead.

will thus be translated as: $p\leftarrow\!\lozenge\boxdot\!\rightarrow s$, $q\leftarrow\!\lozenge\lozenge\!\rightarrow s$, $r\leftarrow\!\square\square\!\rightarrow s$, respectively. For unspecified causals/implications the double-headed arrow may be used ($\leftrightarrow$). Note that the modalities involved here are NATURAL, viz physical, biological, conventional, etc. Thus, [45] is two-way valid only in all those worlds where death is defined in terms of certain bodily functions (*eg* heart and brain functions), not in those worlds where life of higher organisms is brainless (or when we speak of the life and death of plants).

Conditionals in general, and causals in particular, require that relations between facts hold in sets of worlds related by a relation of SIMILARITY. This notion may be defined in terms of sets of propositions. These propositions may have the general status of laws, such as in the case of postulates, or else a specific, limited status. If worlds share (are selected by) the same set of basic postulates they are ESSENTIALLY SIMILAR; if they share the same facts they are ACCIDENTALLY (more or less) SIMILAR. Now, a causal relation like that expressed in [43] requires that the worlds in which jumping from the Empire State building (or any high tower) necessitates death are sufficiently similar to our own, NORMAL worlds.

After this discussion of the truth or satisfaction conditions for actual conditionals, it should finally be examined whether specific CONNECTION CONDITIONS are involved. It may be assumed that causal or conceptual interdependency itself is sufficient to establish the connection between propositions: the facts seem related by the very nature of the connection. It would follow that if either the condition expressed by the antecedent or the consequence is connected with the topic of conversation, the whole sentence is both connected as such and connected with the topic of conversation. Nevertheless, it may be the case that causes or consequences are asserted which are not directly connected with a possible topic of conversation. Take for example the following examples:

[46] The soil has dried out because there were no clouds this summer.
[47] Because Harry is a human being, Mary married him.
[48] John had a flat tyre, because he went to Paris.

Examples with reasons are less easy to find, because people may have the most weird reasons for performing a certain action. This would not make the sentence disconnected but rather the persons talked about. Although in [46] the absence of clouds is, via the absence of rain, a sufficient condition for a dried-out soil, the topic of conversation is rain or water and soil, with which clouds are not directly related. Similarly, in [48] it may well be the case that John would not have had a flat tyre if he had not gone to Paris. Still, we would not qualify it as a relevant cause of the flat tyre, because it is too indirectly dependent upon the flat tyre. From such examples it seems to follow that only those causes and consequences are relevant which are more or less directly related and which are related at the SAME LEVEL OF INFORMATION. Thus, 'major' actions require 'major' decisions or reasons as conditions, and 'major' events require 'major' conditions and consequences, where both antecedent and consequent must be related to the topic of conversation. Thus, that I pay my airport bus ticket would be a minor condition of the (relatively) 'major' fact of travelling to New York. Such a constraint is not yet very explicit, but may be clear from our analysis of the structure of event/action given in Chapter 6. In [47] we observe that a necessary condition need not be a relevant condition for a certain consequence, even if it is part of a process of reasoning, viz as a presupposition of the consequent action. More generally it may be said that presuppositions and necessary consequences of the conceptual type are not normally assertable, because the implications involved are normally supposed to be known by the hearer. In this respect [47] is not only disconnected but also INCORRECT when it is used in a context of communication.

We may now summarize the various truth/satisfaction and connectedness conditions for actual conditionals:

(i) an actual conditional is true/satisfied if both of its connected propositions are true in world w_0; it is false if one or both of the propositions are false (in case both are asserted); it is indeterminate/incorrect if its presupposed antecedent is false.

(ii) a conditional is connected if both propositions are relevant to the topic of conversation;

(iii) the actual conditional is also true iff the consequent is true in worlds selected by, or accessible from, the worlds in which the antecedent is true, such that for:

    a: a necessary consequence, $p\,\square\!\!\rightarrow q$, q is true in any world following a p-world in all subtrees;

    b: a probable consequence, $p\,\square\!\!\rightarrow q$, q is true in all worlds following a p-world in most subtrees;

    c: a possible consequence, $p\,\diamondsuit\!\!\rightarrow q$, q is true in all worlds following a p-world in at least one subtree;

    d: a necessary condition, $p\leftarrow\!\square\,q$, p is true in the world preceding q-worlds in all subtrees;

    e: a probable condition, $p\leftarrow\!\square\,q$, p is true in the world preceding q-worlds in most subtrees;

    f: a possible condition, $p\leftarrow\!\diamondsuit\,q$, p is true in the world preceding q-worlds in at least one subtree.

Similar conditions apply to necessary/probable/possible reasons and conclusions, for inferential conditionals.

(iv) the conditions hold only if each subtree is homogeneous, *ie* has similar worlds in the sense that a given set of (physical and other) postulates hold at each node.

2.5.4 *Hypothetical conditionals*

Interdependencies of facts do not exist only in the actual world, but also in possible alternative worlds, and of course in those (actual) worlds which are not epistemically accessible for the speaker. We may know from experience or knowledge of the language that facts may be or must be connected, but not know whether the facts are realized in some world. The typical connectives used to express such a relationship are *if . . . (then), in case . . . (then)*:

[49] If it does not rain this summer, the soil will dry out.
[50] If it does not rain this summer, we must irrigate our fields.
[51] If he flunked his maths exam, he has not worked hard enough.
[52] If he has not worked hard enough, he will flunk his maths exam.

The connections established here are the same as those for actual conditionals: *ie* in terms of conditions and consequences, etc, where in [51] a probable cause or reason is asserted and in [52] a probable consequence. In this respect the truth/satisfaction and connection conditions for *if . . . then* are the same as for *because*. The main difference, as suggested above, is that the clauses are to be satisfied in an epistemically non-accessible world: future worlds, or past worlds in which either a cause or a consequence is known or assumed but not the corresponding consequence or cause, respectively.

    The specific importance of being able to state relations between facts in any world, makes the hypothetical conditional specifically important in GENERALIZATIONS, and hence in the formulation of laws, principles and rules. This is one of the reasons why it is *if . . . then* which has played such an important role, viz as the MATERIAL CONDITIONAL ($\supset$), in classical propositional logic and philosophy.[23] It has been observed that the material conditional formulates a dependency between truth values (like all truth-conditional connectives) and not between propositions or facts, for which a RELEVANT CONDITIONAL has been introduced ($>$). Truth-value assignment in that case depends on the truth of the antecedent which determines the worlds in which the consequent is true or false. This condition in fact guarantees that the connection involved can be asserted for the world where the antecedent holds, viz the actual world. It is in this sense that the uses of sentences like [49–52] have been called CONDITIONAL ASSERTIONS. This term is somewhat misleading, because the assertion itself is not conditional, but actually made, only with respect to a non-actual (unknown) state of affairs.

Strictly speaking, then, *if . . . then* as such is not a connective, but a (monadic) OPERATOR together with an 'underlying' conditional, because *if* merely indicates that the facts are not to be interpreted in the actually known world. Since the connection expressed is not different from that for the causals and implications introduced above, we may keep the same connectives and add an operator to the sentence as a whole, for which we simply use the symbol 'IF'. A propositional translation of a sentence like [49] would then be: IF $(p \dashv \Box \vdash q)$. Conditionals modalized in this way are called HYPOTHETICAL because a connection is expressed between facts which are hypothetically assumed to be true in the actual world (present, past or future). Thus, the *if*-clause specifies the set of (actual) worlds where the *then*-clause is satisfied.

Assertions about epistemically non-accessible worlds are made with respect to knowledge about fact dependencies in general, holding in all or most possible worlds similar to the actual world. A sentence like [49] expresses a particular instance of the general proposition 'If (whenever) it does not rain, the soil will dry out'. Instead of taking *if . . . then* as a hypothetically modalized causal or implicational connective, we may also take it to represent this implicit INFERENCE, where the *if*-clause indicates the assumed premise and the *then*-clause the asserted conclusion, as in the modus ponens schema given in [43].

Note that there may be a difference between the 'degree' of knowledge in hypotheticals. In [49–50] it is not known at all whether it will rain or not this summer, whereas in [51–52] the *if*-clause nearly has the 'certainty' of a presupposition, *eg* established by information just received from the hearer. The *if* in such cases expresses rather a certain reservation of the speaker with respect to the truth of the proposition expressed by the *if*-clause. Instead of a hypothesis an ASSUMPTION becomes the basis of the assertion.

It is not the case that BOTH antecedent and consequent must be 'unknown'. It may be that under the assumption of a certain consequence a fact is asserted which was already known, but not as the cause of the other fact:

[53] If Peter has flunked his exam (it is because) he went to the movies too
      often with Susan.

Of course, our general knowledge of exams and their conditions of success does not allow us to infer that somebody went too often to the movies with a particular somebody. As such, then, [53] cannot be a particular instance of a general fact. The reason cited must be such that the fact might be a consequence of it, *eg* 'if *x* goes to the movies, then *x* does not study'. This fact allows us to 'search' among the known facts for the most likely cause of the assumed consequence, viz those facts which were a sufficient condition for Peter not to have studied enough.

If . . . then does not only express the IF-modality of causals and implications ('If he is a bachelor, he is not married'), but may also correspond to a much weaker connection, in which the consequence is not necessitated but just a possible fact in some condition or situation as specified by the antecedent, as in 'conditional' conjunctions. Compare for instance the following sentences:

[54] If you go to the store, please buy some sugar.
[55] Go to the store please, and buy some sugar.
[56] I went to the store, and bought some sugar.

Although going to the store may be a probable condition of buying sugar, buying sugar is not a consequence (as defined) of going to the store, because there is no situation in which our being in the store inevitably results in buying sugar. The conditional request of [54] is to be satisfied in an epistemically non-accessible world as specified by the *if*-clause, in which the consequent CAN be realized. The conjunction of [56] may denote the 'same' facts, but only in a known (past) world.

It has already been observed that hypothetical conditionals are particularly used to make GENERALIZATIONS. Instead of making assertions about an epistemically non-accessible world, we may analogously make assertions about NON-SPECIFIED worlds or about SETS of specific worlds:

[57]*a:* If sugar is put in water, it dissolves.
 b: If Archibald wanted to smoke pot, he went to Charlie's.

The generalization over worlds or moments of time more clearly appears in the possible use of *when(ever)* in such sentences.

In the conditional schema $p \rightarrow q$, it is the truth or satisfaction of p which determines q. In the connective *unless* the conditional is combined with negation:

[58] Unless you give me some more liquor, I'll go home.

Unless p, q, or, *q unless p*, is satisfied in an epistemically inaccessible world, where the antecedent is false (or rather: where the negation of the antecedent is true) and a sufficient condition for the truth of the consequent. Hence *unless p, q* is semantically equivalent with *if ~p, then q*, and often implies *if p, then ~q*. The latter formula may not always be equivalent with *unless p, q*, owing to possible presuppositions of asserted negations (denials). Thus, we would only say *If you give me some liquor, then I won't go home*, if the topic of conversation already includes the possibility that I might go home, whereas in [58] the topic of conversation rather includes the fact that I may not get any more liquor. The negation involved in *unless* is even stronger and expresses that some fact is the *only* cause or reason for not doing something: *only if... then not...* It will be shown below that this 'exception' to the normal course of events is also present in *but*. An acceptable paraphrase of *q*, *unless p* would therefore be: *q, but not if p*. No further intricacies of *unless* and of negation and conditionals in general will be discussed here.

2.5.5 *Counterfactual conditionals*

General relations between facts may exist whether they are realized in the actual world or not. This means that we are able to make assertions about conditionals which are true in some alternative world, not in the (un-) known actual world:

[59] If it had not rained this summer, the soil would have dried out.
[60] If Peter were rich, he would buy a castle.

We see that, again, the normal properties of conditionals in general are involved here: possible or probable conditions and possible or probable consequences. The truth conditions are such that the counterfactual *if*-clause must be true in some alternative to the actual world, in which its negation ('It has rained this summer') holds. The consequent must then, for the whole sentence to be true, hold in one of the alternative worlds selected by the antecedent by necessitation as discussed for actual conditionals. We also have the weaker form of conditional as in [60], where the consequent is not necessitated, but made possible or ALLOWED by the truth of the antecedent.

As for the other conditionals, the basic assumption is that the speaker has some more general knowledge about relations and interdependencies of facts (or fact concepts, *ie* propositions). The counterfactual world, therefore, must be relatively SIMILAR to the actual world.[24] In such a world it should still be the case that absence of rain has the drying out of the soil as a probable consequence, and that rich people may have the opportunity and the desire to buy a castle. In this respect, we may speak of ACCIDENTALLY COUNTERFACTUAL WORLDS and ESSENTIALLY COUNTERFACTUAL WORLDS. Probably little or nothing else would change if Peter were rich instead of not rich. The same laws of nature would hold, and only a slight difference in the distribution of probabilities (*eg* in a lottery) would have been sufficient to make an accidentally counterfactual world. More systematically different, however, would have been a world in which lack of rain does not cause drying out, all other things being equal (*eg* no irrigation possible). Essential counterfactuals are of the type: *If I could fly . . ., If the moon were made of green cheese . . .*, etc. Such counterfactuals may become true as long as there are accessible worlds where the connection would hold. Some counterfactuals, however, are IMPOSSIBLE and would hold nowhere (or rather: would hold in some impossible world): *If the ball were both round and square . . ., If John were a bachelor but married . . .*, etc. If the conventional conceptual structure of words were slightly changed in some context, such sentences may of course be assigned a meaningful interpretation and be true in some world. It is difficult to draw a sharp line between accidentally and essentially different worlds, because accidental facts are also particular instances of general facts, in which essential laws, principles or rules may be involved. We therefore have to add the clause 'all other things being equal' (*ceteris paribus*) to the conditions for counterfactuals, although strictly speaking such a clause cannot be true, and would break the normal laws of causality.

According to the number of basic postulates holding in sets of alternative worlds, a DEGREE of similarity and difference may be assigned to sets of worlds. Thus, [60] would be true in a world 'closer' to the set of worlds in which the actual world exists (develops) than [61], or would even be a member of the set of NORMAL WORLDS. Given the basic relations established by the conditional, as for actual/hypothetical conditionals, the counter-factual is also a sentential OPERATOR, determining truth (exclusively) in alternative worlds, or in those actual worlds which are epistemically non-accessible. For instance: at the very moment when I utter [60] Peter may indeed have bought a castle out of his sudden lottery winnings; this would require [60] to hold in unknown actual worlds; or else [60] would be false, although appropriately and correctly uttered.[25]

We shall use the operator CF to denote the counterfactual dimension of the conditional, and translate [59] as $CF(p \dashleftarrow\!\Box\Box\!\rightarrow q)$ and [60] as $CF(r \dashleftarrow\!\Box\Diamond\!\rightarrow s)$. Both the IF and the CF operator will provisionally be required to have compound (conditional) sentences as their scope. The difference between IF and CF in natural language is usually marked with specific tenses and/or auxiliaries. Counterfactuals used in non-compound sentences function as optatives:

[61] If (only) he hadn't flunked that easy exam!

The relation between similarity and counterfactuals may be directly expressed in the connective *as if*:

[62] The whale made a noise, as if it were singing.
[63] You are spending money, as if you were a millionaire.

Characteristic for *as if* is that the antecedent is true in the actual world and the consequent assumed to be false in the actual world (that is, it may be true in a non-accessible actual world), although a certain number of properties are shared with the fact holding in some alternative world (where whales actually sing, and where you are actually rich). The use of *as if* may therefore either be intended as a comparison, as in [62], or denote an APPARENT sufficient condition of the fact expressed in the antecedent, in the sense that it LOOKS AS IF some fact were the case, but that the speaker is not certain whether the fact IS actually the case, as in:

[64] You look as if you have passed your exam.

In the latter case the conditional is clearly involved as may be seen from the sentence:

[65] If you had passed your exam, you would be looking like that.

in which a possible condition is cited for a possible consequence.

2.6 *Contrastives*
2.6.1

Things may be different from how they USUALLY are, *ie* in MOST NORMAL POSSIBLE WORLDS. Although dependencies may hold in general, there may be EXCEPTIONS, owing to particular circumstances. Such exceptions are in principle UNEXPECTED, if the properties and courses of events CONTRAST with the normal expectations about what normal worlds look like. Such unexpected or contrastive relations between facts are expressed by such connectives as *but, though, although, yet, nevertheless, whereas, in spite of, notwithstanding, anyway*, belonging to the category of conjunctions, adverbs and prepositions.

Some examples:

[66] John is very handy, but he made a miserable job of painting his house.
[67] Although we slept late, we were still able to catch the boat.
[68] Peter loves skating. Nevertheless, he wanted to stay at home.

The exception to normal courses of events involved in these examples consists in the fact that the antecedent expresses a sufficient condition for the negation of the proposition expressed by the consequent. Just as in conjunctions, both conjuncts must be true for the whole sentence or sequence to be true, with the proviso that the consequent be false in most alternative possible worlds which can be reached from the antecedent. From this condition it follows that contrastives for just possible consequences are less acceptable in normal contexts:

[69] He fell off his chair, but did not break his neck.

Contrastives do not only indicate exceptional courses of events but also states or events which are merely UNEXPECTED or UNDESIRED (defining their pragmatic aspects):

[70] I went fishing, but I didn't catch anything.
[71] Although Peter is very clever, he is not very kind.

Catching a fish is not necessitated in any situation by fishing, but only possible. Not catching a fish, therefore, is merely in contrast with the purpose of the action described. Similarly, in [71], a 'positive' property of somebody is contrasted with a 'negative' property. Instead of having the additional clause

$p \leftrightarrow \sim q$, we would here have a clause $p \& \sim q$ or $p \& r$ (where $r \not\equiv q$), to be true in at least some possible world compatible with the expectations of the speaker.

Contrastives are also used to express the non-satisfaction of possible, probable or necessary conditions:

[72] Peter wants to buy a car, but he does not have any money.
[73] I wanted to learn Turkish, but it was too difficult.

Note that this use of *but* does not allow the use of subordinative *although* in such sentences as [70] and [72–73]. Similarly, sentence-initial *yet* is less acceptable in such cases. Hence, contrastive and condition-unsatisfied *but* seems to be different from consequence-unsatisfied or unexpected-consequence *but*, which is (semantically) equivalent with *although* and *yet*.

The adverbs *yet* and *nevertheless* may combine with the unexpected-consequence *but*, as in:

[74] We slept late, but nevertheless we caught the boat.

The use of *yet* or *nevertheless* (either with *but* or with *and*) seems required even when a normally expected negated proposition is to be (positively) asserted:

[75] He cannot fish, but nevertheless he caught a lot.

Conversely, the use of *but* with *yet* or *nevertheless* (or of these connectives alone) is less acceptable in more general sentences, in which properties are contrasted and not actual facts (although intuitions are vague here):

[76] The glass was very thick, but nevertheless it broke.
[77] The glass is very thick, but nevertheless it is fragile.

Apparently, the sentence adverbs *yet* and *nevertheless* rather express the unfulfilled expectations (of the speaker) at some moment, whereas *but* merely has the semantic role of contrasting properties or facts, with respect to normal courses of events. As soon as unfulfilled expectations are involved the sentence adverbs may be used in order to denote this pragmatic aspect of the connection. We shall come back to these differences between semantic and pragmatic connectives later.

2.7 *Connectives combined*
2.7.1
A recursive semantic account of natural connectives also must deal with sentences of the following form:

[78]*a: $p * q * r * \ldots$*
   b: $p * (q * r)$
   c: $(p * q) * r$
   d: $(p * q) * (r * s)$

where '*' is any connective. Earlier it has been shown that the usual logical axioms and theorems do not hold for sentences of these forms, at least not always. Given the assumption that even conjunctions and disjunctions may have the asymmetrical nature of (weak) conditionals, and given the conditions on connectedness, where the antecedent may codetermine the topic of conversation, a sentence will in general have different truth or satisfaction conditions when the antecedent or the consequent is simple from when it is compound. This is the reason why [78]*b* is not equivalent with [78]*c* in all models. Sentences of the form [78]*a* are ambiguous in this respect: each proposition may be connected with the preceding proposition or with the whole preceding sequence. Although it is impossible to discuss here all possible combinations of the natural connectives introduced in the previous sections, we may give some examples and indicate briefly how their interpretation is built upon from the interpretation of their parts. It should be admitted, however, that our intuitions about the interpretation of the various examples are not always clear-cut.

2.7.2

Sentences of the form [78]*a* are of the ENUMERATIVE type, and mostly restricted to repeated conjunctions or disjunctions (but not both):

[79] John smoked a cigar (and/or) Peter smoked a pipe, and/or Charles smoked a cigarette.

All but the final connective in such cases may be deleted, preserving the same information. There is no sense in which it can be said that the conjuncts or disjuncts are grouped, other than by linear consecution: smoking a cigar and smoking a pipe do not belong 'closer' together than smoking a pipe and smoking a cigarette. Nor can it be said that either the first or the first and the second conjuncts/disjuncts constitute a situation for the following propositions. It may be asked in which respect these enumerative *and*s and *or*s are binary connectives at all: they do not seem to connect propositions other than by including or excluding them with respect to a set, where the only relation between the propositions is this actual or possible membership in the set.

Conditionals may also occur in such a schema, but in that case the interpretation is normally based on the following schema:

[78]*e*: $(p * q)$ *and* $(q * r)$ *and* . . .

as in the following example:

[80] I overslept, so I arrived late at my office, so John was no longer there, so I had to deal with Mr Robinson alone.

The propositions are connected in pairs here by cause/reason – consequence relations. It may be said that the last proposition is connected with the previous sequence as a whole when it denotes a causal chain, and therefore should be interpreted according to structure [78]*c*. Such an interpretation is acceptable if the causal chain can be taken as a compound fact or event, which as a whole is a sufficient condition for the last proposition. The individual propositions of the sequence alone need not be sufficient conditions in such a case. Hence the schema [78]c is not equivalent in such cases with: $(p \rightarrow r)$ and $(q \rightarrow r)$. It is not easy to decide which type of interpretation should be followed. As such, John's absence from the office is a sufficient condition for my being obliged to deal with Mr Robinson alone, whatever the reasons for John's absence. On the other hand, there are possible worlds in which John would not have been absent had I arrived in time, had I not overslept, such that the worlds in which the last clause is to be interpreted are more restricted in number if the previous clauses codetermine the immediate reason for the last proposition.

2.7.3

A similar example may be devised where a compound condition with conjunctions must be either JOINTLY satisfied (as a complex cause/reason) or DISJOINTLY (where each fact is a sufficient condition):

[81] John didn't come and Mary refused to phone Charles and I couldn't come away in time, so I had to deal with Mr Robinson alone.
[82] John was not there, and Mary refused to see him, and Charles had locked his door, so I had to deal with Mr Robinson.

Clearly, such and other examples given are somewhat artificial. Under some further conditions we would at least have stylistic variations, *eg* use of *while* instead of *and* or the construction of several sentences. In order to be able to differentiate between the structure underlying [81] and [82], additional brackets ('⟨' and '⟩') may be used to denote those compounds which enter further connections as a whole: $⟨(p$ *and* q *and* $r)⟩$ *so s*. In that case the connection may not 'reach' within the brackets and relate to the individual members of the sequence, as in $(p$ *so s*$)$ *and* $(q$ *so s*$)$ *and* $(r$ *so s*$)$. These remarks hold for any connective being able to make compound facts in such a way that the component facts are not as such connected with the fact to which the compound as a whole is related. Disjunctive *or* (not its conditional reading), however, behaves like enumerative conjunction, because it does not derive facts from facts as the other connectives do. Take for example the following sentence:

[83] I will either go to the movies or visit my aunt or take a walk downtown, so I have no time to see you.

Here the structure $(p$ *or* q *or* $r)$ *so s* seems equivalent with $(p$ *so s*$)$ *or* $(q$ *so s*$)$ *or* $(r$ *so s*$)$, even if the latter structure were reduced to the former in surface structure, as in [83].

2.7.4

Since natural language does not use parentheses or brackets to disambiguate strings of the form $p * q * r * s$, there must be other means to express the different possible connections. Although we may have recourse to the use of commas, semi-colons and periods in written discourse, in part corresponding to pause and intonation phenomena in spoken discourse, the main disambiguating factors are syntactic and semantic.

Syntactically, the first rule will be that connections are established first from left to right: $p * q$, $(p * q) * r$, $((p * q) * r) * s$, etc. Secondly, conjunctions and disjunctions are connected before conditionals (including contrastives): $(p \ and/or \ q) \ so/but \ r$, $p \ so/but \ (q \ and/or \ r)$, etc, as in:

[84] I'll go to the movies or I'll visit my aunt, but I won't stay at home tonight.

where the contrastive has the disjoined clause as its antecedent, and not the disjunction a contrastive as its consequent. Thirdly, conditionals connect before contrastives, because we may not have contrastives as compound conditions or consequences, it seems. Hence, we have $(p \ so \ q) \ but \ r$, $p \ but \ (q \ so \ r)$, but not $p \ so \ (q \ but \ r)$, $(p \ but \ q) \ so \ r$:

[85] There was no rain this summer so the soil dried out, but we were able to irrigate the fields before the crop was ruined.
[86] There was no rain this summer, but we were able to irrigate the fields so the soil did not dry out.

More problematic is the disambiguation of repeated conditions or contrastives. In general, the schema $p \ but \ q \ but \ r$ is less acceptable, at least when expressed in one sentence. The same holds for $p \ so \ q \ so \ r$. Syntactic disambiguation may take place either by subordination of one of the clauses, such that subordinate and main clause are connected first and then main clauses with main clauses, or the sequence of propositions is expressed in more than one sentence, where clause boundaries connect before sentence boundaries:

[87] ?John didn't work very hard, but he passed his exam, but his teacher gave him a bad report.
[88] Although John didn't work very hard, he passed his exam. But the teacher gave him a bad report.
[89] ?There was no rain this summer so the soil dried out so we had to irrigate.
[90] Because there was no rain this summer, the soil dried out. So, we had to irrigate.

The differences involved here, *eg* between [89] and [90] are often merely stylistic if the basic connections involved are equivalent. The main criterion in all cases is SEMANTIC: it is at this level where it is decided whether $p * q$ is a condition for r (or for $\sim r$, as in contrastives), or p a condition for $q * r$. The first case would hold if the compound $p * q$ is sufficient to bring about r (or imply r), but not p or q alone, whereas in the second case there must be a situation in which p alone may necessitate the compound fact $q * r$. In $p \ so \ q$

so r-structures like [89] the interpretation will depend on semantic-pragmatic criteria of presupposition or focus, to be discussed later.

2.8 *Connected sequences*
2.8.1

Connectives not only make sentences (propositions) out of sentences (propositions) but may also build SEQUENCES OF SENTENCES:

[91] We all expected him to flunk his exam. And so he did.
[92] We all expected him to flunk his exam. But he didn't.
[93] We may go to the beach and have a good swim. Or we'll have to stay home and prepare for our exam next week.
[94] John is a bachelor. So, he has no wife.
[95] I was ill that night. Therefore I couldn't come!
[96] I'll throw you out soon! Unless you stop talking my head off.

Other examples have been given above. Indeed, the discussion about connection and connectives has not been limited to clausal connection. Connected PROPOSITIONS may be expressed either in composite sentences or in sequences. It will therefore be assumed that the semantic rules and principles holding for the sentential connectives also hold for those occurring in sequences. Of course, only coordinating conjunctions and sentence adverbs may connect sequences, not subordinating connectives like *because*, *although, if . . . then*.

2.8.2

Although part of the semantic conditions for the sequential uses of connectives coincide with those for their sentential use, sequences have an additional number of properties constraining the interpretation of connectives. An important distinction to be made first is between the SEMANTIC and PRAGMATIC functions of connectives. This distinction will be treated in more detail later. The semantic function of connectives is to relate facts, whereas pragmatic connectives relate sentences (or propositions), as for instance in inferences. Thus, in [94] the second sentence not only denotes a necessary consequence of the fact denoted by the first sentence, but the second sentence at the same time functions as a CONCLUSION of a partly implicit argument. The pragmatic function of connectives must be defined in terms of the STRUCTURES and SEQUENCING OF ILLOCUTIONARY ACTS.

The SEMANTIC differences between sentential and sequential connectives are not very clear-cut. In many situations of spoken discourse, it is not even sure whether the sentence-sequence distinction is made. The usual phonological clue for sentence initial (sequence forming) connectives is sentence intonation, and a pause after the connective, mostly represented as a comma in written discourse. The difference involved in sequences like [91] and [92] seems to be that the second sentence is satisfied at a different point of time and for different individuals as the first sentence. Transition to a new sentence allows a CHANGE of world and/or of discourse referent. However, such differences between sentences and sequences hold more in general, and are not to be considered as specific properties of sequential connectives. Similarly, in sentence initial *or* we have a disjunction of propositions which from a certain point of view are dissimilar. That is, *or* then denotes what could be called a STRONG ALTERNATIVE.

Note that sentence-initial *therefore* is ambiguous in the sense that it either indicates a consequence (when it is non-stressed and not followed by a pause) or a cause or reason of the fact denoted by the sentence in which it occurs (stressed, and followed by a pause). In the latter case the second proposition is usually presupposed. Pragmatically, such sequences function as EXPLANA-TIONS of certain facts.

2.8.3

Sequential uses of connectives further allow the connection between sentences (or sequences) with whole previous SEQUENCES, as was discussed above for combined connectives. A fact may be a condition or a consequence of several facts, occurring at the same time or in subsequent moments of time. Similarly, the use of *but* or *however* may indicate a contrast with an expected consequence of a whole series of facts.

The semantics for such cases is straightforward: instead of merely letting p hold at some node we take a set or a sequence $\langle p_1, p_2, p_3, \ldots \rangle$ as antecedent, to be true at some situation in the semantic tree, where q or a sequence $\langle q_1, q_2, q_3 \ldots \rangle$ is the consequence to be true or false at some or all subsequent nodes, somewhere or anywhere in the tree. The major difficulty involved is the interpretation of the antecedent or consequent as some connected 'whole'. That is, we may use a contrastive, for instance, which does not contrast with the (consequences of the) individual sentences of the antecedent, but only with some complex situation as a whole. It should be made clear later how sentences or propositions are related, and thus may denote composite facts, by other means than connectives, so that a basis is provided for the interpretation of this sort of sequential uses of connectives.

2.8.4

Finally, it should be emphasized that sentential and especially sequential connection need not be expressed by explicit connectives. We already have observed earlier that we may use *and* also for stronger connections, if these follow from the connected propositions themselves.

Similarly, the connections between propositions in sentences and sequences may be 'expressed' by the very co-occurrence of the sentences expressing them:

[97] John smoked a pipe. Harry smoked a cigar.
[98] John smoked a pipe. Mary didn't like it.
[99] Peter had an accident. He is in hospital now.
[100] Of course Harry has been in France. He has been in Paris.

It is characteristic of disjunctions and *if*-conditionals that they are not expressed without their explicit connectives because the facts denoted do not necessarily hold in the actual world. In cases where *or* is not used to express disjunction, other modal expressions are used to denote the possible truth of the disjuncts in the actual world (*I may go to the movies. I may visit my aunt . . . Who knows?*). We may adopt it as a general rule that in sequences which do not use connectives (asyndetic sequences), the sentences are interpreted to have truth values with respect to a given topic of conversation, relating them indirectly. As a second general rule it will be assumed that facts thus connected by one topic of conversation are further to be connected in the closest possible way, viz as reason/cause and consequence, *eg* as in [99]. In cases where conditional relations are exceptional, *ie* do not hold in most possible situations, the explicit connective must be used:

[101] John smoked a pipe so Harry smoked a cigar.

One of the further aspects of this rule is the LEFT-RIGHT ORDERING of sentences as expressing linear (before-after) ordering of facts. Hence, first sentences express conditions, second sentences express consequences. In explanatory contexts, this ordering may be reversed, *eg* when we would take [99] in another ordering. Similarly, changes of tense may influence the interpretation of normal orderings. This and similar issues concerned with the ordering and distribution of information in discourse will be dealt with in following chapters.

It goes without saying that the mere absence of connectives does not mean that sentences are asyndetically connected. Especially when we change the topic of conversation or the focus (see following chapter) in a discourse, two sentences may follow each other without being directly connected, although each being connected with different but related topics of conversation.

2.9 *Connection and connectives: conclusions*
2.9.1

Let us summarize the main characteristics of natural connectives as they have been discussed in this chapter.

   (i) Natural connectives are INTENSIONAL. They do not relate truth values but propositions and values of propositions in possible worlds: facts.

   (ii) Natural connectives presuppose that clauses and sentences express intensionally CONNECTED propositions. Propositions are connected if the facts denoted are related in some possible situation and if they are connected with the same TOPIC OF CONVERSATION.

   (iii) The differences between natural connectives are given along the following dimensions:
      a: strictness of the relation between facts (compatibility, probability, necessity);

     b: generality of the relation (holding in some, most, all possible courses of events – subtrees);

     c: intended possible world (the relation exists in the actual world, an epistemically non-accessible actual world, or a non-actual world);

(iv) With the exception of enumerative conjunction and disjunction, natural connectives are of the CONDITIONAL type in the sense that the consequent is to be interpreted in worlds determined by the antecedent (together with the topic of conversation).

(v) The usual axioms holding for LOGICAL CONNECTIVES are not valid for natural connectives (commutativity, associativity, transitivity, distributivity).

(vi) Connectives have both SEMANTIC and PRAGMATIC functions: they denote relations between facts and may indicate relations between sentences or propositions in discourse based on these semantic relations (*eg* in inferences).

(vii) Differences between the SENTENTIAL and the SEQUENTIAL use of connectives are mainly pragmatic or are inferred from meaning relations between the propositions. In general the sentence-sequence differences may be used for CHANGES in topic of conversation, discourse referent, focus or perspective.

(viii) Differences between the SUBORDINATING and the COORDINATING versions of each type of connective are, under normal ordering, related to presupposition and focus distribution in discourse. Hence, *although-*, *because-*, and *if*-clauses express propositions which must be (epistemically) true. Sentences which do not satisfy these conditions may be true/false and connected/disconnected, but INCORRECT.

2.9.2

These general characteristics are certainly not exhaustive. Each of the connectives has more specific semantic, pragmatic (and syntactic, stylistic) properties which have not been discussed. Although some pragmatic aspects have been mentioned briefly, the major focus of the treatment was on the specific semantic aspects of the kind of connection involved for each type of connective. This semantics was given in terms of connected model structures, such that each model structure for a sentence/proposition is determined by the models (structure and interpretation) of the previous sentences/propositions. The model structures, especially the notion of possible topic of conversation, however, have not been analysed further. We have discussed the relationships of facts as whole entities, but it should also be specified what sort of properties do establish such relations between facts. Just as a propositional logic must be complemented with a predicate logic, the study of the semantic relations in discourse requires an analysis of the relations between PARTS of different sentences, *eg* between individuals, properties/relations, operators, quantifiers, etc. Whether a sentence is connected with a topic of conversation, and hence whether a sentence or sequence is connected itself, depends on this internal structure of the respective sentences/propositions. This will be the topic of the next chapter.

Notes

1 Thus a formal semantics may specify the way truth or satisfaction conditions may be given for sentences like *It is possible that Peter is ill and that Mary is visiting him*, *ie* of the following logical form $\Diamond(f(a)\ \&\ g(b, a))$, but it will not specify what *ill* means, nor the conventional relation between *eg* the meaning of *ill* and the meaning of *fever*. The formal semantics will indicate only how each kind of expression is related to a particular kind of value, and how relations between values depend on relations between expressions (as is the case for the logical connectives, for instance). In other words, a formal semantics only specifies certain properties of the notion of meaning of natural language expressions. It is one of the attempts of current logical theory applied in the study of natural language to extend the domain of the study of these 'logical properties' of natural language, *eg* by devising so-called non-standard logical systems. For surveys of linguistic semantics, see Leech (1969, 1974), Steinberg and Jakobovits, eds (1971), Bartsch and Vennemann (1972).

2 The definition of causation has been very much simplified here and conceals many philosophical and logical problems. When we say that A is incompatible with the non-occurrence of B, in some possible world w_i, we thereby mean that both A and B occur in w_i and in all possible worlds similar to w_i (*eg* sharing the same set of physical and biological laws). In other words: A causes B if they are related NECESSARILY at least at some point of time (where A precedes B).

3 We might be more specific still and reserve the notion 'topic of conversation' only for conversations and give it a pragmatic definition (in terms of intentions and knowledge of speakers, for instance), and then use the term 'topic of discourse' in a more restricted, formal and semantic sense, viz as a property of sequences of propositions. Since this distinction is not elaborated in this book, we will use the terms 'topic of conversation' and 'topic of discourse' provisionally as being synonymous.

4 We have used, provisionally, only the theoretical term 'connected', both for relations between propositions in composite sentences and sequences, and for the relation between propositions and topics of conversation. The latter might also be called (semantic) relevance. In that case, propositions would be connected if they are relevant to the same topic of conversation. Since, however, first conjuncts and in general previous discourse may constitute the topic of conversation, we have made no theoretical distinction between connection and (semantic) relevance. The latter term is mostly used in recent work in relevance logics. See references below.

5 A similar 4-value interpretation is used by Groenendijk and Stokhof (1975) in order to account for correctness-conditions (*eg* of modal expressions).

6 One of the crucial methodological problems which cannot be fully clarified in this book is the delimitation of linguistic semantics on the one hand from a cognitive semantics – in particular a theory of the acquisition, representation and use of 'world knowledge' – on the other hand. The system of the knowledge of the world we have is ordered by conventional 'frames' as we will see in Chapters 4 and 5. Connection, coherence and topics of conversation are being determined not only by the general conceptual knowledge exhibited by the language system, but also by our knowledge as represented in cognitive frames.

7 The question arises whether there would not always be such a concept, which would make any topic change acceptable. Formally, this would not be an objection

(if only the relevant concept is specified), but empirically we will want some constraints, *eg* that the concept be rather specific or even expressed in the discourse. In Chapter 5, dealing with macro-structures which are intended to explicate topics of conversation, some further constraints on topic change, *ie* on macro-structure proposition sequences, will be given. In principle the same constraints hold as for the connectedness of any sequence of propositions. In general, it may thus be said (which is empirically warranted) that connection of propositions and topics always holds if there is a proposition relative to which they are connected. If language users nearly always are imaginative enough to establish 'any' connection (in a particular discourse and context) this means that they are able to construct the required topic or common proposition.

8 See Dik (1968) for a discussion of these and other grammatical properties of connectives. The most recent extensive discussion of connectives related to problems of coordination is given in Lang (1973). Some of our semantic notions used in the explication of connection and connectives are similar to those used by Lang. Besides these two monographs little attention has been paid in modern linguistics to natural connectives. Most work has been done within a philosophical and logical framework (see references below). See van Dijk (1973*b*, 1974*a*).

9 For a discussion of phrasal connectives, see Dik (1968), Lang (1973), and references given there. See also R. Lakoff (1971), who also gives a more general discussion of connection conditions (using the notion 'topic').

10 The major monograph about relevance logics, in particular logics of entailment, is Anderson and Belnap (1975). See the numerous references given there.

11 For details of these definitions of compatibility (compossibility), consistency and related notions, see Routley and Meyer (1973).

12 See Stalnaker and Thomason (1970) for a discussion about selection functions in the semantics of (relevant) conditionals. See also Lewis (1973).

13 See Gabbay (1972). Urquhart (1972) also introduces the primitive notion 'piece of information' with respect to which formulae are interpreted in a way similar to our use of the notion 'topic of conversation'.

14 See Groenendijk and Stokhof (1975) for an explication of correctness, which is determined by the knowledge/ignorance language-users should have in order to use sentences adequately. Although the notions involved here are pragmatic, and will be discussed further in Part II, the epistemic relations between possible worlds, as long as truth and connection are involved, are taken as belonging to the semantics (*ie* they are abstracted from the knowledge of language-users in particular communicative contexts). We say that a world w_j is 'epistemically accessible' from a world w_i ($w_i R_K w_j$), if it is known in w_i what is the case in w_j (R_K may be indexed for some individual x).

15 The fact that such 'actual' conditionals as those mentioned may also denote relations between facts in any world selected as a 'point of view', would make the term 'actual conditionals' less appropriate if 'actual' would be understood in the strict sense of the 'actualized' (historical) world (past-now-future), and not the world I am 'actually' talking about. Since these two kinds of worlds will often coincide in natural language discourse we keep the term 'actual conditionals', at least provisionally and for want of a better term, and in order to distinguish them from the non-actual *if*-conditionals.

16 For detailed discussion, both of the pragmatic and the semantic properties of presupposition, see *eg* the contributions in Petöfi and Franck, eds (1973). For recent surveys of the discussions, see Kempson (1975) and Wilson (1975) and the references given there to the large linguistic and philosophical literature about presuppositions.

17 At least this would be one of the natural readings of natural negation or denial. Strictly speaking, as we will see below, we would in such cases have the negation of

the connective, *ie* a denial of the fact that causation is involved. In that case, however, the *connective* must be stressed, viz as a particular comment of the negated sentence.

18 We omit a mathematical (graph-theoretical) characterization of these semantic trees, because we are uncertain of their precise philosophical properties: do they have roots (*ie* where time begins), are all trees connected, or should we postulate a set of possible trees, perhaps with different sets of basic postulates (*eg* time might be flowing faster in other trees, which would be impossible in one tree, according to definition)? One of the properties we would like them to have is that courses of events cannot merge again, on the assumption that once the history of a course of events is different, its future will be also.

19 Clearly, this is not the full philosophical or even semantic picture of causation. Note that the term 'sufficient condition' is ambiguous in the sense of being determined by possibility or necessity (or any value on a continuous scale of probabilities): some fact may be sufficient for another fact to occur in some situation (falling off a chair and then breaking one's neck) or in most of all possible situations (drinking sulphuric acid and then dying). Note also that 'sufficient condition' is defined in terms of consequence, not in terms of (possible or necessary) condition, which may easily lead to confusion.

20 Note that it will simply not do to define causes and consequences in terms of sets of possible worlds or courses of events alone. We must have a 'double' system with (sets of) trees and subtrees, in order to be able to account for the fact that even if some event causes another event only once (speaking of event types), this causation still involves necessity. In that case we require that some course of events may define only (at least) one subtree, but there, given some node p, ALL paths will lead to q-nodes. In a strictly deterministic system, however, it would be appropriate to speak only about necessary consequences. The same holds if we could spell out the members of the set C codetermining q together with p: at any C-node, anywhere in the tree, q would follow in all immediately subsequent nodes. Again, further philosophical intricacies (*eg* regarding determinism) are ignored here. For references about causation, see Chapter 6.

21 In spoken language the explanatory *for* (unlike German *denn* and Dutch *want*) is mostly supplanted by other causal connectives, such as *since* or (*be-*)*cause*. This means that *because* may be ambiguous in the sense of denoting fact relations on the one hand and inferential relations on the other hand. See below.

22 For this kind of non-standard quantifiers, see Altham (1971).

23 From our discussion it follows that the material conditional should not be considered as the formal equivalent of natural *if...then:* firstly the material conditional (unlike the relevant conditional) need not exhibit connection or respect presuppositions or assumptions, secondly, it does not express the modality (viz necessity) and epistemic (non-)accessibility of *if* in natural language. Thus the material conditional is rather an abstraction from natural language conditionals. For a different view, see *eg* Grice (1967).

24 For the notion of similarity between possible worlds within the general framework of a discussion of counterfactuals, see Lewis (1973) and Rescher (1975).

25 Along this dimension counterfactuals would differ from hypotheticals in their epistemic basis: the speaker would know, believe or assume that the antecedent is false in the actual world, whereas in the hypothetical he does not know (believe, assume) the antecedent to be either true or false in the actual world.

Chapter 4

Coherence

1 Aims and problems
1.1

In this chapter we will analyse some properties of the semantic structure of discourse which determine its so-called COHERENCE. The notion of coherence is not well-defined, however, and therefore requires explication. Intuitively, coherence is a semantic property of discourses, based on the interpretation of each individual sentence relative to the interpretation of other sentences.[1] The notion of connectedness, discussed in the previous chapter, apparently covers one aspect of discourse coherence, viz the immediate, pairwise relations between subsequent propositions taken as 'wholes'. Sentences or propositions in a discourse may form a coherent discourse, however, even if they are not all connected to every other sentence or proposition. In particular, they may be related in pairs without being connected in the sense defined earlier, *eg* when relations exist between parts of two or more propositions.[2] In order to be able to delimit the object of our analysis, some examples of coherence relations in discourse will be given first.[3]

1.2

The greatest amount of discussion, both for sentences and discourses, has been devoted to the relation of REFERENTIAL IDENTITY between individuals. Arguments of different propositions may have the same individual as their value, where the argument expressions themselves need not be identical: the same individual may be referred to by the proper name *John*, by the pronoun *he*, or by expressions like *my brother*, *that boy* or *the pupil who has lost a book*.

Such relations of identity can also be established for properties and relations: I may be ill, and *so* may Peter, and I may love Mary, and *so* may John.

In a wider sense, identity is also involved when some fact holds in the same possible world, at the same place and/or at the same time.

In all these cases the model of some sentence S_i is determined by the models of the sentences $S_j, S_k, \ldots$, such that the same individual object, property, or world-place-time is being assigned.

1.3

Since we do not in a discourse continuously say the same thing about the same individuals, a coherent discourse will also have relations of DIFFERENCE and CHANGE. In the first place we may INTRODUCE new individuals into the universe of discourse, or assign new properties or relations to individuals which have already been introduced. Such differences, however, are of course subject to systematic CONSTRAINTS. It seems intuitively reasonable to require that newly introduced individuals are related to at least one of the individuals already 'present'. Similarly, we may expect that assigned properties also are related to properties already assigned. And finally a change of world or situation will also be constrained by some accessibility relations to the world or situation already established.

In other words, changes must somehow be HOMOGENEOUS. That is, they must be operated within the bounds of some higher level principle determining the POSSIBLE individuals and properties of some universe of discourse.[4] The notion of TOPIC OF CONVERSATION, introduced as a primitive notion in the previous chapter, seems to be involved here, and therefore requires further explication.

Note that the semantics to be elaborated should account for these permanent changes in the models. An expression like *the man* in S_i may not have the same referent as the same expression in some other sentence S_j.

1.4

Changes of individuals, properties or relations are to be operated with respect to individuals, properties or relations which are already GIVEN. Thus, in order to express the continuity of a discourse, each sentence will in principle express this relation between OLD and NEW information, viz as TOPIC and COMMENT respectively, along the simplified schema $\langle\langle a, b\rangle, \langle b, c\rangle, \langle c, d\rangle, \ldots\rangle$, or $\langle\langle a, b\rangle, \langle a, c\rangle, \langle a, d\rangle \ldots\rangle$. One of the aims of a serious semantics of discourse is to account for these and other aspects of INFORMATION DISTRIBUTION in the discourse.

1.5

Natural language discourse, unlike formal discourse, is not fully EXPLICIT. Relationships between sentences or propositions may exist without being expressed. This is the reason why the theoretical construct of a TEXT is necessary in order to show how discourses can be coherently interpreted even if most of the propositions necessary to establish coherence remain IMPLICIT, *eg* as entailed propositions of propositions explicitly expressed in the discourse.

The problem at issue, then, is to formulate conditions which allow propositions to remain implicit, and to specify what sort of propositions must be expressed in order for the discourse to be coherent. Propositions which are postulated to establish theoretical coherence of a text but which are not expressed in the discourse will be called MISSING LINKS.

We here touch upon a more general problem of the theory of grammar: in what way are missing links to be called part of the underlying structure or semantic representation of a discourse? Or should we rather assume that they are 'constructed', viz by rules of inference, or by rules and processes defined at the level of pragmatics or in cognitive theory?

1.6

The issues raised above cannot possibly all be treated in their full complexity within the space of one chapter or of one book. Therefore, those issues which are familiar in discussions about the semantic structure of sentences, *eg* those pertaining to referential identity (determining pronominalization, article selection, etc), will be passed over here. The main focus will be upon the different aspects of INFORMATION DISTRIBUTION in discourse: introduction, continuity, expansion, topicalization, focusing, etc.

These specific phenomena of the semantic structure of discourse are GRAMMATICALLY interesting: they are systematically associated with specific syntactic and morpho-phonological structures, which however cannot be treated in this book.[5] On the other hand, some of the close associations with pragmatic structures will receive particular attention in Part II.

1.7

In this chapter we will be concerned with what has been called LINEAR or SEQUENTIAL COHERENCE, *ie* the coherence relations holding between propositions expressed by composite sentences and sequences of sentences. There are also semantic structures of a more global nature, not to be directly characterized by (relations between) individual propositions, but in terms of SETS of propositions, whole sequences and certain operations on sets and sequences of propositions of a discourse. These MACRO-STRUCTURES determine the GLOBAL or overall coherence of a discourse and are themselves determined by the linear coherence of sequences.[6] Thus, as we saw in the previous chapter, coherence relations between sentences are not only based on the sequential relations between expressed or interpolated propositions, but also on the topic of discourse of a particular passage. The notions of topic of conversation and macro-structure will be treated in the next chapter.

2 The semantics of coherence

2.1

In order to characterize the coherence properties of sequences we need an appropriate semantics. Such a semantics is essentially RELATIVE in the sense that sentences are not interpreted in 'isolated' models, but relative to the interpretation of related sentences in related models. The relationship between the sentences is defined in terms of these relative interpretations.

The simplest way to account for relative interpretations would be to interpret the sentences of sequences in the respective models of an ordered MODEL SEQUENCE $\langle M'_1, M_2, \ldots, M_n \rangle$. A discourse is then SATISFIED in some model sequence if each of its sentences is satisfied in the respective model structures for the respective valuations. Such a model sequence will briefly be called a DISCOURSE MODEL.[7]

Coherence relations exist between parts of sentences (or propositions) and the model structures involved must therefore be such that values can be assigned to these parts (operators, quantifiers, predicates, arguments, etc). Characteristic of the discourse model, then, is that these valuations in some model M_i depend on the valuations in some model M_j. The same holds for the respective model structures themselves: they may also depend on each other. We may have identity, intersection or change of the respective DOMAINS (of individuals). 'During' the discourse, individuals may be 'introduced' or even 'eliminated', in the sense that each sentence is to be interpreted with respect to its specific ACTUAL DOMAIN of individuals. As we have seen for the semantics of connection, the POSSIBLE WORLD in which a sentence is interpreted is determined by the interpretation of previous sentences in previous models of the discourse model. Similarly, QUANTIFIERS will also be interpreted for the domains which at some point in the discourse model have been established for the various possible worlds involved: expressions like *all men* normally refer to the men of a certain, previously mentioned group, not to all existing men, universally speaking, nor to all men of a certain world.[8] Finally, PROPERTIES OR RELATIONS, *ie* the values of predicates, will also change for a given individual at different time points and in different possible worlds. A discourse, thus, may have the propositions 'John is ill' and 'John is not ill', without being inconsistent. Less straightforward is our task to account for the fact that properties assigned to individuals in related models should somehow be 'homogeneous'. Thus, being ill and having a fever or calling a doctor are, intuitively, more homogeneous than being ill and being born in London or having red hair. Apparently, part of this homogeneity is to be formulated in terms of conceptual implication and condition-consequence relations between facts. Predicates, or the properties denoted by them, have a certain RANGE, viz the set of possible individuals or individual concepts to which they can be assigned or applied. A sentence like *The boy is ill* is MEANINGFUL if the individual denoted actualizes an individual concept ('boy') belonging to the range of the property 'ill'. Only meaningful sentences, *ie* sentences denoting a possible fact, may be satisfied in some possible world.[9] Now first of all, properties assigned to the same individual must have overlapping ranges, otherwise they could not apply to the same individual. Thus, the ranges of 'flowing' and 'walking' do not overlap such that 'boy' belongs to the intersection. Yet, 'having red hair' and 'being ill' may have overlapping ranges, although these properties are not as such directly related. These properties belong, so to speak, to different DIMENSIONS, *eg* the dimension of 'physical appearance' or 'having colour' and 'health', respectively.[10] A dimension may be seen as a basic category defining sets of properties. Possible individuals may be COMPARED with respect to a certain dimension, and thus be more or less (DIS-)SIMILAR. Thus we call one object blue, *but* the other yellow with respect to the same dimension, viz 'having colour', and will not call an object blue, *but* the other round because two different dimensions are involved here.

Now, in a semantic theory of discourse it should be made explicit how notions such as RANGE, DIMENSION, COMPATIBILITY and SIMILARITY of meaning are involved in the definition of discourse coherence. A formal semantics, however, can only do this in a 'schematic' way, by giving general conditions on possible predication and meaning relations, whereas linguistic (lexical) semantics on the one hand and cognitive semantics on the other hand will have to provide the actual conventional 'content' of sentence and sequence meanings, and the probabilistic expectations based on our knowledge of the world, respectively.

2.2

Whereas we may have some idea what meanings and referents of arguments, predicates and sentences are, such concepts as meaning or referents of discourse are not so obvious. As for composite sentences, it may be assumed, however, that discourses denote certain FACT STRUCTURES, *ie* ordered sets of facts. A simple example of such a fact structure would be a sequence of causally related events, as represented by the tree semantics of the previous chapter. Other fact structures could be the state of a certain street at a certain time point, or the activities of some agent during a certain period.

Important, however, is the fact that only part of the individuals, properties and relations characterizing some state, event or action is being referred to explicitly by the discourse. That is, the description is INCOMPLETE from an ontological point of view.[11] Natural discourse merely denotes those facts which are PRAGMATICALLY RELEVANT, *ie* which the speaker thinks the hearer should know, bring about, etc. On this 'selection' among true propositions there are some specific constraints, *eg* regarding 'level', to be discussed below.

Another aspect of discourse semantics is the relationship between the ORDERING OF SENTENCES and the ORDERING OF FACTS. For actions and events the discourse ordering will be called NORMAL if their temporal and causal ordering corresponds to the linear order of the discourse. For descriptions of states, where the facts all exist at the same time, it will be assumed that a normal ordering corresponds with the general-particular and the whole-part relations between facts.

Under certain conditions these orderings may be transformed. One set of these conditions is pragmatic, pertaining to the communicative importance of certain propositions. Other transformations are, more generally, perceptual and epistemic: not the ordering of the facts themselves, but the ordering of the perceptions and the knowledge about them determines the structure of the discourse.

These pragmatic and other constraints on the ordering of propositions in a representation will be discussed in Chapter 7. In the semantics, strictly speaking, we can only describe the relations between expressions (and their internal structure) and the structure of facts and situations, abstracting from pragmatic and cognitive properties of sequence ordering. This means that notions such as 'normal ordering' are purely theoretical; they do not imply that discourse is usually ordered like this, or that such orderings constitute a norm.

3 Coherence analysis: some examples
3.1
In order to elaborate a theoretical framework for the semantic description of coherence in discourse, some examples should first be analysed.

Consider the following passage from the beginning of a chapter in a crime story:[12]

[1]*a:* Clare Russell came into the *Clarion* office on the following morning, feeling tired and depressed. She went straight to her room, took off her hat, touched her face with a powder puff and sat down at her desk.
Her mail was spread out neatly, her blotter was snowy and her inkwell was filled. But she didn't feel like work (. . .). [*p* 59]

Now, what conditions make such a passage coherent? A first determinant seems to be the INDIVIDUAL IDENTITY in the model sequence:[13] V(*Clare Russell*) = V(*She*). The other individuals, viz V(*office*), V(*room*), V(*hat*), V(*face*), V(*powder puff*), V(*desk*), V(*mail*), V(*blotter*), V(*inkwell*), are related in a less direct way. The relations involved are those of INCLUSION, MEMBERSHIP, PART-WHOLE and POSSESSION: a room may be part of an office, a desk be part of an office-room, mail, blotter and inkwell part of the objects characterizing a desk-'world'; similarly, a face is part of the individual, whereas a hat and powder puff are possible possessions of a human (female) individual. The individuals seem to cluster around two concepts, viz the 'human (female) individual' and the 'office' concepts. A set of individuals thus related by identity or partiality ($\in$) through successive models will be called a SERIES. In some sentences these two series are related, *eg* by verbs. The predicates in the successive sentences should also be related in order for the passage to be coherent. Predicate relations, however, need only exist between predicates assigned to the same individual or to the individuals of one series. Here the predicates are related because they denote a possible sequence of activities, bodily states and mental (emotional) states for the woman series, and related properties (along the 'neatness' or 'readiness' dimension) of the office-desk series. The passage is normally ordered with respect to the activity sequence. Finally, the passage is coherent due to time/period and place identity associated with the activity sequence and the office-desk series.

This is only a very informal and partial characterization of the coherence relations in the passage. The regularities as formulated would allow a great number of possible discourses which would be unacceptable. Further explication, thus, is necessary.

3.2

An important COGNITIVE condition of semantic coherence is the ASSUMED NORMALITY of the worlds involved.[14] That is, our expectations about the semantic structures of discourse are determined by our KNOWLEDGE about the structure of worlds in general and of particular states of affairs or courses of events. For abnormal worlds, we need specific indicators, *eg* the *but* in the last sentence, indicating that not working is abnormal in an office-desk situation under further positive conditions (mail available, inkwell filled, etc). Under these normality conditions the following discourse alternatives would be much less acceptable:

[2] (. . .) took off her clothes (. . .)
[3] (. . .) threw her desk out of the window (. . .)
[4] (. . .) her mail was hanging on the wall (. . .)
[5] (. . .) she drank her inkwell (. . .)

As such, these clauses would express perfectly possible facts (propositions), and could occur in discourses in which such states or events are made plausible. Normality, therefore, is a relative concept.

The set of propositions characterizing our conventional knowledge of some more or less autonomous situation (activity, course of events, state) is called a FRAME.[15] In our example we have an instance of an OFFICE-frame, viz a set of typical office individuals and typical activities in offices. The alternatives [2–5], in this respect conflict with an office frame. Note that such frames include propositions determining the possible orderings of facts, *eg* along the cause-consequence and general-particular or whole-part lines. The following passage would be less acceptable for that reason:

[6] (. . .) came into the office. Her inkwell was filled, and she sat down at her
      desk (. . .)

The office-inkwell-desk ordering is abnormal because the relative dimensions and inclusion relations are not ordered in the whole-part relation, nor the local presuppositions determining the place of the inkwell on the desk.

3.3

The discourse in [1]*a* continues as follows:

[1]*b:* She pushed the mail away and stared out of the window. The sun was
         already hot and the streets looked dusty. Fairview wanted rain badly.
         There was a burnt up, frowsy look about the small, straggly town. (. . .)

The first sentence is directly coherent with [1]*a*: V(*she*) and V(*the mail*) are individuals already introduced in the models of previous sentences. The predicate 'pushing away', denoting a relation between V(*she*) and V(*the mail*), is coherent with [1]*b* because it determines a possible consequence of the fact denoted by the previous sentence (not feel like work). Window is a normal part of the OFFICE-frame, over the general postulates[16]

[7]*a*: $(\forall x)[office\ (x)\ \square\!\rightarrow\!building\ (x)]$
  b: $(\forall x)[building\ \square\!\rightarrow\!(\exists y)(has(x,\ y)\ \&\ window(y))]$

This is the basis for the definite article appearing in the first sentence before *window*, even if window has not been explicitly introduced by previous sentences (or known to the speaker from contextual information). The predicate 'staring (out of the window)' is related to the predicates 'being in the office' and 'not feel like work', assuming that working is incompatible with staring out of the window.

The next sentence is less obviously coherent. First of all an individual is introduced (definitely because of its uniqueness) which does not belong either to the WOMAN- or to the OFFICE-series or -frames, viz the sun. The same holds for the other individuals, viz streets, rain, town. Fairview, the proper name of the town, has been introduced in previous chapters. None of the individuals introduced before re-appear in the models for these sentences. Without further rules, therefore, this passage would be incoherent with [1]*a*. We here have an example of a CHANGE in the TOPIC OF DISCOURSE, which is the discourse-based notion corresponding to the concept of a topic of conversation introduced earlier. Now, the question is whether this change is acceptable, *ie* whether the new topic of discourse can be 'reached' from the established topic.

The link connecting the two topics is expressed by the clause [*she*] *stared out of the window*, which entails that she sees something outside. If an office-building is part of a town, and if towns have streets, etc the implied introduction of the notion 'outside' (a building) allows introduction of the ATMOSPHERE-(sun, dusty, rain, etc) frame and the TOWN-frame. The access to the new topic, established in a locally different 'world', is provided by the looking outside relation, whereas it is understood in such a case that individuals in that world are objects of the seeing predicate.

The new topic of discourse induces the coherence of the next passage and is established by the ATMOSPHERE- and the TOWN- series and their interrelations. Thus a hot sun and absence of rain are probable conditions for the probable consequence of dusty streets, and the 'burnt up' look of the town.

3.4

The new TOWN-topic, however, is 'embedded', as may be seen from the following stretch of the discourse:

[1]*c*: Sitting there, she thought about Harry Duke. Most of the night, she
    had thought about him. Harry Duke and Peter. Peter and Harry Duke.

She had tossed about in the narrow bed, staring into the darkness, remembering all the small details of what had happened. She could see Harry Duke very clearly. She could see his powerful shoulders, his narrow, dark head and his close-clipped moustache. She could almost feel the power in him.

He would only have to stretch out his hand and she would put hers in his willingly. And she knew that he knew it. That frightened her. (...)

The first topic, in which the woman is in an office, sitting at her desk is being 'picked up' again, by the phrase *sitting there*. The local adverb *there* in that case does not automatically refer back to the closest previous place expression, but to the location associated with the position of the woman referred to in the main clause of the first sentence of this passage.

At the same time, however, a new topic is introduced by the 'world-creating' predicate 'to think'. The subsequent sentences, therefore, are to be satisfied in models with worlds accessible by a thought relation. Indeed, the individuals introduced then (Harry Duke, Peter, bed, etc) do not belong to the actual office series. The second sentence is to be satisfied in thought or recall worlds of the past actual world, in which again a thought relation exists. The individual persons, referred to by their proper names, have been introduced in previous chapters of the story. Thus, past thought or recall worlds are coherently introduced if they are related to the present actual world of the agent. The auxiliary *had* indicates this past world, and the past-past world is accessible from the remembering predicate holding in the past world. The *she* in those sentences denotes the same individual as in the previous sentences, or rather the COUNTERPART of V(*Clare Russell*) in the thought and recall worlds. We see that the notion of an individual is an abstraction, viz a function which may take actual or non-actual values in different possible worlds.[17] The same holds for the individual (Harry Duke) which is the object argument of the see-relation. Seeing, here, can only mean 'see in imagination', 'mentally represent', in order to account for the fact that Harry Duke is not really in the office.

The embedded recalled and imagined worlds must, as was observed above, be introduced coherently too. *The night* will refer to the night preceding the following morning introduced in the first sentence of [1]*a*. Night, darkness, and bed form a homogeneous series in normal worlds, and the predicate 'tossing about' is a possible implication of the concept of 'sleeplessness' which belongs to the NIGHT-series. Similarly, such individuals as shoulders, moustache, head and power are essential or accidental properties of the human (male) individual introduced before.

In this imagined world where V(*she*) sees V(*Harry Duke*) another world is initiated, viz a counterfactual world with the same individuals (or rather: their counterparts), and possible interactions, where stretching out a hand and putting a hand in a hand are again to be conditionally related. From the actual point of view of the agent there is access finally to the 'epistemic worlds' of the individual Harry Duke, and from there to the counterfactual world referred to. The anaphorical demonstrative *that* in the last sentence then refers to the content of the epistemic predicate of the previous sentence, viz 'that he knew it', where 'it' refers to the facts in the counterfactual world. Although the relations between the worlds involved here are rather complex, it appears that coherence first of all seems to be guaranteed by the permanence of individuals. The worlds in question are related if the world-creating predicates are coherently introduced for the actual individuals, where for each world there must be a coherent series of activities (reason/cause-consequence) and properties.

Whereas for the coherence relations discussed until now we may use such terms as frames, series, implications or meaning postulates, only part of them can be reconstructed in a (linguistic) semantics. Thus, our knowledge of the world contains information about the typical behaviour of people in love (thinking/seeing the loved one, sleeplessness, etc) or of the probable consequences of mental power, which associate the imagined feeling of power with the counterfactual actions. It is clear that a semantic theory of discourse coherence cannot hope to cope with such particular postulates of normal worlds, unless an encyclopedic data base is elaborated, which is not the task of a grammar. A discourse semantics, then, can only specify the general forms and functions of these constraints, relations, etc determining the coherence of a discourse with respect to such a data base.

3.5

Let us now summarize the main COHERENCE CONDITIONS for this passage:

(i) Each SITUATION $\langle w_i, t_i, l_i \rangle$ of each model M_i of the discourse model (for this passage) is either identical with an actual (represented) situation $\langle w_0, t_0, l_0 \rangle$ or accessible from this situation;

(ii) There is at least one INDIVIDUAL (function), d_i, such that $d_i \in D_i$ (for each M_i of the discourse model), for all counterparts of d_i, or there is an individual $d_j \in D_j$, such that $\langle d_i, d_j \rangle$ is a value of a relation f in some model M_{j-k}, preceding M_j;
In our case: $V(\textit{Clare Russell}) = V(\textit{she}) = d_i$, and the sun or Harry Duke $= d_j$, related to d_i, by seeing or thought relation;

(iii) For all other individuals d_k, there is a SERIES $\langle d_k, d_i \rangle$ or $\langle d_k, d_j \rangle$ defined by relations of partiality (inclusion, part-whole, membership, possession);
Examples: $V(\textit{hat}) \langle V(\textit{she})$, $V(\textit{streets}) \langle V(\textit{town})$, $V(\textit{moustache}) \langle V(\textit{Harry Duke})$;

(iv) For each PROPERTY (or relation) φ_i, applied to the same individual d_i in the successive models of the discourse model, there is a more comprehensive property ψ such that φ_i is a possible component of ψ, or there is a dimension δ such that φ_i is a member of the set characterized by δ.
Examples: $V(\textit{come into} [\textit{the office}])$, $V(\textit{go} [\textit{to one's room}])$, $V(\textit{sit down}$

[*at a desk*]) are components of human working activities, whereas
V(*hot*), V(*dusty*), V(*burnt up*) are members of the tempera-
ture/atmospheric condition dimension.

(v) For each FACT f_i in the subsequent models of the discourse model there
is a fact f_j such that f_i is a condition of f_j, and f_j is a consequence of f_i, or
there is a fact f_k, such that both f_i and f_j are conditions for or
consequences of f_k, in the respective temporally ordered models;
condition/consequence may be weak (possible) or strong (necessity);
Examples: the sun's being hot is a possible condition for the streets
being dusty, it is possible to think for somebody in the situation of
'sitting at their desk', being in someone's power is sufficient reason for
being frightened.

These (still incomplete) conditions hold for identical topics of conversation
or discourse and for actual courses of events. Thus, we need an extra
condition in order to allow COHERENT WORLD AND TOPIC CHANGE:

(vi) A sequence of sentences consisting of two coherent sequences (as
under conditions i–v) is coherent if there is a relation such that
individuals or properties of the two topics or frames satisfy this
relation in the discourse, or if the first sequence contains a predicate
giving possible access to the possible worlds in which the second
sequence is satisfied.
Examples: [*She*] *stared out of the window; She thought about Harry
Duke; That frightened her.*

Especially this latter condition is only a first approximation of the condition
of coherent topic change. In fact, we still need a sound definition of the notion
'topic of discourse' or of the more general notion 'topic of conversation'.

4 Fact ordering and sequence ordering
4.1

After the preliminary analysis of a concrete example we must now try to
refine, step by step, the various theoretical concepts involved. If sentences
denote facts (in some possible world), SEQUENCES OF SENTENCES would
denote SEQUENCES OF FACTS. In some cases the structure of sequences is
structurally isomorphous with the structure of fact sequences, viz in those
cases where there is a one-to-one mapping from a sequence of linearly,
temporally ordered facts onto a sequence of linearly ordered sentences of a
discourse.

In most cases, however, the relation between 'words and the world' is less
straightforward. First of all, a discourse usually mentions only a very small
part of the facts of some situation. Secondly, the ordering of facts may, due to
pragmatic and cognitive constraints, correspond to a different order in the

discourse. Thirdly, facts are often not linearly ordered, but for instance spatially or hierarchically, which raises the issue about their 'canonical' representation in a discourse, if there are ordering constraints involved at all.

4.2

The relation between ACTION SEQUENCES and ACTION DISCOURSE may simply be one-to-one, as in our earlier example

[1]*a:* Clare Russell came into the *Clarion* office (. . .). She went straight to her room, took off her hat, touched her face with a powder puff and sat down at her desk.

The interpretation of this sequence is such that each action referred to occurs in a subsequent model for the respective clauses. This ordering of the discourse has been called NORMAL.

Normal orderings may undergo structural changes of several types. The ordering $\langle S_i, S_j \rangle$, if temporal, may become $\langle before\ S_j, S_i \rangle$ or $\langle S_j\ after\ S_i \rangle$, where *before* S_j and *after* S_i are subordinated to S_i and S_j, respectively. Similarly, a coordinated structure is possible with sentence initial *Previously:* $\langle S_j, Previously\ S_i \rangle$, where *Previously* is followed by a pause (or comma), has specific intonation, and where, as in a subordinated *after*-clause in final position, a pluperfect tense is obligatory:

[8]*a:* She went straight to her room and, before she sat down at her desk, she took off her hat and touched her face with a powder puff.
   b: She went straight to her room and sat down at her desk, after she had taken off her hat and had touched her face with a powder puff.
   c: She went straight to her room and sat down at her desk. Previously, she had taken off her hat and had touched her face with a powder puff.

Although the same sequence of facts is denoted by these alternative versions of the second composite sentence of [1]*a*, there are nevertheless differences due to differences in the presupposition-assertion structures of [8]*a–c*, or differences in topic or focus, to be discussed later. Intuitively, it seems that the embedded clauses are expressing less 'important' information, or information which is already known. In [8]*a* this produces the rather specific effect that taking off one's hat and doing one's make-up is more important in the particular situation than sitting at the desk. If 'importance' is defined in terms of SETS OF POSSIBLE CONSEQUENCES, it would be required that taking off one's hat has more consequences. This is not the case in the present passage, however, where sitting at the desk is a condition for working, which is a normal part of the OFFICE-frame. In [1]*a* itself these acts are at the same (coordinated) level, but it seems as if the final position in compound sentences has more 'informational value' assigned to it than the initial or intermediate positions, at least in normal orderings. The concepts introduced here, such as 'importance', and 'informational value' are vague and need further explication. Part of this explication will have to be given in pragmatic terms, because neither meaning nor truth/satisfaction or reference are involved, but degrees of knowledge and attention of speech participants.

4.3
Another way to change the normal ordering is a change in situation (world-time-place) by the appropriate adjectives, temporal adverbs, verb tenses and verbs, as in:

[9] Sitting there, she thought about Harry Duke. Most of the night she had thought about him.

Verbs like *think, believe, remember*, etc, followed by past tenses or adverbs like *yesterday*, or adjectives like *previous*, give access to past-time models with respect to actual-time models.

In these cases, however, there is no changed representation of the order of the facts, because, the past events are, as it were, 'embedded' in the present. In [9] the sitting and thinking events are normally ordered, where the past events occur in a world which belongs to a SUBMODEL of the model in which the sentence *She thought* (. . .) is satisfied.

4.4
Normal ordering is also used in a stronger form of temporal relations between facts, viz in CONDITION-CONSEQUENCE orderings of facts, discussed in the previous chapter. Initial states or initial events are mentioned before intermediary/final states or events of a course of events. Structural changes are operated with final *because*-clauses, coordinated sentences with initial *Therefore*, or simply with coordinated clauses of which the second unambiguously denotes a conditional fact:

[10]*a:* John was ill. He didn't come.
  b: John was ill, so he didn't come.
  c: Because John was ill, he didn't come.
[11]*a:* John didn't come. He was ill.
  b: John didn't come. So, he was ill.
  c: John didn't come, because he was ill.

The reversed order in [11], as for the temporal examples, also has specific semantic and pragmatic functions. First of all, presupposed propositions will normally be expressed by initial subordinate clauses. Secondly, according to the principle that final position is assigned more informational value, the 'focus' of these sequences is on the cause, reason or condition of some presupposed or asserted fact. In particular, the examples given in [11] are typical for EXPLANATORY contexts in which inductive reasoning is used in order to draw conclusions from present facts about possible or necessary conditions. In the [11] examples it will further be assumed that the first clause expresses a proposition coherent with previous propositions, as in:

[12]*a:* We went to the movies. John didn't come. He was ill.

Here the actions of the first two sentences are coherent along the conditions given earlier. That is, the topic of the discourse is 'going (or not) to the movies'. Being ill, then may be added as an explanation of one of these facts, but is itself not coherent with the topic. This is the reason why [12]*a* seems more natural than:

[12]*b:* We went to the movies. John was ill. He didn't come.

The initial (cognitive) interpretation strategy will first try to link subsequent propositions. Hence, there may arise an interpretation in which John is (became) ill in the cinema. This interpretative hypothesis will be rejected after interpretation of the last sentence, which would be incompatible with the first, hypothetical interpretation. We see that besides semantic and pragmatic constraints, there are cognitive constraints determining the 'optimal' ordering of information in discourse.

4.5
Whereas normal orderings for the representation of courses of events or actions, together with initial and final states, are due to structural isomorphy, the ordering of STATE DESCRIPTIONS must be normal on the basis of other criteria. Again, the main constraint is of course the necessary preceding of presupposed elements: the phrase (*her*) *face* can be interpreted only if a (human) individual has been introduced first, according to general coherence conditions. Some state descriptions have FREE ORDERING:

[13] Her mail was spread out neatly, her blotter was snowy and her inkwell was filled.

An ordering is free if each permutation is equivalent, semantically and pragmatically, with each other permutation of the sentences or clauses. In [13] the objects denoted are all objects located on the desk introduced in the previous sentence, such that no individual or predicate is part of or otherwise related to the individual or predicate in the previous sentence or clause.

The other orderings of descriptions depend on the RELATIONS between individuals or properties denoted by the subsequent sentences. The overall constraints determining normal ordering of state descriptions are the following:

[14]*a:* general – particular
　　b: whole – part/component
　　c: set – subset – element
　　d: including – included
　　e: large – small
　　f: outside – inside
　　g: possessor – possessed

These relations are mapped onto a preceding-following relation over sequences of sentences, and would make the next sequences normally ordered:

[15] Peter always comes late. He won't be in time tonight either.

[16] She could see Harry Duke. She could see his powerful shoulders (. . .)

[17] Many girls had applied for the job. Some of them were invited to a meeting with the staff.

[18] There was a large glass on the table. In it was a pinkish juice.

[19] Peter climbed upon the hill, which was covered with pine trees. Under the trees were thick bushes.

[20] We came to an isolated inn. The lights were already on.

[21] Peter was shabbily dressed. His jeans had large holes in them.

The normal ordering of descriptions as it is assumed here is based not only on constraints of semantic information distribution (presupposition), but also on general COGNITIVE PRINCIPLES, *eg* of perception and attention. Thus we will usually perceive a whole object before its parts, a large object before a small object in its neighbourhood. In general the interpretation of an object or fact requires its 'location' in a spatial context. Thus, we will hardly give descriptions like:

[22] There was a glass in the room. Under it was a table.

[23] There were still some leaves. They were attached to the trees in the park.

Under certain conditions normal orderings of objects or properties as represented in discourse may be CHANGED. A first possibility is again the context of EXPLANATION, in which a particular fact may be explained by asserting a more general proposition:

[24] Peter was late again. He never comes on time.

[25] The house had not been painted for years. In fact the whole town looked dilapidated to us.

Another important condition changing normal ordering, holding both for state and event descriptions is some SPECIFIC order of PERCEPTION or KNOWLEDGE of the facts. There are situations in which the general, the whole or the possessor are identified later, just as we may interpret a certain fact as a cause after having perceived the consequences. Characteristic examples of these epistemic orderings are:

[26] There was a small figure sitting beside the road. It was one of the local gipsies, who settled here last year.

[27] Yesterday I found a gold watch. It turned out that it belongs to Harry.

A specific case of abnormal ordering of information in discourse is perceptual and epistemic FOCUSING. It may be that a particular object is consciously focused upon, *eg* because it has specific properties assigned to it, because it is searched for, etc. Then the identification of the individual object and the predication made about it may precede specification of time, space and conceptual range:

[28] After a search of several days the body of the victim was found. It was hidden under some bushes in the nearby foothills.

[29] We landed on the small airstrip. It had been cut in the middle of the jungle.

Other constraints on ordering, as we said above, are still more clearly pragmatic (to be discussed in Chapter 7).

In the examples given and their tentatively formulated underlying constraints we find ourselves in some ill-defined domain involving semantic, pragmatic and cognitive notions. We have provisionally discussed them in this semantic part of our investigation because the principal notion involved is still reference, viz relations between some kind of expression ordering and the ordering of facts in the world AS THEY ARE MENTALLY REPRESENTED. The latter clause expresses a referential condition of a rather specific type, but there seems to be no a priori reason not to consider it as a component of the interpretation of a sequence.

5 Explicit and implicit information in discourse
5.1

It has been remarked several times that natural language discourse is not EXPLICIT. That is, there are propositions which are not directly expressed, but which may be INFERRED from other propositions which have been expressed. If such implicit propositions must be postulated for the establishment of coherent interpretations,[18] they are what we called MISSING LINKS. The problem at issue is: under what conditions may or should propositions remain implicit in a given discourse? Important from a grammatical point of view would be the question which linguistic properties of sentences and sequences of sentences 'indicate' implicit propositions and allow the inferences involved. We here touch the closely related issue of PRE-SUPPOSITIONS and their role in the semantics of discourse.

5.2

A first distinction should be made between (IN-)COMPLETE and IMPLICIT/EXPLICIT discourse. If a discourse is taken as a state and/or event description, it is complete if all the facts constituting a certain situation are represented. In particular, an action discourse is complete if it mentions all actions of a given course of action. The same holds for state descriptions. The number of facts (all existing individuals, all their properties and relations) characterizing a situation, however, is very large, and discourses are not, and need not be, complete for that reason. If possible at all, full descriptions are impracticable and pragmatically inappropriate: most information would be redundant or irrelevant in the conversation.

Hence, from the large set defining 'possible information' a SELECTION is made. Thus, in the example from the crime story we have been examining, only a few facts (actions) of a possible course of events are mentioned: entering the office, going to one's room, taking one's hat off, powdering oneself and sitting at one's desk. Each of these actions, however, in the fictitious possible world involved, will have initial conditions, component actions, intermediary state descriptions, agent descriptions, such as opening and closing doors, walking up stairs, meeting people, thinking particular thoughts, the physical make-up of the office, and so on. In some discourses such details may be given for aesthetic or practical communicative purposes, *eg* in some modern novel or in a police report. Apparently, there are not only DEGREES OF COMPLETENESS but also LEVELS OF COMPLETENESS. A description of a course of events may be relatively complete for a certain level, but at another ('lower', more specific) level be incomplete. I may relate my actions of the afternoon, but will omit all component actions, descriptions of the environment, etc, as was indicated above. Such a description will be even more incomplete from a physiological, chemical or physical point of view. On the other hand, in the annual report of a big business company, we will not find mention of the particular actions of particular employees on one particular afternoon. At that level the description would be too specific, and in a sense OVER-COMPLETE. The level of description depends on the topic of conversation and, in a wider sense, on the purposes of the communicative act. If the topic is something like 'actions of a big company over a period of a year', the description of actions of one employee during one afternoon, at least if these do not affect the more general conduct of the company, would yield a PARTIALLY OVER-COMPLETE discourse. Differences of temporal, local and causal 'scope' determine that two topics of conversation are involved which cannot appropriately be combined in one coherent discourse. It need not be the case, however, that all descriptions within one discourse are of the same level. In a description about my particular acts on one day, I may insert general statements, *eg* as explanations of particular facts. Conversely, talking about more general facts, *eg* in a sociological treatise, allows mention of particular facts as examples or illustrations. Perhaps each type of discourse, given a certain topic of conversation, has an UPPER BOUND of generalization and a LOWER BOUND of particularization or specification. One of the hypotheses which might hold in this respect is that the constraints on particularization are stricter than those on generalization: some discourses will allow generalization but not specific descriptions of particular ('small') facts.

Completeness and incompleteness may take different forms. A discourse may omit reference to certain facts in a state of affairs or course of events either because these facts were not 'relevant' in the conversational context, or because they are indirectly referred to by a description of a higher level fact of which they are necessary or probable components. In the second case there is incompleteness of LEVELS: more detailed levels of description are not given. In the first case we could speak of SELECTIVE incompleteness (at the same level): only some facts of the same order of generality are selected for description. When we speak of incompleteness we will in general mean this type of selective incompleteness. In those cases where facts are necessary conditions, components or consequences of other facts which have been referred to, we will rather speak of implicitness than of incompleteness.

Some examples may illustrate the distinction made above:

[30] John came home at 6 o'clock. He took off his coat and hung it on the hat-stand. He said 'Hi, love' to his wife and kissed her. He[19] asked 'How was work at the office today?' and he took a beer from the refrigerator before he started washing up the dishes (. . .)

[31] John came home at 6 o'clock and had his dinner at 7.

[32] John came home at 6 o'clock. Walking to the main entrance of the flat he put his hand in his left coat pocket, searched for the key to the door, found it, took it out, put it into the lock, turned the lock, and pushed the door open; he walked in and closed the door behind him (. . .)

Discourse [30] is a relatively complete action discourse: all actions of roughly the same level have been referred to. At the same level [31] is incomplete because it does not mention John's activities between 6 and 7 o'clock. At another level of description these may of course not be relevant, *eg* in a police report describing John's activities of that day. On the other hand [32] would be over-complete relative to the level of description of [30]. All or nearly all component actions are described which are normal constituents of the action of 'coming home'. In this respect [30] is level-incomplete or implicit with respect to the information given in [32] whereas [31] is selectively incomplete with respect to the information given in [30]. In a rather wide sense of 'inference', we may say that [32] can be inferred from [30], in particular from the first sentence of [30], whereas [30][20] cannot possibly be inferred from [31].

Note that the following version of [32] would be level-incomplete and incoherent, because some details are given and other comparable details, necessary components of the complex action, are not given:

[33] (. . .) He put his hand in his left pocket and searched for the key. He turned the lock. He closed the door (. . .)

Apparently, there are some forms of incompleteness which are unacceptable. If a discourse clearly aims at a full description of component actions/doings, all necessary constituents must be referred to. A discourse like [33] may therefore be called UNDER-COMPLETE. If we inserted [32] into [30], we would have an OVER-COMPLETE discourse, because details are given of one action but not of the other actions: there would be 'too much' information, given the level of description established by the rest of the discourse. Both under-completeness and over-completeness are conditions of discourse in-coherence,[21] whereas incompleteness is natural for the pragmatic reasons given above.

The examples given are action discourses. Completeness and incomplete-ness are relative to type. All examples are incomplete with respect to object and situation (place) description: we do not know what John (and his wife) look like, nor his flat, nor the actions (*eg* replies) of his wife, and so on. The same remarks may be made for further state descriptions. We may mention that the flat was big, pleasantly furnished, etc, but also give a more or less precise description of each object. Such state descriptions would only make a coherent discourse together with the action description if these states were conditions or consequences of the actions. If not, they would be irrelevant from the point of view of the action discourse (or conversely). From a pragmatic point of view, given the assumption that action discourse is an essential component of narrative, the detailed description of objects would be inappropriate in the act of narration. Again, these (still rather informal) constraints may be violated under specific conditions, *eg* for aesthetic purposes in novels (*cf* over-completeness of state and action descriptions in the *nouveau roman*).

5.3
Given a relatively complete or (mostly) incomplete discourse at some level of descriptive generality and with respect to some major kind of facts (*eg* actions), what information is or must be EXPLICIT and what information is or must be IMPLICIT and what are the consequences for the coherence of the discourse?

The distinction between implicit and explicit information is not clear-cut. First of all, explicitness of information is to be defined in terms of propositions, and not in terms of pragmatic concepts like the assertion of propositions. Thus, in a sentence like

[34] Peter sent a letter to his aunt.

the proposition 'Peter has an aunt' is expressed without being explicitly asserted. On the other hand, the proposition 'An aunt of y is a female human being x, such that x is the sister of one of the parents of y', is neither asserted nor expressed in [34]. Yet, both propositions are ENTAILED by [34], although in a different way: the truth of the first proposition entailed by [34] may be affected by the falsity or inappropriateness of [34], whereas the truth of the second proposition is not thus dependent on [34]: it holds in general because it is a MEANING POSTULATE of the language. The same holds for the proposition 'If x sends a letter, then x is human', defining 'sending' as a human action. Whether propositions are true or false, they entail meaning postulates: the latter merely determine POSSIBLE PROPOSITIONS. Meaning postulates together with a particular proposition p yield, by modus ponens, the particular implications of p, *eg* 'Peter is human' in [34]. Implicit information will be restricted to the set of PARTICULAR propositions entailed by each proposition of the discourse.

This notion of implicit information, taken as the sets of (non self-) entailed[22] propositions of a given discourse, may be extended from conceptual information to factual information, even if the boundaries between them are hard to make precise. Inferences, however weak, may be drawn

about the further structure of the facts referred to. These inferences are based
not on our knowledge of the conventional meanings of the language, but on
our knowledge of the world. It is likely that, if x sends a letter to y, x has
written this letter, has put the letter into an envelope, put a stamp onto the
envelope, and so on. This information is part of our 'letter-sending' knowledge subset, or FRAME.

The set of conceptual and factual implications of each sentence of a
discourse may be very large and, from a cognitive point of view, most of these
implications are irrelevant for the comprehension of the discourse. In terms
of a formal semantics this means that only a subset of the implicit information may be necessary for the interpretation of subsequent sentences. In
order to keep the notion of 'implicit information' manageable and linguistically interesting, it will be identified with this SET OF IMPLICATIONS
NECESSARY FOR THE INTERPRETATION OF SUBSEQUENT SENTENCES. Thus, in
order to be able to interpret the subsequent sentence [35], following [34],

[35] Owing to the postal strike, it came a week too late.

we should be able to infer the implicit proposition that Peter sent the letter by
mail.
Similarly, the following discourse

[36] We came to a deserted house. White smoke came out of the chimney.

is coherent only if the first sentence implies that houses in general (may) have
chimneys, which identifies the chimney referred to in the second sentence if
the particular inference is made that the particular house also has a chimney.

The linguistic relevance of postulating implicit information is that there
may be grammatical features, *eg* the definite article in the second sentence of
[36], indicating this implicit information.

From examples like [36] it is clear that implications need not be LOGICAL or
necessary, but may also have an INDUCTIVE nature. The set of relevant
implicit information is determined by the interpretation conditions of
following sentences. This means that relevant implicit information of a
discourse, as defined here, is a subset of the set of PRESUPPOSITIONS of the
discourse. Part of the presuppositions of the discourse, *ie* the union of the sets
of presuppositions of each sentence, however, are explicitly expressed in
previous sentences. Other implicit information and presuppositions are
based on the structure of the communicative CONTEXT and will be discussed
later.

Although in many respects textual presuppositions have the same formal
status as contextual presuppositions, there are reasons to distinguish them.
Similarly, some information is textually implicit, other information, *eg* that
entailed by the use of sentences in certain speech acts, is co-textually implicit.

5.4

With the provisional characterization of implicit information in discourse,
we now must try to formulate the CONDITIONS which determine the necessary

or optional implicitness of certain propositions. Why would a discourse like

[37] We came to a deserted house. It had a chimney from which came white
smoke.

be less acceptable than [36]? The most obvious reason is that information
which is necessary or probable need not be specifically expressed and asserted
if it is implied by an asserted proposition. This is not the case for a discourse
like

[38] We came to a deserted house. The old man told us that the next village
was eight miles from there.

from which a proposition like 'An old man was sitting on the porch' has been
deleted, such that [38] becomes incoherent because the referent of the phrase
'the old man', has not been identified. Nothing in the concept of house or our
factual knowledge of (deserted) houses includes the information that an old
man is related to it in some way. This means that in any case we would need a
subsequent sentence like:

[39] (. . .) The old man sitting on the porch told us (. . .)

in which this link is established in the complex noun phrase.
We now have the following conditions:

[40]*a:* a proposition q is (may be) IMPLICIT iff q determines the interpretation
of a subsequent proposition r and if q is entailed (but not self-entailed)
by a proposition p, preceding r;

b: a proposition q is (should be) EXPLICIT iff q determines the interpretation of r and if there is no proposition p such that p entails q (or
if p self-entails q).

What has been formulated here for (conceptual) entailments holds in a
similar way for weaker forms of implication, holding in most normal possible
worlds. Note that these rules do not say that all explicit propositions in a
discourse must determine the interpretation of subsequent propositions:
much of the descriptive details may very well be RELATIVELY IRRELEVANT in
this sense, *eg* the fact that the smoke was white in the previous examples.

In many cases there is not only one implicit proposition necessary to
establish coherence, but a set or sequence of them, *eg* in the example we have
analysed earlier:

[41] (. . .) [she] stared out of the window. The sun was already hot and the
streets looked dusty.

Staring out of the window weakly implies seeing things outside a building,
where one of these things may be the sun, and, if it is further known that the
building is in a town, other things may be the streets of the town. It appears at
the same time that implicit information may be implied by sets of explicit and
(other) implicit information. Thus, the rules in [40] should not mention
individual propositions but sets of propositions.

6 Topic, comment, focus, and their functions in discourse
6.1

In this and the previous chapters the notions TOPIC OF CONVERSATION and TOPIC OF DISCOURSE have been used in order to define connectedness of sentences and coherence of discourse. It has been assumed that such topics are to be defined in terms of propositions, sets of propositions and/or propositions entailed by such sets. At the level of sentence structure another notion of TOPIC has been used in recent linguistics,[23] often in combination with the notions of COMMENT and FOCUS. In that research a sentence may be assigned, besides its usual syntactic and semantic structures, a binary TOPIC-COMMENT STRUCTURE. The definition of such structures is specified both in semantic and pragmatic terms of information and information distribution in sentences and their canonical or transformed syntactic and morpho-phonological expression. The intuitive idea behind the assignment of such structures in a grammar is that in a sentence we may distinguish between what is being said (asserted, asked, promised . . .) and what is being said 'about' it, a distinction closely parallel to the classical SUBJECT-PREDICATE distinction in philosophy and logic.

Thus in a sentence like:

[42] John is rich.

the part 'John' is topic because it denotes the thing about which something is asserted, whereas 'is rich' is the comment or focus of the sentence, denoting the thing (property) said about (predicated of) John. This comment may be much more complex as in sentences like:

[43] John inherited a large estate from his old uncle who lived in Australia.

where *John* could be assigned the topic function and the rest of the sentence would be assigned the comment function.

Now, although our linguistic intuitions about the topic-comment distinction may be correct, the theoretical reconstruction is by no means straight-forward. Confusion about the levels of description and about their appropriate definition is widespread in the literature.

Some of the questions arising are for example the following:

(i) is the topic-comment distinction to be defined in syntactic, semantic or pragmatic terms, *ie* do these terms denote parts or functions of syntactic structures of sentences, of meaning or reference of propositions, or of contextual structures of speech acts, knowledge and information transmission?

(ii) do all sentences have such a structure, and by what explicit rules and procedures can topic and comment be assigned?

(iii) do sentences have topic-comment structure independent of text structure and/or of their use in communicative contexts? In other

words: can the 'same' sentence have different topic-comment structure in different (con-)texts?

(iv) what are the relationships to notions such as 'subject' (grammatical,
logical, psychological) and 'predicate', presupposition and assertion,
etc?

(v) which grammatical, in particular morpho-phonological and syntactic, structures are systematically related to the topic and comment
functions?

(vi) what are the relationships to notions like topic of a conversation or of
a discourse as used semi-technically above?

These questions cannot possibly be answered here in a systematic and explicit
way. Some of them relate to characteristic properties of sentence structure
which are outside the scope of this book. Our attention, therefore, will be
focused upon the role of the topic-comment distinction in the account of
discourse coherence.

6.2

However, some preliminary remarks about the theoretical status of topic and
comment are necessary. From sentences such as [42] and [43] it seems as if the
topic of a sentence coincides with, or is expressed by, the subject of the
sentence, which in turn is normally associated with the left-most (or first)
noun phrase of the sentence, as also in:

[44] The estate John has inherited from his rich uncle is in Australia.

where the topic is expressed by the complex noun phrase. The comment, thus,
would in that case be related to the predicate, or the predicate phrase, of the
sentence. This general, informally formulated, rule holds for what could be
called the NORMAL ORDERING of sentences in English, but not for sentences
such as:

[45] Lóndon is a town I like!
[46] No, Péter has stolen the book.

where the first noun phrases have particular stress. For such sentences the
grammatical subject or the first noun-phrase does not carry the topic
function: the first sentence is not about London but about towns I like, the
second not about Peter but about someone who has stolen a book, intuitively
speaking, whereas it is asserted that London and Peter are individuals
satisfying the particular property or relation, respectively. That is, comments
are normally in second (predicate) position or in positions with particular
stress. In the latter case, the cleft sentence construction (*it was . . .
who/which . . .*) may also be used to make comments out of categories with
topic function. By particular stress assignment or cleft sentences, nearly any
grammatical category can thus be assigned comment function, the rest of the
sentence becoming topic:

[47]*a:* Hárry paid for the book with a ten-dollar bill.
  b: Harry páid for the book with a ten-dollar bill.
  c: Harry paid for the bóok with a ten-dollar bill.

and so on for the major categories (and in some cases also for prefixes, suffixes, prepositions, articles, demonstratives, etc).

Without giving a more precise analysis and syntactic description of these examples, it will be assumed that the notions of topic and comment cannot possibly coincide with or be identical to particular syntactic categories, and that they must at least have a semantic status. This semantic status most clearly manifests itself in a further analysis of the 'intuitions' referred to above: a topic is some function determining about which item something is being said. Similarly, a topic is often associated with what is 'already known' (to the hearer) in some context of conversation, or what is 'presupposed' (to be identified) by some sentence. The comment, then, associates with what is 'unknown' (to the hearer) and asserted. An explication of these terms would have to be framed in a referential semantics and a pragmatic component.

The link between topic and presupposition in the given examples shows in the fact that, for instance, [47]*a* presupposes the proposition 'Someone paid for the book with a ten-dollar bill', and [47]*c* presupposes 'Harry paid for something with a ten-dollar bill', where it is asserted that the variables 'someone' and 'something' are identical with 'Harry' and 'the book', respectively. Note also that comments do not simply denote 'unknown' individuals (objects, properties, relations or facts): both Harry and the book are 'known' in the given examples: they are identified by the hearer (the speaker uses, characteristically, the definite article in the phrase *the book*). It is only unknown that Harry and the book have the specific (complex) property referred to.

By examining the semantic functions of normal sentence orderings or of stress distribution, we may often decide which sentence part expresses the topic and which part expresses the comment. This is less easy in the normal form of [47]*a–c:*

[47] Harry paid for the book with a ten-dollar bill.

It is not at all obvious whether this sentence is about Harry, about the book, or even about both, especially since both referents are 'known'. Could a sentence have two topics or should we perhaps speak of one compound topic, *eg* the ordered pair ⟨'Harry', 'the book'⟩ of which it is asserted that the first bought the second with a ten-dollar bill?

A typical test for establishing the topic-comment structure of sentences is to use preceding questions. If [47] is used as an answer to the question

[48] What did Harry do?

we may conclude that 'Harry' or 'Harry did something' is the topic of [47]. If the question were:

[49] What happened to the book?

it would be 'the book' which would be the topic. Similarly, after a question like:

[50] What did Harry do with the book?

the ordered pair ⟨'Harry', 'the book'⟩ would be the topic. What is being established by questions can be established by PRECEDING DISCOURSE in general:

[51] At last Harry found the book he wanted to give Laura as a present. He paid for it with a ten-dollar bill (. . .)

Characteristically, noun phrases with topic function may then, or must be, pronominalized. Thus topic can be associated with the logical category of BOUND VARIABLES, ranging over both individuals and properties or relations. Less strictly speaking, it may be said that topics are those elements of a sentence which are BOUND by previous text or context. We should therefore investigate how topic-comment structure is to be determined relative to (con-)textual structure.

6.3

In order to understand the topic-comment articulation of sentences and their (con-)textual dependence, some remarks are necessary about the COGNITIVE BASIS OF INFORMATION PROCESSING in communicative contexts.[24]

As will be shown in detail in the next part of this book, sentences (discourses) are uttered within the framework of specific speech acts and speech interaction. Thus, one of the purposes of the act of asserting a proposition is that the hearer be informed about a certain matter. This information increase is an enlargement or other change in his set of knowledge and beliefs, brought about by understanding of the meaning of the perceived utterance. The details of the actions involved here are less important for the moment. The point is that all 'new information' is usually integrated into information already known. Thus, when I say that Peter is ill, it is assumed that my speech participant already 'knows' Peter, *ie* knows that Peter exists, and knows his main properties. In this case, general or specific knowledge about Peter is 'enriched' with the proposition 'that he is ill (now)', to be attached to the complex 'Peter' concept already present in the hearer's knowledge.

Now, the topic of a sentence has the particular cognitive function of selecting a unit of information or concept from knowledge. This may be a more general concept (like love or renting a flat) or an individual concept (Peter, this particular book, etc). In the latter case, the individual referred to may already have been 'introduced' into the context of communication either by direct action or perception of certain objects (*That chair must be painted red*) or by previous sentences of the discourse. In such a way many objects may be introduced into the context, and for each sentence it must be established which of these objects is (again) 'picked up', *ie* referred to, in order to make a statement about it.

Cognitively, this 'topicalization' of certain phrases is probably a process whereby knowledge of certain individuals is 'foregrounded', *ie* taken from long-term memory stores to some working memory, in which the established information may be combined with the incoming new information.

This new information, usually called the 'COMMENT' or also the 'FOCUS' of the sentence, may be in various forms: it may assign a general or particular property to a known and identified individual, or a relation between individuals of which one or more are known (*Peter met a girl. He kissed her*), or the instantiation by one or more individuals of a known property or relation (*Péter hasn't committed the murder*), or the assignment of various higher level properties or operators to events or propositions (*The robbery had been planned cleverly. Your appearance was really unexpected, you know*). From these assumptions it follows that in principle any phrase of a sentence may express topic function, or even several, discontinuous phrases like subject noun phrase and (in-)direct object noun phrase.

6.4

This is roughly the general theoretical basis for the topic-comment articulation in natural language: it is mainly a result of the constraints of effective information processing. Now, what are the implications for the structure and interpretation of discourse?

The first point to be made here is that, according to the principles adopted, certain sentences beginning a discourse or a section of discourse (*eg* a paragraph) may not always have a topic, viz in those cases where no individual object or property known to the hearer is selected for 'comment', as in:

[52] A man was walking slowly along a beach.

Here, individuals (person, place) and a relation are introduced at the same time. Although, intuitively, we might say that this sentence is 'about' a man, according to the canonical topic-comment mapping onto the subject-predicate structure of the sentence, there is, formally speaking, no topic in [52] but topic introduction. In cognitive terms: the hearer's knowledge 'slate' is still clean with respect to a topic of conversation. Note, however, that sentences like [52] are rather unusual, and occur more in literary narrative than in everyday, natural narratives, where we would have something like:

[53]*a:* This afternoon a strange man came to my office (. . .)

Again, we could speak of topic introduction, but there is already established knowledge (time: a specific afternoon, determined by time of context of communication, and place: a particular, known, office), which is formally the topic of [53]*a*. In other words, [53]*a* is not primarily about a strange guy, but rather about what happened this afternoon, to me, in my office.

We see that the notion of ABOUTNESS is not very precise, and, at least for sentences, not always decidable. A sentence like [52] may be about a man, his walk or about a beach, or about all of them. More in general, aboutness should be established in (con-)textual terms, perhaps in such a way that a discourse or a passage of the discourse is about something if this 'something' is referred to by most phrases with topic function. In this case, however, we no longer deal with the topic of a sentence but with a TOPIC OF DISCOURSE or a TOPIC OF CONVERSATION. We here find ourselves at a more global level of discourse description, to be discussed in the next chapter. Such a topic may be 'a strange man' even if in the individual sentences the topics may be 'his cigarette', 'his trousers', 'I', etc, *ie* those referring phrases of which the referents are associated with the strange man. It will appear, however, that aboutness at this more global level is again ambiguous: a story may be about Romeo, about Juliet, about both, about a specific (forbidden or impossible) love or about certain political structures in the middle ages. Often, however, the 'aboutness' pertains to a given individual object or person, if most properties and relations are assigned to one permanent referent or to those objects/persons introduced in relation to it.

Topics are established not only with respect to explicit previous information but also with respect to implicit information as defined above. If we continued [53]*a* with a sentence like

[53]*b:* His nose was nearly purple (. . .)

the phrase *his nose* would be assigned topic function even if its referent has not been explicitly referred to before.[25] However, the concept 'man' entails the meaning postulates of being a human adult male and of having a nose. The proposition '*a* has a nose' is therefore implied by [53]*a*, referred to definitely (by possessive pronoun) in [53]*b*, and therefore implicit. In cognitive terms: the hearer already knows that if there is a man he also has a nose. Topics, thus, may be expressed by any phrase referring to an individual (con-)textually identified by the hearer, but also by all other expressions for individuals or properties belonging to what may be called the EPISTEMIC RANGE of that object.[26]

In this semi-formal framework, topic function may be related to any object of previous models, also to facts or possible worlds. This would explain the notorious difficulty of assigning topic-comment structure to such sentences as

[54] It is hot.
[55] It was raining.

It would express a topic by referring to some particular time-place or world.[27] Similarly, in sentences like [52] which have no apparent topic part, but in which some particular real, fictitious, or narrated world is taken as the (implicit) topic. In fact, the sentence specifies a number of properties of such a world (that there is a man, that the man is walking, that the man/his walking is slow, and that the walking takes place along a beach, in the past).

Note that this textual approach to the problem of sentential topics does not always guarantee that the subject of a sentence is automatically the topic of that sentence, even in normal ordering. After the question "*What happened to the jewels?*", we may have

[56] They were stolen by a customer.

where the topic function is indeed assigned to the first noun phrase (subject), but we may also have a sentence like

[57] Peter has sold them to a diamond merchant from Antwerp.

where the topic is assigned to the predicate noun phrase *them*, although according to some theories of topic the phrase *Peter* would be assigned topic function. Besides syntactic ordering and stress distribution, we thus have indications from definite articles and pronouns about the topic function of certain phrases.

It should be stressed that (con-)textually identified individuals determining topic function need not be 'expressed' by the same lexical units:

[58] Now, Fairview had had its golden age (. . .) The little town's methods of production could not compete with the modern factories (...) [Chase, *p* 5].

In this passage from the same crime story taken as an earlier example, part of the complex noun phrase of the second sentence, viz *the little town* is topic, due to referential identity with Fairview, introduced before. In case the epistemic range of the concept of town includes the existence of factories and hence of methods of production, the whole noun phrase *the little town's methods of production* would be assigned topic function, as is also indicated by the definite article.

In general, topical noun phrases may be used even in those cases where the referent is not an essential (necessary) part of a previously introduced referent with which it is associated. The definite noun phrase in a later passage,

[59] The more progressive businesses had transferred to Bentonville (. . .)

would in such a case receive topic function, although no progressive businessmen have been introduced above.

Theoretically speaking this is possible only if we assume that a proposition like 'Fairview has progressive businessmen' is introduced as a missing link. This would mean that some topics still have an IMPLICIT COMMENT function. Conversely, we might speak of IMPLICIT TOPIC function in those cases where previously identified referents are assigned to a previously identified property or relation:

[60] Paul stole the diamonds!

where the phrase *Paul* (with specific stress) has comment function if the topic is 'Somebody had stolen the diamonds'. In case we should, for theoretical reasons, be reluctant to assign comment function to referring phrases, and especially to those referring to previously identified referents, sentences of the type exemplified by [60] may be considered as having a relation as comment, viz IDENTITY, according to the following logical schema $(\exists x)(\ldots x \ldots) \&$ $(x = a)$, as is also expressed in the natural language variants of [60]:

[61] It was Paúl, who stole the diamonds.
[62] The one who stole the diamonds was Paúl.

Note that in such examples (initial) stress does not only mean that a phrase which would have topic function in normal ordering now has comment function, but also that CONTRAST and implicit DENIAL are involved. In those cases where it is assumed by the hearer that $x = a$, and it is asserted by the speaker that $x = b$, the noun phrase (viz its last main category) referring to b has marked stress. The reverse applies to explicit internal (phrasal) negation, as in:

[63] Paul did not stéal the diamonds.

where *steal* has marked stress: the speaker assumes some belief in the hearer to the effect that the relationship g between Paul and the diamonds, is that of stealing: g = 'steal', and it is asserted in the comment that $g \neq$ 'steal'. Taking natural language negation as an expression of a specific speech act, as the 'converse' of assertion, namely of DENIAL, the whole sentence would have topic function and the 'new' element would be a change in illocutionary force.

6.5

At this point it becomes necessary to say something more about the precise status of such categories as topic and comment. It has been shown that they cannot possibly be syntactic, but must at least have a SEMANTIC nature. It has also been shown that there are no meaning relations involved: phrases may be assigned topic function even if related to phrases with different meaning in previous sentences. The topic-comment distinction essentially is a structure relating to the REFERENTS of phrases: in general a phrase is assigned topic function if its value in some possible world has already been identified as a value of expressions in preceding implicit or explicit (con-)textual propositions.

In a more formal way we may reconstruct this hypothesis as follows. Given a discourse model $\langle M_1, M_2, \ldots, M_{i-1}, M_i, \ldots M_n \rangle$, we take a set Δ_k as the union of all sets of individuals which are the values of any expression of sentence $S_1, \ldots, S_k$, respectively, in the models $M_1, \ldots, M_k$. In other words, Δ_k is the set of all things referred to in the previous discourse. This set includes proper individuals (objects), and also properties, relations and facts.

We then introduce a binary TOPICALIZATION FUNCTION T, taking as arguments any expression and an index i, and having either a value 1 or a value 0. The assignment of value 1 means that the particular expression has topic function, the assignment of 0 that the particular expression has comment function. The basic conditions (to be modified for special cases) are thus as follows:

[64] $T(\varphi, i) = 1$ iff $V(\varphi, i) = \delta$ and $\delta \in \Delta_{i-1}$;
      $T(\varphi, i) = 0$ iff $V(\varphi, i) = \delta$ and $\delta \notin \Delta_{i-1}$.

That is, any expression in a sentence which denotes something denoted before is assigned topic function, whereas the other expressions are assigned comment function.

This is the most general statement about topic-comment functions in sentences. This proposal, however, should be made more specific. First of all, it might be assumed that all (formal) INFORMATION IS PROPOSITIONAL, whatever the precise cognitive implications of this assumption. That is, we reconstruct knowledge as a set of propositions. A simple argument and predicate like 'the book' or 'is open' are not, as such, elements of information, only a proposition like 'the book is open'. For the expression φ in rule [64] this means that it denotes propositions, *ie* an intensional object, taking FACTS as values at some index i of the discourse model. In still simpler terms: at some point i of the discourse the participants know a common set of facts, namely those denoted by the (propositions expressed by the) previous sentences. Note that such atomic propositions may be expressed simply as phrases of sentences. That is, the fact 'that there is a girl' is expressed in the verb phrase of the sentence *Peter met a girl*. In a following sentence *The girl is from Italy* this information is also expressed, or rather embedded in the definite expression *the girl* ('The only x such that x is a girl'). If this proposition denotes the same fact as the one denoted in the previous sentence, then the phrase expressing this proposition is assigned topic function.

This approach to topic-comment structures, however, is clearly too rigid. First of all, it would become problematic to assign topic function to those phrases which are not likely to have underlying propositional structure, like the pronoun in *She is from Italy*. Secondly, the notion of (propositional) transmission of information should rather be made explicit in pragmatic terms. Here we are concerned first of all with giving a semantic characterization of topic-comment structure. Finally, it may be assumed that the assignment of topic function to a phrase, PRESUPPOSES propositional information, without expressing it as such. Thus, even in *She is from Italy* it is presupposed that there exists a certain female human being (or other object pronominalizable with *she*).

We may therefore uphold the hypothesis that all categories may be assigned topic function, where the topic is assigned to contextually bound elements of the atomic or complex proposition. These bound elements may denote objects, but also properties, relations, facts or possibly functions. The 'free' (comment) elements would then be assigned to the expressions denoting properties of (known) objects, relations between (known) objects, objects of (known) properties or relations, properties of facts, etc as was indicated earlier. According to these principles, any phrase with the referential character mentioned would be assigned topic function.

Note that, strictly speaking, this formal condition also holds for those examples where the surface structure phrase denoting an individual which has already been introduced (and which hence is known to the hearer) seems to have comment function, as in *I met him*, where *him* has heavy stress. That is, both the speaker and the referent of *him* have been identified, and hence are assigned topic function. Comment function, then, is assigned to that part of semantic structure which is not yet introduced, that being the fact that, given the propositions $(\exists x)(meet(I, x))$ and $(\exists y)(Peter = y)$, $w = y$. In other words, it is the identity of Peter with the one I met which is the (asserted) comment of this sentence. English has only limited possibilities to express such comments, for instance by stressing the phrase expressing part of the relation. In this case the sense is ambiguous: the stress may either be interpreted as expressing the fact that there were several people I could have met, but that it actually was (the known) man, *eg* Peter, or else it may be interpreted as expressing the fact that the speaker denies or contradicts an assumption of the hearer, in this case $(\ldots) \& x = z$. The first use could be called 'contrastive' or 'selective', the second 'contradictive' or 'corrective', which means that the specific stress is semantically determined in the first usage, and pragmatically in the second. Contrastive selection is not limited to cases where the predicate (relation) is already known, as may be seen in: *Finally I listened to hím, and ignored hér*.

It follows that rule [64] is still theoretically correct if assumed to operate on expressions of some semantic language: topic-comment assignment is not always unambiguous for phrases in surface structure. The rule seems to apply correctly when only one such phrase is expressed:

[65] Peter is ill.
[66] Peter met a girl.
[67] That Peter met a girl was unexpected.

As soon as we have several phrases denoting identified individuals, the situation is less straightforward. Earlier it was suggested that in that case we might assume several topics, or one complex topic:

[68] The boy went with the girl to the cinema.

Here, two or possibly three referents have been identified. The simplest solution is to assume as topic the triple ⟨'the boy', 'the girl', 'the cinema'⟩, and to assign comment function to the predicate this triplet belongs to, viz 'to go' and the past tense. This assumption is not in accordance with the intuitive way in which topics are established, *eg* by question tests like "What about the boy?", or "What did the boy do?", which would identify *the boy* as the phrase expressing the topic function. Instead of assigning a particular relation to a pair or triplet, we then seem to assign a complex property ('going to the cinema with the girl') to a certain object, as in the classical subject-predicate distinction. Along the same line, the pair ⟨'the boy', 'the girl'⟩ would have topic function in [68] when it answers the question "What did the boy do with the girl?". Such questions are means of expressing a certain communicative situation: they indicate where the interests of the hearer are, what he wants to know or expects to be informed about, given a certain context and part of discourse. In an explicit account it should be made clear how such questions 'follow from' a certain part of the discourse. Whereas the knowledge deficit of hearers, or rather the speaker's assumptions about what the hearer may want to know should be treated in pragmatic terms, this account should first of all be semantic.

Take as sentences previous to [68] the following:

[69] Mary was glad to go out that night.
[70] Peter was glad to go out that night.

It is understood that *the boy* and *the girl* (or their pronominal forms) are referentially identical with *Peter* and *Mary*, respectively. Given [69] as previous discourse, we could say that [68] is saying something about the girl, at least primarily. Similarly for the boy after [70]. Apparently, the topicality of 'the boy' or 'the girl' depends on the topicality of referentially equivalent phrases in the previous sentence, as is also the case in the test questions establishing a certain epistemic context. If this sort of 'relative' establishment of topics held, we would have to conclude that 'the boy' is assigned topic in [68] after a sentence like *Peter met a girl this afternoon*, in which 'a girl' is not topic but part of the comment according to rule [64]. And the same for 'the girl' after a sentence like *That afternoon Mary met a boy*. After such sentences, as after [70] and [69], respectively, the sentence [68] would be interpreted as being primarily about the boy or the girl, respectively.

However, apart from other difficulties, the rule of relative topic assignment (if there is more than one topical phrase in a sentence, then the phrase co-referential with the last topical phrase has topic function) meets with difficulties. That is, after the sentence *Peter met a girl this afternoon* we may have the sentence *The girl was very pretty*. According to the rule, this would mean that 'the girl' would be assigned topic function in [68], although it may be maintained that the sentence is primarily about the boy – intuitively speaking at least. This intuition may be based on the fact that the girl has been introduced after the introduction of the boy, and relative to it, viz as the 'object' of the meeting relation. This intuition is not always accurate, as shown by this simple story:

[71] Once upon a time there was an old king.

He had seven daughters.
One of them was called Bella.
She loved her father very much.
(. . .)

Although the daughter Bella has been introduced relative to her father the king, we would not say that *her father* in the fourth sentence has (primary) topic function: the sentence is intuitively about Bella, introduced in the previous sentence. Note that the sentence *He was her best friend* would be unacceptable as a fourth sentence in [71], whereas the sentence *He loved her most of all* would be acceptable, as well as the full version *Her father was her best friend*. The first of the acceptable sentences would re-establish the 'father' as the topic, or at least the pair ⟨'the father', 'the daughter'⟩. In the second acceptable sentence the expression *her father* may not be pronominalized, apparently because it does not express a topic but part of the comment, where *she* or *her best friend* are topic (or derived topic).

The difficulty arising in these cases seems in part due to the fact that the establishment of topic function in individual sentences with several bound elements also depends on what could be called the topic of the passage, or the topic of discourse in general. Thus, in [71] we intuitively know that in the third sentence the topic of the discourse changes to the daughter. This is not the case for 'intermediary' sentences such as *She was very pretty* after which 'Peter' can still stay topic of the discourse taken as an earlier example. How topics of (parts of) discourse are to be defined is a problem for the next chapter. It will be provisionally assumed however that if a phrase has topic function and if a phrase in the next sentence is co-referential with it, then the topic will be 'continued'. A change of topic seems to follow automatically with reference to previously identified things referred to by comment-phrases:

[72]*a:* I am looking for my typewriter.
  b: It is no longer on my desk.

Whereas the contextually identified 'I' is assigned topic function in [72]*a* the topic is changed to the argument referring to the typewriter in [72]*b*. It will however be difficult to maintain that since 'I' is assigned topic in [72]*a* this topic remains the same in the subsequent sentence:

[72]*c:* I do not see it in my office.

which seems to be also about the typewriter (as is indicated by the pronominalization *it*). As before, we thus must assume that sets or ordered pairs may be topics in a sentence (if no further information is established about topicality by the whole passage/discourse).

Note, incidentally, that arguments referring to identified members of the context (*eg* speaker and hearer) need not be explicitly introduced into the discourse in order to be topic. With normal ordering and stress they always have topic function.

Note also that not all definite noun phrases must express topic function. Definite noun phrases are also used in those cases where there is obviously only one object of the kind in the universe of the particular discourse. In order to become topic, however, such individuals must first be introduced into the set of referents:

[73] Leonard ran off with the maid.

Here 'the maid' may well belong to the comment.

6.6

It is not easy to draw unambiguous CONCLUSIONS from these observations about the topic-comment articulation in sentences, not even for sentences in (con-)text. We have a clear formal criterion, viz [64], possibly corresponding to a cognitive principle of information expansion, but our intuitions do not always seem to match with these rules. At the same time it is not simple to distinguish at this point between sentential topics on the one hand and sequential or discourse topics on the other hand. How discourse topics may be defined is a problem for the next chapter. Besides the referential conditions stated above, the assignment of sentential topic function also seems to be determined by rules of topic continuity and topic change, and further by pragmatic factors like 'interest', 'importance' or 'relevance',[28] rather vague notions to be further discussed in Chapter 8. It has been clear in this last section that certain problems of discourse semantics are still very puzzling: even if there are some fairly general rules, there are many very subtle differences which seem to obey other constraints.

Notes

1 Other terms are used to denote similar concepts. Halliday and Hasan (1976) use the term COHESION, though sometimes in a broader way than we use the term 'coherence'. In other writings, especially in psychology and philosopy, the term CONNECTED(NESS) is used to denote discourse coherence. From our discussion it follows that connectedness in our terminology is a very specific kind of coherence, viz the set of conditions determining the relations as pairs, ie interdependencies, between facts, as expressed by composite sentences and sequences, and relative to some possible world and some possible topic of conversation. For a philosophical discussion of coherence and truth, see Rescher (1973).

2 For example, the relations between the following sentences, which are not connected semantically, but which have other coherence relations: *They went to the zoo. Never had they been in a zoo before.* Other examples will be given below.

3 We merely treat some aspects of coherence. An analysis of relations of lexical meaning, reference, etc has been given in our earlier work (*eg* van Dijk, 1972a, and the references given there). We also refer to the inventory of coherence relations given by Halliday and Hasan (1976)

4 Thus in a discourse about a tea party in some flat in London, say, the introduction of protons and elephants as individuals will be most unlikely (except of course in possible discourses produced during that party). Part of this kind of PRAGMATIC unexpectedness will be reconstructed in terms of SEMANTIC coherence, requiring relations between individuals and properties of individuals, on the one hand, and

abstract functions, viz topics of conversation, determining sets of possible facts in which these individuals and properties are involved.

5 See especially Halliday and Hasan (1976) and for some of the grammatical properties of discourse, viz syntactic structures expressing semantic coherence relations in discourse, van Dijk (1972a), Dressler (1970), and the references given in these works.

6 There should be made a methodological and theoretical distinction between the notion of determination in a grammar or a logical system (*eg* semantics) and determination in actual processes of language production and comprehension. As will briefly be explained in the next chapter, a reader starting to read a discourse will not have a full macro-structure at his disposal, but will make hypotheses about the topic of conversation which may be gradually confirmed, changed, or rejected in further reading. In the grammar we only have to do with theoretical dependence, *eg* relative interpretations of expressions with respect to an (also theoretical) topic of conversation 'as if' this topic were already there. In this respect the grammar more closely models the reader's 'final comprehension' – still in a very abstract way – of a discourse or part of it. Further methodological intricacies involved will not be discussed here.

7 For a similar notion (text model) see *eg* Ballmer (1972). It should be noted though that, as yet, the notion of discourse model or other kinds of model sequences is not well-defined in logical theory (see Groenendijk and Stokhof, 1976, however, for a similar concept needed for the interpretation of certain composite performative sentences). Recall that a MODEL STRUCTURE is an abstract semantic reconstruction of 'what there is' (sets of worlds, individuals, properties, etc). Together with a valuation function (relating expressions of a language to these various semantic 'things'), such model structures constitute MODELS (see Chapter 2). Characteristic of a discourse model would be, for instance, the fact that the respective domains of individuals would at least intersect (together defining what most literally may now be called a 'universe of discourse'). See below.

8 For this kind of 'restricted quantification' or 'sortal quantification', see Altham and Tennant (1975), and the references given there to earlier work on that topic. See also van Dijk (1973a) for a discussion about quantification in discourse.

9 See section 6 of Chapter 2 and for formal details on this issue also Goddard and Routley (1973).

10 For the notion of 'dimension' of meaning and similar concepts, see the references given in note 18 of Chapter 2.

11 A COMPLETE DESCRIPTION of a situation would consist of all sentences being true (or satisfied) with respect to that situation. In particular, it might be required that if a proposition p did not belong to the set, $\sim p$ would be a member. In general such sets will be CONSISTENT: if p belongs to it, $\sim p$ does not. They will be MAXIMALLY CONSISTENT if in addition any proposition were a member of the set without making it inconsistent (so, either α is a member or $\sim \alpha$ for any α).

12 The crime story from which we take several examples, here and elsewhere is James Hadley Chase, *Just the way it is*, 1944. We quote from the 1975 Panther Book edition.

13 Recall that the expression $V(a)$ means 'the value of a', *ie* it stands for the thing denoted by the expression a (see Chapter 2).

14 We here touch upon the difficult methodological problem of distinguishing a (formal) semantic characterization of discourse coherence on the one hand, and a specification of pragmatic and cognitive determinants formulated in terms of world knowledge, interpretation strategies, expectations, etc. In the passages that follow we will not always bother to make the distinction explicitly. It should be borne in mind, however, that for the semantics, expectations, world knowledge, etc are merely specific sets of propositions, relative to which sentences are (formally) interpreted. It is NOT the task of a formal or linguistic semantics to spell out these

propositions, but only to formulate the more general interpretation conditions for coherent sequences involving such knowledge/expectation sets.

15 The notion of FRAME comes from recent cognitive psychology and artificial intelligence, and has been coined by Minsky (1975). See further discussion and references in the next chapter. For the relations between frames and discourse interpretation (comprehension), see van Dijk (1976a).

16 The postulates given are one of the possible REPRESENTATIONS of (cognitive) frames. They are given here to indicate the assumption that the office-frame would not itself contain the information that offices have windows, but that this information is subsumed under the more general building-frame. Again, we see that semantic coherence, determining comprehension and hence acceptability, is based on relations between facts as they are conventionally known, and hence present in frames.

17 See the discussion about 'possible individuals' in Chapter 2 and in Rescher (1975). Note that the real Clare Russell as she exists in the past actual world is not strictly identical with the Clare Russell as conceived in some thought-world of the real, present-actual Clare Russell. The philosophical intricacies will be ignored here, the upshot of our analysis being only that 'referential identity' in a discourse may involve identity across several worlds, which must satisfy certain constraints (eg that these worlds are accessible from a given world).

18 Note that the interpretations involved here are those of an abstract semantic theory, viz those assigning intensions and/or extensions to expressions. We do not claim that such a theory can be translated directly into a theory of cognitive semantic information processing (comprehension), but even in such a cognitive theory it should be assumed that language users construct some form of propositional missing link in order to connect superficially disconnected sentences (see Kintsch (1974) for empirical evidence for this assumption).

19 How compelling conventional frames can be in the coherent interpretation of discourse by language users, may be illustrated by the fact that one of the readers of the first draft of this book thought that *he* was a typing error for *she*.

20 This inference would be based on the lexical and frame-like conceptual structure of the concepts in [30]. What we do in fact is operate a certain EXPANSION, viz specify (generally known) details of certain actions at a 'lower' level of representation.

21 It may be argued that completeness of various kinds does not belong to discourse coherence in the strict sense, but either constitutes a different kind of semantic property of discourse or a typical pragmatic property determining appropriateness relative to some context (involving communicative intentions). We do however consider (in-)completeness as a condition of (semantic) (in-)coherence of discourse.

22 Since for any proposition α it holds that it also entails α, (self-entailment), the self-entailed proposition of an expressed (explicit) proposition is of course not implicit.

23 See Dahl (1969), Sgall, Hajičová and Benešová (1973) and the references given there.

24 One of the recent papers in psychology about the cognitive basis of the GIVEN-NEW contract is Clark (1973). See also Dahl (1976) for a linguistic point of view. In fact, most current work on semantic information processing deals with the more general problem of how incoming information is integrated into the already present conceptual structure. See the references in the next chapter, and the discussion in Chapter 8.

25 We here again touch upon the difficult problem of the precise STATUS of the notions of topic and comment, *ie* the levels and terms in which they should be described. Although our discussion is mainly framed in semantic terms (reference), pragmatic and cognitive elements are also involved (knowledge of hearers, etc). Speaking loosely, one may say however, that a syntactic phrase together with a specific stress and intonation pattern are ASSIGNED, or EXPRESS, topic and comment function.

This means that we take these functions to be specific properties of the semantic structure of sentences, viz a property to be defined (at that level, at least) in terms of relative interpretations.

26 The 'epistemic range' of an object is taken to mean the set of propositions known, by someone, to be true of that object. For our purposes this might be strengthened such that only general, conventional knowledge about some individual is involved, but this would exclude the topic-comment functions that operate on the basis of ad hoc or other particular knowledge about objects as it is shared by speaker and hearer in some particular context of communication.

27 This would at least explain the use of *it* in English and the use of similar 'pronouns' in other languages. For languages like Latin, Italian and Russian no such explanation would be necessary, since only a third person ending is used to express impersonal events. There is no reason, however, to assume that such morphemes would not also express topic function (as do the other person morphemes of verb-endings), requiring specific personal pronouns when having comment-function (which, however, is impossible for the impersonal expressions).

28 Parallel to the notion of topic-comment articulation, the Prague School has discussed a still more elusive concept, viz that of COMMUNICATIVE DYNAMISM, required to explain the notions of 'relevance' or 'importance' of certain expressions and possibly correlated phenomena as stress, intonation and word order to be explained in terms of topic-comment transformations or contrast. See Sgall, Hajičová and Benešová (1973) for a discussion of this notion.

Chapter 5

Macro-structures

1 Introduction

1.1

In the previous chapters it has already been indicated that a semantic characterization of discourse structures should also be given on a level of a more global organization, that of MACRO-STRUCTURES. In particular it has been shown that conditions of semantic coherence are to be formulated relative to such notions as TOPIC OF CONVERSATION or TOPIC OF DISCOURSE. In this chapter some of the semantic properties of these and related notions will be made more explicit.

1.2

It is not the aim of this book or of this chapter to provide a sound THEORY of macro-structures, which would certainly be a premature enterprise.[1] On the one hand such a theory would clearly pass the boundaries of the domain of grammars or linguistic theory in general, extending to a more inclusive study of discourse in psychology, the social sciences and poetics, and on the other hand observations and descriptions with respect to linguistic properties of macro-structures are still too vague to warrant theoretical generalization. This chapter, then, will be limited to some observations about the LINGUISTIC, and in particular the SEMANTIC, nature of macro-structures, referring only indirectly to cognitive evidence which has been provided in the last few years for the hypothesis that macro-structures constitute a separate level of linguistic analysis.

1.3

Let us first enumerate some QUESTIONS and PROBLEMS which seem to require a formulation in terms of macro-structures.

First of all, as we mentioned above, it is necessary to clarify the status of such concepts as TOPIC OF CONVERSATION and TOPIC OF DISCOURSE. In the previous chapter, where the notion TOPIC for sentences has been discussed, we tried to answer questions like "In what respect can we say that a sentence is 'about' something?". Similar questions may be formulated for sequences of sentences and whole discourses. Our linguistic behaviour shows that we can say that a discourse, or part of it, was 'about' something. That is, we are able to produce other discourses, or parts of discourses, expressing this 'about-ness', *eg* in summaries, titles, conclusions or pronouncements in any form.

Now, the question is whether this notion of discourse topic can be made explicit in semantic terms and, if so, whether we are able to establish systematic relations between such a notion and the semantic representation of the sentences of the sequence or discourse. Should we speak about one (theoretical) topic of a passage or discourse or may we distinguish several, theoretically possible, topics of the same passage or discourse? What is the relation between the respective topics of discourse-parts and what is the relation between such a topic structure and the macro-structure of a discourse? And finally, what linguistic (grammatical) evidence can be found for introducing the notion topic of discourse?

1.4

In a broader sense, it should be investigated whether it is possible to formulate general RULES relating sentence and sequence structures with macro-structures of discourse. And assuming macro-structures to have semantic status, it should be asked whether specific CATEGORIES should be introduced to characterize macro-structures in general and macro-structures of specific types of discourse in particular. And again: what intuitions or other manifestations of linguistic 'knowledge' in conventional language utterances indicate the presence of macro-structural rules and categories?

1.5

Another set of problems which has had little attention in linguistics concerns the RELATIONSHIPS BETWEEN DISCOURSES, both systematically ('para-digmatically', as we used to say in classical structural linguistics) and in conversation ('syntagmatically'). On the one hand, how do we assign a summary, an abstract or a paraphrase to a discourse, and how can we say that a given sentence or discourse is ENTAILED by another discourse, which again presupposes that we can significantly apply the notion of truth to discourse. On the other hand, just as sentences combine with sentences to form discourses, discourses combine with discourses in order to form DIALOGUES and CONVERSATIONS: which relations between discourses in conversations require a macro-semantic characterization? In the next part of this book it should also be investigated which properties of discourse and conversation structure are to be given in PRAGMATIC terms.

2 Topics of discourse
2.1

Instead of starting with a speculative hypothesis about the status and structures of macro-levels, or about the cognitive constraints on complex semantic information processing, the notion of macro-structure will be approached from a more concrete point of view, viz the explication of the intuitive notion of TOPIC. In this respect the discussion provides a necessary basis for the coherence conditions given earlier and at the same time completes the discussion about the notion 'topic of a sentence'.

2.2

The notion TOPIC OF DISCOURSE (or TOPIC OF CONVERSATION, two terms which for the moment we take to be synonymous) seems to be even more vague than the notion 'topic of a sentence'. For the latter notion we at least are able to assess certain phonological and syntactical structures indicating an assumed topic-comment articulation. On the other hand, terms like 'topic', 'theme' or 'being about' are intuitively applied to longer stretches of discourse and conversations. It is also in the latter sense that, even in sentences, it is (con)textually determined whether the topic is, for example, 'John', or 'Mary', or ⟨'John, Mary'⟩ or 'making a trip around the world'. Sentential topics, as we have seen, determine the distribution of information along sequences of sentences, whereas discourse topics seem to reduce, organize and categorize semantic information of sequences as wholes.

2.3

In order to make these intuitive assumptions more precise let us examine some examples.

The beginning of the crime story by Chase, of which we analysed the first passage of Chapter 9, runs as follows:

[1] Fairview was dying. In the past, it had been a go-ahead, prosperous little town and its two large factories, specializing in hand-tools, had been a lucrative source of wealth.

Now, Fairview had had its golden age. Mass production had seen to that. The little town's methods of production could not compete with the modern factories that had sprung up overnight in the neighbouring districts.

Mass production and Bentonville had put paid to Fairview. Bentonville was a rapidly expanding manufacturing town some thirty miles away. It was a mushroom town. A town for the younger generation with brightly painted shops, neat, cheap little bungalows, swift trolley cars and a young, vigorous beating heart of commerce.

The youth of Fairview had gone either to Bentonville or farther north; some even went to New York. The more progressive businesses had transferred to Bentonville as soon as the writing appeared on the wall. Only the less enterprising smaller shops were left to carry on as best they could.

Fairview was defeated. You could see it in the shabby houses, the unkept roads and the quality of goods in the shop windows. You could see it in the dignified shabbiness of the small colony of retired business people who had done well in the golden age and were content to live out their days in this sad, stagnating little town. And you could see it particularly in the numbers of unemployed who gathered at street corners, indifferent and apathetic.

Asked what the topic or theme of this passage is, or more simply 'what this passage is about', a native speaker will in general be able to answer something like: "*Fairview, a little town*", "*The decline of Fairview*", "*The decline of Fairview due to mass production and to competition from a neighbouring town, Bentonville*", and such answers would be intuitively and conventionally acceptable. The question is: what are the (semantic) rules or procedures underlying this ability of language users?

An obvious beginning would be to indicate that the topic of this passage is expressed; in fact it is expressed several times:

[2] Fairview was dying.
    Fairview had had its golden age.
    Mass production and Bentonville had put paid to Fairview.
    Fairview was defeated.

These somewhat metaphorical sentences are quasi-paraphrases of the same underlying semantic representation. Yet, how do we know that just these sentences express the topic of the whole passage?

Similarly, taking "Fairview" as topic, we may say that it is also functioning as topic in many sentences of the sequence. But again, such a purely 'quantitative' answer to the problem would hardly be satisfactory.

The specific status of sentences like those of [2] must be sought in the relation between their meaning and the meaning of the other sentences of the sequence. More particularly, we may say, intuitively, that the other sentences SPECIFY this meaning. Thus the concept of 'decline' (of a town, country or culture) implies that of previous economic and/or cultural prosperity and that of actual stagnation. This content of the concept of decline is indeed expressed in the passage (*In the past . . . Now . . .*). At a still more detailed level of specification the reasons for components of this prosperity and stagnation are expressed. Here our semantic (conceptual) knowledge and our knowledge of the world allow us to relate the concept of economic prosperity to the existence of lucrative factories. Similarly, we know that competition may be a sufficient condition for economic decline, and that in turn mass production is a possible component of successful competition. Futhermore, the consequences of economic decline are possibly the appearance of the town (shabbiness of houses, streets) and a socio-economic state as unemployment, in turn causing indifference and apathy. Conversely, if B successfully competes with A, it follows that B becomes richer, a property which may show in urban expansion, appearance, etc of B. Finally, the concept of 'economic progress' is related to that of 'modern', 'young', 'vigorous', that of 'decline' to 'old', 'old-fashioned', 'retired', 'sad', etc.

In other words, a concept or a conceptual structure (a proposition) may become a discourse topic if it HIERARCHICALLY ORGANIZES the conceptual (propositional) structure of the sequence.

It will be assumed that the abstract notion of discourse topic is to be made explicit in terms of PROPOSITIONAL STRUCTURES (or formally equivalent structures). This means, for our passage, that the topic would not be *Fairview* or *decline*, but at least *decline* (*Fairview*) or *decline* (*a*) & *town* (*a*) & *small* (*a*) & (*a* = *Fairview*). From the informal discussion given above it then follows that given a discourse sequence Σ_i, and a proposition α, α is the TOPIC of Σ_i, iff Σ_i ENTAILS α. In our example this is trivially the case because α is also a member of the propositional sequence Σ_i. In general the definition must also hold, however, for those sequences where α is not an element of Σ_i. In that case we require that the ordered sequence Σ_i of propositions JOINTLY and non-trivially entails α. In a formal description we would have to PROVE that such a relation is indeed satisfied. This would require explicit statement of a set of meaning postulates and a set of propositions representing conventional knowledge of a part (here: socio-economical structures) of the world, of which some examples have been given in a natural language version above. Instead of such a (very complex) proof we may give a hierarchical representation of the conceptual and factual relations involved.

As a hypothesis we take the complex proposition underlying the sentence *A* (*little*) *town* (*called Fairview*) *is declining because it cannot compete with another town* (*called Bentonville*). In somewhat more formal notation the underlying proposition would in that case be something like:

[3] $town(a)\ \&\ town(b)\ \&\ [\sim \mathrm{CAN}_a\ (compete\ with\ (a, b))](e)\ \&$
$cause\ (e, f)\ \&\ [decline(a)](f)$.

This is a simplified notation, in which the constants e and f are event constants,[2] and where the causal relation is expressed by a two-place predicate over events (instead of a specific causal connective as used in Chapter 2). Now, the proposition *decline*(*a*) entails the following proposition:

[4] $prosperous(a, t_i)\ \&\ \sim prosperous(a, t_{i+j})$

Given certain propositions from the set F of factual knowledge, we may infer:

[5] $[town(a)\ \&\ prosperous(a)] \leftarrow\Box\ \Box\rightarrow [have(a, c)\ \&\ industry(c)\ \&\ lucrative(c)]$

Note that the semantic relations can be established both ways: on the one hand it is (economically) necessary or at least probable that lucrative industry in a town implies that this town is (economically) prosperous, and on the other hand it may be possibly concluded that if a town is prosperous it has lucrative industry. On the basis of the first relation the establishment of the topic is operated. The second relation determines hypothesis formation in the interpretation process concerning POSSIBLE CONTINUATION of a discourse. That is, once we know a town is prosperous, we may reasonably expect the information that it has lucrative industry. In other words, we may expect information about the CONDITIONS of a certain event.

Similarly, the notion of 'competition' involves methods of production, and 'modern factories' implies 'modern methods of production' which, with further factual information, yields:

[6] $\sim CAN_a(compete\ with(a,\ b))$.

In addition to [4] we may infer from [3] that

[7] $prosperous(b,\ t_{i+j})$,

a proposition which follows from a joint sequence of propositions like

[8]a: $expand(b)$
     b: $have\ (b,\ heart\ of\ commerce(d))\ \&\ vigorous(d)\ \&\ beating(d)$.

The set of these and further propositions expressed in the passage form what has been called a FRAME, *ie* a subsystem of knowledge about some phenomenon in the world like economic prosperity and decline. In more specific terms such a frame contains information about COMPONENT states, actions or events, about NECESSARY OR PROBABLE CONDITIONS and CONSEQUENCES, as defined in the previous chapters. Thus, the propositions expressed in the third paragraph of this passage, describing the town Bentonville, JOINTLY imply that this town is prosperous (*cf* [7]) owing to the information in the frame associated with the concept of economic prosperity. The same holds for the description of decline of Fairview in the fifth paragraph, *eg* by

[9] a: $[shabby(a')\ \&\ part\ of\ (a',\ a)]\ \Box\!\!\rightarrow\ shabby(a)$
     b: $shabby(a)\ \Box\!\!\rightarrow\ \sim prosperous(a)$

In the COMPETITION-frame we would further expect information about the transfer of business and preference of employees to work for the successful competitor. Finally, the fact that the decline of *a* is indeed caused by the inability to compete with *b* follows from the propositions in the second and third paragraph ('had put paid', 'had seen to that').

In this slightly more precise way we have given an indication of how we may 'derive' the components of the complex proposition [3] functioning as a topic of this passage. Sufficient propositional information is given in the respective sentences to infer the specific conceptual frame (PROSPERITY, COMPETITION) and individual (small-scale, micro-) proposition (*prosperous(a)*). The connections and hence the inferences (entailments) involved are to be defined with respect to the specific subset of actual postulates defining the set of worlds in which this story is satisfied, viz the set of socio-economic laws of a capitalistic society.

2.4

We have reconstructed the notion of topic of (a part of) a discourse as a proposition entailed by the joint set of propositions expressed by the sequence. In case there is more than one proposition satisfying this requirement we may speak of alternatives. The set of these alternatives will be called the TOPIC SET of that part of the discourse.

According to our definition the topic must be entailed by the sequence as a whole. This is true also for the atomic parts of the topical proposition if that is complex as in [3]. And indeed, it may also be said that this passage is about a town, about two towns, about the decline of a town, or about competition. We see that this use of the notion of topic is to be construed as a component atomic proposition of the topic. In such cases we will speak about SUBTOPICS or ATOMIC TOPICS. That such subtopics cannot be the whole topic is shown by the fact that other sequences of sentences of the passage entail further atomic propositions. This means that only those propositions entailed by (a part of) a discourse are topics which DOMINATE all semantic information of the sequence:

[10] A proposition T is TOPIC of a sequence of propositions
$\Sigma = \langle p_1, p_2, \ldots, p_n \rangle$ iff for each $p_i \in \Sigma$ there is a subsequence Σ_k of Σ such that $p_i \in \Sigma_k$, and for each successive Σ_k there is a P_j such that $\Sigma_k \Rightarrow P_j$ and $T \Rightarrow P_j$.

In fact this definition[3] should be formulated in a recursive way, because it may be the case that there is a sequence of entailed propositions $\langle P_i, P_{i+1}, \ldots \rangle$ which in turn entail a proposition Q_i entailed by T. Thus, in our example, the subset of propositions expressed in the last paragraph entails the proposition 'The town is declining', which is part of (entailed by) the complex topic of the whole sequence.

Sentences expressing (sub-)topical propositions directly, as those in [2] will be called TOPICAL. Such sentences NEED not occur, but are often given to emphasize the topic. They have a specific function in the cognitive processing of discourse: they either 'announce' the topic of a passage or, after a passage, confirm the hypothetical topic established by the reader. In this sense the other sentences may be viewed as 'explicating' or 'specifying' the information of the topical sentences.

2.5

The definition of topic given above needs some further specification. One of the provisos to be built in is that the entailed propositions are not too GENERAL. Thus, in our example, Fairview is a town, but this in turn implies that Fairview is an inanimate thing. Similarly, that Fairview is declining, implies that Fairview is subject to a certain process. In order to keep the topic of a discourse as SPECIFIC as possible, we must require that the entailment relations involved are DIRECT or IMMEDIATE, *ie* define the SMALLEST SUPERSET of a set. The concept defining this smallest superset will be called the IMMEDIATE SUPERCONCEPT of a given concept.[4] Thus, the immediate superconcept of 'house' is 'building'. The same will be required to hold for the assignment of frame concepts: given the description of a state, action, event, etc they will be integrated into the smallest possible frame. Thus, the occurrence of houses, shops and streets will be assigned the TOWN-frame, and not the COUNTRY-frame.

2.6

The characterization of the notion of topic of (a part of) a discourse given above is identical with what we intend MACRO-STRUCTURES to have. That is, a macro-structure of a sequence of sentences is a SEMANTIC REPRESENTATION of some kind, viz a proposition entailed by the sequence of propositions underlying the discourse (or part of it). First of all, this assumption implies that the macro-structure of simple sentences may be identical with their underlying propositional structure.[5] The macro-structure of the discourse *Peter is going to Paris next week* would then simply be its underlying proposition, something like [*go to* (Peter, Paris)]*e* & *next week*(*e*).

Secondly, we should speak of several LEVELS OF MACRO-STRUCTURE in a discourse. Given the definition, any proposition entailed by a subset of a sequence is a macro-structure for that subsequence. At the next level these macro-structural propositions may again be subject to integration into a larger frame, *ie* entail, jointly, a more general macro-structure. Thus, the last paragraph of the passage we analysed has as a hypothetical macro-structure a proposition like 'Fairview is (economically) declining' or 'Fairview is not prosperous'. The latter proposition, together with the proposition entailed by the first paragraph ('In the past F. was prosperous'), would yield 'Fairview is declining'. Now, when we speak of THE macro-structure of a sequence we refer to the most general macro-structure, entailed by the other macrostructures, 'dominating' the whole sequence.[6] The proposition 'Fairview is declining' could not as such be THE macro-structure of our passage because it does not contain the information that decline was due to competition with another town, nor any information about this other town.

2.7

Before we can apply our observations to macro-structures in general, we should at least give a tentative analysis of another passage. Whereas the Fairview passage is 'descriptive', *ie* pertains to a certain state of an object, it should be investigated whether the assessment of a discourse topic is also possible for action and event discourse, *eg* for narrative. Consider, for example, the following passage from Boccaccio's *The Decameron* (Second Day, Fourth Story):[7]

[11] This Rufolo, then, having made the sort of preliminary calculations that merchants normally make, purchased a very large ship, loaded it with a mixed cargo of goods paid for entirely out of his own pocket, and sailed with them to Cyprus. But on his arrival, he discovered that several other ships had docked there, carrying precisely the same kind of goods he had brought over himself. And for this reason, not only did he have to sell his cargo at bargain prices, but in order to complete his business he was

practically forced to give the stuff away, thus being brought to the verge of ruin.

Intuitively, the topic of this passage may be expressed by a sentence like *A merchant wants to trade but is ruined by competition*. The topic, as we see, is partially identical with that of the previously analysed passage, viz 'ruin due to competition'. The differences are that here the competition is not industrial but mercantile, and that it happens to a person instead of a town.

The procedures by which the topic for this passage is obtained are similar. First of all, the complex concept of 'trading', as an action, is constructed from the first propositions of the sequence: if *x* wants to trade, he will have to make calculations, buy goods, transport them or have them transported, and will try to sell them at a higher price than he bought them at. This is, in a succinct form the content of the TRADE-frame. We see that such an action frame consists of the following elements: PREPARATORY ACTIONS (making calculations), AUXILIARY ACTIONS (purchasing a ship), and COMPONENT ACTIONS, according to the definitions of these terms given in Chapter 6. The component actions are those which are necessary parts of the compound or complex action: they define the concept in question. Here: buying cargo, and trying to sell it. The component of transport is spelled out here by the propositions '*a* sailed to Cyprus' and '*a* arrived in Cyprus'.

The next event, viz the fact that R. is meeting competition, is constructed from the proposition 'that there are others with the same cargo', which is a necessary component of mercantile competition. Finally, the event of his being ruined is composed by propositions like '*a* had to sell his cargo at bargain prices' and '*a* practically had to give the stuff away'. As is expressed in the passage itself, these two events constitute probable CONDITIONS of mercantile failure, which is itself a probable CONSEQUENCE of the conditioning events. Again, we see that information implied by a sequence of sentences may also itself be expressed in the discourse (*thus being brought to the verge of ruin*). On the other hand, neither the concepts of trading nor that of competition are themselves directly expressed: they are implied by the successive subsequences of this passage.

2.8

Language users not only have the ability to produce or interpret (parts of) discourses with respect to a given topic, they are also able to CHANGE a topic and to perceive such a topic change in a discourse or conversation. We are now in a position to make this intuitive notion more precise. The obvious road to take is to make use of the formal criterion that for a sequence to have a topic, each sentence (or its underlying propositions) must 'satisfy' this topic, directly or indirectly. A sequence with this property is coherent with respect to topic or, more broadly, to MACRO-STRUCTURE. Thus, we may expect a change of topic to occur if one of the sentences of a discourse no longer 'belongs to' a given topic and if the sentence is the first member of a sequence with a different topic: that is, if a sentence introduces an argument or a predicate which cannot be subsumed under higher order arguments or predicates of the given topic.

In our Fairview passage we thus witness the introduction of a new subtopic with the introduction of a new individual in the first sentence of the third paragraph,[8] viz the town Bentonville. Although Bentonville is an argument of the topic of this passage, we do not know yet whether this argument is 'local' or more global. In the latter case, Bentonville would occur as an argument also in other topics of the story, as will in fact turn out to be the case.

A characteristic example of a topic change is the sentence following the Fairview passage [1]:

[12] But there was still one spark of life to be found in Fairview (. . .) when Fairview was at the peak of its prosperity Harman had founded a newspaper for the town (. . .)

In this passage first of all a new individual is introduced, viz a newspaper, and secondly it is asserted that it constitutes an exception to the decline of the town. That is, the predicate ('x is a spark of life') cannot be subsumed under the topical predicate of decline of the first passage. That this newspaper has topical function will appear from the rest of the passage initiated with [12]: a description of the newspaper, viz its history, building and editors are given. In the same way, the topic then changes to/with the introduction of the 'main character' of the story, as follows:

[13] (. . .) The staff consisted of the editor, Sam Trench, Al Barnes, three somewhat inefficient clerks and Clare Russell.

Clare was the mainspring of the *Clarion*. The office, the staff and the copy revolved round her. She was responsible for the small spark of life that remained in the newspaper (*p* 6).

Although it is a normal part of a TOWN-frame that there is a newspaper, this newspaper is specifically 'thematized'. It is not only introduced like the 'unemployed' in the previous paragraph, but a series of predicates are assigned to it, such that it acquires independent topical character. Similarly, Clare Russell is not merely named as one of the editors, but she acquires topical 'independence' by an elaborate description of her career, her character and her appearance. Since she will re-appear throughout the whole story, she is not only locally topical, but more globally so. Moreover, her local topical role is further assessed by the fact that she is the cause of the specific exceptional property ('spark of life') of the newspaper in Fairview, just as Bentonville is the cause of Fairview's decline.

One clear surface manifestation of underlying 'global structures' such as topics, is the use of *but* at the beginning of [12]. According to our satisfaction conditions for natural *but*, we expect it to connect propositions. In this case, *but* does not connect the last proposition in [1] with the first in [12], but in fact connects the whole sequence of [1] with [12], not individual propositions of

[1]. It will be assumed, then, that there is a contrast of the first proposition of [12] with the TOPICAL PROPOSITION 'Fairview is declining'. This would also be the case if the first passage did not have topical sentences like 'Fairview was defeated', etc, so that we cannot construct *but* as a connective of these particular sentences. This is one clear LINGUISTIC reason why the assumption about semantic macro-structures in discourse must be made. Below, we will give some more evidence of this kind.

Changes of topic are subject to certain constraints within the same discourse or conversation. Whereas in casual everyday conversations topics may follow each other without much of a systematic connection (often a common argument or predicate is sufficient as a condition of change: "*By, the way, talking about Harry: . . .*", "*Now you talk about unemployment: . . .*", etc), topic sequencing in discourses following stricter conventional rules must satisfy a number of conditions similar to those determining the linear connection and coherence of sentences. In our example we see that although the predicate of the topic changes, there is at least a common argument (Fairview). Expressed in a simpler way: the story continues about the same town. More particularly, the argument introduced in the second topic, viz the local newspaper, is a regular element of a normal TOWN-frame. Finally, the two topics are connected by the contrastive relation 'decline'/'spark of life' underlying the use of *but*. In more formal semantic terms: 'In most possible worlds where a town would be declining, its newspaper (among other things) would also be declining' is the presupposition of such a use of contrastive *but*.

These relations between topical propositions are the familiar semantic (referential and conceptual) relations discussed in the previous chapters. They are the linguistic basis for another kind of structural relations determining the specific super-structural (or schematic) properties of various sorts of discourse, *eg* of narratives, arguments, etc, to which we will turn below.

2.9

Although it is not the aim of this book to present a theory of DIALOGUE and of CONVERSATION in general, it should be assumed that the remarks made above about topics and macro-structures are also valid for the identification of TOPICS OF CONVERSATION. Much in the same way as (monologue) discourse is to be globally coherent, a dialogue is coherent due to the assignment of the various utterance meanings to one macro-structural topic. Take for example the following conversation from James Joyce's 'Ivy Day in the Committee Room' (*Dubliners*) between Mr O'Connor and Old Jack, the caretaker. We quote a slightly edited version, where some descriptive phrases of the situation and the speech context (*eg . . .*," *said Mr O'Connor*") have been deleted:

[14] OLD JACK

Ah yes, it's hard to know what way to bring up children. Now who'd think he'd turn out like that! I sent him to the Christian Brothers and I

done what I could for him, and there he goes boozing about. I tried to
make him somewhat decent. Only I'm an old man now I'd change his
tune for him. I'd take the stick to his back and beat him while I could
stand over him – as I done many a time before. The mother you know,
she cocks him up with this and that.

MR O'CONNOR

That's what ruins children.

OLD JACK

To be sure it is. And little thanks you get for it, only impudence. He takes
th'upper hand of me whenever he sees I've a sup taken. What's the world
coming to when sons speaks that way to their fathers?

MR O'CONNOR

What age is he?

OLD JACK

Nineteen.

MR O'CONNOR

Why don't you put him to something?

OLD JACK

Sure, amn't I never done at the drunken bowsy ever since he left school?
"I won't keep you," I says. "You must get a job for yourself." But sure
it's worse whenever he gets a job; he drinks it all.

Although this conversation is from a literary short story, it comes close to
casual everyday conversations, which of course should constitute the empirical basis for a sound theory of conversation.[9]

Intuitively, we would say that the possible topics of this dialogue are Old
Jack's son, the difficulty of bringing up children, or a form of self-
justification. Evidence for the second topic is the initial topical sentence,
announcing the content of the brief narrative of Old Jack. At the same time,
this topic ('It is difficult to know how to bring up children') may be said to
'follow from' the narrative, much in the sense of a MORAL or general
implication. The narrative, within this perspective, is an instantiation of this
general truth, but has as its own topic something like 'Although I did my best
(for him), my son turned out a drunk'. The first proposition is expressed in
the discourse, and subsumes propositions like 'I sent him to the Christian
Brothers' and 'I beat him'. The second proposition is also expressed (*he goes
boozing about*) and subsumes the assumed reason for the son's behaviour: the
actions of his mother. This explanation is confirmed by the general statement
of Mr O'Connor, which is in turn accepted by Old Jack. The EDUCATION-
frame also contains the information that in certain situations the unacceptable behaviour of children is punished, which requires the excuse of being too
old to beat him now. Another possibility of correction, suggested by Mr
O'Connor, is work, whereupon Old Jack supplies the information that this
did not work out either. Note that the question of O'Connor about the age of
Old Jack's son pertains to the information necessary for O'Connor to make

his suggestive question. In the next chapters of this book it will be analysed how sequences of speech acts are thus related to the distribution and communication of information in conversations. The point here is that the statement and questions of O'Connor are topically related to the semantic structure of Old Jack's narrative in the way described in the informal paraphrase given above, and summarized in the following informal and partial representations of frames:

[15] EDUCATION
    x brings up y
    x sends y to school
    x tries to make y decent
    if y shows unacceptable behaviour then x punishes y
    if y is spoilt then y has unacceptable behaviour
    y must respect x
    if y is grown up, x sends y to work

    DRUNKENNESS
    – is often hereditary
    if x is a drunk and if x has money, x drinks his money.

These tentatively formulated 'facts of the world' (known to the particular speech participants) together with general semantic postulates, yield the summarizing global information 'I tried to bring up my son decently' and 'My son became a drunk'. The semantic information would for example specify that beating is a form of punishment, and punishment a corrective act after misbehaviour. Clearly, these sorts of postulates give general information which cannot always be distinguished from the factual, *ie* more incidental information about the world. In that case the meaning of punishing is the ESSENTIAL part of a possible PUNISHMENT frame, which may, for example, contain the information that punishment may be executed by beating someone, and that beating is often executed with a stick: *ie* nonessential information about punishment. Characteristic of this kind of (narrative) dialogue is that the addressee, with his general frame knowledge, has certain assumptions about the development of the narrated events, and thus may ask questions seeking confirmation for his anticipatory hypotheses, or give confirmation of events by invoking general truths from the respective frames.

It will be investigated below what other properties such dialogues and conversations have. We now have a first indication, however, that they also may have topical macro-structures, just like monologue discourses. One of the systematic differences in that case is that in (oral) conversation, discourse referents need not always be introduced explicitly. The presence of some object or property in the conversational situation may be sufficient to identify these for the hearer, and may also be sufficient reason to be included in the topic of a conversation, at least under some further pragmatic conditions.

3 Macro-operations and semantic information reduction

3.1

It will be suggested below that one of the cognitive functions of macro-structures is the ORGANIZATION, in processing and memory, of COMPLEX SEMANTIC INFORMATION. In particular, it will turn out that language users can not, and need not, store all the propositional information of a given discourse in verbal processing. Hence, this information will, at least in part, be REDUCED to the macro-structures as they were discussed above. A certain number of examples of this sort of semantic information reduction have been given. The general property holding for this reduction is that the reduced information must be entailed by the 'full' semantic information of the discourse. In this section, we shall attempt to specify the relationships between the propositional structure of sequences and macro-structures.

3.2

First of all it should be emphasized again that macro-structures are not merely postulated in order to account for cognitive information processing. The hypothesis is that they are an integral part of the meaning of a discourse, and that, therefore, they are to be accounted for in a semantic representation. The basic idea is that the meaning of a sequence is not merely the 'sum' of the propositions underlying the sequence, but that, at another level, we should speak of the meaning of the sequence as a whole, hierarchically ordering the respective meanings of its sentences.

It is a sound principle of explicit semantic theories, however, that the meaning of compound or complex units is to be defined in terms of the meanings of their component units. Both the 'sequential' meaning and the global meaning of a discourse have been represented by an ordered set of propositions. It will be assumed therefore that macro-structures are related to micro-structures – as we may briefly call the semantic structure of the sequence of sentences – by sets of SEMANTIC MAPPINGS. In other words: in order to obtain macro-structures of any sequence we must apply a number of operations. Since, as we saw, a certain amount of more detailed information gets 'lost' during these operations, we may speak of operations of SEMANTIC INFORMATION REDUCTION. On the other hand information is not just 'deleted' in such operations, but also INTEGRATED. That is, a certain number of propositions may be replaced by one (macro-)proposition 'subsuming' the more detailed information at a MORE GLOBAL LEVEL OF REPRESENTATION. It is this macro-proposition which then accounts for the fact that the original sequence of propositions forms a semantic unit RELATIVE TO the level of the macro-proposition.

3.3

The various operations and their specific conditions will be tentatively formulated with respect to the examples discussed earlier in this chapter.

A first general constraint, holding for all rules, is as follows:

[16] For any sequence $\Sigma = \langle p_1, p_2, \ldots, p_n \rangle$ of propositions of a discourse and for any $p_i \in \Sigma$: if there is a proposition $p_j \in \Sigma$, such that p_i is a presupposition of p_j, then p_i may not be deleted by macro-operations.

More particularly [16] may be given in terms of presuppositions holding between topics (macro-structures), such that the rule guarantees that the semantic macro-structure is semantically 'well-formed'. Thus, in our first example [1], we may not omit the information that a (Fairview) is a town, because this is presupposed by further information about the presence of factories, shops, streets, etc. Similarly, at the macro-structural level, this topical proposition may not be deleted because it is a presupposition for the following topics in the story (about the local newspaper).

A first rule of information reduction is, very simply, DELETION: information is simply left out, along the following schema[10] (where → denotes the semantic mapping):

[17] $fx \& gx \to fx$

Example:

[18] town(a) & little(a) → town(a)

The disadvantage of this traditional logical representation is that we cannot read from the formula that 'little' is an ATTRIBUTE of 'town', so that we can not, more specifically, formulate the rule to hold for certain attributes. Note, incidentally, that a need not be little in general, but only relative to the normal size of towns. It is not our aim to provide a sound formal language and logic for attributes, so the traditional notation will have to do. Now, only those propositions may be deleted according to [17] which have an attributive predicate, and not those which have what may be called an 'identifying' or 'conceptual' predicate. The latter predicates identify a thing, assign it to a category of things of a certain kind, defined by a number of essential properties. Attributive predicates will provisionally be characterized as those referring to accidental properties (not holding in all possible worlds/times). Rule [17] may apply to example [18] because the size of the town is an accidental property (it may grow, for example), and because the proposition 'little(a)' is not a presupposition of any other proposition in the sequence, as is specified by constraint [16].

The same rule would apply in our passage to such information as:

[19] the factories are specializing in hand-tools
    Bentonville is a manufacturing town
    Bentonville is thirty miles away

This sort of ACCIDENTAL INFORMATION may be left out without changing the meaning or influencing the interpretation of the subsequent sentences of the discourse.

Note that information deleted by [17] is IRRECOVERABLE, given its macro-structural result. That is, the mappings are unlike syntactic trans-formations such as those in generative-transformational grammar: after semantic deletions of this kind we do not know which propositions have been deleted.

There is another deletion rule, but operating under different conditions. Here the information which is deleted is not 'accidental' as described above, but is CONSTITUTIONAL of a certain concept or frame. That is, it specifies normal or expected causes and consequences of events, reasons and con-sequences of actions, preparatory and auxiliary actions, normal component events, actions or objects, and the 'setting' (time, place, world) of the object, action or event. The schema for this rule would be something like:

[20] $\langle fx \& gx \& hx \rangle \rightarrow gx$
$\quad\quad\quad$ Condition: $gx \;\square\vdash\; \langle fx \& gx \& hx \rangle$

The brackets in the antecedent of operation [20] denote any ordering between the facts (cause, consequence, part of, etc). The condition makes it that in most situations the facts $*fx$[11] and $*hx$ will co-occur with $*gx$. That means that the deleted information is at least INDUCTIVELY RECOVERABLE – which will have its consequences in cognitive processing.
Examples in passage [1] to which operation [20] may apply are:

[21] a has factories
$\quad$ the factories are the source of a's prosperity
$\quad$ the (other) factories are in the neighbouring districts
$\quad$ b (Bentonville) has shops
$\quad$ b has trolley-cars
$\quad$ b's shops are brightly painted
$\quad$ a has shabby houses
$\quad$ etc

These propositions need not be taken up into the macro-structure if there are propositions weakly implying the propositions in [21]. Thus, it is normal that towns have factories, and that if the town is prosperous the factories are one of the causes of prosperity. Similarly, in most normal worlds, towns have shops and streets, and bright paint is a normal sign of prosperity, whereas shabbiness is a normal sign (component) of decline.

A third operation is that of SIMPLE GENERALIZATION. Whereas in the previous operations the information deleted was accidental and con-stitutional ('normal'), respectively, the information deleted in generalizations is essential. Thus, if we generalize from a cat to an animal, we abstract from inherent properties of the cat species. The interesting macro-semantic role of this rule is that several objects or properties of the same superordinate class may be referred to, globally, with the name of the superordinate class: *there were toys lying around* would express a macro-proposition for a sequence like *There was a ball, a doll, a toy-car, ..., lying around*. The schema for this operation would be:

[22] $\langle fx \& gx \rangle \rightarrow hx$
      Condition: $(fx \square \vdash hx) \& (gx \square \vdash hx)$

As for the first rule, the information in this case is irrecoverable.

The last operation is also a form of generalization and also involves essential information, but, as in the second operation, this deleted information denotes essential properties, causes, components, consequents, etc of a higher level fact. That is, the information is not as such deleted but COMBINED or INTEGRATED. Thus, the sequence ⟨*I bought wood, stones and concrete; I laid foundations; I erected walls, I made a roof . . .*⟩ may for example be subsumed under a proposition like 'I built (a house)'. The essential information of the sequence is in that case recoverable, because it is part of the more general concept or frame. The tentative schema for this operation of integration is:

[23] $\langle fx \& gx \rangle \rightarrow hx$
      Condition: $hx \square \vdash \langle fx \& gx \rangle$

Note that all operations satisfy the ENTAILMENT relation. That is, after the application of any operation the resulting macro-propositions are entailed by the micro-structure (*ie* the sequence of sentence-propositions). We now see that the macro-operations are indeed reducing information by several kinds of ABSTRACTION: irrelevant detail, normal properties or constituents, subset specifications, or necessary properties and constituents are not referred to by the macro-propositions. In other words: the operations define what is RELATIVELY IMPORTANT in a passage. On the one hand this importance is relative to information occurring in the same sequence, and on the other hand this importance is a property of a (macro-)proposition relative to the propositions of the original sequence, *ie* of the WHOLE with respect to the PARTS. Note also that the first and the second rule are SELECTIVE, whereas the third and the fourth rule are CONSTRUCTIVE. The selective operations are of the deleting type, whereas the constructive operations are of the substituting type.

The macro-rules formulated above are RECURSIVE: whenever there is a sequence of propositions satisfying the conditions a new macro-structure at a more general level will be formed. This means that a text may have several LEVELS OF MACRO-STRUCTURE $m_1, m_2, \ldots, m_n$, where m_n is the 'general' macro-structure of the text as a whole (in a macro-structurally non-ambiguous text). It has already been emphasized that m_n must be the LEAST GENERAL macro-proposition, in order to guarantee enough specific 'content' in a macro-structure. That is, the component macro-propositions in m_n are not themselves, individually, further generalized. For example, from the proposition 'a town is declining' we do not generalize to 'something is declining' or 'something has some property'. Constraint [16] in this case will guarantee that no macro-propositions are deleted or generalized which are presuppositions of other macro-propositions at the same level. Furthermore, the operations will apply only if the input is at least two propositions (see note 5 below).

3.4

A certain number of restrictive remarks should be added to the principles of information reduction formulated above.

First of all, at this moment it cannot be proved that the various operations are SUFFICIENT for an adequate account of semantic information reduction in grammar (and/or cognition). At the same time it may turn out that the rules are too POWERFUL, and that further constraints must be supplied.

Secondly, it should be emphasized that the formation of macro-structures, although theoretically based on a relation of entailment and thus having a 'deductive' nature, may in fact often have an INDUCTIVE nature. It may be the case, for example, that a macro-proposition ψ is entailed by the sequence $\langle \varphi_1, \varphi_2, \varphi_3 \rangle$, but that, eg, only a sequence $\langle \varphi_1, \varphi_3 \rangle$ is expressed in the discourse, which, as such, does not entail ψ. Now, in case proposition φ_2 is a normal consequence of φ_1, or a normal condition or presupposition of φ_3, we may inductively INFER φ_2 from $\langle \varphi_1, \varphi_3 \rangle$, and hence also $\langle \varphi_1, \varphi_2, \varphi_3 \rangle$ such that the macro-proposition ψ can be constructed. This inductive procedure is normal in all sorts of information processing: we make hypothetical con- clusions with partial evidence. At the level of perception and (inter-)action we may observe somebody building walls, etc and conclude he is building a house even if we do not yet see him making a roof for example. The same holds in the actual interpretation of discourse: we do not need all essential components of a concept or frame in order to infer the general concept.

A third restriction pertains to the generality of the proposed principles. Although it may be maintained that they are general principles of semantic information reduction, information reduction and hence macro-structure formation may be different for various TYPES OF DISCOURSE. In more concrete terms: what is 'important' information in one discourse or con- versation may be less important for other types of discourse. It may be assumed that in narrative discourse, for example, event and action de- scriptions are more important (with respect to macro-structures) than state descriptions. This means that the macro-structure of a narrative should also contain several action/event descriptions and not merely a description of the initial and/or final state of an episode. As we shall see below, narratives also have narrative 'macro-structures'. It will therefore be necessary to provide for the possibility that the various discourse types each have their own constraints in the application of the principles, even if the principles themselves are type-independent.

Finally, the principles are not only general, but also 'ideal' and theoretical. They do not indicate how individual language users will in fact construct macro-structures from a given discourse. Due to various cognitive factors, the actually constructed cognitive macro-structures may be different for different language users, or different for the same language user in different pragmatic contexts or social situations. Again the actual APPLICATION of the rules may be variable (within certain bounds) but the rules themselves are general (grammatical) and thus may only provide theoretical predictions of actual behaviour or processing. We here again touch upon more general methodological problems of psycho-linguistics, the empirical nature of grammatical theories and their relation to cognitive models.

4 Macro-structures and the conditions of connection and coherence

4.1

In previous chapters we have discussed a set of conditions determining the linear connection and coherence of pairs and sequences of propositions. One of the elements in the formal semantics of connectives in natural languages, however, remained undefined, viz the notion TOPIC OF CONVERSATION. It was argued that for two propositions to be connectible with a connective the facts denoted by these propositions must be related. This relation should hold in the same possible world or situation, or in otherwise related or accessible worlds. At the same time it was pointed out that this relation between facts is not a sufficient condition of natural connection: propositions are connected only with respect to a topic of conversation. In this chapter this notion has been treated in more detail, and we now must see in what ways topics of conversation/discourse, *ie* macro-structures, really determine linear connection, and the coherence of sequences.

4.2

In order to illustrate our hypothesis we may construct the following example of a compound sentence:

[24] The houses in the town were shabby, and a lot of unemployed people were hanging around at street corners.

Now, the two main clauses can be said to be connected first of all because of the identity of worlds or situations or of certain individuals ('town'), but it is further required that the facts referred to be related. Such a relation between the shabbiness of houses and unemployment and its consequences does not exist, at least not in a direct way. Still, sentence [24] is perfectly acceptable. We therefore will have to assume that the clauses are connected by the topic of conversation of the particular passage, viz 'The town was declining'. In that case, both propositions are probable consequences of the macro-structure proposition. To use other terms: they both belong to the same frame, viz that of economic (urban) decline.

On the other hand, the sentence

[25] John was born in Manchester, and we are going to the beach.

will be disconnected if there is no macro-proposition defining a topic of conversation with respect to which both are relevant, whereas

[26] John was born in Manchester, and he went to primary school in Birmingham.

[27] John was born in Manchester, but his parents were from Scotland.

are acceptably connected by a superordinate topic like 'the major events of John's life'.

4.3

Similar remarks may be made about the coherence of a sequence of sentences in general. We have seen that referential identity, both of individual objects or of properties, or identity or other relations between worlds, are not sufficient to establish coherence. Thus, the following sequence appears unacceptable in most contexts, although there are semantic relations between its underlying propositions:

[28] I bought this typewriter in New York. New York is a large city in the USA. Large cities often have serious financial problems . . .

Sequences of this type may perhaps be said to be linearly coherent, but at another level of comprehension they do not make sense owing to the lack of a specific topic of conversation. In [28] the topic of conversation must at least contain the concept of a typewriter, or of buying typewriters, but such a topic does not contain information about large cities in the world or specific financial issues.

On the other hand, a passage such as that about Fairview at the beginning of this chapter is linearly coherent also because it has a macro-structure. In fact, such a macro-structure even allows subsequent sentences to be semantically unrelated if both are related to the same macro-structure.

5 Linguistic evidence for macro-structures

5.1

Some brief remarks are necessary about the status of the LINGUISTIC evidence for our hypothesis that, at the semantic level, the coherence of discourse is determined also by macro-structures.

Often the question of evidence for certain rules, categories or levels of description is formulated in terms of certain linguistic 'forms', such as properties of morpho-phonological or syntactic structures of sentences. That is, for example, semantic or pragmatic differentiations should only be made in a theoretical framework if such differentiations can be or are regularly and conventionally 'expressed'. Conversely, in a FUNCTIONAL view of language, it is assumed that systematic morpho-phonological and syntactic differences correspond to semantic and pragmatic differences.

Within the perspective of this chapter it might therefore be asked whether macro-structures have direct linguistic manifestations. If not, such structures might be of interest only in a cognitive account of information processing, for example.

Besides the evidence drawn from linguistic 'form', however, we should also admit evidence from implicit or explicit linguistic knowledge (intuition) of language users, and the actual USE which is made of language in production-interpretation processes. To this kind of evidence belong the specific re-actions to the sequences lacking a macro-structure: "What are you talking about?", "You are all mixed up!", "That does not make sense", etc. Such reactions are typical for specific SEMANTIC deficiencies of the utterance as they also appear in judgements about semantically less acceptable, *ie* less interpretable, sentences. Hence the first sort of empirical evidence we have is the trivial fact that the set of sequences which do not have macro-structures is normally unacceptable in communicative contexts.

5.2

The other sort of evidence for semantic properties of utterances is, as was indicated above, what 'shows' in the UTTERANCE itself, viz in intonation, stress, syntactic structure and lexical units. Sentences and clauses thus express propositions and properties of propositions, *eg* certain relations between arguments, predicates, modal operators, etc. Macro-structures, however, are much less directly related to actual sentences because they are higher level properties of sequences of propositions. A certain number of surface structure phenomena will however now be listed which seem to indicate the presence of macro-structures.

In the passages we have been analysing it occurred that macro-propositions are sometimes directly expressed, viz as what we called TOPICAL SENTENCES, often at the beginning or at the end of a passage. The cognitive function of such sentences is obvious: they directly provide the macro-structure of a certain passage instead of leaving the construction of the macro-structure to the hearer/reader, *ie* they facilitate comprehension. Such sentences also have specific grammatical properties however. As we said they typically occur at the beginning or at the end of a passage. Moreover, they do not seem to directly belong to the sequence of propositions, as in the case of the first or the last member. Such sentences cannot be embedded in neighbouring sentences, and cannot be connected with them by even the most general connective *and:*

[29] Fairview was dying and in the past it had been a go-ahead, prosperous little town (. . .)

A sentence like [29] is unacceptable because the propositions following the first sentence/proposition are specifications of this more general content. It follows that sentences expressing macro-propositions have a specific gram-matical status.

A second piece of evidence has already been mentioned before: if macro-structures of passages are to be constructed as propositions, we may expect these propositions also to be CONNECTED. Such macro-connections may indeed be expressed by natural connectives like *furthermore, but, however, so,* etc. In [12] we saw that *but* does not connect the sentence *But there was still one small spark of life to be found in Fairview* with the previous sentence, but with the macro-proposition underlying the first passage ('Fairview was dying'). In fact this *but* connects the first passage with the whole second passage, *ie* a macro-structure with a macro-structure.

The third way in which macro-structures appear in linguistic structure is through REFERENCE: we may use pro-forms and demonstratives to denote facts referred to earlier only by a macro-structural proposition, as in:

[30] Fairview was defeated. You could see *it* in the shabby houses (. . .)

where this proposition is previously expressed, but also in those cases where this is not the case and where no particular referent would be established without a macro-structure:

[31] He would only have to stretch out his hand and she would put hers in his willingly (. . .) She knew that the moment of meeting had done something to both of them (. . .)

It had never happened to her before. She had been in love several times (. . .).

The pronoun *it* apparently refers to the fact that she (Clare Russell) had fallen in love, which is indeed the macro-proposition inductively entailed by the previous passage: the sentences of that passage clearly express the conventional information of the FALLING IN LOVE-frame. There is no word, proposition or sentence with which *it* could be co-referential in the previous passage, and the hypothesis that it must be some sort of 'implicit' (entailed) information is confirmed by the next sentence *She had been in love several times* which in this context presupposes that she is or might be in love now, or at least that 'being in love' is now the topic of conversation. Besides the pronoun we therefore also may have PRESUPPOSITIONS which are only macro-structurally present in the text.

In fact, what may be expressed by a pronoun may also be expressed by a noun phrase with a 'full' noun. In that case we would expect the noun phrase to be DEFINITE, even if there has not been a co-referential expression in the previous part of the discourse. Take for example the following example:

[32] A man in a fast car stopped before the bank. He quickly got out and ran into the bank. He drew a pistol and shouted to the cashier to hand him the money in her desk (. . .) *The* hold-up did not last longer than three minutes.

The definite article in the last sentence can only be explained if we assume that the previous passage contains an argument or predicate which is co-referential with respect to the same event as the word *hold-up*.

We see that not only full macro-propositions may be expressed in the discourse itself, but also parts of it, viz the macro-structural predicates. This means that there is also LEXICAL evidence for the existence of macro-structures, viz in the expression of the concept containing the concepts in the rest of the passage, at least in some sort of relational structure (frame: 'x requires money', etc).

This is probably the most conspicuous and straightforward way macro-structures are expressed: they determine for a discourse or part of it the range of possible CONCEPTS which may be used and thus are a global constraint on lexical insertion. Thus, for instance, the HOLD-UP-frame will not usually contain the concept of 'daisy', whereas the LOVE-frame will not usually contain the 'North Pole' or the 'elephant' concepts. Those concepts which do not belong to the frames initiated by the macro-structure must then belong to frames initiated by concepts belonging to the macro-structure frames. That is, there must always be an INDIRECT link with the macro-structural proposition and its concepts.[12]

Finally, there may be macro-structurally determined identity of time, place or modality. A passage giving a narrative will normally be in the past tense, or we may give part of our personal plans in a counterfactual mode or we make guesses which are pertaining to facts which are only probable. The modal nature in such cases may belong to the sequence as a whole, and need not always be expressed in each sentence of the sequence, *eg* when I tell about what I dreamt. Besides MODAL OPERATORS we also have specific PREDICATES (nouns, verbs) determining the possible world in which a whole sequence must be interpreted, *eg* in the mentioned dream example. It may be assumed that such predicates and operators have macro-structural propositions as their 'scope'. The macro-structural proposition may in that case also be referred to by a pro-form, as in:

[33] I dreamt it.
[34] That is impossible.

That in [34] may refer to one fact, denoted by a previously expressed proposition, but also to a more global fact, expressed by a whole passage (of which each of the propositions, taken alone, might have been possible).

5.3

We have enumerated some strictly linguistic indicators of propositional information entailed in the meaning representation of discourses, but not made explicit: specific topical sentences, pro-forms for macro-propositions and predicates from such propositions, the use of connectives between macro-propositions, definite articles without explicit co-referential ante-cedents, macro-structural presuppositions of sentences, and the general constraints on the conceptual structure and the mode/modality, including time/tense, of passages of a discourse.

Besides these types of syntactico-semantic evidence there are various sorts of MORPHO-PHONOLOGICAL and GRAPHICAL indications of macro-structural organization of discourse. First of all, in writing, we have rules for PARAGRAPH indentation which have a macro-structural nature: they mark sequences which somehow 'belong together', *ie* which belong to the same topic. A new paragraph thus indicates (sub-)topic change. In spoken language we have pauses, intonation and specific particles like 'now', 'well', etc to indicate such paragraphs. Other languages have specific morphemes in order to mark beginnings and endings of stretches of discourse which are to be theoretically defined in terms of semantic macro-structures (see note 8). Finally, there are PRAGMATIC properties of communication requiring macro-structures: speech acts may have a whole sequence as their scope (see Chapter 9).

6 Macro-structures and discourse types
6.1

In principle, the macro-structures discussed thus far characterize any discourse of natural language. They were taken as general properties of complex semantic structures and as principles of semantic information reduction.

Macro-structures may in turn be subject to certain rules and constraints varying for different TYPES OF DISCOURSE. For example, a macro-structural proposition may be assigned to a certain CATEGORY representing a specific FUNCTION in the discourse. These categories and functions, although based on linguistic (semantic) macro-structures, do not themselves belong to linguistic theory or grammar proper, but are to be defined within the framework of a more general THEORY OF DISCOURSE or subtheories, like the theory of narrative, the theory of argumentation, of the theory of propaganda, belonging to various disciplines, eg poetics, rhetoric, philosophy or the social sciences. Such theories would require separate monographs and we therefore may only briefly discuss the relation with linguistic macro-structures as they are treated in this book.

6.2

The first passage of the crime story analysed above could be assigned a macro-structure like 'A town, Fairview, is declining owing to competition from another town, Bentonville'. In the particular discourse, a specific type of NARRATIVE, such a proposition may have a function within the discourse as a whole, or rather within the NARRATIVE STRUCTURE[13] as a whole (the discourse may express several narrative structures). For instance, the town Fairview may become the setting of a certain number of events and actions. In a narrative, then, we may postulate a specific category subsuming those elements indicating time, place or other circumstances of a certain episode, eg the theoretical category SETTING. The specific function of such a category would also be, for example, the introduction of the characters of the story. In our example, we thus witness the introduction of Clare Russell, after the introduction of the local newspaper. Time, place and individuals are at the same time assigned one or several specific and identifying properties, eg the decline of Fairview, the spark of life in the newspaper and the smartness of Clare Russell. These properties are CONDITIONS for certain events and actions described later in the discourse.

Note that the individual sentences or propositions do not, as such, have this narrative function, but only the macro-structural proposition entailed by a sequence of propositions. It is possible in that case that the sequence determining a macro-proposition with such a specific narrative function is DISCONTINUOUS. Characterizing properties of times, places, backgrounds, characters, etc may be given throughout the whole story, thus either conditioning or explaining certain actions and events.

In the same way the structural analysis of narrative has postulated categories or functions such as COMPLICATION and RESOLUTION defining the EPISODE of the story, which may be followed by an EVALUATION and a MORAL. Similarly, in fairy tales or other simple narratives, we may have more specific 'semantic' functions like *arrival of the hero*, *departure of the hero*, *trial of the hero*, *reward*, etc. These are proper macro-categories because they dominate sequences of propositions of the narrative discourse, or rather the macro-proposition related to such a sequence.

The narrative rules and categories, abstractly defining the narrative expressed by the discourse (or by some other semiotic language, *eg* pictures), may be RECURSIVE. Narratives may be embedded under various categories of a higher level narrative. In the SETTING we may have the story about Fairview's decline or about Clare Russell's career. This narrative grammar will not be further specified here. What matters are its relationships to the semantic structure of the discourse.

Certain narrative categories have specific constraints on their macro-structural basis. A SETTING in a narrative structure will for example be 'expressed' by a state description or a process description, like 'Fairview is dying', 'There is still a small spark of life'. On the other hand, a COMPLICATION requires a sequence of propositions together interpreted as an event description, whereas the RESOLUTION must at least 'contain' an action description. It must be stressed that these constraints pertain to macro-structures, because in the actual sequences of the discourse we may well have state descriptions in the COMPLICATION or RESOLUTION parts. The same holds, in a more particular way, for narrative 'content' categories like ARRIVAL, DEPARTURE or TRIAL. The macro-rules defined above are able to explicitly link the sequence of sentences of a story with these particular narrative categories or functions.

Together with the macro-structures on which they are based the narrative categories determine the overall structure of the discourse. Without the narrative categories we could produce a linguistically acceptable, *ie* an interpretable discourse, but such a discourse would have no 'point'. In our example, we could in that case have a discourse which only gives a detailed description of the decline of Fairview, the exact causes and consequences, and so on, and the story would no longer be a narrative but some sort of socio-economic report. We see that the type of categories and rules determining the overall organization of a discourse at the same time identify the TYPE of discourse involved. They enable us to differentiate between a

story and a political article in the newspaper, between an everyday conversation about the weather and an advertisement. Note that the categories
involved are not only STRUCTURAL ('syntactical') – determining the linear
and hierarchical ordering of macro-structures of a discourse – but also
CONCEPTUAL ('semantic'): they stipulate what the discourse is about (actions
of heroes, world politics, the weather or certain products).

6.3
The remarks made about a well-known type of discourse, the story, could be
extended for other discourse types. All sorts of argumentative discourses
have global categories like PREMISES and CONCLUSION, possibly with additional subcategories like WARRANT or CONDITION. Psychological articles
have a linear structure like INTRODUCTION-THEORY/PROBLEM-EXPERIMENT-
COMMENT/CONCLUSION, with the subcategories DESIGN, METHODS,
MATERIAL, RESULTS within the EXPERIMENT category.[14] Generally, scientific discourse may be assigned a global structure like INTRODUCTION-
PROBLEM-SOLUTION-CONCLUSION with embedded argumentative structures
of various kinds. It is the task of a general theory of discourse to classify and
define such categories, rules and their specific textual functions. If discourse
types were merely differentiated according to different semantic content
(topic), we would have a potentially infinite number of discourse types. It is
more interesting to elaborate a more abstract theory which relates structural
categories to conceptual categories. The structure of an argument, for
example, should be assigned independently of whether it is about engineer-
ing, linguistics or child-care.

Finally, such a theory would also have to include rules of a more
PRAGMATIC kind, pertaining to the specific FUNCTIONS of discourse types in
certain contexts and social situations. The intentions, knowledge, beliefs and
preferences of speakers and hearers are different when they tell stories from
when they try to convince each other with an argument. This will be a topic in
Part II.

7 The cognitive basis of macro-structures
7.1
Finally, some brief remarks are necessary about the COGNITIVE BASIS of
linguistic (and non-linguistic) macro-structures, ie about the role macro-
structures play in the production and comprehension of discourse. Research
in this domain has just begun, but a certain number of interesting provisional
conclusions may already be made.[15]

Whereas cognitive psychology and psycho-linguistics have addressed
themselves first to the processing of words and phrases and of syntactic and
semantic structures of sentences, the question now arises: what specific
models should be postulated for the processing of discourse and, more in
general, of COMPLEX INFORMATION.

For discourses, this means an account of how we understand them, which information from the discourse is stored, how this information is organized in memory, and how it is retrievable for different tasks, such as recognition, recall, problem solving, inference and action.

7.2

Whatever the precise properties of these processes may be, there are a certain number of constraints which are beyond doubt typical for any sort of complex information processing.

First of all, as is the case for (longer) sentences, surface structures (morpho-syntactic structures) are only used in order to organize semantic (*eg* propositional) information. Most of the surface structure is therefore stored only in short-term memory and soon forgotten, whereas only semantic information may be processed such that it can be stored in long-term memory.[16] There are a number of exceptions in which surface information, *eg* of a stylistic kind, may also be stored. There is little insight into the conditions of this kind of (episodic) memory, however, and they will not be discussed here.[17]

The major problem at issue for discourse is however whether all propositions are stored in memory. This is clearly not the case when we look at free recalls of discourses of more than about 200 words.[18] That is, beyond a certain threshold a language user hearing or reading a discourse can no longer retrievably store all the semantic information of the discourse as a set or sequence of propositions. Still, in most cases, even for very complex discourses like novels, the reader still knows what the discourse is about, and still is able to establish coherence relations with the previous part of the discourse. It follows that these relations cannot possibly be established with all previous propositions individually, but must be based on information which can easily be stored and which is necessary and sufficient for the interpretation of the rest of the discourse. Similarly, having interpreted the whole discourse, structures must be available for the accomplishment of recognition, recall or problem solving tasks.

7.3

It may be assumed, then, that the processes and tasks mentioned above are to be accounted for in terms of macro-structures. That is, the amount of information presented must somehow be REDUCED. This reduction has been theoretically reconstructed by the rules given above. In a cognitive process model based on that theory we therefore would postulate processes in which certain propositions are deleted and *n*-tuples of propositions replaced by other propositions. The operations would maintain the semantic 'core' of a certain passage by constructing, during input, a macro-proposition representing the most 'important' information of that passage. As was specified above, this information would at the same time provide the necessary presuppositions for the interpretation of subsequent sentences and sequences.

In ACTUAL PROCESSING these operations are however HYPOTHETICAL or PROBABILISTIC: during input and comprehension of a certain sentence and underlying propositions the language user tentatively constructs the macro-proposition which most likely dominates the proposition in question. This hypothesis may be confirmed or refuted by the rest of the discourse. In case of refutation another macro-proposition is constructed.

We have seen already that the discourse itself will often give certain CLUES for such a hypothetical process of macro-structure formation, *eg* by the expression of macro-propositions or macro-predicates.

What is stored in memory, then, is at least the macro-structure of the discourse. Or rather, the highest levels of macro-structures constructed of the discourse. Depending on the length and the complexity of the discourse most individual propositions of the discourse will in that case no longer be directly retrievable. The rules we have formulated however will in some cases make certain types of detailed information RETRIEVABLE BY INFERENCE. If we remember that somebody built a house, we might remember by specification of components of the associated frame, that he made walls and a roof. And remembering that a town was declining we may by probable inference conjecture that the shops, streets and houses were shabby or dirty. If these hypotheses are correct, it follows that macro-structures not only enable the comprehension of highly complex information during input, but at the same time ORGANIZE the information in memory, thus at the same time serving as retrieval cues for more detailed information weakly entailed by it.

7.4

Experiments have shown that these assumptions are indeed correct. Subjects reproducing a story will produce a discourse which mainly contains macro-propositions. In immediate recall more detailed information is still connected with this macro-structure, but after several weeks the reproduction does not contain much more than the macro-structure or fragments of macro-structure.

It is interesting to notice that when subjects are requested to give a SUMMARY of a discourse, the structure of this summary is very close to that of a delayed recall protocol. That is, a summary is a type of discourse providing (a personal variant of) the macro-structure of the discourse it summarizes. Just as topic sentences may directly express a (sub)topic of a passage, the summary will express the general macro-structure of the discourse as a whole. This assumption provides us with an EMPIRICAL decision procedure for judgements about the textual character of discourses. If a sequence of sentences cannot be summarized it is likely that it does not have a macro-structure so that the sequence does not have discourse character. In fact, sequences which do not have a macro-structure of any kind are much less well recalled than discourses: it is easy to reproduce the gist of a story, or even a full story if it is not too long, but very difficult to reproduce a set of unrelated sentences. Such insights are familiar from experiments with word lists and with sentences having, or not having, syntactic and semantic structures.

7.5

It should be added that comprehension, organization and recall of complex information not only depends on linguistic rules of semantic information reduction, but also on rules and categories determining the global organization of the particular kind of discourse. In our example, not only a macro-proposition like 'Fairview/a town is declining' is constructed – or, as in our case, taken from the discourse as the macro-proposition – but at the same time this information is further organized according to NARRATIVE rules and such categories as SETTING. The narrative structure will then in the same way determine comprehension and organization in memory, and hence recall; more easily so if this structure is closer to conventional narrative structures.[19] In recall, the elementary categories/rules for the narrative discourse are already present (as general rules of story production) and need only be 'filled in' with the macro-structural content, which in turn may retrieve more detailed information.

In all these processes there are very complicated sets of specific factors determining comprehension, organization and recall, *eg* the specific FAMILIARITY of the topics, the structural COMPLEXITY of the linguistic or non-linguistic overall structure of the discourse, cognitive and PERSONAL properties of the subjects, the kind of TASKS and task CONTEXTS (cues, motivation, etc) involved, DELAYS in reproduction, the presence of (similar) semantic or narrative structures and the experience of processing them, etc. These aspects of processing cannot be dealt with here.

7.6

The main point to be made here is that macro-structure formation in complex discourse is a necessary property of cognitive information processing. Large amounts of detailed information must be reduced and organized so as to remain available for retrieval in recall, in integration of incoming information, and in problem-solving.

The same, of course, holds true for the processing of all sorts of other information about the world, *eg* in PERCEPTION and ACTION. Although we observe a great number of facts every day, only some of them are important for our permanent knowledge and for future action. Much in the same way as in discourse comprehension, our interpretation of the world requires the deletion of many elements (propositions and/or images) of information, the integration of such elements into higher level elements, and generalization of an inductive kind. Little is known about this type of complex information processing but it may be assumed that the principles underlying it also determine the rules and categories of discourse processing.

Note, incidentally, that our remarks hold not only for comprehension/interpretation of discourse, but also for the PRODUCTION of complex discourse. In order to be able to execute the formidable task of keeping a discourse coherent, to produce sentences expressing propositions contributing to a macro-proposition and satisfying certain narrative rules, the speaker must already have a first 'sketch' or 'schema' or 'plan' available for the global semantic organization of his discourse.[20] That is, he will begin with the construction of a (first) macro-structure, at least for the beginning of the text. At later stages of production this macro-structure may be corrected or replaced by another macro-structure. The processes involved here are of course different in spontaneous everyday conversation, in public speeches, in novel writing or newspaper article production, but the same general principles are necessary for monitoring the production of any kind of complex information.

The same again holds for other cognitive tasks, *eg* in the planning and execution of ACTION and INTERACTION, and hence for speech acts as we will see below. Research on such complicated cognitive problems as complex action planning/execution, and their relationships to language and visual perception is only in its first stages. This chapter has tried to show that such tasks cannot possibly be accounted for at the level of linear processing of micro-information, but that hierarchical rules and categories and the formation of macro-structures are necessary. A sound theory of macro-structures, as now becomes obvious, has a linguistic (grammatical) component that accounts for notions like topic and in general for semantic relations in discourse; it has other components of a theory of discourse (*eg* theory of narrative) and a general cognitive basis that accounts for macro-processing in language production/comprehension, perception, action, problem-solving and other human abilities.

7.7

Some final remarks are in order about the notion of FRAME, a theoretical primitive, cited as one explanatory component of linear and global coherence. The concept, which has been coined in recent work in artificial intelligence, belongs to cognitive theory.[21] It denotes a conceptual structure in semantic memory and represents a part of our knowledge of the world. In this respect a frame is an ORGANIZATIONAL PRINCIPLE, relating a number of concepts which by CONVENTION and EXPERIENCE somehow form a 'unit' which may be actualized in various cognitive tasks, such as language production and comprehension, perception, action and problem solving. Thus, in a RESTAURANT-frame would be organized the conventional, *ie* general but culture dependent, knowledge that a restaurant is a building or place where one can eat publicly, where food is either ordered from a waiter/waitress or taken at a counter, etc. That is, a frame organizes knowledge about certain properties of objects, courses of event and action, which TYPICALLY belong together. We have seen that propositional knowledge from frames is necessary to establish the explicit coherence between sentences of a discourse, under the assumption that propositions belonging to a frame, and hence having a more general nature, need not be expressed in the discourse. This explains among other things that in a sentence like *We went to a restaurant, but the waitress was too busy to take our order immediately*, the noun phrase *the waitress* may be definite although no waitress need have been referred to by previous expressions in the discourse.

Similarly, such frames provide knowledge about normal conditions, components and consequences of states, events and actions, all of which are necessary in the operation of MACRO-RULES.

Due to their general conceptual nature, frames may have VARIABLE INSTANTIATIONS, which allows the application or use of frames in concrete cognitive contexts: there are many ways to 'execute' the action of going to and eating in a restaurant, but they will all belong to, or be subsumed by, the same RESTAURANT-frame. Similarly, in perception we will recognize a table or some specific table, whatever the visual transformations of the table due to varying positions.

It may be assumed that frames themselves are also organized in a HIERARCHICAL way. That is, some information seems to be essential for the frame, other information more or less specific and accidental. Thus, it seems essential for a shop to be a public place, usually in a building, where one can buy something, but less crucial whether there are baskets for self-service. Thus it seems that the higher-level information of the frame will always be actualized, whereas the lower-level information will only be actualized if needed for specific tasks. Besides the frame-structure itself, we thus need rules or principles determining the USE of frames in actual cognitive behaviour. Since frames may be represented as sets or rather as ordered sequences of propositions, which may be highly complex, we surmise that they also have a MACRO-STRUCTURE, in which the level and importance of the information contained are defined.

Although there is little theoretical and experimental insight into the precise status, structure and use of frames, it may be concluded that they have hierarchical (macro-)structure, that they organize conventional and typical knowledge, that this knowledge pertains both to states (properties) and to actions and events, *ie* to procedures which are goal oriented, that they have an essential and a probabilistic (inductive) component, in which variables (or variable terminals) occur as 'slots' to be filled in different cognitive contexts.

For a linguist it might be tempting to ask how such frames differ from the conceptual knowledge of a LEXICON of the language, a question which for the psychologist is less relevant since there seems no cognitive/behavioural difference between knowledge of the language and knowledge of the world. It might be proposed, though, that the top-level, essential information of frames, is the conceptual information associated with the lexically expressed concepts of a language.

The analyses here and in the foregoing chapters should make it plain that a clear distinction between general MEANING POSTULATES of the language and FRAME INFORMATION is hard to make. Nevertheless, in semantic theory formation, we may abstract from the variable or ad hoc properties of the actual representation, use, formation and transformation of frames, and postulate a set F of frames $f_1, f_2, \ldots$, each consisting of an ordered sequence of propositions, on which macro-rules may operate. Sentences, sequences of sentences and discourse, then, would not only be interpreted, FORMALLY, with respect to a model structure (or sequences of model structures) containing sets of possible worlds, individuals and possibly properties and relations, but also a set of frames, of which a specific frame f_0 is the actual frame in the actual context of speech.

Given the MONEY-frame, for instance, the sentence *I went to the bank* would be assigned a non-ambiguous intensional meaning and extensional reference. On the set *F* of frames we would further need a BINARY OPERATION which would allow us to CHANGE to or initiate ('actualize' in cognitive terms) another frame, similar to our change operator for topics of discourse. Note, however, the difference between frames and topics (macro-structures): frames are general and conventional, topics are particular for a specific discourse or conversation.

The point of introducing frames into model structures[22] is that the interpretation of sentences would no longer be relative only to the sequence of previous sentences of a discourse, but also relative to the set of propositions of a particular frame. The previous sentences, then, would denote what actually was the case, the frame information would denote what will normally or could possibly be the case. We have seen that a convincing semantics of discourse needs both components in order to explicate the notions of linear and global coherence. It does so, however, only by formulating abstract semantic constructs, rules and conditions, leaving to pragmatics and cognitive psychology the specification of the communicative intentions, specific processing and memory structures.

Notes

1 The notion of macro-structure as it relates to the structure of discourse was first introduced (briefly) in Bierwisch (1965*b*) – with respect to the plot of a story – and has since then been treated in literary theory and various attempts at constructing text grammars (see, *eg*, van Dijk, 1971*a*, 1971*b*, 1972*a*, 1972*b*, 1973*c*).Whereas of course literary theorists are, by the nature of the phenomena they describe, viz structures of literary discourse, interested in macro-structures, there has been little interest in linguistics for an analysis of the linguistic (semantic) properties of macro-structures of discourse. Below we will refer to recent developments in cognitive psychology and artificial intelligence. It is clear from this remark that a theory of macro-structures is still very much in its first tentative stages, even more than a theory of connection and coherence at the sequential (linear, local) level.

2 For further details about individual variables, constants and quantification over events, see Reichenbach (1947), Davidson (1967) and Bartsch (1972) among others. In our notation in [3], which is ad hoc – no precise semantics is given, nor tenses, nor specific connectives, etc – [*decline* (a)](f) would read 'the fact *f* has the property that *a* declines', for instance. Note that we have also used constants (*a, b, c, . . .*) instead of bound variables, in order to avoid problems with *eg* the adequate logical representation of indefinite articles.

3 This definition is still far from perfect and does not make explicit all the intuitive notions we are trying to capture under the concept of a 'topic of discourse'. Thus, several formal requirements should be met in order to guarantee that the sequences

are ordered, not overlapping, that there are no gaps, etc. Further the notion of entailment for sequences of propositions should be made explicit.

4 Just as for the definition given in [10] it should be assumed that there actually IS an immediate superconcept, and hence a topical proposition for a sequence of propositions. Provisionally we take the rather strong view that if that is not the case, the particular passage does not have a 'global meaning' or topic of discourse.

5 Although this possibility must be left open, because there is no reason why a one-sentence discourse should not have a macro-structure, we may later require the macro-rules to operate non-trivially only on sequences where $n \geq 2$.

6 Just as sentences may be AMBIGUOUS, so may discourses, also at the macro-level. In that case we could have several, alternative (highest) macro-propositions for a given discourse. This does not mean that in actual language use and cognition a discourse with one theoretical macro-structure could not be assigned different topics by different language users, depending on a number of factors (knowledge, interests, etc) to be discussed briefly below. Similarly, a theoretically ambiguous discourse, at the macro-level, may be unambiguous in context.

7 This story has been analysed in detail for the cognitive experiments on discourse recall and summarizing by van Dijk (1975c), Kintsch and van Dijk (1975), van Dijk and Kintsch (1977) and Kintsch (1976) – see below for some results. The text of the story is from Giovanni Boccaccio, *The Decameron* (ed and trans G. H. McWilliam, Penguin Books, Harmondsworth, 1972, *pp* 136–41).

8 This may be one of the semantic conditions determining the conventional use of paragraphs in written discourse or similar units (marked by specific pauses, intonation or morphemes) in spoken discourse. The unit of the paragraph in discourse has not been given special attention in this book. For recent work in this area, see the work done by Longacre and his associates (*eg* Longacre, 1970).

9 See for instance the work on conversation done by the ethnomethodologists mentioned in Chapter 1, note 17.

10 For a more precise formulation and for further discussion of these macro-rules, see van Dijk (1976a).

11 By *fa we denote the fact which is the value (in some w_i) of the expression *fa*. Hence $*fa = V(fa, w_i)$.

12 At this point the condition may become too powerful, however, because there are no (linguistic) THEORETICAL limits on these indirect semantic relations. The additional constraints to be formulated, then, are cognitive: the search for a possible link between concepts in related propositions must be feasible (either under general conditions on distance or under ad hoc personal links between concepts).

13 See note 16, Chapter 1.

14 For a detailed macro-analysis of a scientific discourse (viz a paper on social psychology), see van Dijk (1976b) and forthcoming work by Kintsch and van Dijk.

15 Recent work in cognitive psychology and artificial intelligence about processing and memory representation of discourse goes back to Bartlett's seminal research (Bartlett, 1932). From the large number of papers and monographs now being published we may mention (also for further references): Kintsch (1974), Meyer (1975), Thorndyke (1975), Freedle and Carroll, eds (1972), Crothers (1975), Carpenter and Just, eds (1977), van Dijk (1975c, 1976a), Kintsch and van Dijk (1975), van Dijk and Kintsch (1977), Kintsch (1976), Rumelhart (1975), Barnard (1974), Charniak (1972), Schank (1975).

16 See the various chapters in Tulving and Donaldson, eds (1972), Kintsch (1974), Norman and Rumelhart, eds (1975), Bobrow and Collins, eds (1975) for empirical evidence and theoretical models for this assumption.

17 See Janice Keenan (1975).

18 See van Dijk (1975c), van Dijk and Kintsch (1975), Kintsch and van Dijk (1977).

19 Thus, Kintsch (1976) found that American Indian stories, which have a narrative

structure which is different from that of our conventional 'Western' stories, are harder to recall for (non-Indian) subjects than the traditional Boccaccio stories. This may also be one of the reasons why Bartlett (1932) found that so much was lost in the recall of such Indian stories, especially those elements which are unfamiliar. See also Paul (1959), who replicated the Bartlett experiments and focused on personal differences of 'cognitive style' in recall and on the effect of familiarity of the topic of the discourse.

20 This insight for sentence comprehension and for 'higher' cognitive tasks in general has been elaborated especially by Miller, Galanter and Pribram (1960).

21 As was remarked earlier, the notion of frame has been studied frequently since Minsky (1975). See, especially, the contributions in Bobrow and Collins, eds (1975), eg Winograd (1975), Kuipers (1975).

Other, but similar concepts, such as DEMON, SCRIPT, SCHEMA, SCENARIO, etc have also been used. See Charniak (1972, 1975), Schank (1975), Rumelhart (1975).

For a discussion about frames and macro-structures, see van Dijk (1976a).

22 See Urquhart (1972) for a brief suggestion about a similar proposal, involving information sets (though these would also include more particular, contextually determined, information).

PART II
PRAGMATICS

Chapter 6

Some notions from
the theory of action

1 Introduction
1.1

There is another domain from which a certain number of concepts will be used in this book: the THEORY OF ACTION. It goes without saying that a sound analysis of speech acts, which is a central task of pragmatics, cannot be carried out without previous understanding of the notion of an act or action. Insight into the structure of action at the same time provides a basis for the semantic interpretation of action discourse, *ie* discourse in which actions are described, stories for example.

1.2

It should be emphasized that an application of results from the philosophy and logic of action in the analysis of speech acts is not a marginal topic in linguistic theory. That, by speaking we DO something, that is, something more than merely speaking, is a simple but important insight from the philosophy of language.[1] It should be added that the use of language is not only some specific act, but an integral part of SOCIAL INTERACTION. Language systems are CONVENTIONAL systems. Not only do they regulate interaction, but their categories and rules have developed under the influence of the structure of interaction in society.[2] This FUNCTIONAL view of language, both as a system and as an historical product, in which the predominant SOCIAL role of language in interaction is stressed, is a necessary corrective to a 'psychological' view of language and language use, where our competence in speaking is essentially an object for the philosophy of mind.[3] To be sure, our knowledge of the language is a complex mental system. But, this mental system, like all conventional systems, on the one hand has been formed by the requirements of effective and successful social behaviour, and on the other hand is used and changes under these constraints.

1.3

In this chapter we must provide some elementary concepts in order to be able to draw the consequences of this view for linguistic theory and grammar. We must define what actions are, and what are not actions, what the conditions of successful action are, show how actions may constitute sequences of actions and how they are part of interaction, both verbal and non-verbal, and finally how interaction depends on norms, conventions, obligations and needs.

In the next chapters we will use this more general understanding of (inter-)-action in the characterization of speech acts and communication.

2 Events, actions, processes

2.1

Although there is an enormous literature about action, it cannot be claimed that we at present possess a fully elaborated theory of action. The notions discussed below come from various studies, both from a philosophical and from a more logical approach to the various problems.[4] All of these concepts would require book-length treatment in order to understand their full intricacies, and it will therefore be impossible to enter into detailed discussion of exceptions or complications in the definitions given below.

2.2

The notion of action is usually treated in close connection with that of EVENT. A brief intuitive 'definition' of action already shows this relationship: AN ACTION IS AN EVENT BROUGHT ABOUT BY A HUMAN BEING. We will see below what is lacking in this 'definition', and will first try to be more precise about events.

One basic concept involved in the definition of the notion of event is CHANGE. This change may be viewed as a relation between, or an operation on, possible worlds or states of affairs. More particularly, a change implies a DIFFERENCE between world-states or situations and hence requires a TEMPORAL ORDERING of worlds. For our purposes, we shall divide time into units described as previous or subsequent in the linear sequence of time. Each time unit is associated with a set of possible worlds, viz one actual possible world, and a set of alternative possible worlds. Possible world-time point pairs, *ie* states of affairs or situations, may be represented by STATE DESCRIPTIONS, where a state description is a set of propositions. Differences between situations are thus represented as differences between state descriptions. A change occurs in a possible world, or rather between the situations $\langle w_i, t_i \rangle$ and $\langle w_i, t_{i+1} \rangle$, if their descriptions are different. A change will be called MINIMAL if these descriptions differ only in one atomic proposition, viz having $\sim p$ instead of p, or p instead of $\sim p$ (or: not having p instead of having p, or having p, instead of not having p, if we only admit 'positive' state descriptions), all other things being equal. Thus, if at $\langle w_i, t_i \rangle$

the proposition 'The door is open' holds, and at $\langle w_i, t_{i+1} \rangle$ the proposition 'The door is not open' or 'The door is closed', we say that an event has OCCURRED or TAKEN PLACE or that something has HAPPENED. The change in question may affect various properties of possible worlds, viz the coming into existence or disappearance of a particular individual object, the acquisition or disappearance of some property of an object, or the establishment or destruction of some relation between objects. We assume that NO change has occurred if the descriptions of $\langle w_i, t_i \rangle$ and $\langle w_i, t_{i+1} \rangle$ are identical; this guarantees that no intermediate events have taken place between t_i and t_{i+1}. If an event occurs 'between' $\langle w_i, t_i \rangle$ and $\langle w_i, t_{i+1} \rangle$ these situations are usually called the INITIAL STATE and the FINAL STATE of the event, respectively. Events, just like objects, properties and (static) relations, may be defined according to CHANGE or EVENT DESCRIPTIONS, and they may have conventional names. Since events accomplish or affect objects, they may be represented as n-place predicates. In our simple example the event type may be represented with the predicate 'to close'.

The IDENTIFICATION of events is closely linked with the conventional means we have in language for the description of events, which, as we have earlier stated, depends on the functions of such descriptions in interaction. We have a predicate 'to close' in order to denote the event between an 'open' initial state and a 'closed' final state, but no specific predicate to denote the event of opening (or closing) something one inch, or one inch more. Yet, the opening of a door is an event taking place GRADUALLY in (continuous) time. This holds, physically, even for the 'click' or sound of the opening or closing door, identifying the initial or final state, respectively. Although events may be assigned properties (opening wide, opening slowly, etc), we still have one predicate (or several synonymous predicates) for the event of opening (or closing) as one distinct event 'unifying' the infinite series of intermediary PHASES of the event, because only the initial state/final state difference is RELEVANT for our actions and interactions: we may, eg, enter an open door, but not a closed door. Hence, the identification of events (as types) is not based on physical time and motion alone, but also on cognitive and conventional units.

It is also in this perspective that we may speak of a COMPOUND EVENT, ie an event which is constituted by several events which are linearly ordered but which are perceived or conceived of as ONE event at a certain level of description. In this case, the component events may in other situations occur independently or as components in other (compound) events. In compound events the initial state is identical with that of the first component event (the initial event) and the final state is identical with that of the last component event (final event). If the final stages of the component events are identical with the initial states of the following component events, a compound event will be called CONTINUOUS. Otherwise, it is DISCONTINUOUS. The event of 'crashing' may be called compound, because it is at least composed of the event of 'moving' and the event of 'breaking'. Crashing, moreover, is continuous, whereas the event of 'thunder' may be discontinuous, because there are temporal 'gaps' between the component events (during which other events may occur).

2.3

The notion of PROCESS is not easily defined, and perhaps should not be accounted for in terms of events at all. For reasons of simplicity we take processes as continuous events, occurring during a PERIOD $\langle t_i, t_{i+j} \rangle$ of time, of which intermediary events cannot be, or are not conventionally, distinguished. Raining is a typical example. In process perception and description the focus of attention is on the properties of the change itself rather than on the difference between the initial and the final state. As soon as an initial or final state of a change and some difference are indicated, as in 'it started raining' or 'it stopped raining', we speak of events not of processes. It follows that if we consider events during one moment (unit) of time, we observe them as processes, because we do not distinguish intermediary events. This means that we may take processes as the basic concept, and identify events that constitute discrete (parts of) processes by distinguishing initial and final states and a change between them.

2.4

Changes in possible worlds need not be minimal. Several events may occur at the same time. The same holds for processes, and for events and processes. Similarly, we may speak of SEQUENCES OF EVENTS, *ie* series of distinct events following each other in time. If such a sequence is perceived or conceived of as one unit, we called it a compound event. This distinction between one compound unit and a sequence of units will be important not only for actions but also for the theory of discourse. This is one of the reasons why the term 'sequence of events' will be used in a stricter sense, in order to denote a subset of the set of possible series of events. A SERIES of events may consist of events which are completely INDEPENDENT. In a sequence the events are not only linearly ordered but also related by DEPENDENCE.

The highly intricate notion involved here is that of CAUSATION.[5] A series of events will be called a sequence if the events are causally related. This causal relation (or operation) may have various forms. Either each event causes each next following event, or a subsequence of (causally related) events causes some following event (or again sequence of events), or some series of independent events causes one event (or sequence of events). That is, an event may have a SIMPLE CAUSE or a COMPOUND CAUSE. The event(s) caused by an event or sequence of events will be called a CONSEQUENCE. Events may have several, independent causes or consequences. If a consequence immediately follows the causing event, it will be called a DIRECT consequence; otherwise it is INDIRECT. We see that the notions of cause and consequence are RELATIVE: an event is a cause relative to its effected consequence(s).

These definitions imply that causation only holds between events, not between states or between events and states. This is different from the expression of 'cause' in ordinary language. We say that the heat caused the fire, or that the accident caused John's being in bed now. However, closer analysis shows that natural language and cognition make shortcuts over sequences of events and the initial and final states of events. Thus, the fire is caused by a change of temperature, and John's being in bed now is the FINAL STATE of a series of events (and actions) caused by the accident. Such a final state of a causal sequence of events is often called a RESULT.

In Chapter 3 we tried to give a simplified semantic analysis of cause-conditional connectives. The proposal made there will have to be based on a serious analysis of causal relations between facts, of which however only a few notions can be touched upon here.

We first assumed that causation is involved in COURSES OF EVENTS, characterizing state changes, not states. If we say that some state is 'caused', we mean that an event is caused which has that state as final state, viz as a result. Similarly, I may 'cause' the state that a glass does not fall (viz by holding it), but again this state is rather the result of my action itself, not part of a consequence of my act. Secondly, it is assumed that courses of events are ordered in TIME, such that if A causes B (or some part A' of a A causes some part B' of B in case of non-momentaneous events), A precedes B. Thirdly, a course of events is a member of a set of POSSIBLE COURSES OF EVENTS, of which one course will be called ACTUAL (or historical) and the others the non-actual alternatives. This kind of set-up may be represented with the trees as given in Chapter 3: from each node in the tree, defined as a particular state of a particular world, several paths lead to different subsequent nodes.

Given these preliminaries, various KINDS of causation may be defined. Above, for instance, we saw that we may have single and multiple causes, unique or exclusive and concomitants causes, etc. Similarly, a cause may be such in just one situation or in several or in all possible situations. Given our scheme of world-time and courses of events, we define a simple kind of cause in terms of SUFFICIENT CONDITION. A condition is sufficient for a subsequent event if it NECESSITATES the subsequent event. In other words, at some node t_j of the tree it is INEVITABLE that, given A occurs in $\langle w_i, t_j \rangle$, B occurs at all subsequent situations (at t_{j+1}) which can be reached from $\langle w_i, t_j \rangle$. Note that this may hold just for this particular occasion, provided that all other things remain the same (this is the well-known *ceteris paribus* clause in definitions of causation). That is, John may break his neck falling off his chair only on this occasion – where indeed his falling causes his breaking his neck – but not at the numerous other occasions he has or might have fallen off his chair. On those occasions the event would not have been sufficient. It follows that some event is a cause only together with a number of specific properties (or other events) of a certain world, *eg* the brittleness of John's bones and the reaction speed of his muscles, together with the specific properties of the event (change) itself: the exact way John fell NOW made a fractured spine physically/biologically necessary. We see that here the cause holds only in one (at least one) subtree of the universal tree.

Causing events may or may not be NECESSARY CONDITIONS: taking water is a cause for a plant to grow, and it is also a (biologically) necessary condition, but breaking my neck is not necessarily a cause of my death. Thus, *B* has *A* as a necessary condition if in ANY (sub)tree we must pass an *A*-node in order to reach a *B*-node.

Different kinds of causation may depend of the FORCE of the causing event, *ie* on the fact whether the cause is sufficient in at least one, many, most or all possible (sub)trees of the universe. Thus, in the (sub)tree in which our actual world is developing, being shot through the head will on nearly all occasions cause death. This means that in the definition of causation we need a set of basic POSTULATES (laws, basic properties, etc) defining the actual world and the set of possible worlds compatible with it. That is, I can cause a book to change place only in those worlds where gravity is similar to that in our world(s). A causing event is more forceful than a sufficient condition in that it brings about some other event in a way more independent of co-occurring events and initial conditions. In natural conversation, then, we normally will ask for further, specific, conditions in cases of weak causes (how did he fall off his chair?), but not with strong causes (he fell from the Empire State buildings (as a cause of his death)).

From our brief discussion of causality it follows that causation involves necessity (of consequences), viz the fact that – given the circumstances – *A* will lead to *B* whatever else may happen (independently), *ie* in all possible worlds which have *A* occurring in an immediately previous state (in this particular subtree).

We will see below that in a specific kind of courses of events, viz in (courses of) action, further intricacies, *eg* regarding agency, intentions, purposes and goals become relevant, but we now are in possession of some elementary notions about events, sequences of events, processes and causation, which will be necessary in an account of action.

3 Doings, acts, actions
3.1
Above we gave a brief intuitive characterization of action as 'an event brought about by a human being'. If BRINGING ABOUT has the same meaning as 'causing' this characterization is already incorrect as it stands, because we have stipulated that only events (not objects or persons) may cause events. So, either 'bringing about' is not 'causing', or actions are not events.

Intuitively, at least a set of actions involves events. The action of 'opening a door' clearly 'contains' the event of 'opening', with an initial state where the door is closed and a final state where the door is open. In the ACTION of opening a door, however, there is another event involved, viz the movement of the arm of the one who opens the door. This is an event because in an initial state the arm is in a different position from that in subsequent states. Such an event may, according to definition, cause the event of opening, viz if moving my arm, on this occasion, necessitates the opening of the door.[6]

The event of opening may also have been caused by other events, *eg* by a movement of air (wind), but intuitively we do not say of the wind that it performs an action, or acts, when it causes a door to open. Actions are usually predicated only of HUMAN BEINGS (and perhaps of animals). In the example given, this action contains a movement of a part of the body causing a movement of a door, and we will say that it is the movement of the body which is 'brought about' by a human being. On the other hand, we also speak of action when only a bodily event is involved without another event as a consequence, *eg* when I greet somebody, or when I am speaking or walking. Note that in both cases we may speak of actions only if a human being brings about an event in his OWN body. If somebody moves my arm when I am asleep, we do not say that *I* have moved my arm, or that *I* have acted, but somebody else has. Similarly, if somebody pushes me against a door and the door then opens, we do not simply say that I opened the door.

The problem remains whether bringing about a movement of part of my body is the same as CAUSING this movement. It might be said that bringing about a certain movement of my muscles causes my arm to move in a certain way. But then the question arises how the movement of muscles is caused.

At the same time we may have the situation that I move (part of) my body when I am asleep. Although it may be said in such a case that I DID something, it is usually not said that I performed some action. Similarly, I may listen to a lecture and at the same time play with a pencil without noticing that I am doing so.

3.2

Apparently, a movement of my body alone is not a sufficient reason for calling it an action: I must be AWAKE and CONSCIOUS, and AWARE of what I am doing. Actions, thus, involve certain MENTAL components, or at least require certain mental preconditions. These mental conditions are of a very specific sort. I may stumble and fall against a door, thereby causing the door to open. Although I am awake and although I may be conscious of what I am doing, or rather what happens (to my body and the door), we would not say that I performed the action of opening a door. One of the criteria seems to be here that I did not WANT to stumble, nor did I want the door to open by falling against it: I had no INTENTION of opening the door at all.

A number of conceptual distinctions seem relevant to this intuitive analysis. An action involves a BODILY EVENT, but since a bodily event might not be brought about by myself but by somebody else or by another event, we need the concept of a DOING for a bodily event brought about by myself. Similarly, I may do something without thereby performing an action because I did not specifically want or intend to perform that doing nor did I want or intend the following events to happen as a cause of that doing. SO, ONLY DOINGS BROUGHT ABOUT INTENTIONALLY MAY QUALIFY AS ACTIONS.

3.3

At this point philosophical complications abound. We still have the 'bringing about' problem, and additionally have such things as intentions and wants.

The simplest solution for the first problem would be to let intentions cause doings. In that case, intentions must be events, which requires a change of state. Assuming a mind to be some object, part of my body, this mind may undergo a change of state. That is, at some point t_i it 'has' no intention and at t_{i+1} it 'has' an intention. It is a long way, however, between such an assumed 'mental event' and a bodily event. First of all, I may have the intention to move my arm, but may DECIDE not to do it. This would be impossible if intentions directly caused doings, or if doings were necessary consequences of intentions. If doings are only accidental consequences of intentions, we need other conditions in order to let intentions cause doings in at least some cases. Secondly, I may intend to do something, but not actually do anything: if intentions are changes of my body, and if they are brought about consciously, they are themselves actions. Actions, however, were provisionally defined as requiring 'causing' intentions. It follows that if intentions are actions, viz so-called MENTAL ACTS, they would in turn require intentions, and so on, ad infinitum. So, either intentions are not actions or not all actions need be 'caused' by intentions. Thirdly, if intentions may be 'cancelled' by things like decisions, what other events should be postulated 'between' intentions and doings?

3.4

Before we can discuss these problems about the mental conditions of actions, some further remarks are necessary about the observable part of actions, viz about doings and their consequences. Apparently, there are at least two types of actions, viz those which only consist of a doing (greeting, walking, waggling one's ears) and those which consist of a doing plus some event as a consequence (opening a door, smashing a window, eating an apple). In reality, however, actions are often much more complex. When I eat breakfast, build a house, govern a country, or study linguistics, these doings may be qualified as actions, but these actions are at least COMPOUND or should be considered as SEQUENCES of actions, in the sense defined above for events. In such compounds and sequences we must have intermediary states, to be considered as INTERMEDIARY RESULTS of the component actions, as well as a FINAL RESULT of the action(s). Characteristically, it is often this final result or consequence of a simple or composite action we 'have in mind'. To wit, when I open a door, I will hardly think of, *ie* consciously intend, moving my arm and hand in a certain way; what I want and probably think of is getting the door open so that I may enter or may let somebody enter. In such cases we normally speak of the PURPOSE of an action. Whereas an intention has the action itself as its scope, a purpose will be taken as a mental event in which an agent represents the GOAL(S) of the action. A statement of purpose answers a Why-question about action. I may intend to go to Paris. The purpose of this rather complex action may differ from case to case: I may want to visit my friend Pierre, or want to attend some congress, or visit the Louvre. From this formulation it appears that purposes are also closely related to wants and should therefore be further discussed in the framework of mental structures.

Purposes of actions are crucial in the organization of our activities and interaction. It sometimes happens that we accomplish some actions, *eg* go into a room, but at the same time 'forget' our purpose (What was I going to do?). There are cases where intentions and purposes seem to coincide, viz in the accomplishment of those actions which are done just for their own sake. In that case the doing or its result are themselves a satisfaction of my wants or desires, and not some further consequences of this doing.

3.5

The analysis of actions, and especially of compound actions and action sequences, requires another concept, viz that of the SUCCESSFULNESS of actions. I may have the intention of opening a door, performing a certain doing, but without the intended result(s): the action fails, because *eg* the door is locked. As for events, doings may cause certain consequences only if some further CONDITIONS are satisfied. An action will be called FULLY SUCCESSFUL if the final consequence or final result is identical with the purpose. Since however the occurrence of a consequence may depend on conditions or events which are beyond my control, there is also a more restricted notion of successfulness, viz that of the intended doing. If I succeed in travelling to Paris but do not meet my friend Pierre, my purpose may not have been realized, but my action of going to Paris itself at least was successful. A distinction between INTENTION-SUCCESSFULNESS (or I-successfulness) and PURPOSE-SUCCESSFULNESS (P-successfulness) is therefore relevant. Thus, I may accomplish some doing and thereby TRY to open a door which is locked, but if the full doing of opening cannot be performed, the action fails, and is I-unsuccessful. Trying is not of itself an action, but the accomplishment of the initial doings of a (compound) action, which then did not lead to I-success (unexpectedly) or of which I-success is doubted by the agent.[7]

Note that in a great number of action types the accomplishment of a doing nearly co-occurs with an event affecting an object. The doing of opening a door or painting a wall can be I-successful only if the door opens and the wall becomes white. Although strictly speaking we have two (or more) events which are (nearly) co-occurring, viz a doing and a change of the properties of some object, we may say that the object-event is an integral part of the doing. That is, doings are not only qualified and identified by the type of bodily movements but also by the types of objects and object-changes effected. It is the final state of this object-change which is the I-RESULT of an action: the door is open, the wall is white, the car is repaired, the cigar is reduced to ashes, etc.

There are a certain number of detailed complications in the SUCCESS or FAILURE of actions. These details are not unimportant because an action which fails is not an action, and hence conditions of success are at the same time existential conditions for actions. Above, for example, we have defined P-success as the realization of a purposed event or state of affairs. This goal of an action may occur, however, also independently of the doing. At the same time as I want to open a door, the wind may blow it open. My purpose is then satisfied, but *I* did not open the door. It should therefore be further required that an action is fully P-successful if it also is I-successful and if the doing is the cause of the purposed events or state of affairs, and if the agent wants and knows that the doing as accomplished causes the realization of the purpose. Thus, my car may break down; I do not know anything about motors but nevertheless pull some cables, as a consequence of which the motor un-expectedly runs again. My doings were intended, I had the purpose that the car would run again, and this purpose is realized. Nevertheless it can hardly be said that I *repaired* the car. Hence the doing must be intended AS a specific cause of a specific purposed consequence. We will say that intentions of actions are under the SCOPE of purposes of actions.

From these few examples it appears that successfulness of actions in the strict sense requires the satisfaction of various types of initial conditions. These are not only properties of the 'environment' (*eg* of the objects affected) of the action, and not only intentions and purposes, but also KNOWLEDGE about both these initial properties of objects and environment and the CAPACITIES and ABILITIES of the agent, concepts to which we will return below.

3.6

We are now in a position to have a better understanding of compound actions and sequences of actions, in that conditions of success may now be given for them.

Compound actions consists of SIMPLE ACTIONS. A simple action is defined as an I-successful doing with *one* intended result. In general, this doing will itself consist of several doings but, as was the case for events, there are cognitive and conventional reasons for considering some continuous doings as one doing, of which only the initial and final state are relevant. Doings which are continuous over a period of time, and which satisfy the conditions of processes, will be called ACTIVITIES (walking, smoking). Similar remarks may be made here about events and processes. It should be said that in normal circumstances agents are in 'continuous action'. They do not accomplish one action and then some time later, another action, etc, but their permanent activity is ANALYSED as a series of discrete actions and sequences of actions.

Above, a simple action was defined in terms of I-successfulness and the realization of one result of one doing. This result may consist in an effected change of our body together with a co-occurring change in an immediately affected object. A simple action, however, may also be defined with the additional requirement of P-success. When I cash a cheque at the bank, I may have performed all the necessary doings successfully, but if the bank refuses my cheque, it can hardly be said that I actually cashed the cheque. That is, the action was I-successful but not P-successful. In order to be able to distinguish between these two 'dimensions' of activity, I-successful doings may be called ACTS, and those acts which require the occurrence of further consequences in order to be P-successful may be called ACTIONS. However, this distinction will not be made systematically in this book.

The intended results of acts may become sufficient or necessary conditions not only for following events but also for following acts. Now, a COMPOUND ACT is a sequence of acts such that the result of act a_i is a condition for the successfulness of act a_{i+1}. Moreover, a compound act is ONE act by virtue of the fact that the 'intermediary' results (or rather their corresponding intentions) are under the scope of ONE GLOBAL INTENTION realized by the accomplishment of the whole compound act. Global intentions will be called PLANS. Building a house is a compound act. It consists of a sequence of acts, each of which may be carried out successfully (or fail), but they are intended as parts of the realization of a plan. A compound act is successful if its plan has been realized.

The difference between a compound act and a SEQUENCE OF ACTS is that a compound act has a clearly identifiable intended (planned) result. The development of the acts is determined by one plan (which may be changed during execution of the sequence), and the component acts are conditions for following acts. In a sequence of simple and/or compound acts there is a given purpose, but the acts may be relatively independent in the sense that even when they condition each other these relations are not planned to realize a specific result. I may take a holiday with the purpose of bettering my health, and the holiday may consist of a sequence of acts, such that at each point I may choose which act to perform, *eg* visit some town or go to the beach. There need not be a definite plan nor a precisely identifiable result, and the acts may be relatively independent. The sequence is unified (is not an arbitrary series of acts) under the identity of agent(s), a continuous period of time, and the execution of the various acts under one purpose. As for all purposes, such a purpose may involve a whole SET of wanted changes or states.

Finally, it is useful to introduce AUXILIARY ACTS. An auxiliary act is an act of which the result is intended as a sufficient condition for the successfulness of a (main) act. A composite act of which some act(s) are auxiliary acts, is called a COMPLEX ACT. Component acts of COMPOUND acts, however, may also be conditions of following acts. What, then, qualifies as a main component act, and what as an auxiliary act? Do we consider building a wall a main component act of building a house, and mixing concrete as an auxiliary act? One of the possible differences may be that building a wall is a NECESSARY component of the act of building a house, which is not the case for mixing concrete (I may use stones as foundations and have wooden walls). That is, normally speaking, I do not build a house at all when I do not build walls. As an essential part of the compound act, building a wall must be represented in the plan. Characteristically, auxiliary acts may be carried out also by HELPERS. Lighting my pipe is an auxiliary act which somebody else may do for me, although I am still the one who smokes the pipe. A component act, thus, is carried out by the agent himself and is carried out with the intention to make the whole compound act successful, whereas an auxiliary act is carried out only to make one component act succeed.

These are only tentative suggestions for a distinction between composite (complex or compound) acts and act sequences, and between auxiliary acts and (necessary) component acts, and it is obvious that these distinctions require further explication.

4 Mental structures of action

4.1

It has been made clear above that a serious account of acts and actions cannot be given in purely behaviouristic terms, *ie* in terms of doings and their consequences alone. A number of MENTAL concepts, like consciousness, awareness, knowledge, wants, desires, intentions, purposes and decisions, have been used. Although little is known about the precise status and the mutual relations between these concepts, some brief remarks about them are necessary.

4.2

It has been shown that acts and actions may succeed only if a certain number of conditions are satisfied. These conditions may consist of properties of worlds in which the agent is acting. Since acts involve results of changes in the body of the agent as well as changes in properties or relations of objects, the agent must KNOW about the actual state of his body and of the objects to be affected. He must know about the POSSIBLE changes of worlds, changes compatible for example with the laws of physical and biological nature, as well as about the possible consequences of doings. The agent must have a rich data base of information consisting of his KNOWLEDGE and BELIEFS. A knowledge set or EPISTEMIC SET consists of propositions which are 'true', in the conventional sense of the term. That is, these propositions are 'warranted' by conventionally accepted truth criteria (perception, correct inference, information from reliable sources). Beliefs are propositions, which need not be true but which the agent thinks to be true or which he thinks to be probably true.

Knowledge and beliefs pertain to all kinds of facts, both particular and general, viz about properties of, and relations between objects, both actual and possible, and about particular and general relations between facts or fact concept. Knowledge and beliefs are productive in the sense that there are RULES of deductive and inductive inference which enable an agent to derive new information from old information.

4.3

Whereas knowledge and beliefs provide the data base for the agent about the world as it is, or as it could be or could become, our DESIRES and WANTS provide the actual motivation for our action, because they pertain to the structure of the world as it should be. If an agent desires or wants the state p to be realized, it is presupposed that he believes that at that moment p is not the case. One of the intuitive differences between desires and wants is that I may desire p although I know that p is not possibly realizable in a normal world, whereas from my desires I may select some of the states which I think realizable; in the latter case it is said that I want something. I may also want p to be the case without directly desiring p to be the case, but only because, for example, somebody else desires p. The wanting of p, then, is indirectly determined by my desire to satisfy the desires of somebody else. Similarly, I may desire p, but know that p has q as a possible consequence, but where q is undesirable. Then, if p is less desirable than q is undesirable I will not want p. If of two states (or events) p and q, p is more desirable than q, we say that the agent PREFERS p over q. In that case preference is directly based on desires. If it is based on our actual wants, it is more complex. Although as such I may desire p more than q, and hence prefer p over q, I may know or believe, as in the example given above, that p has more undesirable (*ie* stronger and/or more numerous) consequences than q. In that case I will want q, *ie* REASONABLY prefer q over p. Note that wants and preferences need not pertain to actual state of affairs, they may also relate to other possible worlds, *eg* in generic preferences. I may prefer an apple to a pear even if I do not make an actual choice in order to eat an apple. I then prefer it for any imagined world in which I would make a choice.

One of the crucial concepts briefly mentioned above is that of REASON. We assumed that our wants and preferences based on them are RATIONAL (whereas our desires need not be). Obviously, this concept involves processes of inference in which certain desires are 'controlled' by our knowledge and beliefs about possible consequences, further conditions, desires and wants of others, and so on.

4.4

If I want or prefer a certain state or event, there are several possibilities to realize this want. I may wait until the state is realized by the normal course of events and by the actions of other agents, or I may act in such a way that this state is realized. In my knowledge set I have information about what types of action will most probably have the wanted state or event as a consequence. Then, if this particular act cannot reasonably be expected to have (stronger) undesired other consequences, the agent will transform his want to a PURPOSE OF ACTION. That is, a purpose is a state of mind in which I have a representation of a wanted future state of affairs or event together with the instruction that this goal must be brought about by an action (of myself). If there is more than one course of action leading to this goal, the agent must DECIDE which course to take, *ie* he must make an actual CHOICE. This decision, if it is rational, is based on a calculation of preferences and RISKS of failure of the different courses of action. A decision is OPTIMAL if it results in a course of action realizing a maximum of the desired states or events. It is obvious that in real action our decisions are not always optimal, especially not if failures can easily be corrected or if they do not have serious undesired consequences.

Given a certain purpose and the result of the process of decision-making ranging over possible courses of action, the agent may form a particular INTENTION of action or a PLAN of action, to be executed in a specific situation (time, place, conditions). Whereas plans and purposes are formed before compound acts and sequences of action, respective intentions may be formed immediately before the execution of part of the compound act or the sequence. When I plan to go to Paris, I do not normally already have the intention of sitting on a certain seat in a certain carriage. I may not even be able to decide about such a possible action, owing to a lack of information. After the formation of an actual intention, new unexpected information may become available which may result in the cancelling of the intention or even of the purpose and want. We again make a decision, viz whether to execute the concrete intention or not. If this decision is positive the information contained in the intention is given to the motor systems of our body which, in the appropriate sense, 'cause' the doing.

4.5

This reconstruction is of course speculative and far from precise. An exact model would be needed for the flow and processing of information in various mental 'regions', and experiments would have to provide the necessary empirical data. Much of our actual knowledge does not go beyond systematic speculation based on introspection, and based on conceptual distinctions made in ordinary language. The speculations may be made more explicit by devising various LOGICS for the assumed mental systems: epistemic logic, doxastic logic, preference logic, decision logic, and boulomaeic logic.[8] Such logics have very serious difficulties in choosing appropriate axioms and in establishing inference rules. In many cases the theorems derived account for 'ideal' aspects of the systems. For example: must we know all implications of what we know? Are beliefs consistent? Are our doxastic and epistemic systems complete in that we always either know or believe p or $\sim p$? Some characteristic truths of these systems are for example (where K: Know, B: Believe, W: Want, I: Intend):

  (i) $Kp \supset p$
 (ii) $(Kp \,\&\, Kq) \equiv K(p \,\&\, q)$
(iii) $Kp \supset Bp$
 (iv) $Wp \supset B \sim p$
  (v) $I(DOp) \supset B \Diamond (DOp)$

Whereas we may have the following rule of inference:

 (vi) From $K(p \supset q)$ and Kp infer Kq.

Note, that the operators of mental states have an INTENSIONAL character: If Kp and $p \equiv q$, then it need not be the case that Kq.

4.6

The knowledge about necessary conditions for actions must also be about what we are in principle able to do. We must know our ABILITIES and

CAPACITIES. We will not plan actions we know we cannot accomplish, either due to our physical limitations (fly, jump ten feet high), limitations of our learning (read Chinese, repair our car), or to the essential or actual impossibility of the doing (paint a wall white and black all over at the same time, prevent all wars). We are unable to accomplish certain acts, but are in principle capable of at least learning to accomplish them (learning Chinese). The set of ABILITIES is strictly time-dependent. It contains the acts (or rather concepts) we would be able to accomplish at a given moment given the appropriate conditions. The set of CAPACITIES may be viewed as a larger set, also containing the actions which we would in principle be able to do, given further training. We further say that we are (un-)able to do something when we refer to conditions beyond our control: physical restrictions (my arms are tied), psychological restrictions (fear), social restrictions (permissions, norms, obligations, rules). Some of these will be further discussed below.

Earlier, those doings were disqualified as actions which cause the realization of a result or consequence by chance. We now see that a doing is an act only if it is CONTROLLABLE, *ie* if I can initiate and terminate the doing when I want, given certain conditions.

5 Negative action
5.1
In the previous sections we discussed only acts and actions which have a 'positive' character, *ie* consisting of real and observable doings, which involve one or more changes of properties of possible worlds. Note that these changes need not only affect states, they may also affect changes of states, viz events or processes. I may act in such a way that a certain event, process or action of somebody else, changes, either by stopping it or by giving it another property (slowing down, accelerating). Characteristic here are acts of PREVENTION: I know that something will happen, have the purpose that it shall not, and perform an act with the consequence that the event will not take place which would have taken place if I had not acted. Here again the COUNTERFACTUAL element of action comes up. An action is sometimes said to be successful if its consequences would not have been realized without the doing causing it. Here, an event would not have taken place in the actual world, whereas in prevention an event would have taken place.
5.2
These types of 'positive' action also have 'negative' counterparts. There are circumstances where NON-DOINGS may also count as acts, viz as FORBEARANCES and LETTINGS. I may forbear to take my breakfast this morning, or forbear to save a child from the canal. After such acts, I may be questioned about my not accomplishing these acts and I may also be held RESPONSIBLE for this. Typical of forbearances is that the corresponding positive act is somehow normal, expected, morally necessary, according to my habits,

conventions, norms and obligations. Given a certain situation I would have to follow the normal course of action and form the appropriate purposes and intentions. In such a case, a decision is necessary not to accomplish the expected act, on the basis of some desire, want or preference. I have reasons for forbearances as I have for positive acts. My non-acting is strictly speaking also observable, because due to the earlier indicated properties of permanent activity, I do something else INSTEAD of the expected act. Forbearances are not based on an absence of a particular intention, but on a present intention not to execute a particular intention. Even here, a CHANGE is involved in the act, viz a change in the normal course of action. Not only may I bring about changes in possible states or courses of events, but I may also intentionally change a habit, break a law norm or obligation.

As a counterpart of preventions, LETTINGS have the same conditions as forbearances; it is normal that I prevent some course of events, but forbear to change or prevent it: I (intentionally!) let things happen. The reason for lettings may be very simple: I may assume that a purposed state of affairs will come about without my doings and be brought about by the natural course of events or by actions of other agents.

6 Interpretation and description of action
6.1
An essential component in the definition of action turned out to be the various mental structures 'underlying' the actual doing and its consequences. This means that actions cannot as such be observed, identified and described. We have access to them only by the INTERPRETATION of doings. Such observable parts of acts, however, may be highly 'ambiguous'. When I see somebody move a pen over a piece of paper such that the white surface of the paper is partly covered with black lines, I may say that he is writing, that he is trying out his new pen, that he is writing his signature, that he is signing a document, that he is buying a house, that he is making his wife happy, and so on. One single doing, thus, may lead to various (sometimes disjunct) interpretations of the activity going on: we ASCRIBE actions to somebody.

The process involved may be compared with that of understanding an utterance, which also involves assigning a meaning to observable utterance structures. We understand what somebody 'does' only if we are able to interpret a doing as a certain action. This implies that we reconstruct an assumed intention, purpose and possible further reasons of the agent. Of course, this is no pure guess-work. Many kinds of action, much like the discourses of a language, are carried out according to conventions. The execution of certain doings may have quite straightforward connections with their corresponding actions: when we see that an agent is holding a glass of beer to his mouth in a certain position, we CONCLUDE 'that he is drinking beer'.

In many such cases where rather elementary actions are carried out on observable objects (hammering, throwing a ball, breaking a glass, climbing a tree) the interpretation will have this obvious nature. Intentions are reconstructed by the observation of the execution of the doing by assumption that an agent carries out the doing according to plan. Reconstructing purposes is a step more complex, as the observer may not be sure whether all the consequences of the doing are wanted by the agent, or because consequences are not yet evident. If I see somebody hammering, I may ask "*What are you doing?*", thereby meaning 'what are you hammering *for*', and thereby requesting information about purposes. Further questions may be raised concerning the reasons for such a purpose ("*Why are you making a new dog-kennel?*"). An immediate interpretation of doings will be easier if the observer has had previous information about the intentions and purposes of the agent, and/or if he knows about the basic wants and preferences of the agent, as may be the case between close friends or man and wife. Conversely, it may be more difficult to interpret actions in cultures where part of the conventions are unknown to us.

6.2
In the writing example in the preceding paragraph it was shown that actions may be differentiated also at several LEVELS. I write my name on a contract, and THEREBY have bought a house, WHEREBY I may make my family happy. The buying of the house legally coincides with writing my signature. Making my family happy is more a consequence of house-buying. In the first case, then, we may speak of SECOND ORDER acts. Actually, the action of house-buying may for me consist of a whole series of acts, of which the signature is just one (decisive and essential) component. Given a doing, interpreted as a single first order act, the assignment of 'further' acts or actions may be given depending on the situation: we may identify the compound act of which the simple act is a component, we may ascribe a more global compound action if further consequences have been realized of the act, or may interpret the act at a second order level or even third order level.

6.3
Descriptions of action are given in ACTION SENTENCES and ACTION DISCOURSES. Crucial here is the point of view of the description. In first person descriptions I may express the desires, wants, reasoning, purposes and precise intentions of a doing describèd. In (non-literary) third person descriptions we may only assign conventional interpretations of actions, or else it must be expressed or implied that the agent of which the actions are described also provided information about mental structures. Action descriptions may also imply EVALUATIONS of actions. Instead of describing the act 'John painted his house pink', I may describe the 'same' doing as 'John spoiled his house'.

7 Action logic
7.1

Explicit descriptions of actions may be given in an ACTION LOGIC, of which some principles have been elaborated in the last few years.[9] A first requirement, and difficulty, is to devise an appropriate ACTION LANGUAGE. With such a language, and with a convincing semantics for it, we would have to formulate action-logical axioms and derivation rules, in order to be able to prove theorems about the structure of action and action sequences.

There are several possibilities for constructing an explicit action language. One approach is to try to explicate the logical structure of action sentences in natural language, *eg* with a specific predicate calculus. In that case we require that action sentences are formally different from non-action sentences. Thus, *Hit (John, Peter)* or $(\exists x)(Nail\ (x)\ \&\ Hit\ (John,\ x))$, for example, are inadequate because we have the same structure for predicates like 'see', 'is beside' or 'are different', which are not action predicates. If we want to express the specific nature of actions, we may for example introduce specific variables in our language, such that the variables are interpreted as specific individuals,[10] viz actions, *eg* as follows: $(\exists u)([Hit(John,\ Peter)](u))$ or $(\exists u)((Hit,\ John,\ Peter)(u))$, where $u, v, \ldots$, would be variables ranging over actions. The advantage of having such variables would be that we could add time and place indications and predicate modifiers (adverbs): $(\ldots)\ \&\ Yesterday(u)\ \&\ In(u,\ London)\ \&\ mean(u)$. In such a notation an act is interpreted as an individual 'thing' with the property that 'John hit Peter', or that a relation between John, Peter and an action has the property 'hit'. Such an account would be parallel to that for events.

There are, however, a number of important difficulties in such an approach. Actions, owing to their mental components, are INTENSIONAL objects. If the 'action' variables $u, v, \ldots$ only refer to doings, we do not account for actions at all. If, for example, $u = v$, it may not be concluded that the acts are identical: I may give my signature and thereby buy a house, but on another occasion I thereby merely finish a letter. The identification and differentiation of actions cannot be separated from purposes and intentions, or interpretations of these. Moreover, the logical explication of natural language expressions does not give insight into the conceptual structure of actions, so that necessary implications cannot be formulated in terms of the logical structure alone.

Some of this logical structure can be made explicit in a propositional language with a specific CHANGE OPERATOR over pairs of states of affairs. Thus, $p\ T \sim p$ could be read as 'the state characterized by p changes into a state characterized by $\sim p$'. This would account for the event (change) involved in actions. But much more would be needed, *eg* the aspect that the event is brought about by an agent, which might be expressed by a *DO*-operator with indexed variables for agents as follows: $DO_a(p\ T \sim p)$. But again this is a notation for doings, not necessarily for actions. Moreover, the KIND of change operated is not expressed in such formulas: there are many ways to change one state into another. Some of them are doings (I drop a glass) others actions (I throw a glass on the floor). Similar problems will occur in the semantics for such formulas: how will operators like *DO* be interpreted?

7.2

Even if a convincing language of actions has been developed, problems arise with the formulation of its LOGICS, viz axioms, derivation rules, validity, etc.

Axioms like $(DOp \& DOq) \equiv DO(p \& q)$, $DOp \supset p$, etc seem reasonable and have correlates in other modal logics. However, the antecedent of the first axiom seems to denote a sequence of acts (or doings) and the consequent one compound act, which were shown to have different properties. In any case, since actions are intentional objects, an unequivocal use of truth-functional connectives is not possible. Thus, a formula like $((p \supset q) \& DOp) \supset DOq$ will not be valid, not even on a causal interpretation of the conditional. What would be required, at least, is that the agent knows that $p \supset q$, so that he knows that if he does p, q will 'follow'. In that sense only, he (indirectly) also does q. (In this highly simplified notation propositional letters denote intended doings, *ie* events). Other possibilities and difficulties of action languages and action logics will not be discussed here.

8 Interaction
8.1

Most philosophical and logical investigations into the nature of action are limited to analyses of actions performed by one agent. Indispensable to a theory of action that seeks to explain the nature of communicative acts is, however, an account of the nature of INTERACTION. Several agents may be involved in the accomplishment of one simple or compound act, or in a course of action where each agent accomplishes his own acts but where the acts are mutually related (lifting a table, playing chess, building a house). In fact, most of our activities have social implications, and our acts are therefore often part of interactions.

8.2

It is necessary to distinguish first of all various TYPES OF INTERACTION, and to separate action from interaction. The presence of more than one person does not imply interaction: like other objects, persons may be affected by acts (John hits a nail, John hits Peter). Such acts may be part of interaction, but are not themselves 'interacts'. Of interacts it may be required that at least two persons are agents at the same time or, in sequences, agents in subsequent points or periods of time.

One type of interacts consists of those where the agents TOGETHER accomplish one (simple or compound) act. Although their respective doings are distinct they have the same result in mind, that is they have IDENTICAL INTENTIONS, and they know this of each other. In such a case, we may speak of a COLLECTIVE AGENT. The condition of mutual knowledge is crucial. It may be the case that A has an intention i and that B also has the intention i, and both carry out the intention, possibly even affecting the same object, but in that case A and B need not be interacting with each other (A goes to the beach, and so does B). Note that identity of intentions must pertain to the same result. A as well as B may be sitting by a canal, both may have the intention of 'catching a fish', and may even know this of each other; yet, they need not be interacting, because the success of the doing of A does not imply success for B. In intuitive terms: A and B are not COLLABORATING, as they would be in lifting a table together. In such cases the acts of either of the agents may be necessary and/or sufficient conditions for the successfulness of the interact. I may not be able to lift the table alone, and cannot possibly marry alone. Some acts only succeed as interacts.

A bit more complex is collaboration in compound acts. Co-agents may perform different acts for which they each have the appropriate intentions, but each of these acts is a sufficient or necessary component in a compound act, for which the agents have the SAME PLAN (as in building a house together). COORDINATION of acts is rather complicated here, because each of the agents must know precisely what the other agents are doing at a certain moment, or what belongs to the TASKS of the other agents. A task will simply be seen as a set of acts which are necessary or obligatory for an agent in order to realize a goal. Collaborating interaction need not be with co-agents, but may occur between (co-)agent(s) and HELPER(S), *ie* agents of auxiliary actions. Helpers need not have the same plan as the agents of the compound act, or may even not know of this plan.

Although intentions and plans of co-agents may be identical such that they bring about the same result, they need not have IDENTICAL PURPOSES. We may go to the movies together, *ie* execute similar or identical intentions, but each of us may go for DIFFERENT REASONS, one because he wants to see a particular film, the other mainly because he is tired and wants to relax (with any film). In such a case the realizations of different purposes are COMPATIBLE. Intentions may be incompatible or even inconsistent. If A and B play chess, they play together, and the acts of each one of them constitute an essential condition for a game of chess to take place; both may have the intention of playing chess, but at the same time have the intentions 'A wins' and 'B wins', respectively. These intentions cannot be realized at the same time. Purposes, however, may be identical in this case: that the game be enjoyed by both players. Purposes may also be incompatible, as is the case in fights, where the consequences of winning and those of losing realize the desires of only one agent. Doings may occur at the same moment and be correlated although the agents have different intentions and different purposes, both successful for both agents, as in buying-selling interaction.

8.3

The different types of often highly complex interaction briefly characterized above are based on the successful coordination of doings. Besides the ability to coordinate such doings physically, this requires knowledge and/or assumptions about the wants, purposes and intentions of other agents. Interaction, however, would not always be effective even if this mutual insight were extensively expressed before co-acting. Nor is it always possible to deal with possible conflicting wants and intentions. We must know of each other what it is we would normally do in particular situations. We must have CONVENTIONS.[11] These may be so restricted that they exist between just two persons for just a few interactions (*eg* meetings), but they may also exist for large groups for an indefinite period of time, at many places, and for many interactions (*eg* traffic). What is essential is that each agent knows how other agents will normally act under certain conditions so that doings can be successfully coordinated. Similarly, the convention may indicate as what act a certain doing should be interpreted. If a policeman raises his hand at a road crossing, I know by conventional RULE that he wants me to stop, and do not interpret the signal as a friendly greeting.

Conventions may be explicitly codified (traffic rules, language rules) or be mainly implicit (rules of politeness). They may have varying degrees of STRICTNESS: some have strong OBLIGATIONS others have weak obligations.[12] Breaking strong obligatory rules may be punishable by law. In social interaction we are held RESPONSIBLE for our actions. In principle our actions should not have consequences which are heavily incompatible with the JUSTIFIED wants of other persons. Legal consequences of our doings are intimately connected with the conditions for acts given above. We are punished only for acts for which we are responsible, and we are only responsible if our doing was conscious, intended with permitted purposes, controlled or in principle controllable, and if we had no POWER over its (non-permitted or undesired) consequences, *ie* were unable to prevent those consequences.

Many other interactions are not strictly formulated, but nevertheless conventional,[13] although we may not be aware of them: how we pass each other in the street, walk with somebody, look at each other, touch or kiss each other, and of course how we speak to each other, a topic to be treated in detail in the rest of this book from the standpoint of its predominantly rule-governed action properties.

Notes

1 Although this idea appears in various philosophical writings, both in the analytical and phenomenological paradigm, its major proponent has undoubtedly been Austin (1962).
2 See Kummer (1975) for an elaboration of this view, which is not only a functional conception of language, but also a materialistic one.
3 As it is the case, typically, in the generative-transformational philosophy of language, especially in Chomsky's writings (*eg* Chomsky, 1966, 1968). The functional view of language has been propagated predominantly in the Prague

School and the London School and in recent sociolinguistics. See, *eg* Firth (1957, 1968), Halliday (1973), and Labov (1972a, 1972b).

4 For philosophical further reading and references, see Care and Landesman, eds (1968), Binkley, Bronaugh and Marras, eds (1971), and White, ed (1968).

For a more logical approach, see especially von Wright (1963, 1967) Davidson (1967) and other readings in Rescher, ed (1967), Pörn (1971), Brennenstuhl (1974).

5 For introductory readings and further references about causation, see Sosa, ed (1975). See also von Wright (1957, 1963).

6 Sometimes causation of events and actions is formulated in *counterfactual* terms : the event/action A brings about a state S if S *would* not have come about without A. See *eg* von Wright (1967) and Lewis (1973). The reason for such a formulation is that even if both A at t_i and S at t_{i+1}, S might have been brought about by other causes. There are some problems with this formulation which will not be discussed here, but which are apparently evaded in our account of relative necessity.

7 Notions such as trying, beginning, finishing or continuing are not so much actions, but rather certain PROPERTIES (or perhaps MODES) of action, that is, we predicate them of actions.

8 There is a large literature in philosophy about the properties and logic of preference and decision making. See Rescher, ed (1967) and the references given there.

For epistemic logic, see especially Hintikka's (1962) monograph. We do not know of any extensive attempt at establishing a boulomaeic logic – a logic of 'wants' or 'wishes' (insofar as it would be different from a logic of preference). See Rescher (1968) for a discussion of these and other non-standard logical systems.

9 See von Wright (1967), Brennenstuhl (1974), Kummer (1975), Davidson (1967).

10 For this kind of 'event-splitting', see Reichenbach (1947), Davidson (1967) and Bartsch (1972).

11 See Lewis (1968) for conventional action.

12 For a discussion of obligations and permissions, see von Wright (1963), the readings in Hilpinen, ed (1971) and the references given there.

13 Study of these kinds of (semi-)conventional interactions has been made in recent sociology, especially by Goffman. See *eg* Goffman (1971) and Laver and Hutcheson, eds (1972).

Chapter 7

Contexts and speech acts

1 The aims of pragmatics
1.1
Whereas the aims of syntax and semantics and their place in the grammar are relatively clear, the tasks of PRAGMATICS and its contribution to linguistic theory are by no means decided issues. Pragmatics, not unlike semantics fifteen years ago, has become the waste-paper basket of the grammarian, although its possible relevance is no longer denied. The situation, however, is different for pragmatics from what it was for semantics. With the possible exception of contextual semantics, pragmatic theory has hardly drawn inspiration from logic. It draws mainly upon philosophy of language and the THEORY OF SPEECH ACTS in particular, as well as the ANALYSIS OF CONVERSATIONS and of cultural differences in verbal interaction as viewed in the social sciences. As a brief preliminary to the following chapters, this chapter will introduce some of the notions and problems of current linguistic pragmatics and some of its theoretical links with both grammar and action theory.

1.2
As the third major component of any SEMIOTIC THEORY, pragmatics would have the task of studying 'the relationships between signs and their users'.[1] If pragmatics is distinct from psychology and the social sciences, this tells us little about the precise object of description and explanation. In any case, if a pragmatic theory yet to be developed should be part of a theory of language, it will have to account for SYSTEMATIC phenomena within the domain of the latter theory, and it must be interrelated with other parts of the theory. That is, pragmatics must be assigned an empirical domain consisting of CONVENTIONAL RULES of language and manifestations of these in the production and interpretation of utterances. In particular, it should make an independent contribution to the analysis of the conditions that make

utterances ACCEPTABLE in some situation for speakers of the language. The syntax (and morpho-phonology) provides the well-formedness conditions for utterances, the semantics meaningfulness and reference conditions; what PRAGMATIC CONDITIONS make utterances (un-)acceptable? The answer from philosophy of language has been based on the insight that the production of utterances is an ACT, which may be SUCCESSFUL or not.[2] So, whereas the grammar provides an explanation why the OBJECT-utterance is acceptable, one of the tasks of pragmatics is to provide successfulness conditions for the utterance-ACT, and explain in what respect such an act may be a component in a course of interaction in which it is either accepted or rejected by another agent. A second task, thus, is to formulate the principles underlying such courses of verbal interaction, which must be satisfied for an utterance act to be successful. Third, since our empirical data are largely available only in the form of utterances, it should be made clear in pragmatics how conditions of success for the utterance as act, as well as principles of communicative interaction, are connected with the structure or interpretation of the discourse.

1.3
This is a general view; we must formulate the empirical domain, precise tasks and specific problems. On the other hand, such a formulation requires some concept of the FORMAT of a pragmatic theory: what are its types of rules, categories or other constraints, how does it formally reconstruct its empirical objects?[3]

A suggestion for this format can be drawn from formal semantics, which has sentences from the syntax as 'input' and is expected to provide recursive truth definitions of these sentences in some possible world, or rather in a MODEL (STRUCTURE). Instead of having the 'real' world as a basis for interpretation, a semantic theory gives a highly abstract reconstruction of the 'real' world (and of other possible worlds) in this model structure, which contains precisely those objects (sets of individuals, properties, relations, possible worlds, etc) required to interpret each part of each sentence of the language. A similar course may be followed in pragmatics.[4] The input, here, are sentences (or discourses) as specified in the syntax plus their semantic interpretation as given in the semantics. Such discourses are OBJECTS and as such cannot be called successful or non-successful. A first task of pragmatic theory, therefore, is to turn these objects into acts. In other words: what has been the abstract structure of the utterance-object must become the abstract structure of the utterance-act. It would be nice if the structure of the former could somehow be maintained in the structure of the latter, just as rules of semantic interpretation respect the categories of syntactic structure. The operation turning discourse into acts might also be called a PRAGMATIC INTERPRETATION of utterances.

A second task of pragmatics would then be to 'place' these acts in a situation, and formulate the conditions stipulating which utterances are successful in which situations. That is, we need an abstract characterization of this 'situation of speech interaction'. The technical term we use for such a situation will be that of CONTEXT. Similarly, we need a specific term in order to denote the 'systematic pragmatic successfulness' of an utterance, because there are many other aspects of success (grammatical but also psychological and sociological). For 'pragmatic success' the term APPROPRIATENESS will be used. Now, appropriateness conditions must be given in terms of abstract properties of contexts, specified in PRAGMATIC MODEL STRUCTURES.

Whereas a COMMUNICATIVE SITUATION is an empirically real part of the real world in which a great number of facts exist which have no SYSTEMATIC connection with the utterance (either as an object or as an act), such as the temperature, the height of the speaker, or whether grass is growing, a context is a highly idealized abstraction from such a situation and contains only those facts which systematically determine the appropriateness of conventional utterances. Part of such contexts will for example be speech participants and their internal structures (knowledge, beliefs, purposes, intentions), the acts themselves and their structures, a spatio-temporal characterization of the context in order to localize it in some actual possible world, etc.

Before one can sensibly work out a FORMAL SYSTEM of pragmatics in the shape of the format sketched above, a systematic ANALYSIS of its various components is necessary. Appropriateness conditions can be formulated only if we know the structure of communicative acts and of the contexts in which they are functioning. Taking up the notions from the theory of action given in Chapter 6, we will have to make clear that speech acts really are acts. In following chapters, it must then be shown what sort of linguistic problems can be formulated and in principle be solved in such a pragmatic framework.

2 The structure of context
2.1
In a communicative situation there are at least two persons, one an actual agent, another a possible agent, ie a speaker and a hearer, respectively. Both belong to at least one speech community, ie a group of persons with the same language and related conventions for interaction. During a certain period of time the activities of two (or more) members of the community are coordinated, in the sense that a speaker produces an utterance with certain consequences for the hearer, after which the hearer may become agent-speaker and produce an utterance or he may merely become agent and accomplish a certain number of actions. Such may be a relatively intuitive description of some features of the communicative situation. Which of them must be theoretically reconstructed in terms of context structure, and how?
2.2
A first property of context to be emphasized is its 'dynamic' character. A context is not just one possible world-state, but at least a sequence of world-states. Moreover, these situations do not remain identical in time, but *change*.

Hence, a context is a COURSE OF EVENTS. Such a course of events has, according to the theory of events of Chapter 6, an initial state, intermediary states and a final state. Since contexts must be theoretically identifiable they must have limits: we must know what conditions a possible world must satisfy in order to qualify as initial or final state of context, even if a finite context need not have a limited length.

We have an infinite set of POSSIBLE CONTEXTS, of which one will have a specific status, viz the ACTUAL CONTEXT. The actual context is defined by the period of time and the place where the common activities of speaker and hearer are realized, and which satisfy the properties of 'here' and 'now' logically, physically, and cognitively. An actual context, as well as each of its intermediary states, has a set of alternatives. Some of these are NORMAL and satisfy the basic postulates of communicative courses of events. Others are possible, imaginable, but not normal. In such contexts the basic principles of communication are violated, at least from the point of view of normal contexts. Contexts are courses of events and thus are defined by an ordered set of 'here-now' pairs $\langle\langle t_0, l_0\rangle, \langle t_1, l_1\rangle, \ldots \rangle$: the context changes from moment to moment. This change must affect (or effect) objects in the successive states of context. Most conspicuous is the 'coming into existence' of an utterance token, $|u_i|$, which at $\langle c_0, t_0, l_0\rangle$, where c_0 denotes the actual context and $\langle t_0, l_0 \rangle$ its initial state, does not yet exist, and which changes its properties (eg its dimension) in the subsequent states. Utterance tokens are actual realizations of utterance types, which are conceptual structures, and hence functions, of which utterance tokens are values in some context. Hence, we need a set of utterances U, and a specific member u_0, denoting the actual utterance, of which $|u_0|$ is the actual utterance token.

This seems unduly complicated but even so methodological problems concerning the precise 'objects' or 'units' of a pragmatic theory are not fully solved. First of all, it should be recalled that utterance tokens are unique, in a strict physical (phonetic) sense: at a single moment, a person can produce only one (oral) utterance token; if he 'repeats' the utterance, he produces another utterance token of the same utterance type. Yet, at the same moment he COULD have uttered other utterance tokens of the same utterance type (viz in alternative contexts), and these would all have been acceptable given the 'same' contextual conditions. The pragmatic theory, thus, does not differentiate between utterance tokens but is only interested in the abstract utterance type and its conditions. Secondly, the theory will further make abstractions from utterance types in the sense that repeatable variations in pronunciation (of a certain person, as determined by sex, age, socio- or dialectical colouring, etc) are neglected. In this sense the utterance of a sentence like:

[1] May I borrow your bike tomorrow?

is still a CLASS of possible utterance types – each defining a set of utterance tokens. That is, we recognize differences when John pronounces this sentence and when Laura does, for instance. And even this class of possible utterance types is not simply identical with a type of uttered sentence, because the same holds for possible utterance types of non-sentences like:

[2] Tomorrow I borrow may bike your.

That is, the set of utterances corresponding to utterances of sentences and discourses of a certain language is a subset of the class of possible utterance types. In particular, it may be said that the utterance of [2] cannot be appropriate in any possible context, as it is to be defined (even if there are concrete SITUATIONS in which the utterance can be understandable and acceptable, *eg* if spoken by a foreigner).

The upshot of these distinctions is that there are several stages of generalization and abstraction between a concrete, empirically observable, utterance token on the one hand and the kind of abstract unit, corresponding to a sentence or discourse of a language, which we call UTTERANCE or UTTERANCE TYPE. It is at this theoretical level that we say that an utterance is appropriate in one (abstract) context, and that the 'same' utterance is inappropriate in another context. Note also that this kind of abstraction allows us to relate utterances to units at other levels of linguistic description, *eg* sentences. Whereas we say that a proposition REPRESENTS a fact, that a sentence EXPRESSES a proposition, we now say that an utterance act REALIZES a sentence. Since in principle I may realize any sentence in any situation, the pragmatics is required to formulate the conditions determining when these realizations are appropriate and when they are not, viz as acts of language and acts of communication. Having pointed out some problems of the precise status of pragmatic units, we will further ignore the methodological intricacies involved.[5]

2.3

What else changes in a context? Obviously, certain RELATIONS. At $\langle c_0, t_0, l_0 \rangle$ nobody PRODUCES an utterance, which however is the case in subsequent states. The same holds for the relation of PERCEPTION. These relations of which the utterance is one 'term', require other objects, viz PERSONS. Below it will be made clear that these persons are POSSIBLE AGENTS and POSSIBLE PATIENTS. Of the set of persons P, a subset exist in c_0: they are the ACTUAL PARTICIPANTS. Participants are selected from the set of persons by their characteristic properties, *eg* their doings, in the actual context. Two functions are important in this respect, the SPEAKING-FUNCTION and the HEARING-FUNCTION, defining for each state in the context which participant person is speaking and which participant person is hearing. The values of these functions are distinct in each state of context: no participant may be speaking and hearing at the same time, although there are psychological arguments for letting speakers hear their own utterances. Conforming to traditional terminology, a participant satisfying the speaking function will simply be called a SPEAKER and the participant satisfying the hearer function will be called the HEARER. The values of the latter function are SETS of participants. This set in our case will not be empty: we need at least one hearer, but may have more. If we let one participant satisfy both functions, we would include cases where the speaker speaks 'for himself'. There are theoretical motives not to consider such cases as belonging to communicative situations. Also empirically, speech is essentially interactive, and speaking alone is derivative – satisfying only the 'expressive function' of language – or pathological.

The various participants and their actual function will be denoted simply as follows $S(a)$, $H(b)$, $H(a)$, $S(b)$, ... Although in some very specific cases several speakers may produce the same utterance (*ie* different utterances tokens – of the same utterance type – which are co-occurring), only one participant will be allowed to produce the utterance. In reality, several speakers may produce different utterances (types) at the same time, but such speech will be theoretically unacceptable (and in most cases is conventionally so, too).

The properties of speaking and hearing which participants have are in the strict sense only DOINGS: I may speak in my sleep, and hear but not pay attention to 'what is said'. Hence, in order to reconstruct communicative interaction, these doings must be 'interpreted' as ACTS (as was indicated above) such that utterances become RESULTS from acts of speaking. It will be shown below how complex acts of speaking/hearing, what types of act, and of which order, are involved here. So, in the theoretical reconstruction of the situation, our context structure further needs a set (or set of sets) of acts plus its (their) specific member(s) actualized in some context.

It should be mentioned that these acts require characterization not only of their typical doings with typical results (utterances), but also of their full MENTAL STRUCTURES as discussed earlier in Chapter 6 for action in general: wants, knowledge, purposes, intentions. From the KNOWLEDGE SET, at least three subsets must be actualized: (i) knowledge of the WORLDS in which the utterance is interpreted (ii) knowledge of the various states of the CONTEXT (iii) knowledge of the LANGUAGE used, *ie* of its rules and of possible uses of rules, as well as knowledge of other systems of interactional CONVENTIONS. Without this knowledge, the utterance cannot be processed as a type, and hence cannot be produced and interpreted, and without this knowledge the participants do not know what is spoken about or why there is any speaking at all. Nor would it be possible to monitor the acts of speaking or to coordinate the interaction. Without the information from the epistemic data base there could be no question of (inter-)action at all, let alone communicative interaction in which this information is specifically transmitted. A crucial part of context structure, then, will be the change operated in the epistemic sets of the participants. It is in terms of this epistemic change that initial and final state of the context can be defined.

2.4

The concepts superficially introduced above seem at least necessary components in contexts, but it remains to be seen whether they are sufficient to completely define conditions of appropriateness. That the task of a pragmatic theory is several times more complicated than that of semantics may already be measured by the number of elements 'with respect to which' utterances are to be 'evaluated'. These complications will especially appear in the complexity of speech acts and communicative interaction as analysed below. Let us summarize the categories we now have:

C: a set of possible contexts
c_0: the actual context $\in C$
T: a set of time points
L: a set of places (locations)
$\langle t_0, l_0 \rangle$: 'here-now' pair defining the 'states' of $c_0 \in T \times L$
P: a set of persons or possible agents/participants
P_0: a subset of P, containing the actual participants
U: a set of utterance types
u_0: the actual utterance type $\in U$
$|u_0|$: the actual utterance token of u_0
A: a set of (communicative) acts
S: a speaking-function (act of speaking), $\in A$
H: a hearing-function $\in A$
$S(\ )$: the actual speaker $\in P_0$
$H(\ )$: the actual hearer $\in P_0$
$K, \ldots$: several sets of actual relevant knowledge, beliefs,
        wants/wishes, intentions.
CON: the set of communicative conventions of the speech community P.

3 Acts of language
3.1

A first issue requiring attention is the ACTION character of speech and communication. It has been assumed that realizing a sentence or discourse of a language is an act, but that statement encompasses a great deal of theoretical complexity of which only some partial aspects can be dealt with here.

What is usually meant by saying that we DO something when we make an utterance is that we accomplish some specific social act, *eg* making a promise, a request, giving advice, etc, usually called SPEECH ACTS, or more specifically, ILLOCUTIONARY ACTS. Obviously, however, there is a long way between producing some sounds on the one hand, and accomplishing a complex social act on the other hand. Yet, in a strict extensional way of speaking, the production of sounds or graphs and the accomplishment of an illocutionary act seem to co-occur. This means, as we have seen earlier, that the same DOING, call it SPEECH, should be described at several levels of action. In this sense we may speak of first, second, . . ., n-th ORDER acts, such that an i-th order act is accomplished BY accomplishing an $(i-1)$th order act. A global differentiation between the various kinds of acts involved is made by the distinction between a LOCUTIONARY ACT, a PROPOSITIONAL ACT, and ILLOCUTIONARY ACT, and, in some cases, a PERLOCUTIONARY ACT.

3.2

Under a LOCUTIONARY ACT we should understand a complex act, itself consisting of several orders of action, viz at the phonetic, phonological, morphological and syntactic levels. The basic DOING is given in phonetic (or graphic) terms, but an ACTION is involved only given some specific intention, control and purpose, which however cannot possibly be purely phonetic. We may want to pronounce an /a/ or an /f/, but can intend to do so only at the level of abstract types, *ie* on the phonological level (although specific variations between realization classes of the same phoneme may be intended, *eg* when I imitate the vowel pronunciation of some dialect).

It should be emphasized that the phonological act and the other acts involved in the complex locutionary act will in general qualify as acts by the criteria of intention, purpose and control, even if the individual acts are in fact not individually conditioned by these criteria, but AUTOMATIZED, *ie* executed under control of fixed rules and routines, which however MAY be de-automatized by conscious execution of separate acts (I may decide on, intend and execute the pronunciation of an /a/).

COMPOSITE phonological acts, thus, constitute the basis of next higher order morphological acts, *eg* the uttering of the word/morpheme *man*. Similarly, composite morphological acts, viz the utterance of morpheme sequences, may constitute the basis of syntactic acts, *eg* by using the sequence *the man*, as a definite noun phrase, as a subject or as a direct object. Details need not be given here, only questions asked regarding the precise PRAXEOLOGICAL (*ie* action-) nature of the various levels of speaking.

We here start the analysis of speech, beginning with the phonetic level (as in an analysis-grammar). This does not mean, of course, that the formation of intentions for sound production comes first: on the contrary, a speaker will first make decisions and form intentions with respect to what a hearer should do or know, *ie* he plans the particular speech act first, then its precise semantic 'content', and only after that does he give a syntactical, morphological, phonological and phonetic 'form' to this content. That is, the control of the lower acts comes from the higher order, social acts. Similarly, our theoretical reconstruction of acts of language does not respect the precise cognitive processes and strategies involved: morphological, syntactic and semantic acts are planned in a mingled way, as is also the case in language comprehension.

3.3

By the realization of morphemes and syntactically structured morpheme sequence (sentences) we at the same time accomplish, thereby, certain ACTS OF MEANING, *ie* intensional acts. That is, we assign some conceptual meaning to our expressions or, conversely, express some meaning by uttering certain morphosyntactic structures. It is probably at this level where the acts of language become really conscious in the sense of being individually intended and executed: choosing our words is choosing our meaning(s). Those meaning acts which may serve as the basis for further acts, *eg* that of assertion, are usually called PROPOSITIONAL, although it is not clear whether propositional acts are to be seen as intensional or also as extensional, viz as regarding truth values through REFERENCE to facts. In any case, SEMANTIC ACTS are of the two kinds: we may express a MEANING by uttering a sentence without necessarily REFERRING to some specific individual or property. Hence, reference is a higher order act: we may refer to a specific table by uttering the phrase *the table* by assigning it the intensional meaning of (a particular) 'table'. The same holds for properties, relations, propositions and compound propositions. The possibility that the act of reference is further contextually specified by auxiliary acts, *eg* pointing, direction of looking, etc, will not be considered here. Note also that the propositional act, whether intensional or extensional (referential), is composite, and might be analysed into possible acts of 'predication', structurally combining reference to individuals and reference to properties.

3.4

The upshot of the discussion above is that before we can actually speak of ILLOCUTIONARY ACTS, *eg* as the central object of study for pragmatics, we should realize how complex their 'actional deep structures' are: we give a piece of advice BY referring to a certain fact (a future action of the hearer, as we will see later), BY meaning a certain proposition, BY expressing some clause or sentence, BY expressing some morpheme sequence, BY expressing phonemes, BY accomplishing a phonetic doing. So, illocutionary acts are at least fifth-order acts, and the act of utterance as characterized earlier, viz the act relating a sentence of the language to an utterance (product and act) of the language, should thus be analysed according to our general discussion given above. The utterance function relating semantics and pragmatics, thus, stands for a highly complex, composite function.

The complex acts of language underlying an illocutionary act are SUCCESSFUL if the result of the (phonetic) doing, viz the utterance, is an acceptable token of the utterance type INTENDED (*ie* planned, due to its hierarchical complexity). This kind of success is however one-sided, and merely a part of communicative (inter-)action: a speaker will have PURPOSES. That is, he wants that his utterance has specific consequences. These consequences, in the first place, pertain to specific modifications in the HEARER, more in particular, modifications of the KNOWLEDGE SET of the hearer: $H(b)$ knows that $S(a)$ realizes an /a/, realizes the morpheme *man*, etc . . ., knows that $S(a)$ means 'that the man is ill', thereby referring to a particular man, having a particular property, now (at the moment of utterance). At each level of action, thus, the speaker has corresponding purposes with respect to desired recognition (comprehension) of the hearer. These purposed consequences will in normal circumstances come about due to the conventional nature of the acts involved – and the conventional nature of units, categories and rules of the structure of the product of an accomplished utterance. The philosophical complications involved in the recognition and comprehension of utterances by hearers who postulate certain intentions and purposes of the speaker will be disregarded here.[6] An act of language, then, is P-successful, if a hearer recognizes the intended meaning/reference of the utterance, and if the speaker had the purpose that this particular hearer should form this recognition.

3.5

Theoretical difficulties arise at the level of ILLOCUTIONARY ACTS. Strictly speaking, such acts would be Intention-successful if the underlying act of language is I-successful, if the speaker has a particular illocutionary intention, and if this intention is carried out, viz if the illocutionary act is actually performed BY the execution of the act of language (according to some specific constraints which the illocutionary act imposes on the meaning of the utterance). Now, although we may speak for/to ourselves under certain circumstances, it remains to be seen how we may accomplish illocutionary acts by ourselves: do we make a promise if no hearer is (assumed) to be present simply by making an utterance which WOULD have been a promise if such a hearer would have been present? In other words, is there a point in speaking of SOCIAL acts if we could accomplish them without thereby somehow changing or confirming a relation with other individuals of the same community of language? We will take the view that indeed there is no point in speaking of illocutionary acts outside this socially determined context, ie a context in which a hearer is present and in which a change is brought about in the hearer, conventionally in accordance with the intentions/purposes of the speaker. This means that I-success is now to be defined in this broader sense, viz such that the RESULT of the illocutionary act is not some utterance (product) but some intended state brought about by the (comprehension of the) utterance in the hearer, where the state change involved is EPISTEMIC: the hearer now knows that the speaker promises, advises, . . . that (. . .). In this case we say that the illocutionary act is FULLY I-successful. It would be not fully, but eg PARTIALLY I-successful, if the hearer failed to understand the illocutionary intentions of the speaker, although understanding what is said.

A next step is required in order to define illocutionary acts as COMMUNICATIVE ACTS, viz in terms of Purpose-successfulness. For instance, if a speaker accomplishes the illocutionary act of an assertion, eg by realizing the sentence *The man is ill*, the hearer may change his knowledge such that he knows that the speaker wants him to know that the man is ill. However, it may be the case that the hearer does not change his epistemic set with respect to this fact, eg because he does not believe the speaker or because he already knew about this fact. In that case the PURPOSE of the speaker with his illocutionary act of assertion is not realized. Only in those cases where this purpose is realized do we speak of a P-successful illocutionary act, also called a PERLOCUTIONARY ACT. Hence a perlocutionary act is an act of which the conditions of success are given in terms of purposes of the speaker with respect to some change brought about in the hearer AS A CONSEQUENCE OF the illocutionary act. An advice is perlocutionarily successful, for instance, if the hearer FOLLOWS the advice, acts UPON the advice, as purposed by the speaker and as a consequence of the recognition of the illocutionary act. Whether the hearer does so is beyond the control of the speaker and beyond the conventional norms of communicative interaction – although being subject to other social conventions of interaction. This is one of the reasons why perlocutionary effects are also beyond the domain of a linguistic theory of pragmatics: we stop so to speak at the recognition by the hearer of the illocutionary intentions of the speaker. Whether the hearer believes an assertion, executes an order, complies with a request, etc is not a subject of PRAGMATIC rules.

3.6

Now, it is one of the tasks of pragmatic theory to formulate the general and particular CONDITIONS determining the full I-successfulness of illocutionary acts. These conditions are to be formulated in terms of constituents and structures of the communicative context. One complex set of conditions has now received a preliminary analysis, viz those defining the illocutionary act as being based on a complex act of language: I illocutionarily do x by doing (speaking-meaning/referring) y.

The second set of conditions pertains to the mental underlying structures of speakers and hearers involved in communicative interaction, viz their wants, beliefs/knowledge, intentions and purposes. These conditions, as for action in general, may be classified according to their FUNCTION: they may be preparatory (necessary or probable preconditions), components or consequences. The PREPARATORY conditions are mainly ASSUMPTIONS of the speaker with regard to the initial state of the context: knowledge of the hearer, inclination of the hearer to listen, ability to hear, etc, of which the last condition pertains to the successfulness of the underlying act of language (speech). We shall not go into this further here.

Thus, one of the conditions of success for assertions is the assumption of the speaker that the hearer does not yet know that/whether p: $B_{S(a)} \sim K_{H(b)} p$ (at $\langle t_0, l_0, c_0 \rangle$). Similarly, the speaker must assume that the hearer either wants to know whether p, or at least does not want NOT to know whether p: $B_{S(a)} W_{H(b)} K_{H(b)} p$, or $B_{S(a)} \sim W_{H(b)} \sim K_{H(b)} p$. These latter conditions may be called the WILLINGNESS conditions of communicative interaction in general, or of assertion-like illocutionary acts in particular.

Two other sets of more general conditions are those of SINCERITY and CREDIBILITY, which are necessary because acts of language are related only by convention, not by law, to meanings and intentions. Hence sincerity is a general normalcy condition requiring that we say "p" when we mean 'p' and thereby express that in fact we believe 'p': $B_{S(a)} p$. [7] Similarly, from the point of view of the hearer it must be clear that the speaker is sincere: $B_{H(b)} B_{S(a)} p$, which in its stronger form $B_{H(b)} K_{S(a)} p$ defines the credibility of the speaker for the hearer, according to further conventional criteria dependent on the status, function or position of the speaker and ad hoc situational criteria (personality of the speaker, specific circumstances, corroborating evidence, compatibility with the extant knowledge of the hearer, etc). Note that these conditions are preconditional in the sense that when they are not satisfied the illocutionary act either becomes pointless (*eg* superfluous) or fails by non-acceptance by the hearer.

With each specific illocutionary act, then, a set of CHARACTERISTIC or ESSENTIAL conditions must be satisfied, distinguishing it from other types of illocutionary acts. For assertion, again, this would be the condition $W_{S(a)}K_{H(b)}p$. We see that such a condition pertains to the specific change wanted by the speaker, not to the actual change having taken place or not (as a perlocutionary effect): it is relevant for us merely to reconstruct the systematic rules and conditions determining how the hearer understands what is meant (in a broad sense) by the speaker. Similarly, in a request the essential condition is $W_{S(a)}DO_{H(b)}p$. In both cases we may embed these conditions in the schema $B_{H(b)}$ –, because it must be generally assumed (see above) that the hearer believes what the speaker wants, intends and says. Theoretically, this embedding is RECURSIVE: the speaker must in turn believe that the hearer believes him, etc. The RECOGNITION clause $B_{H(b)}$ – is the consequence part of the illocutionary act, defining its ultimate illocutionary success.

The various sets of conditions for different (classes of) illocutionary acts need not be spelled out here since they have been extensively discussed in speech act theory. What is relevant for our discussion is the set of theoretical primitives needed to be able to characterize them. What else do we need beyond wants, beliefs, wants and bringing about (*DO*)?

One further kind of condition is necessary in the characterization of illocutionary acts such as reproaching, accusing, praising, condemning, congratulating, etc, viz that the speaker thinks or finds that something (an object, event or action) is GOOD or BAD, relative to himself, relative to the hearer, or relative to some community or norm of the community. In the examples given, the presupposition is $PAST(DO_{H(b)})$, embedded in $B_{S(a)}$ –. Introducing two types of EVALUATION operators, viz E^{pos} and E^{neg}, denoting positive and negative evaluation (like and dislike), respectively, one of the essential conditions to be added is $W_{S(a)}K_{H(b)}E^{pos}_{S(a)} PAST(DO_{H(b)}p)$ or its negative variant.

Other differences between the examples of this class of illocutionary acts are to be sought in further presuppositions with respect to the DEGREE of certainty of the speaker, the degree of like or dislike, the ACTUAL EXISTENCE of the object, event or action (dis-)liked, the degree of sincerity of the action, etc. Furthermore, there is an important condition to be formulated in terms of STATUS, POSITION and POWER, defining the AUTHORITY of the speaker. These are again specific functions taking participants in some specific context: only AS a judge may a participant condemn/acquit another participant – having the function of the accused: $S(a) = Y(a, c_0)$, where Y is some position function, defining the role of a in c_0. In this case, we no longer are dealing with internal structures of language users, but with their SOCIAL FUNCTIONS, which hence should be added to the list of categories of the pragmatic context as specified above.

Systematic research is necessary to determine which further categories are necessary in order to define the various illocutionary acts. Methodological problems will certainly arise in that respect, because some differences may not be based on clear pragmatic criteria – relating to the structure of the context – but to other social properties of the situation where the distinction between pragmatics and social theory is admittedly vague. Thus, for instance, would the important notion of POLITENESS be a pragmatic notion or a notion characterizing certain properties of social behaviour in general? Linguistically, the notion seems required in order to differentiate the use of second-person pronouns in many languages (German, French, etc) and other phrases, *eg* in *Would you please be so kind as to give* ... versus *Please give* ... versus *Give* ... In this case the delimitation between pragmatics on the one hand and STYLISTICS/RHETORICS on the other hand adds further confusion. The pragmatic condition would pertain to APPROPRIATENESS of an utterance, whereas the stylistic/rhetorical variations define the degree of EFFECTIVENESS of an utterance, underlying the willingness of hearers at the perlocutionary level. I may have various options to make an appropriate request, but certain requests will be more likely to be complied with than others, according to the degrees of politeness, the measure of preparation of the request (see Chapter 9), and the degree of freedom left to the hearer. At this point of the study of language USE, pragmatics, stylistics and sociology intermingle.

3.7

Whatever the precise delimitation of pragmatics and the set of categories defining pragmatic contexts, the main aim of research should be kept in mind, viz to account for certain systematic properties of language use. As an expedient strategy, then, we only are paying attention to those categories which systematically differentiate the pragmatic functions of certain linguistic expressions. In other words: a pragmatic theory should not merely give independent appropriateness conditions for utterances, but specify which properties of utterances (realized sentences and discourses) depend on these conditions.

Perhaps the most obvious relationship between semantics and pragmatics is exemplified by PERFORMATIVE SENTENCES, such as *I promise to come, I advise you to go*, etc which denote the illocutionary act executed by the very utterance of these sentences in the appropriate context. That is, in the present tense and first person they are pragmatically self-verifying: they are true by the simple fact of being uttered in some appropriate context.[8]

A more general relationship between pragmatics and semantics (and hence with the other grammatical properties of sentences) is constituted by the constraints of the pragmatic conditions with respect to the PROPOSITIONAL CONTENT of the illocutionary act. Thus, in promises and threats the proposition expressed must denote a future act of the speaker, in reproaches and accusations a past act of the hearer, in orders, requests and advices a future act of the hearer, etc. Hence personal pronouns, predicates and tenses must be such that those propositions may be satisfied.

In the case of INDIRECT SPEECH ACTS, such as *Could you lend me some money?* and *There is a bad tyre on that car*, COUNTING AS a request and a warning, respectively, the propositional content corresponds to some necessary condition of the illocutionary act, *eg* pertains to abilities of the hearer or some dangerous state of affairs.[9]

Finally, syntax, intonation and particles may be used as INDICATORS of certain illocutionary classes, even if this relation need neither be necessary nor sufficient: thus, the indicative syntactic structure and intonation may correspond to assertion-like or assertion-based illocutionary acts, the interrogative with question and request-type acts, and the imperative with commands, threats, etc. In some languages, such as German, Dutch and Greek, specific pragmatic structures may be expressed by PARTICLES. Thus one function of German *doch* is to express the fact that the speaker assumes that the hearer knows (or should know) already the proposition asserted by the speaker.[10]

In the subsequent chapters we will be interested in particular in the systematic relations between certain properties of discourse structure, *eg* connectives, and properties of illocutionary acts and act sequences. In order to be able to do this, some final remarks are necessary about composite speech acts and sequences of speech acts.

3.8

Illocutionary acts, typically, do not come alone. They are part of SEQUENCES OF ACTION in general or of SEQUENCES OF SPEECH ACTS in particular. These sequences must satisfy the usual conditions for action sequences. Thus, it may be required that the final state (result) of some speech act is a necessary condition for the successfulness of a following (speech) act. In this sense, an illocutionary act may be an AUXILIARY ACT in a course of interaction. If I want to have some book in the possession of a participant in the social situation, I may expect that he will give me the book without my interference, or I may take the book, or I may give some conventional signal to the effect that the book be given to me. In the latter case an utterance of natural language will be the most prominent means to satisfy my wishes. Similarly, changes in the social situation may be brought about by illocutionary acts such that the appropriate conditions are satisfied for other actions of the hearer: the hearer may act upon the OBLIGATIONS instituted by the illocutionary act. This reaction may again be an illocutionary act, thereby constituting a sequence of CONVERSATION. *A* accuses *B* of *p*, whereupon *B* rejects the accusation or makes excuses for having done *p*. The conversational sequence, as we said above, must satisfy the requirement that the final state s_i

after illocutionary act F_i is an appropriate initial condition for the illocutionary act F_{i+1}. I may apologize for having done p if I assume that my hearer knows that I have done p and disapproves of p, which assumption may have been (perlocutionarily) brought about by the successful accomplishment of a previous accusation by my hearer, which implies the initial conditions of my apologizing. Note, however, that such sequences of illocutionary acts need not as such be 'necessary': each illocutionary act is, in general, successful with respect to a specific structure of the context, whether this actual context is brought about by an illocutionary act or by another act or event. Therefore, we cannot simply say that an apology PRESUPPOSES an accusation or reproach, unlike the case of QUESTION and ANSWER, which however are not specific illocutionary acts but certain structural functions of illocutionary acts: I may answer a question BY all kinds of illocutionary acts. On the other hand, there are examples in which the interactional sequence is practically wholly verbal. A judge may acquit somebody only after an accusation and after assertions that are sufficient conditions for acquittal.

In the following chapters it will be investigated how an analysis of sequences of illocutionary acts relates to sequences of sentences in discourse, and thus how pragmatic coherence may codetermine the semantic coherence of a discourse. Similarly, as for semantic macro-structures, it may be the case that sequences of illocutionary acts are to be described at an additional level of global speech acts, which would be a justification of not merely wanting to study isolated speech acts with respect to a context, but whole conversations with respect to a context.

Notes

1 After Peirce's work (see Peirce 1960), it has mainly been Morris (1946) who has formulated the task of a pragmatic component of semiotic theories. For discussion, see Lieb (1976).

2 See Austin (1962) and Searle (1969) as the two basic works that have given rise to further developments in philosophical and linguistic pragmatics. In the following we take for granted that the basic results in the philosophical theory of speech acts are known.

3 For recent advances in pragmatics, especially linguistic pragmatics, see Bar-Hillel, ed (1972), Kasher, ed (1976), Cole and Morgan, eds (1975), Sadock (1975), Wunderlich, ed (1972), van Dijk, ed (1975), Wunderlich (1976).

4 A similar approach is taken in Groenendijk and Stokhof (1976).

5 For a discussion of the notion of 'utterance', see Kasher (1972).

6 For instance it may be asked in what sense we may MEAN something without – at least tacitly – realizing some language expression. Secondly, increasingly complex cases may arise in which, ad hoc or under special agreement, we may mean q although we express p, or mean certain implications of p as given by specific pragmatic rules of conversation. For detail of these and similar problems, see current work in the philosophy of language, *eg* Grice (1971, 1967), Schiffer (1972).

7 In addition there is a subset of specific constraints on the epistemic set of speakers. For instance for certain utterances involving modal sentences it must be the case

that neither p nor $\sim p$ is part of the epistemic set, *eg* if I assert *Perhaps Peter is ill.* Similarly, in composite sentence utterances it may not be the case that one part has epistemic preconditions conflicting with those of other parts of the utterance, as in *Peter is ill, but I know he isn't,* or *Maybe Peter is ill, but I know he isn't.* For details and formal treatment, see Groenendijk and Stokhof (1975, 1976), who have called these kinds of conditions CORRECTNESS conditions, which are pragmatic and given parallel to the normal truth conditions of sentences, whereby sentences may be true but incorrect, or false but correct. Note that correctness conditions are a specific subset of pragmatic appropriateness conditions, because they are formulated in terms of structures of language users in contexts.

8 For details see Groenendijk and Stokhof (1976) and the references given there to further philosophical work on performative sentences, a notion first discussed by Austin (1961, 1962).

9 See Searle (1975*a*) and Frank (1975) for the notion of an indirect speech act.

10 See Franck (1977) for a discussion of the specific pragmatic function of particles, especially in German.

Chapter 8

The pragmatics of discourse

1 Aims and problems of discourse pragmatics
1.1
In this and the following chapter we are concerned with the pragmatics of discourse, *ie* with the systematic relations between structures of text and context. This means, on the one hand, that we must try to make explicit which specific properties of discourse are determined by the structure of language users, illocutionary acts and information processing in conversation. On the other hand certain discourse structures, when uttered in conversation, may themselves establish part of the communicative context.

The same distinction as has been made for the semantics will be made at the pragmatic level, viz between LINEAR STRUCTURES and GLOBAL MACRO-STRUCTURES. Whereas the latter will be treated in our last chapter, this chapter will investigate the relations between the linear, sequential structure of discourse and the linear structure of context, viz between SEQUENCES OF SENTENCES and SEQUENCES OF SPEECH ACTS.

The reason for this approach is the following. Relations between propositions or sentences in a discourse cannot exhaustively be described in semantic terms alone. In the first part of this book it has become clear on several occasions that conditions imposed on connectives and connection in general, as well as coherence, topic, focus, perspective and similar notions, also have a pragmatic base. In other words: not only do we want to represent certain facts and relations between facts in some possible world, but at the same time to put such a textual representation to use in the transmission of information about these facts and, hence in the performance of specific social acts.

1.2
One of the first problems to be treated in such a framework is that pertaining to the differences between COMPOSITE SENTENCES and SEQUENCES OF

SENTENCES in discourse. At the semantic level, we were primarily concerned with relations between propositions, whether these are expressed within the same composite sentence or within several sentences. Although sentences and sequences may be semantically equivalent they may reasonably be expected to have at least different pragmatic functions. Other systematic differences in the use of sentences and sequences are stylistic, rhetorical, cognitive and social, and will not be discussed here. It will be argued that the pragmatic distinction between the expression of information in composite sentences versus the expression of information in a sequence of sentences depends on the intended illocutionary acts, on their internal structure, and on the ordering of such acts.

1.3

The problem of the DISTRIBUTION OF INFORMATION in discourse is not only semantic. In processes of communicative interaction this ordering depends on what we know and believe and on our beliefs about the knowledge of our conversation partners. Similarly, the information ordering is subject to our own wishes and intentions for action and our assumptions about those of the hearer. TOPICS OF CONVERSATION are initiated and changed under these constraints. Information may be more or less 'relevant' or 'important' with respect to a context thus defined. The same facts may be described from different points of view or under different 'propositional attitudes'. It is within such a framework, then, that notions like PRESUPPOSITION (*eg* versus ASSERTION) and TOPIC-COMMENT require further explication, viz as principles of social information processing in conversational contexts.

1.4

Besides these and other pragmatic properties of connection, coherence, information distribution, sentence and clause sequencing, perspective and relative importance in discourse, this chapter must focus on their relevance for the accomplishment of SEQUENCES OF ILLOCUTIONARY ACTS. That is, we want to know what necessary or sufficient conditions must be satisfied in order for speech acts to be combined, which acts are 'presupposed', focused upon, directly or indirectly intended, and in general how sequences of speech acts are connected and coherent.

2 Sentences and sequences
2.1

Let us start our inquiry into the pragmatics of discourse with a problem of immediate grammatical importance, viz the difference between COMPOSITE SENTENCES and SEQUENCES OF SENTENCES. In later sections the more general theoretical background for such a distinction will then be developed.

Consider, for instance, the following pairs of examples:

[1]*a:* Peter had an accident. He is in hospital.
   b: Peter is in hospital. He had an accident.

[2]*a:* Peter had an accident. So, he is in hospital.

   b: Peter had an accident, so he is in hospital.

[3] Peter is in hospital, for he had an accident.

[4]*a:* Because he had an accident, Peter is in hospital.

   b: Peter is in hospital, because he had an accident.

Apparently, there are various morpho-syntactic ways to express the 'same' information about an ordered sequence of facts. In all these examples, reference is made to the fact that Peter had an accident and that Peter is in hospital (now) and that the first fact caused the second fact. In other words, the different expressions are semantically equivalent at least in one sense of semantic equivalence: they have the same truth conditions.

Yet, at another level of analysis the equivalence does not hold. The differences appear both between sentences with distinct syntactic structure and between sentences and sequences.

Taking the last examples first, we see that subordinated causal clauses may either occur in 'first' or in 'second' position, viz precede or follow the main clause. Sentence [4]*a* however may be used in a context in which (the speaker assumes that) the hearer knows that Peter had an accident, whereas [4]*b* is used in a context in which the hearer knows that Peter is in hospital.[1] That is, the APPROPRIATENESS of the respective sentences depends on the knowledge and beliefs of speech participants at a certain point in the conversational context. On the other hand, examples [1–3] are normally used in those contexts in which the speaker has no such assumptions about the knowledge of the hearer, or rather in which he assumes that the hearer does NOT know either of the facts referred to. This means that [1]*a*–[3] would be inappropriate answers to any of the following previous questions of the hearer:

[5] Why is Peter in hospital?

[6] Where is Peter? They say he had an accident.

Sentence [4]*b*, however, is appropriate after question [5], whereas [4]*a*, although perhaps a bit awkward, is appropriate after [6].

The complex sentence, apparently, has properties which are similar to that of the TOPIC-COMMENT articulation: 'known' elements come in first position, 'new' elements in second position. Since the known element in this case is a proposition, we may say that the first clauses in [4] are PRAGMATICALLY PRESUPPOSED.[2] Hence, one of the differences between the sequences and the coordinated compound sentences is that relating to the well-known ASSERTION-PRESUPPOSITION distinction: in [1–3] each proposition expressed by the utterance of the sentence or sequence is asserted, whereas in [4] only the second position propositions are asserted and the first position sentences presupposed (in the pragmatic sense of this term, *ie* assumed by the speaker to be known to the hearer). Yet, there is a difficulty, because we may also maintain that both [4]*a* and [4]*b*, taken as a whole, are assertions. Below, we therefore will have to find out whether two different meanings of the term 'assertion' play a role here.

2.2

More crucial for our discussion, however, are the differences between [1]*a*, [1]*b*, [2]*a*, [2]*b* and [3]: what implications does the ordering of sentences have, if not presuppositional, and in what respect are compound sentences different from their corresponding, *ie* semantically equivalent, sequences?

Although [1]*a* and [1]*b* are equally appropriate in many contexts, there are also contexts in which the first seems more natural than the second, *eg* after a question like

[7] What happened to Peter?

eg on seeing his car badly damaged. On the other hand [1]*b* seems more appropriate after a question like

[8] Why doesn't Peter answer his telephone?

That is, the reason he doesn't answer his telephone is the one requested by the previous speaker, and in the answer this information is given first. The second sentence in [1]*b* then gives an EXPLANATION of the fact referred to by the first sentence. In [1]*a* no such explanation is given, only a representation of the facts, implying that the first fact caused the second. This relation between the ordering of facts and the ordering of clauses or sentences in a sequence will be further discussed below.

It might be argued that [2]*a* merely explicitly expresses the causal connection which in [1]*a* is only 'expressed' by syntactic ordering,[3] and that the same holds for [2]*b*. Again, however, there are different contextual conditions, hence pragmatic differences between [1]*a*, [2]*a* and [2]*b*. Sentences like [2]*a* are typically used when CONCLUSIONS from certain facts are to be drawn RELATIVE TO A GIVEN SITUATION. If during a board meeting several members do not show up, the president may say "*Harry had to meet Pierre Balmain. So, he is in Paris*", and then utter sentence [2]*a*, possibly by stressing *Peter* and *he*. In this respect, [2]*a* shares a pragmatic function with [1]*b*, viz it draws attention to the fact which is of primary importance or RELEVANCE FOR A CERTAIN SITUATION, but in [2]*a* this fact is not only referred to as a factual consequence but also as a conclusion drawn explicitly by the speaker. This is typically the case in those cases where only indirect factual evidence is present, *eg* in *Peter's car is damaged. So, he must have had an accident*. This does not hold for interclausal *so* in [2]*b*, which only expresses, coordinatingly, the causal connection between the two facts referred to by the respective clauses.[4] Hence, in [2]*b so* is a proper SEMANTIC CONNECTIVE, whereas in [2]*a* sentence initial *So*, followed by a pause, rather relates utterances or illocutionary acts, viz those of premise and conclusion.[5] In that case we may speak of a PRAGMATIC CONNECTIVE.

In some languages, *eg* in Dutch and in German, the difference between semantic and pragmatic *so* (*dus* and *also* respectively) may also show in the syntax. Inter-clausal (semantic) connectives are followed by Verb-Subject ordering, whereas sentence-initial connectives followed by a pause may also have normal Subject-Verb ordering.[6]

Finally, we may use interclausal *for* in order to relate a fact which has, so to speak, 'pragmatic prominence' focused on its cause or reason, much in the same way as [4]*a* – although *for*-clauses cannot be presupposed. The difference with [1]*b* is that *for*-clauses do not have an explanatory function; they merely state a condition of another fact stated before, in the same way as interclausal *so* states a consequence of a fact stated before.[7]

2.3

Until now we have met the following differences between sentences and sequences, *eg* in [1–4]: different presuppositions, *ie* different knowledge-belief structures of the context, focus on the reason/cause or on the consequence, the relevance or importance of a certain fact for the present context, *eg* the interests of the hearer, indications of conclusion or explanation as specific acts. Some of these differences are rather vague and require further definition. The notion of RELEVANCE or IMPORTANCE, with respect to a certain context, should for instance be defined in terms of the action theoretical semantics used earlier in this book. In that case a fact, and hence the knowledge of such a fact, is important relative to a context or in general to a situation if it is an IMMEDIATE CONDITION for a probable event or action (or prevention of these) in that context or situation. In the board meeting situation, the proposition 'Peter can't come' is more directly important for that meeting than the reason 'Peter is in hospital', which is in turn more relevant than the fact that he had an accident. On the other hand, in a situation in which Peter's wife is informed of the events, the information about the accident may well be much more important than the fact that he is in hospital, which are both more important than the fact that he did not have dinner that night.

Similarly, notions like that of FOCUS and PERSPECTIVE must be made explicit to account for the differences. Thus, a sequence of facts may be described from the point of view of the time, place and involved agents of the action or event, but also from the point of view of the observer or 'informant' at the time-place of the context. In the first case we may have compound sentences with semantic connectives, in the latter case, a sequence with a pragmatic connective may be more appropriate:

[9] I felt ill, so I went to bed.

[10] Peter is ill. So, he won't come tonight.

Typical for pragmatic connectives, which may be considered as INFERENTIAL ADVERBS, is that they cannot be preceded by *and*, whereas semantic *so* can be preceded by *and*. Sentence initial *So*, used to make inferences is also typically used in dialogues, as in:

[11] *A*. Where is Peter?

  B. He is in hospital. He had an accident.

  A. So, he won't come tonight. Let us start.

That is, speaker *A* draws an inference from the facts presented by *B*, such that the conclusion is a condition for the actual events of the situation. In some occasions we may have semantic *so* in a dialogue at the beginning of a response, but in that case, it rather continues, by assertion or question, a sentence of the previous speaker:

[12] *A*. John went to the pub.

$$B. \begin{cases} \text{So he is drunk.} \\ \text{So he is drunk?} \end{cases}$$

The differences with pragmatic *So* are expressed by stress, pause and intonation. Note that inferential *So*, and sometimes also sentence-initial *Therefore*, with rising-falling intonation and followed by a pause (in writing by a comma), not only introduce conclusions denoting consequences of certain facts, but may also introduce INFERRED reasons or causes (often together with *must*):

[13] John was drunk that night. So, he went to the pub again.

Given the correct presuppositional structure, we may also use *because* for such 'backward' inferences:

[14] John was (must have been) in the pub, because he was drunk.

Sentences like [14], however, may be ambiguous. On a first reading the first clause is asserted and the second, if presupposed, gives an explanation, by specifying a reason for believing the first proposition. On a second reading, the first clause is presupposed, and the second is asserted as a warrant for a (known) conclusion. Just as for the other examples, our intuitions may be rather weak for these examples, but we must find the theoretical conditions and rules at least to explain the clear cases.

3 Connectives, connection and context
3.1
The discussion in the previous section about the assumed pragmatic differences between compound sentences, complex sentences and sequences, has been based on examples with causal and inferential connectives, such as *so*, *because*, *since*, *therefore*, *for*, etc. We now must see whether similar differences hold for other connectives.
3.2
Taking the basic conjoining connective, *and*, we first of all should recall that *and* is essentially coordinative, so that it cannot be related to syntactic differences expressing presuppositional differences, as was the case with *because*. Secondly, the major use of *and* is interclausal, which seems to make it an exclusively semantic connective. In such cases, clausal ordering must parallel temporal, causal, or conditional orderings of the facts:

[15] Peter had an accident, and he is in hospital.
[16] We visited the Johnson's, and played bridge.
[17] Peter is in hospital, and he had an accident.
[18] We played bridge and we visited the Johnson's.

Clearly, [17] and [18] are unacceptable under the same meaning as [15] and [16], respectively, especially if in [15] and [16] the first clauses determine the topic of discourse with respect to which the second clause is to be interpreted. In [17] and [18] the clauses are not connected because the denoted facts are not conditionally related (in that order). Sentence initial *And* typically occurs in examples like:

[19] Peter was not at the party. And Henry said that he was in hospital because he had had an accident.
[20] Laura ran off to Paris. And she did not even let mè know.
[21] No, I don't need the month's bestseller. And please do not call next month either.

Sentence initial *And* may introduce propositions denoting preceding facts. Just like *moreover* it does not denote conjoined facts, but rather it conjoins utterances, viz by indicating an ADDITION or CONTINUATION of a given statement. Secondly, *And* is used in order to change the topic or perspective of a sequence. Thus, in [19] from Peter's absence at the party to Henry's explanation of that fact, and in [20] from Laura's action to my reaction of surprise. In [21] *And* may be used to relate DIFFERENT SPEECH ACTS, viz a refusal and a request. In that sense we might say that *And* relates, implicitly, the actions involved, viz '(not) trying to sell a book now' and '(not) trying to sell a book next month', as may also be seen from the specific use of *either*.

More generally, *And* may be used as an indirect connective, *eg* in ENUMERATIONS, of facts which are not directly related, but which occur during a certain time or in a given situation, typically in everyday narrative, *eg* of children:

[22] We went to the Zoo. And, daddy gave us an icecream. And, we had fun.

3.3
Similar remarks may be made for sentence initial *Or* as opposed to interclausal *or*, disjoining facts in alternative possible worlds:

[23] Peter won't come of course. Or didn't you know that he is in hospital?
[24] Peter must be ill. Or perhaps he got drunk again.
[25] Let's call the police. Or no, we'd better not tell them.

Whereas *And* has an 'additive' nature, pragmatic *Or* may indicate HESITATION and CORRECTION. In [23] the disjunction does not pertain to denoted facts but to the speech acts performed. The first sentence presupposes that there is (known) evidence for Peter's absence. Having uttered the sentence, the speaker however may have some doubt about the knowledge of the hearer and therefore 'corrects' his assertion by asking whether the presupposed knowledge is present. More accurately, it may be supposed that *Or* relates the pragmatically implied proposition 'you know that Peter is in hospital' with the expressed 'you do not know that Peter is in hospital'. Such corrective uses of *Or* occur when the speaker is not sure whether the conditions of a performed speech acts were satisfied.

Similarly, in [24] a 'disjunction' of the facts alone would require a compound sentence, so that we must assume that [24] should be taken as a 'disjunction' of conclusions, along the 'or else' meaning of *or*. Since both speech acts are actually performed, we could hardly speak of a real disjunction, so that the second sentence also has a corrective nature, by presenting the possibility of an ALTERNATIVE explanation of some fact. The corrective use of *Or* clearly appears in [25], where an exhortation is really cancelled by an exhortation not to execute the requested action.

3.4

More complicated are the interclausal and intersentential differences among the concessives and contrastives *but*, *although*, *yet* and *nevertheless*, of which *although* is subordinative, the others coordinative, *but* a proper interclausal conjunction, and *yet* and *nevertheless* sentence-initial adverbs.

Note, first of all, that the various connectives of this class do not always have the same meaning. *But* may denote (i) unexpected consequence (ii) unfulfilled conditions and (iii) contrast, as in:

[26] John is rich, but he didn't pay for his beer.
[27] We want to go to the movies, but we have no money.
[28] He wouldn't order a gin, but he had a beer.

We may only use *although* and *yet*, however, in the first meaning of *but*, viz the unexpected consequence. The following sentences show a shift in acceptability or meaning:

[29] Although we have no money, we want to go to the movies.
[30] He wouldn't order a gin. Yet, he had a beer.

Unlike conjunctions and causals, concessives may not be expressed by mere coordination of sentences:

[31] John is rich. He didn't pay for his beer.

That is, in general asyndetic coordination may be used to 'express' either a natural consecution of events, a causal relationship, co-occurrence, or else a natural sequence of speech acts, such as an assertion and an explanation, an addition or a conclusion.

What are the differences between interclausal *but*, and sentential *yet* when having the 'unexpected consequence' meaning? One of the differences seems to be the following, although again intuitions are rather weak for such cases: *but* essentially relates two events which are, as such, somehow incompatible, in the sense that the second fact is an 'exception' to the normal consequences of the first fact:

[32] He is very clever, but he couldn't prove the theorem.

The same holds for relations between more general facts:

[33] The glass is very thin, but it is unbreakable.

We use *yet*, however, in those cases not only when one fact is incompatible with another, *eg* physically or otherwise, but also when actual knowledge is incompatible with justified expectations of the speaker or at least with those the hearer presumes the speaker to have.

[34] He cannot fish. Nevertheless, he caught a pike.
[35] Peter is ill. Yet, he'll come to the meeting.

In such examples the speaker refers to facts which occur but which were not expected, *ie* such connectives rather indicate PROPOSITIONAL ATTITUDES than relations between facts. This pragmatic nature of *yet* and *nevertheless* also appears in dialogues:

[36] *A*. This glass is really very thin!
     B. And yet, it is unbreakable.

In such cases we also use sentence initial *But*, often followed by *nevertheless*. Its function is to *deny* or CONTRADICT certain expectations implied by utterances of a previous speaker. As for the other pragmatic connectives, the contrastives/concessives may characterize certain SPEECH ACT SEQUENCES.

4 Speech act sequences
4.1
In our analysis of the differences between composite sentences and sequences which are semantically equivalent, and of the corresponding differences in the use of connectives, we have observed a number of constraints requiring the use of sequences instead of composite sentences, and conversely. One of these conditions was that new sentences and certain connectives indicate specific speech act sequences, *eg* an assertion followed by an explanation or addition, an assertion followed by a correction or alternative, or an assertion followed by a denial or contradiction.

In general it can be argued that sentence boundaries are particularly appropriate to express boundaries between speech acts. Now, at first sight this assumption seems to be inconsistent with examples in which two speech acts are apparently accomplished by the utterance of one sentence:

[37] I'll give you the money, but you don't deserve it.
[38] I wouldn't go to Italy at the moment, because the weather is very bad there.

In [37] we have a promise and then an assertive evaluation, whereas in [38] we have a piece of advice followed by an assertion.

On the other hand, there are many examples where speech acts cannot easily be performed by the utterance of one sentence:

[39] It is cold in here and please shut the window.
[40] Because I am busy, shut up!
[41] Because I have no watch, what is the time?

The reason [39–41] are unacceptable is that the connectives used have a semantic interpretation: they relate denoted facts. However, no such relation exists in these sentences: my being cold and your shutting the window, my being busy and your shutting up, and my having no watch and your telling me the time are not directly related. Rather, we should say, my being cold is a condition for making a request, my being busy a condition for giving an order,[8] and my not having a watch for asking a question. That is, the first speech act provides a CONDITION of the next speech act, much in the same way as a proposition may be a condition of interpretation or presupposition of a following proposition in a sequence. In all cases, the preliminary assertion provides a motivation for the request, command or question. What is needed, then, are pragmatic, sentence initial connectives or simply new sentences for cases like [39–41]. The conclusion from these examples would be that a change of illocutionary force requires the utterance of a new sentence.

There remain such counterexamples as [37] and [38]. Consider also:

[42] Please shut the door and turn the heater on!
[43] Please shut the door and please turn the heater on!
[44] Please shut the door or please turn the heater on!

The question is: one or two speech acts? That with sentences like [42] we accomplish only one request, viz to do two things, may be concluded from the inappropriateness of [43] and [44]. If we had two requests, the repetition of please would be acceptable. Similarly, in the disjunction we perform one request, viz that the hearer executes one of two alternative actions. Similarly, in [37] the second clause does not primarily intend to contradict the promise, but rather it denotes a normal condition for (not) promising. In [38] the state of the weather itself is a condition for (not) going to Italy, not primarily for the advice. In fact I do not motivate my advice but give a reason for the hearer why a certain action should not be undertaken. Of course, KNOWLEDGE of such conditions or reasons is a necessary element of appropriate advices. Yet, [38] does not make an assertion when uttered but counts as a piece of advice, just as [37] counts as a promise.

4.2

In order to provide a sound basis for these assumptions we should look somewhat closer into the nature of (speech) act sequences. In the theory of action we have postulated single acts and composite acts; the latter may either be compound, viz if they consist of components acts at the same level, or complex, viz if some act is embedded in one of the component major acts, *eg* as an auxiliary act. A sequence of actions is interpreted as ONE action if they can be assigned one global intention or plan, and on a more general level this action can in turn be a condition or a consequence of other actions. In other cases, we just speak about SEQUENCES of actions.

The same distinctions hold for speech acts. We may have sequences of speech acts, but some of such sequences may be interpreted as one speech act, consisting of several component or auxiliary acts. In the next chapter, we shall also speak of macro-speech acts, *ie the global speech act performed by the utterance of a whole discourse, and executed by a sequence of possibly different speech acts.*

Let us give some examples of composite speech acts:

[45] Please shut the window. I am cold.
[46] You have done your best. I'll give you a new bike.
[47] Peter is in hospital. Harry told me.

It may be maintained that [45] does not PRIMARILY want to make an assertion about my physcial state but to make a request, although it cannot be denied that the utterance of the second sentence of [45] counts as an assertion. Hence, for [45], AS A WHOLE, to be interpreted as a request, the assertion must in some sense be part of the request. For requests to be appropriate, they must be sensible in the sense that they are motivated, such that satisfaction of the requested action by the hearer at the same time satisfies a desire of the speaker. By specifying a 'justification' for my request I make it more 'acceptable', in the strict sense of that term: the probability that the hearer will comply with my request may be enhanced.[9] In certain contexts, in which politeness is required, such a 'justification' of a speech act is essential.

Similarly, [46] is primarily a promise, not an assertion. First of all, the hearer already knows that he did his best so he need not be told. The first sentence therefore functions as a praise and as a recognition of the merits of the hearer by the speaker, who, thereby, establishes a certain obligation with respect to the hearer. Once this condition is fulfilled, the hearer is able to make a promise. Again, the assertion is used to express a part of the promise conditions, viz the obligation of the speaker.

Example [47] has a different character. As a whole it functions as an assertion (that Peter is in hospital), consisting of two assertions. That Harry told me is probably of secondary importance. Assertions, however, also need 'justification'. That is, the SOURCE of our knowledge must be reliable and, if necessary, be specified. Besides direct observation and inference, the basic source of our knowledge is information obtained from others. The second assertion of [47] specifies the source of information which justifies the first. The more reliable a given source, the higher the credibility of the assertion based on it.

In the three examples, then, we have speech acts, viz assertions, which somehow function as a condition, part or basis for another speech act. It should however be specified whether the whole speech act is compound or complex, *ie* whether the assertions are essential components or merely auxiliary actions of the ('main') speech act.[10]

Although the distinction between component acts and auxiliary acts is perhaps not always clear cut, we might say that the motivation in [45] is a component part of the request, in some contexts even an essential component, because it expresses an essential condition of the act of requesting, viz that we have some wish or desire. Characteristically, the sentence *I am cold*, may independently be used as an INDIRECT SPEECH ACT, viz as a request to shut the window, given the appropriate context. Conversely, the second assertion in [47] seems to have auxiliary function: it indicates how I got the information and thus how I could make another assertion, but is not itself part of it, as for example the condition 'I want you to know that *p*', in:

[48] Peter is in hospital. I thought you might want to know.

where the second assertion gives a motivation for making the first one: assumed interest is essential for information.

More problematic is [46]. In a sense, the first sentence expresses a motivation for the promise. At the same time it satisfies a preparatory condition for promises, viz that the speaker is in a certain state of gratitude, obligation or admiration. Yet, although previous praise may be a sufficient condition to establish the context for a promise, it is certainly not necessary. On the other hand, I only promise to do something for somebody if my action is beneficiary for the hearer. That means that the second assertion in the following example may be used to express part of the conditions for promising:

[49] I'll give you a bike. You need one.

Along this line of reasoning, [46] would be a complex speech act, in which the first prepares the second. It might however also be argued that [46] is not a composite speech act at all, but a proper sequence, viz of praise and a following promise, if the speaker wants both to praise the hearer and to make a promise.

The distinctions made above are admittedly subtle, but it should be kept in mind that the structure of illocutionary acts and of interaction in general has certain properties which are very similar to those of propositional structure. Acts simply do not merely follow each other at the same level: sequences of acts may be taken as one act, and some acts may have secondary rank with respect to others, viz as preparatory or auxiliary acts. By uttering sequences like [45] for example in a train situation, I primarily have the intention that somebody should close the window for me (given the condition that I can not do it myself), not to inform him that I am cold, because my fellow passenger, if a stranger, may well not be at all interested in whether I am cold or not.

That is, the assertion that I am cold has the function of a motivation for another speech act, viz the request.

4.3

With these theoretical assumptions about the structure of speech act sequences we must return to the sentence versus sequence problem, and try to answer the question whether the utterance of sentences like [37] and [38] counts as one single or one composite speech act or as a sequence of speech acts.

For [37] we can say at least that even if the utterance of the second clause were a separate speech act, viz an assertion, it is not preparatory, auxiliary or otherwise part of the promise executed by the utterance of the first clause. At most we could take it as a qualification of the promise (*cf* also conditional promises, see below). If we had the sentence

[50] You got the money, but you didn't deserve it.

we would have the 'same' state of affairs represented, but this time as the assertion of a fact (of which the first, incidentally, is known to the hearer). Hence, we could say for [37] that there is one promise, but taking a compound sentence, representing a compound fact, as its argument, viz that I give you the money in a possible world which normally depends on 'you deserve it'. This tentative solution seems more acceptable, however, for the case in which the concessive clause is subordinated:

[51] Although you don't deserve it, I'll give you the money.

in which the first clause is pragmatically presupposed and hence not an independent assertion, so that one promise is made by the utterance of a complex sentence. Similarly for [38]: I give just one piece of advice, viz not to go to Italy because of the bad weather; that is, the advice is based on a complex proposition. The problem there, however, is that the subordinate clause carries the 'new information', viz the comment of the sentence, but at the same time the first clause cannot be presupposed, pragmatically, because it 'carries' the advice, which is also 'new'. So, we have an additional problem, viz that concerning the relations between topic-comment or presupposition-assertion on the one hand, and (composite) speech acts on the other hand. This problem will receive specific attention below.

4.4

A special problem is the illocutionary status of CONDITIONAL SENTENCES, *eg*

[52]*a:* If I go to Italy this summer, I'll send you a postcard.
    b: If you go to Italy this summer, you must visit San Gimignano.

The utterance of such sentences counts as a conditional promise and as a piece of conditional advice, respectively. These terms, however, may be misleading. They should not be understood to mean that a promise or the giving of advice is performed only if the conditional clauses are satisfied. In both cases the utterance of the conditional sentence counts as a proper promise or piece of advice, but only the DOMAIN OF VALIDITY of the promise is restricted. That is, I only send a postcard in those possible worlds which are determined by 'I go to Italy (this summer)' – possible worlds. The same holds for the advice. Hence, the *if*-clause does not pertain to the speech act, but to the acts referred to in the main clause, viz as a necessary or sufficient condition for these acts.

The situation is somewhat similar with that of MODAL EXPRESSIONS, *eg* in *Maybe I'll send you a postcard*, which may also count as a promise, but the domain of validity is restricted to at least one possible world.[11] In fact, the actual satisfaction of denoted acts does not influence the correct performance of illocutionary acts: I have made a promise, even if for some reason I cannot execute it. The necessary condition is that, at the moment of making the promise, I sincerely believe that I will execute the promised action. For conditionals and modals I also sincerely promise, but not simply to do A, but to do A in w_i or w_B.

Although *if . . . then* is a very specific connective, which presumably has a modal status and hence is not properly interclausal or intersentential, stressed *if* (often preceded by *at least* or *that is*) may be used at the beginning of a next sentence in order to restrict the domain of validity of a promise made by the utterance of the previous sentence:

[53] I'll send you a postcard this summer. At least, if I go to Italy.

Again, the connective here does not merely introduce a semantic restriction, but at the same time operates as a pragmatic connective, linking a promise with a CORRECTION or SPECIFICATION of the promise.

The *if*-conditional illocutionary acts shed some light on our earlier problem with the illocutionary status of composite sentences. Thus, as we suggested, the *because*-clause in [38] specifies a reason for the advised action (not to go to Italy), and hence specifies the domain of validity of the advice. If my hearer finds out that the weather is not bad in Italy so that my information is wrong, he is no longer 'committed' to my advice, because he only had to follow it in those possible worlds determined by the 'bad weather in Italy'-worlds. If we just had advice followed by an assertion, the advice would still hold even if the assertion turned out to be ill-founded. Nor can we say that I dissuade somebody from doing something, *because* I assert something. Yet, in the context for [38], the speaker obviously must assume that the hearer does not know that the weather is bad in Italy. In intuitive terms, then, we could still claim that an assertion is made by [38]. So what is the relationship between information processing and illocutionary acts?

5 Pragmatic information processing
5.1
The basic idea of pragmatics is that when we are speaking in certain contexts we also accomplish certain social acts. Our intentions for such actions, as well

as the interpretations of intentions of actions of other speech participants, are based however on sets of KNOWLEDGE and BELIEF. Characteristic of communicative contexts is that these sets are different for speaker and hearer, although largely overlapping, and that the knowledge set of the hearer changes during the communication, ideally according to the purposes of the speaker. Trivially, when we make a promise or give advice, we want the hearer to *know* that we make a promise or give advice. This knowledge is the result of a correct interpretation of the intended illocutionary act. At the same time we want the hearer to know 'what' we are asserting, promising or advising, viz what is the case, what we wish to be the case, what is to be done or what we will do, in some possible world (mostly the actual one). By uttering the sentence *John is ill* I may express the propositional concept 'that John is ill', and in so doing accomplish a referential act if I denote the fact that John is (now) ill. These, as we saw, fairly complex acts have a social point as soon as I have the intention to demonstrate that I have this particular knowledge about this particular fact. But as long as my observer-hearer also has this knowledge, there is little more than such a demonstration, and nothing changes beyond the fact that my hearer understands that I have some knowledge. My semantic acts acquire a pragmatic function only if I have the additional assumption that the hearer does not possess certain knowledge (about the world, about my internal states) and the purpose to CHANGE the knowledge of my hearer as a consequence of the interpretation of my semantic (meaning, referential) act, by which I express my knowledge or other internal state. If this purpose is realized I have accomplished a successful COMMUNICATIVE act, that is I have been able to add some propositional INFORMATION to the knowledge of my hearer.[12]

5.2

This picture is well-known. But, as soon as we try to analyse the details of such communicative acts, problems arise. In previous chapters we have already met the difficulty of distinguishing, within the sentence, 'old' from 'new' information, and topics from comments. In a simple sentence like *John is ill*, with normal intonation, this seems quite straightforward: 'John' is or expresses the topic, because the phrase or argument refers to a known referent, whereas 'is ill', which has comment-function, refers to an unknown property of John.

Yet, we have assumed that information comes in propositional chunks, so that the new information is indeed 'John is ill', or perhaps '*a* is ill' if John has been referred to earlier in the conversation and if $a =$ John. In any case, the noun phrase *John* not only identifies, and refers to, a specific referent, but at the same time indicates what the sentence, or the discourse, is ABOUT.

Cognitively, this means presumably that part of our knowledge-set, viz the 'John'-part, is activated, containing general and accidental knowledge and beliefs about John. The new information 'John is ill (now)' may then be added to our actual knowledge about John.

If this epistemic change takes place according to the purposes of the speaker and through the interpretation of his utterance, we say that this change is a consequence of the basic pragmatic act of an ASSERTION.

Somewhat more complicated is the situation with composite sentences, *eg Because John is ill, he won't come tonight*. The question is: does this WHOLE sentence, when uttered in an appropriate context, count also as an assertion, or only the second clause? In the latter case: what act is performed by the utterance of the first clause? If above we assumed for such sentences that the proposition underlying the first clause is 'pragmatically presupposed' by the utterance of the sentence, we thereby meant that the proposition is already in the knowledge set of the hearer, at least according to the beliefs of the speaker. It follows that, following our characterization of assertion given above, no assertion needs to be made in order to inform the hearer about this fact. The fact that the proposition is nevertheless expressed in the given example must therefore have another pragmatic function. Much in the same way as we say that a topic indicates what an assertion is about, a subordinate clause may 'point' to the existing knowledge into which new information must be integrated. And in the same way the expression of such a first proposition counts as reference to a known 'object', viz some fact in some possible world. 'About' this fact, so to speak, we then may say that it caused another fact, which was unknown to the hearer. Hence we need an assertion to inform the hearer about this fact. Similarly, we also need an assertion to inform him that this second fact (John won't come tonight) is a consequence of the first fact (John is ill).

At this point of our argument we may choose two roads. Either we say that in our example TWO new facts are made known and hence TWO assertions are necessary, possibly making one composite assertion, or we say that we make known two new facts, possibly constituting one 'compound' fact, by ONE assertion.

As a working hypothesis we take the second road: the utterance of a complex sentence of this kind is ONE assertion. If not, we would need assertions for each new information of a clause. The sentence *Peter kissed a girl*, when uttered, would under an atomic propositional analysis, constitute several assertions: that Peter kissed someone, that the someone is a girl, that the kissing took place in a past world, etc. Of course, such propositions may be expressed, and hence be asserted separately. If we heavily stress the noun phrase *a girl*, we assume the other atomic propositions known but not that 'the one whom Peter kissed is a girl'. Similarly, we take '*p* causes *q*' as a proposition denoting one fact, viz that two facts are in a certain relation, which requires one assertion. In other words: by interpreting ONE assertion we may nevertheless acquire knowledge about *several* facts in the world, because a proposition may entail other propositions.

The question is whether our one-sentence = one-assertion approach is also satisfactory for compound sentences, *eg, John was ill, so he went to bed*. Unlike the example with the subordinate and pragmatically presupposed clause, there is no propositional information present in the knowledge of the hearer in order to link the second part of the sentence. In fact, he did not yet know that John was ill, so he cannot not even appropriately interpret the second clause without knowledge of the first clause. We therefore are inclined to consider the utterance of the first clause as a proper assertion. Once this knowledge has been acquired (and the related topics, *eg* John, or illness), a second assertion can be made with respect to this knowledge, viz that the first fact had a certain consequence. Unlike the atomic propositions mentioned above, the first proposition here is what we may call 'world-determining'. It determines the set of worlds in which the second proposition of the compound sentence is to be interpreted. Typically, the clauses here could also have functioned as independent assertions, *eg* if only John's illness or his being in bed is contextually relevant. It may therefore be concluded that for compound sentences of this type, we have ONE COMPOUND ASSERTION. The assertion is compound because it consists of (at least) two assertions which are both essential for the main assertion: the first must necessarily be made in order to be able to make the second (. . . caused him to go to bed), because the required knowledge is not available in the hearer's memory.

5.3

Whereas an assertion, as we have defined it, is an illocutionary act, PRESUPPOSITION or 'presupposing' does not seem to be an act because there is no intended communicative change operated in the hearer due to an 'act of presupposing', which is rather a mental act, viz an assumption about the knowledge of the hearer. Of course, such an assumption may be EXPRESSED by various linguistic means. But as such assuming knowledge about a fact is not much different, pragmatically, from assuming knowledge of an object. In that sense, 'presupposing' would be if anything a part of a propositional act or SEMANTIC ACT. Of course, we could give a more or less pragmatic turn to this reasoning, by saying that the knowledge of speakers and hearers is involved. And we would make it an 'illocutionary' act, if the speaker intends to act in such a way that the hearer knows that the speaker has some information, but in that case it falls together with the act of assertion. As opposed to proper pragmatic (illocutionary) acts, presupposing, as an assumed act, does not have any obvious purposes defined in terms of consequences of changes brought about in the hearer (as distinct from those of assertions).

According to this argument we can no longer speak of a presupposition-assertion articulation of sentences or utterances.[13] First of all, presupposing, if an act at all, is semantic, whereas an assertion is a pragmatic act. Secondly, the act of assertion is based on the sentence as a whole, not only on the 'new'-information part of the sentence.

Yet, such a binary articulation of sentences seems useful if we keep the distinction between old and new information. In that case we need another term for the introduction of new information, viz the term INTRODUCTION itself, whereas presupposing is the act of reference to known objects and facts. The act of introduction, similarly, may pertain to new objects, new properties of old objects, and to new facts. In general the presupposition-introduction distinction is also grammatically expressed or else to be inferred from existing information, *eg* from previous sentences in a discourse. The illocutionary act of assertion, then, is the pragmatic instruction to use this semantic information for epistemic change, such that a set of presupposed propositions is expanded with a set of introduced propositions.

It should be emphasized that these proposals are merely tentative for the moment, and intended to underline some pragmatic difficulties involved in the usual presupposition-assertion distinction (if assertion is taken here as an illocutionary act).

5.4

This discussion about semantic and pragmatic information processing is also relevant for a further analysis of our earlier difficulties with different speech acts (or not) within the same composite sentence. Take for example the following sentence:

[54] I'll send you a postcard this summer, because I am going to Italy.

Superficially speaking we could say that by uttering this sentence we accomplish first a promise and then an assertion. Note, however, that the sentence is ambiguous. Due to its initial position, the main clause may express a presupposed proposition (I may just have made a promise with the some content). In that case, the subordinate clause in final position expresses the introduced proposition, providing the reason of my (known) future action. This makes the utterance of the sentence an explanatory assertion. The second reading arises when the first proposition is not presupposed, but simply an announcement about future action, also followed by an explanatory assertion of this future action. Both propositions are introduced in that case. The same would hold for a third reading in which the contextual conditions for a promise are satisfied (a certain obligation of the speaker with respect to the hearer). This is possible only, however, if the specific content of the promise is introduced in the sentence. In other words: presupposed elements of a sentence cannot as such 'carry' a speech act. Trivially: promising to do A is senseless if the hearer already knows that I will do A. But as soon as a promise is involved, we no longer have a 'mere' assertion. We have a promise with the propositional base 'to send a postcard because I will be in Italy', much in the same way as the promise 'to send a postcard from Italy'. As for the conditional promises, we could say that the domain of validity of the promise is restricted: if unexpectedly my trip to Italy is cancelled, I am no longer committed to my promise.

Note, incidentally, that there are cases of complex or compound sentences which convey COMPOSITE SPEECH ACTS, viz in those cases where not the facts are related, but a fact with a speech act, or two speech acts:

[55] I'll send you a postcard this summer, because I know that I'm going to Italy.

[56] I'll send you a postcard this summer, because I know that you like postcards.

In these cases, the second clause expresses an explanatory assertion for the promising act, accomplished by the utterance of the first clause: they express necessary conditions for appropriate promising. On the other hand, if we add *I promise that* to [54], the *because*-clause does not express a cause of my promising (or only when it entails 'I know that'). Similarly, we may have *When I am in Italy, I'll send you a postcard,* but not *When I know that I'm going to Italy, I'll send you a postcard,* whereas *When I know that I'm going to Italy, I (can) promise you to send a postcard* is again acceptable.

6 The pragmatics of representation in discourse
6.1
Until now we have only discussed semantic aspects of meaning, reference and representation, and the conditions of presupposition and introduction of propositions. There are different ways, however, to 'represent' existing, future or wanted facts. Sometimes the ordering of propositional representation is parallel to that of the facts themselves. We have analysed examples, however, where this is not the case, viz where subsequent propositions denote preceding facts. Part of the constraints on representation – which might be taken as the converse relation of denotation, reference or interpretation – have a pragmatic nature. They are determined by properties of social information processing in conversation, beyond the semantic ones discussed in Chapter 4.

6.2
The determinants of the order of representation are the following:

  (i) The order of the fact-sequence
 (ii) The order of observation/perception/understanding of the fact-sequence
(iii) The order of information transmission
(iv) The order of illocutionary acts

Constraints (i) and (ii) are semantic, whereas (iii) and (iv) are pragmatic. If a sequence of propositions is expressed along an order parallel to the order of the facts themselves, we said that the representation ordering is NORMAL. Example: *John bought flowers. He gave them to Sally.* That is, if the fact ordering is $\langle *p, *q \rangle$, the semantic representation, and its morpho-syntactic expression, is $\langle p, q \rangle$, where $*p$ is the fact denoted by the proposition p. Conversely, if no specific indications are given in a sequence, it will be interpreted as a direct mapping of the fact sequence.

The principle of normal ordering is also important for COGNITIVE reasons: not only do we try to represent, mentally, a sequence of facts in their temporal and causal order, but this representation will also constitute the basis for our discourse about these facts. Yet, these cognitive constraints at the same time allow different ordering, according to (ii). As such, the facts do not determine our representation of facts, but rather our observation/perception and interpretation of these facts. In that case our observation of a fact $*q$ may occur prior to the observation of a fact $*p$, or rather, having observed $*q$, we may infer that this fact is a consequence of a fact $*p$, which as such we may or may not have observed. That is, in our interpretation of the world, we may first focus ATTENTION on $*q$ and after that on $*p$, or on the specific relation $\langle *p, *q \rangle$. This ordering will be called COGNITIVE. Note, that in many cases the cognitive ordering may be identical with the normal ordering. Examples of cognitive ordering are *John was drunk, because he had been in the pub*, and *She is also at the party, because she had an invitation*, and *John's radio is playing. So, he must be home*, where the TENSES allow the corresponding interpretation of the fact-orderings.

The third determinant of ordering, viz that of information processing, has been discussed already in the previous section. Whereas principles (i) and (ii) depend on the facts and our understanding of the facts, the third constraint determines that the 'facts be represented' in an order dependent on the structure of the communicative context, viz my intentions and assumptions about the knowledge of the speech participants. Assuming that I want my hearer to be informed about the fact $*q$, it may well be that the hearer can only interpret q (or "q") if I first inform him about a fact $*p$, either because of reasons of presuppositions or because the hearer will certainly be interested in conditions (causes or reasons) of a certain fact ("*Why did he go to bed?*"). Hence, given a sequence of facts $\langle *p, *q \rangle$, the representation in actual discourse will also depend on whether the hearer already knows about $*p$, or about $*q$. It is this ordering which defines the presupposition-introduction structure of the sentence. Example: *He had that accident, because he was drunk* (with normal final position stress).[14]

Finally, we have the purely PRAGMATIC constraints on representation orderings. They determine an ordering of representation with respect to the CONTEXT beyond simple information transmission. The wishes and intentions/purposes of the speaker, the sequencing of illocutionary acts, and the known and assumed wishes, interests or intentions of the hearer are involved here.

First of all, speech act sequencing may determine that facts occurring earlier are asserted later in order to give an explanation, a correction, a restriction or similar second-position illocutionary acts following any other speech act, as in *I'll give you the money, but you don't deserve it; I'll go to the USA if I get that grant*, etc.

Secondly, we have the interests and needs of the hearer as determinants of orderings, *eg* in replies to questions, requests and commands, or in general the requirements of the present situation. If John doesn't show up in a formal meeting, we will first assert, ideally, that he is unable to come, then that he is in hospital, then that he had an accident, then, perhaps, that the road was slippery with frost. We do not answer, in such a case, by beginning a narrative: *"Well, it was freezing, and the road was slippery; and John was driving to London* (. . .).*"* Up to a certain degree, such indirect answers are possible, but only in specific contexts, and often with specific effects. The conventional order is first to provide the requested information, and then give further explanation. Thus, the topic of conversation also determines the possible orderings. This means that those propositions must be uttered first which are 'closest' to the topic, after that propositions indicating conditions or consequences. If we are talking about road accidents, we first say *"John (also) had an accident last week"* and only then *"He is in hospital"* or *"The road was slippery"*. Thirdly, not only requested information or topics of conversation order our contributions in a dialogue, but also the STRUCTURE OF (INTER-)ACTION. So, we may have both *"He won't make it. Let's give him a hand"*, and *"Let's give him a hand. He won't make it"*. The first is a description of a fact which is a sufficient condition for a speech act (adhortation), the second is the adhortation followed by an explanatory assertion about the reason for the speech act and the reason for helping. Note, finally, that speech acts are also facts. Hence, a speech act ordering is, itself, normal, if those acts are ordered along the condition-consequence line.

6.3

There are various ways to express these orderings. The schemata we have been discussing in this and the previous sections are the following:

(i) $\langle [p]. [(So,) q] \rangle$

(ii) $\langle [q]. [(So,) p] \rangle$

(iii) $\langle [p, so\ q] \rangle$

(iv) $\langle [q, so\ p] \rangle$

(v) $\langle [[because\ p], q] \rangle$

(vi) $\langle [q, [because\ p]] \rangle$

In these schemata '$\langle$' and '$\rangle$' are sequence boundaries, '$[$' and '$]$' are sentence boundaries, '[' and ']' enclose subordinate clauses, '(' and ')' enclose optional connectives, and *p* and *q* are clause variables. According to these schemata, and given an ordering of facts $\langle *p, *q \rangle$, (i), (iii) and (v) would be normal orderings, the other would be cognitive, communicative and pragmatic. The connectives in (i) and ('i) are pragmatic, the others semantic. Subordinate clauses in initial position often express pragmatic presupposition, the second position main clause the propositional introduction. With special intonation, ordering (vi) is possible for introduced main clauses, *eg* for special emphasis. In general, sentence boundaries are also speech act boundaries, although there are cases in which the compound constructions (iii) and (iv) admit compound speech acts.

The schemata have been given for cause/reason – consequence relations between facts, and premise-conclusion relations between speech acts. Similar schemata may be given for the other connectives and connections.

6.4

Part of the pragmatics of representation is a further explication of notions such as FOCUS and PERSPECTIVE, although these notions are also, or even primarily, to be accounted for at the level of semantics.

The notion of FOCUS is ambiguous. COGNITIVELY, it could be reconstructed in terms of selective information processing. Specific ATTENTION for some object (thing, property, relation, fact) would probably involve conscious processing, fast selective perception, fast recognition, better organization in memory and enhanced retrievability (better recall), and probably presence in the (semantic) processing stores. It will be assumed that focus is PROPOSITIONALLY based in that case.[15] We do not, presumably, just focus (attention) on Peter, on illness or kissing, but on certain facts, *eg* that Peter is ill, or that Peter kissed Mary. The specific focus function of such facts would then consist in their role in a specific network of relations. Certain other facts would be viewed in relation to the fact under focus, viz as conditions, consequences or components.

At the SEMANTIC level, focus has been discussed mostly in terms of 'comment' (of a sentence), as opposed to topic. If it is to be different from topic it should not be identified with 'old information' or 'identified objects', but rather with new, introduced information as it was discussed earlier.[16] Probably, the notion CHANGE OF FOCUS would on this level be more interesting from a linguistic point of view and for our discussion, for example if such a change would require a new sentence. A change of possible world (place, time, circumstances) and a change of involved objects, could be taken as the basis for such a change in semantic focus. Together with the sentence boundary, we would have specific sentential adverbs, tense and modal expressions as indications of focus change.[17] In particular, the notion of focus would apply under the semantic (referential, representational) constraints discussed above. Sequence ordering and propositional embedding, as we saw, can express certain properties of semantic and cognitive information processing. Thus, a fact under focus, although occurring later, may be represented first, or conversely.

PRAGMATICALLY the notion of focus could also be constructed in terms of our treatment of representation. Facts under pragmatic focus would be those which are immediately relevant for illocutionary acts and interaction in the context and communicative situation, where the notion of RELEVANCE was defined in terms of direct conditions and consequences of (speech) acts. Instead of propositions/facts under focus we could at this level also speak of illocutionary acts or forces being under focus. A speech act would be under focus if it is the main act intended in a sequence of speech acts, such that the other speech acts are components or auxiliary/preparatory for that act, as demonstrated in the examples treated above. Just as, on the semantic level, information under focus seems to be close to what we have called topic of discourse, made explicit as macro-structures, the pragmatic notion of focus thus becomes akin to that of the global speech act of a discourse, as will be discussed in the next chapter. We therefore provisionally conclude that a specific notion of semantic or pragmatic focus need not be postulated in the theory, because it covers various phenomena which have been defined in other terms. The only SPECIFIC application of the notion would be to the four principles of representation determining discourse ordering.

Another notion which lies on the boundary of semantics and pragmatics is PERSPECTIVE, which certainly has interesting linguistic implications although hardly any systematic research has been done on it.[18] Sequences of facts may be represented in various ways, according to the factual, cognitive, communicative or pragmatic constraints discussed above. Independent of such orderings, however, we may describe the facts from various perspectives, *eg* the perspective of a certain point of time, place, person involved in the facts, an observer of the facts, or just from the point of view of a speaker/reporter of the facts. Such differences may show of course in the use of different pronouns (*I hit him* and *He hit me* may both describe the 'same' fact, viz that John hit Peter, but differ according to who is reporting the event), the use of different indexical expressions in general, different verbs *buy* versus *sell*, *come* versus *go*, etc.

The notion is interesting in the framework of this book if perpective and perspective change is to be defined in terms of discourse structure. Apart from specific rules in literary narratives, there are indeed strict constraints on perspective in discourse.

Perspective can be taken both as a semantic and as a pragmatic notion. Whereas truth/satisfaction is a notion determined by possible worlds and models, SEMANTIC PERSPECTIVE is a part of a model structure RELATIVE TO which truth in a world is defined. It is this perspective which determines which worlds are in fact ACCESSIBLE from a certain world. Thus, in our crime story, sentences like *She took off her hat* have different perspectival status from *She felt depressed* or *She knew that he knew it*. The latter examples are typical in many novels, where internal mental states are described with third person subjects, instead of first person subjects. Thus, some sentences can only express the perspective of an observer (who may or may not be identical with the speaker/reporter), *eg She seemed unhappy* or *You look fine today!*, whereas others, in normal discourse, may only express the point of view or 'awareness' of the age..t of an action described, as in *I wanted to hit him*. There are languages which use specific morphemes to express differences in perspective.[19]

PRAGMATIC PERSPECTIVE does not determine truth, satisfaction or accessibility, but the appropriateness of discourses, and hence should be defined in terms of context, viz point of view, attitudes, etc of speech participants. For pragmatic or contextual semantics this means first of all that sentences which are asserted are true in worlds accessible from the knowledge/belief worlds of the speaker. For pragmatics proper it means that the utterance of a sentence is appropriate relative to the wishes, intentions and goals of the speaker of the utterance, as in assertions, commands and requests. Perspective is also relative to the wishes, aims and knowledge of the hearer in promises, advices, etc. More generally, the identification or interpretation of utterances as certain speech acts may be different for speakers and hearers: in context c_i, the utterance u_i may be a promise for A but a threat for B. Appropriateness thus depends on perspective.

Similarly, as in such typical examples as *John pretends that he won a million dollars*, the assignment of speech act verbs depends on the beliefs of the speaker relative to the truth, appropriateness or purpose of the represented speech (agent). These and other properties of linguistic perspective, especially those relating semantics and pragmatics, need further investigation.

7 Text versus context
7.1
One final issue which should receive some attention is that concerning the similarities and differences between TEXT and CONTEXT. Especially in this chapter we have studied discourse at the level of sentence sequences and speech act sequences. One of the natural questions to ask in such a framework would be whether the structure of discourse, at least from a grammatical point of view, could also be accounted for in terms of (simple and composite) sentences on the one hand, and the structure of speech act sequences and of context on the other hand.[20] In other words: as soon as we have a pragmatics accounting for CONTEXTUAL structures, such as know-ledge and beliefs, intentions, actions, etc, why do we still need a specific discourse-level of analysis, and not just a SENTENCES-IN-CONTEXT de-scription? For example, in order to provide the necessary relative in-terpretation of sentences, *eg* for the correct identification of individuals, with respect to previous sentences of the discourse sequence, we could also interpret a sentence relative to the sentence previously uttered in the same context of conversation. Such previous sentences, when uttered, would have changed the knowledge of the hearer, and the hearer would be able to interpret any new input-sentence with respect to this knowledge acquired from the interpretation of previous sentences.

Although it cannot be denied that such an approach is interesting, and would certainly be valid from the point of view of cognitive processing, there are serious arguments why an independent linguistic (grammatical) analysis of sequences and discourse remains necessary even within a pragmatic framework.

7.2
A first argument concerns specific MACRO-STRUCTURES. Just as a sentence, because of its hierarchical structure, is taken as a theoretical unit of a

grammar and not as a sequence of (utterances of) individual words (morphemes or phrases), so global structures of discourse require at least one level of linguistic analysis at which discourses, or paragraphs, are taken as THEORETICAL UNITS. More specifically, macro-rules do not operate on the contents of belief/knowledge of language users, but on sequences of sentences or propositions. In this respect we maintain a distinction between grammatical or logical rules and constraints on the one hand and cognitive strategies, processes or operations on the other hand. The latter are of course based on linear linguistic input, viz sequences of words, phrases and sentences.

Similar remarks may be made for structures of sequences. First of all it should be emphasized that preceding discourse cannot always be 'represented' by context. A limited number of individuals and properties may be available for direct, indexical, reference in the context. All other individuals, properties and relations require introduction by previous discourse. More specifically, the RELATIVE INTERPRETATION of sentences in a sequence should be defined whether the sequence is actually uttered or not. That is, identity, continuity or difference of modalities, tenses, individuals or predicates is to be defined for sequences of sentences or propositions and cannot be given only in terms of what speech participants know or believe at a certain moment of a context in which such a sequence is uttered. Certain worlds are accessible only through the explicit presence of expressions of previous sentences. The same holds for the use of predicates like *to précis*, *to conclude*, and *to summarize*, and their corresponding nominalizations, as well as for discourse adverbs such as *consequently*, *thus*, *on the contrary*, etc.

7.3

From these few examples it follows that discourses should not only be described at the pragmatic level, but require an independent level of (relative) semantics for sequences and macro-structures.

Conversely, a pragmatic component of description, having specific categories, rules and constraints, should not be reduced to semantics by the mere fact that some speech acts can be performatively represented in the discourse itself.

Notes

1 This difference holds only with normal sentence intonation and stress. As soon as we assign specific stress to *accident* in [4]*a*, the two sentences [4]*a* and [4]*b* become again pragmatically (epistemically) equivalent, in the sense that the proposition 'Peter is in hospital' is assumed by the speaker to be known to the hearer. However, in such a TOPICALIZATION there are other pragmatic differences, for instance the fact that, by contrast, the speaker denies an assumption of the hearer with respect to the reason why John is in hospital.

2 By pragmatic presupposition of an (uttered) sentence *S*, we mean to say any proposition expressed by *S* which the speaker assumes to be known to the hearer.

Derivatively we may also say this of the clause expressing this proposition in *S*. For further discussion of presupposition, see below, and – also for further references, *eg* about the distinction between semantic and pragmatic presupposition – Kempson (1975), Wilson (1975), Petöfi and Franck, eds (1973).

3 It may seem unusual to contend that a syntactic structure alone may EXPRESS a connection such as causation. Although it is obvious that the meaning of propositions co-determines a causal interpretation of co-ordinated clauses, it should be stressed that clause ordering itself also requires semantic interpretation, *eg* temporal or causal ordering of facts. See below.

4 The kind of phenomena we study here are sometimes very subtle, and our reflective intuitions not always clear cut. Therefore, some of the differences discussed in this chapter are open to challenge from (but also among) native speakers of English. Thus, a distinction between semantic (interclausal) and pragmatic (intersentential) *so*, may be blurred by the very close relationship between causal relations and 'causal' explanations, *ie* between (implicational) connectives and inference. Yet, not only in logical theory but also in grammar, it is necessary to distinguish between connection and operations of inference. See our discussion in van Dijk (1974*b*, 1975*a*).

5 For reasons of simplicity we briefly assume here that 'presuming' or 'assuming' and 'concluding', as expressed in the premise and conclusion structure of a proof or argument, are illocutionary acts.

6 See van Dijk (1975*a*) for some examples. Intuitions may again differ here. We would be inclined to say in Dutch *Peter is ziek. Dus, hij komt niet* [Peter is ill. So, he does not come], but in coordinated clauses: *Peter was ziek, dus kwam hij niet* [Peter was ill, so he didn't come], where in the first example we have SV ordering and in the second VS ordering. In any case, the normal SV ordering is imperative when *hij* [he] is stressed. After German *also* we normally have inversion, but normal SV ordering after heavily stressed sentence initial *Also* followed by a pause. Thus, although there are slight differences, these syntactic observations seem to corroborate our distinction between semantic and pragmatic connectives in English.

7 This does not mean that sentences with *for*, denoting causal relation, are not used in explanatory contexts, but only that *for* as such is purely semantic, not an inferential (pragmatic) connective. Unlike *So*, we may not begin a sentence or a dialogue turn with it. As was remarked earlier, however, there are other connectives taking over the role of *for* in spoken English. The same holds for German *denn*, which is also more and more replaced by *weil* [because]. In Dutch however, *want* [for] is very much used in spoken language, viz as the normal co-ordinative causal (semantic) connective besides *omdat* [because]. For details of German coordination, see especially Lang (1973).

8 Typically, therefore, pragmatic connectives would be acceptable in many such cases, although it was assumed that then we should rather speak of two independent sentences than of one compound sentence: *I am busy. So, shut up!* Note, however, that in those cases where semantics and pragmatics run parallel, as in explicit performative sentences, semantic connectives in compound sentences may be used, because the facts connected there are the speech acts performed: *I promise that I will bring the money, but I ask you to wait for me until at least two o'clock*. See Groenendijk and Stokhof (1976) for correctness conditions on compound performatives.

9 We are here at the boundary of what may still be called appropriateness conditions and other conditions of 'success'.

10 Although the parallel with main clause and subordinate clause is metaphorically instructive, it is not so easy to give precise criteria for a definition of 'main' and 'subordinate' (auxiliary) acts within one 'composite' action. See Chapter 6 for some tentative remarks about this distinction.

11 As for several other examples in these sections other interpretations of the

phenomena are possible here. Thus, modalized sentences denoting future actions of the speaker which the hearer would appreciate might also merely count as (announcing) assertions (*eg* because *maybe*-'promises' need not be kept, or accounted for, in the same sense as full promises). Yet, in the same sense in which we say that the utterance of a sentence such as *Maybe Peter is ill* counts as an assertion, we consider *Maybe I'll visit you* as a (weak) promise.

12 There are a number of theoretical intricacies which are ignored here. For instance, we should speak of DEGREES of success in these (and other) cases, not only because only part of the knowledge may be successfully transmitted according to purpose, but also because knowledge/belief may, theoretically, be mutually recursive: the speaker must believe that the hearer believes what he (the speaker) said, etc. Note that according to our earlier stipulations, a communicative act as defined here is perlocutionary, not merely illocutionary.

13 For a discussion of this issue, see the standard and recent papers collected in Petöfi and Franck, eds (1973), Kempson (1975), Wilson (1975) and the references given there.

14 Note that in a sentence like *Because he was drúnk he had an accident*, or *It was because . . .*, the introductory (comment) part of the sentence occurs in the foregrounded, initial position, in order to mark contrast or contradiction, which apparently is an additional (pragmatico-stylistic) criterion for sentence and sequence ordering.

15 There are perhaps a few marginal counter-examples against this assumption, *eg* in those cases where we give or request all information related to a certain concept: *Tell me all about Peter*, *Can you tell me something about event-splitting?*, etc.

16 For the notion of 'focus' – in the sense of comment and related notions – see Sgall, Hajičová and Benešová (1973), and the references given there to other work.

17 For example, *on the other hand*, *in the meantime*, *suddenly*, etc.

18 See however Fillmore (1974) and Kuroda (1975) and the references given there. In particular, there has been some research on 'perspective' in narratives, *eg* in relation to the problem of free indirect style. See Banfield (1973). For the literature, see Stanzel (1964) and Hamburger (1968) among others.

19 For example, Japanese. See Kuroda (1975).

20 For a discussion of this problem, see van Dijk (1974c).

Chapter 9

Macro-speech acts

1 The global organization of communicative interaction

1.1

One of the most expedient heuristic strategies in theory formation is the construction of parallels between disciplines, methods, problems, domains and structures. Thus, in the same way as we made a distinction between the micro-semantics and the macro-semantics of discourse, it seems necessary to distinguish between the structure of individual speech acts and the linear structure of speech act sequences on the one hand and the GLOBAL, OVERALL STRUCTURE OF COMMUNICATIVE INTERACTION on the other hand. Such a distinction may be supported by a corresponding differentiation in the discipline, viz of MICRO-PRAGMATICS versus MACRO-PRAGMATICS. Such a terminological distinction, however, should be handled with care. Under macro-pragmatics we understand the study of the overall organization of communicative interaction, viz of a sequence of speech acts and contexts and their relation to the structure of discourse. Another domain of investigation which could be labelled 'macro-pragmatics' would have to deal with problems of SOCIAL INFORMATION PROCESSING, viz of how communication takes place between groups and institutions. This type of macro-pragmatics should be compared with macro-sociology and macro-economics. In this chapter we are concerned, however, with the sociological micro-level of (face to face or individual) communicative interaction.

1.2

The macro-analysis of communicative interaction pertains to the following aspects and problems

    (i) can sequences of speech-acts be subsumed under more global speech acts and is there a pragmatic macro-structure?

(ii) if so, what is the pragmatic function of global speech acts?

(iii) what is the cognitive and social (and action-theoretical) basis for the distinction?

(iv) in what respect are global speech acts systematically related to textual macro-structures?

(v) what is the empirical evidence for the assumption that (communicative) interaction also has a macro-structure?

These and related questions should be tentatively answered in this last chapter.

There are several reasons for asking such questions. First of all, we know and use lexical expressions in order to denote speech acts (*eg* of commanding, convincing, advising, etc) which do not consist of commands, 'convincings' or 'advisings' alone, but also of other types of speech acts. That is, the sequence of (various) speech acts AS A WHOLE has the function of a command, advice, etc.

Secondly, it has been observed that the planning, execution and interpretation, viz processing in general, of complex information requires the formation of macro-structures. The same holds for the planning, execution and interpretation of action, and hence for complex sequences of speech acts.

Thirdly, many conventional types of discourse (stories, advertisements, etc) are associated with global speech acts rather than with component individual speech acts.

2 Macro-action
2.1

Like meanings, actions are intensional objects. They are assigned to observable doings just as meanings are assigned to utterances. Just like meanings, actions are combined with other actions to form compound and complex actions and sequences of actions. Finally, it will be assumed that actions, just like semantic information, are organized in higher level units and structures. More specifically, sequences of doings are assigned hierarchical action structures, planned and interpreted as such, at various levels of macro-organization.

These assumptions are based on COGNITIVE necessities. We are unable to plan in advance sequences consisting of a great number of actions, some of which are auxiliary, some component and hence essential, some preparatory. In order to monitor the execution of such a complex sequence we need PLANS OF ACTION.[1] Such plans are not simply the intentional counterpart of the sequence, organized in some hierarchical way. They rather consist of a hierarchical structure for the GLOBAL organization of the sequence. Under the global control of this plan the individual actions may be chosen/intended and executed. Certain steps, as we have indicated, will in that case be necessary, others are only optional but probable, others optional but improbable. Plans, thus described, are macro-structures of action. They determine which subsequences of actions belong together, how such subsequences are related, and how subsequences may be assigned to one macro-action.

2.2

Let us first informally discuss a concrete example: When I want to go to Paris, a certain number of actions will be planned. Globally, first of all: 'I'm going to Paris' or 'Next Tuesday I'm going to Paris', or even 'Next Tuesday I'm going to Paris by train'. This will be the, propositionally represented, macro-action determining the actual sequence of actions. Macro-actions are related to (macro-) PURPOSES: I may intend to go to Paris in order to visit my old aunt Françoise. Given the overall plan of my action, I may proceed to execute it at some point in place and time. This means that the macro-actions must be 'translated' into lower-level action structures. Thus, 'going/travelling to Paris' will activate the TRAIN/JOURNEY action frame, containing the 'reserving seats', 'buying tickets', 'going to the railway-station', etc as preparatory actions, 'getting into the carriage,' 'choosing a seat', 'disposing of luggage', 'reading a newspaper' or 'talking with co-passengers' as obligatory or optional component actions. These actions will very often be intended just before execution: when I plan to go to Paris and visit my aunt, I may perhaps think already of taking the car or taking the train, or even whether I will take the TEE-train, but not whether I will read a novel or a newspaper during the journey, for example. Just before beginning the journey, however, I may execute preparatory actions of later component actions, like buying a newspaper or novel at the news-stand of the station. In many cases the optional actions depend on the accidental initial situations: if there is little time left to catch my train I may take a taxi, otherwise my bike or a tram. These situations cannot and need not always be foreseen so that the actions to be carried out in those situations are not initially planned. Under the most general node of the macro-action 'I'm going to Paris next Tuesday', or rather 'I'm going to Paris at day t_i' (in order to make the action context-independent, except for the 'I', the fixed 'ego' of each action and action plan), the first global auxiliary or preparatory action, as a SUBGOAL, is planned, eg 'I go to the station at time t_i'. Given some initial situation, consisting of the knowledge of the facts 'I have so much time', 'I have so much money', 'I have so much luggage', and such and such are my preferences of transport under such and such weather conditions, the major action of the preparatory action is selected, viz taking a taxi or taking the tram, etc. At this level again auxiliary or preparatory actions are required at a more 'detailed' level, viz 'phoning a taxi' or 'walking to the corner', etc. At a certain level of action organization, depending on experience and abilities, actions are no longer consciously planned, but automatized in a fixed ROUTINE, which is only consciously executed in specific circumstances, eg when something goes wrong, or when normal initial conditions are not satisfied. I normally do not have to decide which foot I first put on the step of the train-door, but may well be aware of this mini-task when my leg is broken and in a plaster cast.

From this example it is clear that actions must be organized in the same hierarchical way as meanings, and that the control of such enormously complex structures requires macro-processing.

2.3

Actions are not normally macro-actions as such, but only RELATIVE TO other actions. In one situation an action may be the major macro-action, whereas in another situation it is only a component or preparatory action, eg my going to the station to meet my aunt, or my going to the station in order to begin my journey to Paris, whereas at a still more general level of activity going to Paris may be an optional component of the action of taking holidays in Europe or of presiding over some EEC commission.

Theoretically, macro-actions are obtained by a number of OPERATIONS on action sequences, similar to the operations of propositional information reduction. Thus, in action sequences we may delete optional component actions, normal preparatory actions and consequences, auxiliary actions and individual mental planning of those actions. Similarly n-tuples of actions may be substituted by one global action. In all these operations no action may be deleted or substituted which is a NECESSARY CONDITION for the successfulness of a following (macro-)action. What propositions and interpretability or truth or satisfaction are for discourse sequences of sentences, necessary conditions and successfulness are for sequences of actions. This account has a theoretical nature. In actual processing of action, the operations must be represented as certain EXECUTION STRATEGIES for macro-actions, consisting of the choice of most expedient or most preferred components, auxiliary actions and preparatory actions, as described in the previous section. On the other hand, from the point of view of control and from the point of view of the observation or the interpretation of action sequences, the operations represent control and interpretation strategies of agents and observers. When I observe that somebody at a newspaper-stand takes some money from his pocket, showing a newspaper to the seller, giving the money, etc, I interpret this sequence as 'Somebody is buying a newspaper'. Whether the buyer takes the money from his left or right pocket, or from his purse or wallet, whether the seller gives back some change or checks the price on the newspaper (which requires the exchange of the paper if the buyer has taken it himself from the pile), may be as such observed and interpreted for some reason in some contexts, but in general these specific actions are generalized/deleted under 'the buying/selling' concept or frame.

Similarly, at a more general level of action, I may be able to interpret and understand certain actions only by inserting them into a macro-action schema, eg when I see somebody leap into the canal and only afterwards see or hear that he was saving a child. It is in the latter case also where we may speak of TOPICS OF ACTIVITY, just as we introduced discourse topics or topics or conversation to denote, theoretically, what a sequence is ABOUT. That is, at each point in a sequence of actions we may ask what the sequence 'is about', *ie* what is being done. Observing a series of different actions I will all the time assign the action 'He is saving a child from the canal'. This will also be the answer to my question "*What is he doing?*", when seeing somebody jump into the canal.

2.4

That complex action sequences are hierarchically organized in planning and interpretation and that they constitute macro-actions at several levels of planning and interpretation seems a plausible hypothesis by now. A more difficult problem is the question whether these macro-structures of action are also organized by specific MACRO-CATEGORIES or FUNCTIONS, in a way similar to the macro-organization of meaning under narrative categories and constraints. And, if such categories exist, it should further be shown that they have specific cognitive and/or social functions.

Whereas a narrative structure identifies a discourse as a certain discourse TYPE, of which the patterns and rules are conventionally known, thus facilitating production, interpretation, processing and storage, specific macro-categories of action would have to identify certain actions as action types with conventional properties, thus facilitating planning and interpretation of actions.

A first, rather trivial, answer to this query is the assignment of each action to the FUNCTION this action has in the action as a whole, according to the theory of action of Chapter 6, viz PREPARATORY ACTION, AUXILIARY ACTION, COMPONENT ACTION, etc. The specific, conventional properties of these categories of action can be deduced from this function in the action structure. In most situations we are able to infer for each action which role it has in a more global action. If we see a passenger taking a taxi, we may infer that this is an auxiliary action in a preparatory action: viz choosing a means of transport in order to do something somewhere else (visit somebody, go to work, take a train).

These distinctions, however, are not very refined. At the level of discourse they nearly have the triviality of saying that a discourse, like an action, has a 'beginning', and an 'end'. More precise categories indicating properties of complex actions can, however, be introduced. Besides the category of HELPING we could introduce that of OBSTRUCTING or PREVENTING. At the same time an action may be intended to STIMULATE or to DISCOURAGE another action. Besides beginning and finishing we further have various MODES of action execution. First of all we may just TRY to execute some action, HESITATE to execute the action or in executing the action; we may SLOW DOWN and CARRY ON, and so on.

These action categories may be assigned specific conventional 'meanings', *eg:* '*x* stimulates action *A* of *y*' = '*x* approves of *A*, and *x* thinks *A* should be continued by *y*, and *x* thinks that by doing *B*, *B* may be auxiliary for *A*, or that by doing *B*, *y* will understand that *x* thinks *A* is good and *A* should be continued'. Of course such 'definitions' should be made more precise, and a fixed set of primitive and defined terms should be used in such definitions.

A certain number of these categories are just PROPERTIES of any action or may be so (begin, slow down, carry on, etc). Others are typical for INTERACTION, like stimulate and discourage. Typical examples of the latter subset are also to PUNISH and to REWARD. Note that these are really CATEGORIES of action, not actions 'as such': we may only punish or reward 'by doing something else', *eg* by hitting or kissing, paying or not paying, etc. That is, under some conditions, a kiss may COUNT AS a reward.

2.5

The important thing about this set of categories is that they are not only interactional, but that they have clear SOCIAL implications. Such categories not only 'organize' so to speak the execution of the action – both in cognitive planning and control and in interpretation – but also define the social function of a given action, by specifying for example the commitments, rights, and duties produced or changed by a particular action. Thus, some conditions for punishment are the following:

[1]*a:* x does A (at t_i)

   b: y does not want (like, prefer . . .) A

   c: y believes that if y does B then x will probably not do A (at t_{i+k})

   d: y believes that x does not like B

   e: y does B

The practical argument involved would in that case allow the ideal social conclusion to be 'x omits doing A in the future'. Other components in such a definition could be the specific roles and functions of the agents. Thus, in punishments, the agent must have a certain, conventional (teacher-pupil, etc) or ad hoc imposed authority. In this way, a great number of interactions may be assigned to specific social (functional) categories defining the roles and relations of the agents, the establishment of rights, duties, obligations, commitments, etc. Thus, in helping somebody, I thereby create the moral obligation for his thanking or rewarding me, even if I did not have this particular purpose: the consequence holds by convention. In the same way as the more general categories of action like 'preparation', 'auxiliary', 'trying', etc, these categories of social interaction give a certain STRUCTURE to a sequence of actions. If some action is intended and accepted, hence counts as a reward, this implies that the other agent has previously executed an action which is judged 'good' by the rewarding agent, who at the same time will expect the thanks of the rewarded agent to follow. Similarly for the series: $\langle x$ prohibits A, y does A, x punishes $y \rangle$, where the punishment is based on the violation of an established interdiction.

The categories, according to our intention, do not merely dominate single actions, but may of course dominate subsequences of actions. Transgression of prohibitions, punishments or obedience may consist of highly complex actions. This means that we now have at least two sets of macro-categories for action, namely the more strictly cognitive and action theoretical categories and the interactional and social categories determining the function of an action with respect to other actions.

3 Macro-speech acts
3.1
Just like actions in general, speech act sequences require global planning and interpretation. That is, certain sequences of various speech acts may be intended and understood, and hence function socially, as one speech act. Such a speech act performed by a sequence of speech acts will be called a global speech-act or MACRO-SPEECH ACT.[2]

Let us give some examples of such macro-speech acts:

[2] A telephone conversation between neighbours:

    A. Hello?

    B. Hello Peter. This is Jack!

    A. Oh Hallo Jack. How are you?

    B. Fine. Listen Peter. Do you still have that old bike of Jenny's which she doesn't use any more?

    A. Yes. Why?

    B. Well, you know, our Laura has her birthday next week, and she needs a bike. And I thought if Jenny doesn't use hers any more, perhaps I could buy it and paint it and give it to Laura as a birthday present.

    A. That's OK with me. Of course I must ask Jenny, but I'm sure she will be glad to help you. When do you want it?

    B. That's terribly nice of you. Shall I drop in tomorrow? And you ask Jenny?

    A. All right. See you tomorrow.

    B. Bye then, and thanks.

    A. Bye.

This somewhat artificial conversation consists of various speech acts of both participants, viz greetings, questions, assertions, thanks, proposals, etc. The whole conversation, however, may properly be summed up as the REQUEST of A to buy B's wife's old bike. Indeed, B, reporting the conversation to his wife may just say: *"Jack phoned and asked if we would sell him your old bike"*. Similarly, the following sequence will in general be interpreted as a PROMISE:

[3] Father looking at a painting done by his little son:

    A. But this is a fantastic painting! Did you do this!?

    B. Of course I did!

    A. It's terrific. I like it. But I see you need some more paints.

    B. Yes. The blue and the red are nearly empty.

A. Tomorrow I'll buy you some new ones.
B. Don't forget them again!
A. No! I'll tie a knot in my handkerchief.

Again the conversation consists of various speech acts, such as praise, question, assertion, suggestion, confirmation and promise, but the whole functions as a promise or perhaps as a combined praise-promise.

The question is: under what conditions may sequences of speech acts in monologue or dialogue conversations be assigned to one global speech act?

3.2

In order to be able to answer this question we should recall the operations postulated for semantic information reduction, both for propositions and action sequences. These operations delete irrelevant or predictable information and combine several units into a higher level, more general unit. For speech acts as well as for actions in general, this would mean that preparatory and auxiliary speech acts may be deleted, as well as those component speech acts which, taken together, define the essential component of the resulting global speech acts. Similarly, expressions of mental states and context descriptions may be deleted, although they may determine the acceptability (politeness, credibility, etc) of the speech act. Finally, those speech acts establishing, maintaining and concluding the sequence, *ie* the communicative interaction in general, may also be dropped in macro-interpretation.

Thus, in our first example, the conversation between neighbours, we may delete the speech acts establishing and concluding the conversation ("*Hello!*", "*Bye!*"), the necessary identification of the speech participant ("*This is . . .*"), expressions of politeness and friendship, viz the greetings ("*Hello!*", "*How are you?*") and their responses, communication maintaining and topic indicative adhortations ("*Listen!*"). Then, in order to construct the context for the request, B must first make sure that the object to be requested is still in the possession of A, which is a necessary condition for (request of) a buy-sell interaction. This preparatory part of the request is executed, typically, by a question, followed by a affirmative answer, followed by a question ("*Why?*") of the addressee A because of the expectations raised by the specific question of B with respect to the bike. The core proper of the request-conversation may then follow, embedded in politeness, hedging and indirectness formulas ("*Well*", "*you know*", "*I thought*", "*perhaps*") and conditionals ("*If Jenny doesn't use it any more . . .*"): "*Can I buy it?*" in the polite *could*-form. These politeness forms are required because requests for selling something are normally more unusual than offers to sell in such situations, and because B cannot be sure whether A will not have other plans for that bike, and therefore tries to leave the decision of complying with the request fully open to A. The (local) request in the conversation is further embedded in a motivation: in order to be able to ask for an object it should be indicated why I want to have/buy that object, viz by declaring that I want to give it as a present, which in turn presupposes a statement about somebody's birthday and the existing needs motivating the particular present. After this compound request, A may give his conditional compliance with the request, accompanied with the reassuring expressions ("*Of course . . ., but . . .*", "*I'm sure . . .*", "*. . . will be glad . . .*") taking away B's hesitations. And, in order to emphasize his willingness to help B, A immediately prepares the necessary consequent actions of the request, viz the exchange of the requested object, by asking about the time of the exchange. Before B then proposes such a time, he first must show his gratitude to A. The proposal (again in question form, not in direct indicative form) is then accepted and confirmed by A, and the conclusion of the discourse initiated by indicating the time of the next interaction, viz the consequence of this request-conversation. Finally, repeated thanks from B and conclusion of the conversation. This more or less detailed, though still rather informal, description of the sequence shows that certain speech interactions are intensively prepared and embedded in socially necessary acts of politeness and hesitation. As such, these acts are not part of the request itself, which might in a quite other context have been made as follows:

[4] A. Hello?
    B. Hello Peter. This is Jack. Listen. Do you want to sell me that old bike of Jenny's?
    (. . .)

Besides these acts of what might be called social 'decorations' or social 'wrapping', the proper request is made in several steps:

[5]i : establishing a necessary condition: the possession by A of requested object;
  ii : motivating the request;
    a: establishing a necessary condition: birthday;
    b: intended action for which the object is needed: giving as a present;
  iii : stating a condition: request to be complied with only if the requested object is for sale/is not used;
  iv : request-proposition;
  v : statement of intentions with respect to the object as repeated motivation.

Both for the social decoration as for the optional and necessary steps of the request, the macro-rules reformulated above are valid. The only information remaining for A is [5]iv and perhaps [5]ii: the preparatory and component speech acts together are integrated into the one speech act of (polite) request.

A similar description may be given for the praise-promise conversation between father and son in [3]. The praise, first of all, is conventionally followed by the 'it is unbelievable' game, in which agents, especially parents and children engage in order to enhance the praise. The praise, again traditionally, establishes a weak obligation for the one giving praise, viz a form of recompense. Such an act of recompense is successful only when an act is performed which benefits the praised/recompensed person, *eg* when a wanted present is given. This need must first be made conscious by a suggestion like "*But I see you need some more paints.*" If this suggestion is accepted, the one making the suggestion is committed to giving a present, a commitment expressed by the promise to buy it in the near future. By an ironical question, presupposing the breach of a past promise, the son then tries to strengthen the commitment of the father, who then must guarantee the proper execution of his promise. In this conversation, two major speech acts are connected in the usual way: the final state of the former (a weak obligation) may become the initial state of the latter (preparing the promise). Again, a macro-speech act is performed if all speech acts of the sequence are optional or necessary preparatory or auxiliary speech acts, or normal component speech acts, such that the context is established (the required knowledge, needs, intentions, duties, expectations, etc) for the 'main speech act'. Both examples satisfy these conditions of the macro-operations.

3.3

Macro-structures have two major cognitive functions: they REDUCE/ INTEGRATE information and at the same time ORGANIZE the information according to certain macro-categories determining the FUNCTION of a sub-sequence (or its macro-structure) with respect to the sequence as a whole. For actions, first of all, this function may be the role of the action in the action as a whole, viz a preparatory, auxiliary, protagonistic, antagonistic, stimulating, or component action. Secondly, the function may be determined by the social situation in which the action is executed or established by the action, resulting in a change in duties, rights, obligations, roles, etc, as was the case in punishing and rewarding somebody. The same distinctions hold for speech act sequences and their macro-structures. We have seen that each speech act has a specific function in the accomplishment of the main speech act, *eg* a preparatory, auxiliary, initiating/concluding or emphasizing function. Since speech acts are conventional, however, each act is part of a social interaction during which a social situation is changed or established. If I ask somebody whether he still has object *a*, the hearer will interpret my question as a preparation for another speech act, *eg* a question or request: he will modify his expectations accordingly and ask "*Why?*". Similarly, requests are more acceptable if plausible motivations for the request are given, whereas compliance with the request requires the expression of gratitude, *ie* the execution of a conventional obligation.

The same is true for the macro-speech act. That is, the change in the social situation operated by the discourse/sequence of speech acts as a whole identifies, delimitates or defines the macro-speech act involved. Only the commitments, duties or obligations established by the speech act as a whole are valid for subsequent action and interaction. Thus, in our first example, B has the right to expect that A will keep his promise to ask his wife about the bike, but at the same time is committed to A because of A's willingness to help B; conversely, A is committed to execute the promised action.

Parallel to these and other SOCIAL RELATIONS between the participants, we also have global changes in the 'mental' states of *knowledge and beliefs* of the participants. A knows that B needs a bike, and B knows that A is willing to sell him the bike. More particularly, the next day, A will be expecting to see B drop in in order to have the final decision and to conclude the transaction. This knowledge will exclude, for example, A's question to B the next day when B comes by: "*Hello Jack, what do you want?*". Such a question – after one day – would highly embarrass B.

Note that after the conversation A will have a whole set of information, *eg* that his neighbour's daughter Laura has her birthday next week and that Jack intends to paint the bike, but due to the rules of information reduction, this information will have a hierarchically subordinate place in the memory structure of the conversation, being dominated by a macro-proposition like 'Jack needs a bike'. If needed, Peter may of course in later situations retrieve the more detailed information through the macro-information, by inverse application of the macro-rules, *eg* by trying to recover the motivation of Jack's wish and request. Similarly, Peter may also draw all logical and inductive implications from the macro-proposition stored, *eg* that Jack has no bike for his daughter, or has no money to buy a new one. At the macro-level, however, the most important information for the success of future (inter-)action of both participants is that A knows that B needs a bike, and that B knows that A is willing to sell one. In a still broader framework of action, the complex request, executed in a sequence of speech interactions, functions itself as a preparatory action for the auxiliary action of B, viz buying a (cheap) bike, which is a normal condition for the main intended action, viz giving a bike as a present to his daughter. It is this main action which satisfies the wish, need or duty of B. The request is, as a whole, merely a preparation for the main action. In PLANNING this complex action, at least the following steps are executed:

[6]*a:*   i Laura has no bike, but needs one.
  b: ii Her birthday will be a good occasion to give her a bike.
  c: iii I will/wish to give her a bike for her birthday.
  d: iv I have no bike to give her.
  e: v How do I get a bike to give her?
  f: vi I must buy a bike.
  g: vii A bike is expensive, and I have no money.
  h: viii Could I get a cheap bike?
  i: ix Used bikes are cheap.
  j: x Where do I get a used bike?
  k: xi Jenny next door has an old bike she doesn't use.
  l: xii I'll ask her to sell it to me.

These are (some of) the steps in a strategy of everyday problem-solving needed in order to be able to execute a preferred action (giving a present). These premises of the practical reasoning will lead to the practical conclusion that Jack phones his neighbours, in order to execute the planned preparatory action: the request. Most probably, the precise 'content' of the conversation is not planned in detail. Which would be impossible because the context, especially the responses of the other participant, cannot fully be predicted. Hence, in the initial plan, the agent will only take up the MACRO-ACTION 'I'll ask the neighbours to sell me the bike' as a specific macro-speech act. In this (macro-)plan, the agent will only have to take into account the final state and the consequence of the request, viz 'The neighbour wants to sell me his bike', implying that I get the bike, which is a necessary condition for the execution of the main action (giving it as a present to my daughter).

We see that macro-speech acts have their functions in the planning and execution of global actions. Relevant in this broader context of interaction are only the final mental and social states brought about by the speech act as a whole.

4 Macro-speech acts and discourse
4.1
After an account of the cognitive and social functions of global speech acts, assigned to sequences of speech acts, we should briefly consider what is the relevance of these hypotheses in a pragmatics of discourse.[3] It seems natural, at this point, to try to relate SEMANTIC MACRO-STRUCTURES to PRAGMATIC MACRO-STRUCTURES, just as we systematically related sequences of sentences to sequences of speech acts in the previous chapter. One of the intuitive reasons for such an attempt is the fact that discourses such as dialogues and conversations may be assigned their global coherence and identification, and hence their global function, within the framework of a macro-speech act. We know that the conversation between Jack and Peter above is a coherent and acceptable dialogue because the utterance of such a dialogue text involves the accomplishment of one speech act. In fact, one of the bases for distinguishing different TYPES OF DISCOURSE, such as narratives or advertisements, is the possibility of assigning one, simple or complex, macro-speech act to the production of such a discourse.

4.2
From the analysis of the examples of global speech acts proposed above, it has already been seen that the meaning of a discourse is closely related to the speech act accomplished by the utterance of that discourse in a context of conversation. This is particularly obvious in the macro-operations yielding a global meaning of a passage or of the whole discourse. In Chapter 5 it has been shown that these semantic macro-operations define which information in a discourse is relatively important or relevant, viz by deletion or integration of less important information. It has been emphasized, however, that these operations also depend on certain pragmatic parameters, connected with the type of discourse involved. That is, what is important information not only depends on the semantic structure of the text but also

on the pragmatic functions of the discourse. Thus, we know intuitively that a (state) description in an everyday story is conventionally less crucial than the description of the main actions. The crime story beginning, for instance, with a description of the town only provides a setting for such major actions. The converse is true, however, in a tourist guide. Here the description of a town, building or landscape is more relevant than incidental personal actions or events of the writer. This is true for communicational reasons. The pragmatic function of the tourist guide discourse is to provide information for the reader about places he might want to visit. Such a discourse provides factual conditions for possible future actions of the reader. In story-telling conversations, however, there need not be such conditions. The function of narratives may be just to operate a change in the knowledge set of the hearer/reader and a change in his evaluation set with respect to the speaker/narrator, with respect to actions narrated, or with respect to the style of the story. Moreover, both participants may know that the events narrated only take place in some alternative world, so that no direct practical information about the actual world is transmitted (in fictional narrative).

Given a certain context of comprehension in which indications, such as title, name of author, preface, publisher, outer form of book/magazine/ newspaper, etc, are available, it is possible to infer the provisional hypothesis that the discourse is a story (or novel), tourist guide or newspaper bulletin. The hearer/reader will appropriately choose the macro-operations to apply to those parts of the discourse which are pragmatically most relevant.

Similarly, in the telephone conversation used in this chapter, pragmatic and social conventions will determine at the same time a semantic selection among the offered information. Since we do not normally phone people only to say *"Hello"* or *"How are you?"* – at least not neighbours we see every day – the meaning of the greeting will probably be marginal with respect to other meanings in the discourse. Similarly, we do not just ask somebody whether he still has his old bike, but only as a presuppositional preparation of another speech act, *eg* a request. This means that, semantically also, the proposition 'A has an old bike' is hierarchically subordinated to the proposition(s) underlying the sentence expressing the request-core: 'A wants to sell his bike to B'. In this respect the formation of semantic macro-structures is also a function of the pragmatic macro-structure.

4.3

On the other hand, it may more specifically be argued that the semantic macro-structure in turn determines the successfulness of the global speech act. Trivially, the macro-act must also have its specific 'content'. We do not just request something, but request somebody to do something (for us). It may well be the case that this particular content is not directly expressed in a particular sentence of the discourse, but is macro-entailed by the discourse as a whole. Typically so in indirect (polite, political/diplomatic) requests, advices, etc. In that case, the macro-proposition defines the specific content of the global speech act.

4.4

The most obvious ways in which macro-structures or macro-functions of discourse may appear is direct expression of such structures or functions in the discourse itself. Thus, at the beginning or end of a story we may typically have introductory formulae like "*Do you know the story of . . .*", "*I'll tell you about . . .*" or "*This was the story of . . .*" or simply "*This is the end of the story*".

The same holds for speech acts proper (we do not discuss here whether narration is a global speech act or not).[4] At the beginning of a longer speech we may say "*I'll give you some good advice:*", or at the end: "*This is a promise*". Such expressions are what we might call MACRO-PERFORMATIVES: the sentences themselves are not performative, but they express the illocutionary force of the discourse as a whole.

The same holds of course in the non-performative, descriptive use of speech act predicates, typically in summaries of discourse/speech acts: "*He warned me . . .*", "*She promised me . . .*", or "*He asked her . . .*". These predicates may refer to the macro-speech act performed by a speaker referred to and its content will in that case be the macro-structure of the original discourse, not necessarily one particular sentence from it.

4.5

That the pragmatic function of an utterance is often somehow expressed in the grammatical structure of a sentence is well known. The same may hold for the expression of macro-speech acts through the discourse as a whole. Given a command context, we may expect typical uses of pronouns (*eg du* in German), imperative syntactical structure, selection of typical lexical units, (the absence of) hedging, indirectness, etc, as a global constraint on the sequence. Similarly, the sentence will globally have to refer to an action of the hearer in the near future. We can make the general, albeit still vague, assertion that each global speech act determines the STYLE of the discourse, viz the set of grammatical structures resulting from choice-operations on semantically equivalent options. That such stylistic differences imply pragmatic differences appears from such pairs as "*Pass me the salt*" and "*Please, pass me the salt*" or "*Could you please pass me the salt?*".

4.6

Discourse type categories themselves may be pragmatically based. Whereas a SETTING in a story is part of a hierarchical structure which, as such, has no pragmatic function, there are discourse types where similar global structures at the same time organize the global speech act, *eg* in arguments. Thus, the PREMISE-CONCLUSION structure not only has semantic properties (*eg* implication of the latter by the former), but also determines the structure of the ACT of arguing: a conclusion is drawn, an inference made. It is exactly this property which differentiates connectives like *because* from sentence initial *so*. Similarly, we may give EXPLANATIONS by referring to causes or reasons for some event or we PROVE that some proposition is true or false.

At another level we have conventional organizations of discourse like

INTRODUCTION-PROBLEM-SOLUTION-CONCLUSION, in which the structure also parallels that of the corresponding global speech acts, and of action (*eg* problem solving) in general.[5]

4.7

We may conclude that the assignment of a global speech act to a discourse, and in particular to dialogue discourse in conversation, also contributes to the COHERENCE of such a discourse. There are connections not only between sentences (semantic) and macro-structures (propositional), but between the acts performed in uttering sentences and expressing macro-structures (linear and hierarchical). The content of a greeting, as such, need not be related to the semantic structure of the rest of the discourse, but the act of greeting may be a necessary condition for the accomplishment of a request, viz as a social wrapping and preparation of the goodwill of the hearer.

Just as we say, in the semantics, that a discourse has this topic or theme or is about such and such, we may say, in the pragmatics, that it had this 'point' or 'purpose' or 'function', thereby referring to the global speech act performed by uttering the discourse in the appropriate context. Indeed, as we said above, semantic and pragmatic macro-structures must run parallel in production, monitoring and interpretation: in communication the hearer must be made to know what major speech act is performed, and at the same time what the global content of the assertion, promise, request, advice or prohibition is.

4.8

The few remarks in this final chapter have been tentative and unsystematic, but at the same time, programmatic. Until now, little analysis has been given of the interdependence of global discourse structures and their pragmatic and social functions, and our observations are intended to demarcate a broad array of problems, both for linguistics proper and the theory of discourse in general. The crucial fact is that the cognitive constraints on information processing, which require the formation of semantic macro-structures and which organize acts and speech acts in global units, at the same time have social implications: they determine how individuals wish, decide, intend and plan, execute and control, 'see' and understand, their own and others' speaking and acting in the social context. Without them the individual would be lost among a myriad of detailed, incoherent pieces of visual, actional and propositional information. Operations, strategies, rules and categories are necessary to connect, generalize, organize, store and use that information in interaction. It is a major task of linguistics, discourse studies, psychology and the social sciences in the coming years to account for this systematic interdependence of meaning and action, *ie* of text and context.

Notes

1 The psychological basis for PLANS of action is discussed in Miller, Galanter and Pribram (1960). See also van Dijk (1976a).
2 There has been little explicit reference to macro-speech acts in the philosophy of speech acts. Fotion (1971) has discussed 'master speech acts', though from a different point of view.
3 The idea that utterances are to be studied as an integral part of the social situation in general, and of communicative interaction in particular is of course not new. It has its tradition in classical work by Malinowski and linguists influenced by this tradition (eg Firth, 1957, 1968). The most comprehensive theoretical framework in this sense is that of Pike (1967). Our discussion has tried to contribute insights into the more precise kinds and levels of coordination between language use and interaction, and to specify how sentences/speech acts function within global structural units.
4 See Searle (1975b) and van Dijk (1975d).
5 See van Dijk (1976b).

Bibliography

ALTHAM, J. E. J. (1971) *The Logic of Plurality*. London: Methuen

ALTHAM, J. E. J. and TENNANT, NEIL W. (1975) 'Sortal Quantification', in Keenan, ed, 46–58

ANDERSON, ALAN ROSS and BELNAP, NUEL D. (1975) *Entailment. The Logic of Relevance and Necessity*. Vol 1. New Haven: Princeton UP

AUSTIN, J. L. (1961) *Philosophical Papers*. London: Oxford UP

AUSTIN, J. L. (1962) *How to do things with words*. London: Oxford UP

BALLMER, THOMAS (1972) 'A Pilot Study in Text Grammar', Technical University of Berlin, mimeo

BANFIELD, ANN (1973) 'Narrative Style and the Grammar of Direct and Indirect Speech', *Foundations of Language*, 10, 1–39

BAR-HILLEL, YEHOSHUA, ed (1972) *Pragmatics of Natural Languages*. Dordrecht: Reidel

BARNARD, PHILIP JOHN (1974) *Structure and Content in the Retention of Prose*. PHD Diss, University College London

BARTLETT, F. C. (1932) *Remembering*. London: Cambridge UP

BARTSCH, RENATE (1972) *Adverbialsemantik*. Frankfurt: Athenaeum

BARTSCH, RENATE, and VENNEMANN, THEO (1972) *Semantic Structures*. Frankfurt: Athenaeum

BAUMAN, RICHARD, and SCHERZER, JOEL (1974) *Explorations in the Ethnography of Speaking*. London: Cambridge UP

BERNSTEIN, BASIL (1971) *Class, Codes and Control*. London: Routledge & Kegan Paul

BIERWISCH, MANFRED (1965a) 'Review of Z. S. Harris, *Discourse Analysis* reprints', *Linguistics*, 13, 61–73

BIERWISCH, MANFRED (1965b) 'Poetik und Linguistik', in H. Kreuzer and R. Gunzenhäuser, eds *Mathematik und Dichtung*. Munich: Nymphenburger. English transl. in Donald C. Freeman, ed *Linguistics and Literary Style*. New York: Holt, Rinehart & Winston, 1970, 96–115

BINKLEY, ROBERT, BRONAUGH, RICHARD, and MARRAS, AUSONIO, eds (1971) *Agent. Action. Reason*. Oxford: Blackwell

BOBROW, DANIEL G., and COLLINS, ALLAN, eds (1975) *Representation and Understanding. Studies in Cognitive Science*. New York: Academic Press

BRENNENSTUHL, WALTRAUD (1974) *Vorbereitungen zur Entwicklung einer sprach-adäquaten Handlungslogik*. Technical University, Berlin, Diss

CARE, NORMAN, S., and LANDESMAN, CHARLES, eds (1968) *Readings in the Theory of Action*. Bloomington: Indiana UP
CARNAP, RUDOLF (1956) *Meaning and Necessity*. Chicago: University of Chicago Press
CARPENTER, PATRICIA, and JUST, MARCEL, eds (1977) *Cognitive Processes in Comprehension*. Proceedings of the XIIth Carnegie-Mellon Symposium on Cognition. Hillsdale, NJ: Erlbaum
CHARNIAK, EUGENE (1972) *Towards a Model of Children's Story Comprehension*. PHD Diss, MIT, Cambridge, Mass
CHARNIAK, EUGENE (1975) 'Organization and Inference in a Frame-like System of Common Sense Knowledge'. Castagnola: Istituto per gli Studi Semantici e Cognitivi
CHOMSKY, NOAM (1966) *Cartesian Linguistics*. Cambridge, Mass: MIT Press
CHOMSKY, NOAM (1968) *Language and Mind*. New York: Harcourt, Brace & World
CLARK, HERBERT H. (1973) 'Comprehension and the Given-New Contract', Paper contributed to the Symposium 'The Role of Grammar in Interdisciplinary Research', Bielefeld
Communications 4 (1964) *Recherches sémiotiques*. Paris: Seuil
Communications 8 (1966) *L'analyse structurale du récit*. Paris: Seuil
COLE, PETER, and MORGAN, JERRY L., eds (1975) *Syntax and Semantics*. Vol 3, *Speech Acts*. New York: Academic Press
COPI, IRVING M., and GOULD, JAMES A., eds (1967) *Contemporary Readings in Logical Theory*. New York – London: Macmillan
CRESSWELL, M. J. (1973) *Logics and Languages*. London: Methuen
CROTHERS, EDWARD (1975) *Paragraph Structure Description*. Boulder: University of Colorado, Dept of Psychology

DAHL, ÖSTEN (1969) *Topic and Comment*. Stockholm: Almqvist & Wiksell
DAHL, ÖSTEN (1976) 'What is New Information?', in Nils Erik Enkvist and Viljo Kohonen, eds *Approaches to Word Order*, Reports on Text Linguistics, Åbo, 37–50
DAVIDSON, DONALD (1967) 'The Logical Form of Action Sentences', in Rescher, ed, 81–120
DAVIDSON, DONALD, and HARMAN, GILBERT, eds (1972) *Semantics of Natural Language*. Dordrecht: Reidel
DASCAL, MARCELO, and MARGALIT, AVISHAI (1974) 'A new "revolution" in linguistics? – "Text grammars" versus "sentence grammars"', *Theoretical Linguistics*, 1, 195–213
VAN DIJK, TEUN A. (1971a) *Moderne Literatuurteorie* [Modern Theory of Literature]. Amsterdam: van Gennep
VAN DIJK, TEUN A. (1971b) *Taal. Tekst. Teken* [Language. Text. Sign]. Amsterdam: Athenaeum, Polak and van Gennep
VAN DIJK, TEUN A. (1972a) *Some Aspects of Text Grammars*. The Hague: Mouton
VAN DIJK, TEUN A. (1972b) *Beiträge zur generativen Poetik*. Munich: Bayerischer Schulbuch Verlag
VAN DIJK, TEUN A. (1973a) 'Text Grammar and Text Logic', in Petöfi and Rieser, eds, 17–78
VAN DIJK, TEUN A. (1973b) 'Connectives in Text Grammar and Text Logic' Paper contributed to the Second Int. Symposium on Text Linguistics, Kiel. To appear in: van Dijk and Petöfi, eds, 1977
VAN DIJK, TEUN A. (1973c) 'A Note on Linguistic Macro-structures', in A. P. ten Cate and P. Jordens, eds *Linguistische Perspektiven*. Tübingen: Niemeyer, 75–87

VAN DIJK, TEUN A. (1974a) '"Relevance" in Grammar and Logic', Paper contributed to the Int. Congress on Relevance Logics, St. Louis

VAN DIJK, TEUN A. (1974b) 'Philosophy of Action and Theory of Narrative', University of Amsterdam, mimeo. *Poetics* 5 (1976) 287–338. Short version "Action, Action Description, Narrative" in *New Literary History*, 6, 1975, 273–94

VAN DIJK, TEUN A. (1974c) 'A Note on the Partial Equivalence of Text Grammars and Context Grammars', University of Amsterdam, mimeo. To appear in Martin Lofin and James Silverberg, eds, *Discourse and Inference in Cognitive Anthropology*. The Hague, Mouton, 1977

VAN DIJK, TEUN A. (1975a) 'Issues in the Pragmatics of Discourse', University of Amsterdam, mimeo

VAN DIJK, TEUN A. (1975b) 'Formal Semantics of Metaphorical Discourse', in Teun A. van Dijk and János S. Petöfi, eds *Theory of Metaphor*, special issue *Poetics* 14/15, 173–98

VAN DIJK, TEUN A. (1975c) 'Recalling and Summarizing Complex Discourse' University of Amsterdam, mimeo

VAN DIJK, TEUN A. (1975d) 'Pragmatics and Poetics', in van Dijk, ed, 23–57

VAN DIJK, TEUN A. (1976a) 'Frames, Macro-structures and Discourse Comprehension', Paper contributed to the XIIth Carnegie-Mellon Symposium on Cognition, Pittsburgh. To appear in Carpenter and Just, eds 1977

VAN DIJK, TEUN A. (1976b) 'Complex Semantic Information Processing', Paper contributed to the workshop on linguistics in documentation, Stockholm, University of Amsterdam, mimeo

VAN DIJK, TEUN A., ed (1975) *Pragmatics of Language and Literature*. Amsterdam: North Holland

VAN DIJK, TEUN A., and KINTSCH, WALTER (1977) 'Cognitive Psychology and Discourse. Recalling and Summarizing Stories', in Dressler, ed

VAN DIJK, TEUN A., and PETÖFI, JÁNOS S., eds (1977) *Grammars and Descriptions*. Berlin – New York: de Gruyter

DIK, SIMON C. (1968) *Coordination*. Amsterdam: North Holland

DONELLAN, KEITH S. (1970) 'Proper Names and Identifying Descriptions', *Synthese*, 21, 335–58

DRESSLER, WOLFGANG U. (1970) 'Textsyntax', *Lingua e Stile*, 2, 191–214

DRESSLER, WOLFGANG U. (1972) *Einführung in die Textlinguistik*. Tübingen: Niemeyer

DRESSLER, WOLFGANG U., ed (1977) *Trends in Textlinguistics*. Berlin – New York: de Gruyter

DRESSLER, WOLFGANG U., and SCHMIDT, SIEGFRIED J. (1973) *Textlinguistik. Eine kommentierte Bibliographie*. Munich: Fink

FILLMORE, CHARLES (1974) 'Pragmatics and the Description of Discourse', *Berkeley Studies in Syntax and Semantics*, Vol I, Ch 5

FIRTH J. R. (1957) *Papers in Linguistics*. London: Oxford UP

FIRTH, J. R. (1968) *Selected Papers of J. R. Firth 1952–1959*, ed by F. R. Palmer. London: Longman

FOTION, N. (1971) 'Master Speech Acts', *Philosophical Quarterly*, 21, 232–43

VAN FRAASSEN, BAS C. (1967) 'Meaning Relations among Predicates', *Noûs*, 161–79

VAN FRAASSEN, BAS C. (1969) 'Meaning Relations and Modalities', *Noûs*, 3, 155–67

FRANCK, DOROTHEA (1975) 'Zur Analyse indirekter Sprechakte', in Veronika Ehrich and Peter Finke, eds, *Beiträge zur Grammatik und Pragmatik*. Kronberg: Scriptor, 219–32

FRANCK, DOROTHEA (1977) *Grammatik und Konversation*. Diss, University of Amsterdam. Kronberg: Scriptor

FREEDLE, ROY O., and CARROLL, JOHN B., eds (1972) *Language Comprehension and the Acquisition of Knowledge*. Washington, DC: Winston/Wiley

GABBAY, DOV M. (1972) 'A General Theory of the Conditional in Terms of a Ternary Operator', *Theoria*, 38, 97–104

GEACH, PETER THOMAS (1962) *Reference and Generality*. Ithaca: Cornell UP

GERBNER, *et al*, eds (1969) *The Analysis of Communication Content*. New York: Wiley

GODDARD, LEONARD, and ROUTLEY, RICHARD (1973) *The Logic of Significance and Context*. New York: Halsted Press/Wiley

GOFFMAN, IRVING (1971) *Relations in Public*. New York: Harper & Row

GREENBAUM, SIDNEY, ed (1977) *Language and Acceptability*. The Hague: Mouton

GRICE, H. PAUL (1967) *Logic and Conversation*. Harvard, Henry James Lectures, mimeo

GRICE, H. PAUL (1971) 'Utterer's Meaning, Sentence-Meaning and Word-Meaning', in John R. Searle, ed *The Philosophy of Language*. London: Oxford UP

GROENENDIJK, JEROEN, and STOKHOF, MARTIN (1975) 'Modality and Conversational Information', *Theoretical Linguistics*, 2, 61–112

GROENENDIJK, JEROEN, and STOKHOF, MARTIN (1976) 'Some Aspects of the Semantics and Pragmatics of Performative Sentences', in R. Bartsch, J. Groenendijk and M. Stokhof, eds *Amsterdam Papers in Formal Grammar*, Vol 1, University of Amsterdam

✓GUENTHNER, FRANZ (1975) 'On the Semantics of Metaphor', *Poetics* 14/15 199–220

GUMPERZ JOHN D., and HYMES, DELL, eds (1972) *Directions in socio-linguistics. The ethnography of communication*. New York: Holt, Rinehart & Winston

HALLIDAY, M. A. K. (1973) *Explorations in the Functions of Language*. London: Arnold

HALLIDAY, M. A. K., and HASAN, RUQAIYA (1976) *Cohesion in English*. London: Longman

HAMBURGER, KÄTE (1968) *Die Logik der Dichtung*, 2nd edn. Stuttgart: Klett

HARRIS, ZELLIG S. (1963) *Discourse Analysis Reprints*. The Hague: Mouton

HILPINEN, RISTO, ed (1971) *Deontic Logic: Introductory and Systematic Readings*. Dordrecht: Reidel

HIMMELFARB, SAMUEL, and HENDRICKSON EAGLY, ALICE, eds (1974) *Readings in Attitude Change*. New York: Wiley

HINTIKKA, JAAKKO (1962) *Knowledge and Belief*. Ithaca: Cornell UP

HINTIKKA, JAAKKO (1971) 'Semantics for Propositional Attitudes', in Linsky, ed, 145– 67

HINTIKKA, JAAKKO (1973) *Logic, Language Games and Information*. London: Oxford UP

HINTIKKA, JAAKKO., MORAVCSIK, J. M. E. and SUPPES, P. eds (1973) *Approaches to Natural Language*. Dordrecht: Reidel

✓HOLSTI, OLE (1969) *Content Analysis for the Social Sciences and the Humanities*. Reading, Mass: Addison Wesley

✓HOVLAND, CARL I. *et al* (1957) *The Order of Presentation in Persuasion*. New Haven: Yale UP

HUGHES, G. E., and CRESSWELL, M. J. (1968) *An Introduction to Modal Logic*. London: Methuen

HYMES, DELL (1972) 'Models of the Interaction of Language and Social Life', in Gumperz and Hymes, eds 35–71

KASHER ASA (1972) 'A Step toward a Theory of Linguistic Performance', in Bar-Hillel, ed, 84–93

KASHER, ASA, ed (1976) *Language in Focus: Foundations, Methods and Systems*. Dordrecht: Reidel.

KEARNS, JOHN T. (1975) 'Sentences and Propositions', in Alan Ross Anderson, *et al*, eds *The Logical Enterprise*. New Haven Yale UP, 61–86

KEENAN, EDWARD L., ed (1975) *Formal Semantics of Natural Language*. London: Cambridge UP

KEENAN, JANICE (1975) *The Role of Episodic Information in the Assessment of Semantic Memory Representation for Sentences*. PHD Diss, University of Colorado, Boulder

KEMPSON, RUTH M. (1975) *Presupposition and the Delimitation of Semantics*. London: Cambridge UP

KINTSCH, WALTER (1974) *The Representation of Meaning in Memory*. Hillsdale, NJ: Erlbaum

KINTSCH, WALTER (1976) 'Comprehending Stories', Paper contributed to the Twelfth Carnegie–Mellon Symposium on Cognition, Pittsburgh. To appear in Carpenter and Just, eds, 1977

KINTSCH, WALTER, and VAN DIJK, TEUN A. (1975) 'Comment on se rappelle et on résume des histoires', *Langages*, 40, 98–116

KRIPKE, SAUL (1972) 'Naming and Necessity', in Davidson and Harman, eds 253–355

KUMMER, WERNER (1975) *Grundlagen der Texttheorie*. Hamburg: Rowohlt

KURODA, S.-Y. (1975) 'Reflections on the Foundations of Narrative Theory – from a Linguistic Point of View', in van Dijk, ed 107–40

KUIPERS, BENJAMIN K. (1975) 'A Frame for Frames: Representing Knowledge for Recognition', in Bobrow and Collins, eds 151–84

LABOV, WILLIAM (1972*a*) *Language in the Inner City*. Philadelphia: University of Pennsylvania Press

LABOV, WILLIAM (1972*b*) *Sociolinguistic Patterns*. Philadelphia: University of Pennsylvania Press

LAKOFF, GEORGE (1968) 'Counterparts or the problem of reference in a Transformational Grammar', Paper LSA meeting, July, mimeo

LAKOFF, ROBIN (1971) 'If's, and's, and but's about Conjunction', in Charles J. Fillmore and D. Terrence Langendoen, eds *Studies in Linguistic Semantics*. New York: Holt, Rinehart & Winston, 115–50

LANG, EWALD (1973) *Studien zur Semantik der koordinativen Verknüpfung*. Diss, Akademie der Wissenschaften, Berlin, DDR

LAVER, JOHN, and HUTCHESON, SANDY, eds (1972) *Communication in Face to Face Interaction*. Harmondsworth: Penguin Books

LEECH, GEOFFREY N. (1969) *Towards a Semantic Description of English*. London: Longman

LEECH, GEOFFREY N. (1974) *Semantics*. Harmondsworth: Penguin Books

LEWIS, DAVID (1968) *Convention*. Cambridge, Mass: MIT Press

LEWIS, DAVID (1970) 'General Semantics', *Synthese*, 22, 18–67

LEWIS, DAVID (1973) *Counterfactuals*. Oxford: Blackwell

LIEB, HANS-HEINRICH (1976) 'On Relating Pragmatics, Linguistics and Non-semiotic Disciplines', in Kasher, ed, 217–50

LINSKY, LEONARD (1967) *Referring*. London: Routledge & Kegan Paul

LINSKY, LEONARD, ed (1971) *Reference and Modality*. London: Oxford UP

LONGACRE, ROBERT E. (1970) *Discourse, Paragraph and Sentence Structure in Selected Philippine Languages*. Santa Ana: Summer Institute of Linguistics

MARANDA, PIERRE, ed (1972) *Mythology*. Harmondsworth: Penguin Books

MASSEY, GERALD J. (1970) *Understanding Symbolic Logic*. New York: Harper & Row

MARTIN J. (1975) 'Facts and the Semantics of Gerunds', *Journal of Philosophical Logic*, 4, 439–54

MARTIN, R. M. (1967) 'Facts: What they are and what they are not', *American Philosophical Quarterly*, 4, 269–80

MEYER, BONNIE F. (1975) *The Organization of Prose and its Effects on Memory*. Amsterdam: North Holland

MILLER, GEORGE A., GALANTER, EUGENE, and PRIBRAM, KARL H. (1960) *Plans and the Structure of Behavior*. New York: Holt, Rinehart & Winston

MINSKY, MARVIN (1975) 'A Framework for Representing Knowledge', in P. Winston, ed *The Psychology of Computer Vision*. New York: McGraw Hill

MONTAGUE, RICHARD (1974) *Formal Philosophy*. ed by Richmond H. Thomason. New Haven: Yale UP

MORRIS, CHARLES W. (1946) *Signs, Language and Behavior*. New York: Prentice Hall

NORMAN, DONALD A., and RUMELHART, DAVID E., eds (1975) *Explorations in Cognition*. San Francisco: Freeman

PAUL, I. H. (1959) *Studies in Remembering*. *Psychological Issues*, Monograph Series 1, 2

PEIRCE, CHARLES SANDERS (1960) *Collected Papers*, Vol 2. Cambridge, Mass: Harvard UP

PETÖFI, JÁNOS S., and FRANCK, DOROTHEA, eds *Präsuppositionen in der Linguistik und Philosophie/Presuppositions in Linguistics and Philosophy*. Frankfurt: Athenaeum

PETÖFI, JÁNOS S., and RIESER, HANNES, eds (1973) *Studies in Text Grammars*. Dordrecht: Reidel

PIKE, KENNETH L. (1967) *Language in Relation to a Unified Theory of Human Behavior*. The Hague: Mouton

PLETT, HEINRICH F. (1975) *Textwissenschaft und Textanalyse*. Heidelberg: Quelle & Meyer, UTB Taschenbücher

PÖRN, INGMAR (1971) *Elements of Social Analysis*. Uppsala, *Filosofiska Studier*, Uppsala University, Dept of Philosophy

PROPP, VLADIMIR (1968) *Morphology of the Folk-Tale* [1928] transl from the Russian. 2nd edn. Bloomington: Indiana UP

REICHENBACH, HANS (1947) *Elements of Symbolic Logic*. London: Macmillan

RESCHER, NICHOLAS (1968) *Topics in Philosophical Logic*. Dordrecht: Reidel

RESCHER, NICHOLAS (1973) *The Coherence Theory of Truth*. London: Oxford UP

RESCHER, NICHOLAS (1975) *A Theory of Possibility*. Pittsburgh: Pittsburgh UP

RESCHER, NICHOLAS, ed (1967) *The Logic of Decision and Action*. Pittsburgh: Pittsburgh UP

ROMMETVEIT, RAGNAR (1974) *On Message Structure*. New York: Wiley

ROUTLEY, RICHARD, and MEYER, ROBERT K. (1973) 'The Semantics of Entailment', in Hughes Leblanc, ed *Truth, Syntax and Modality*. Amsterdam: North Holland, 199–243

RUMELHART, DAVID E. (1975) 'Notes on a Schema for Stories', in Bobrow and Collins, eds, 211–36

SADOCK, JERRY M. (1975) *Toward a Linguistic Theory of Speech Acts*. New York: Academic Press

SCHANK, ROGER C. (1975) 'The Structure of Episodes in Memory', in Bobrow and Collins, eds, 237–72

SCHIFFER, STEPHEN R. (1972) *Meaning*. London: Oxford UP

SCHMIDT, SIEGFRIED J. *Texttheorie*. Munich: Fink (UTB)

SEARLE, JOHN R. (1969) *Speech Acts*. London: Cambridge UP

SEARLE, JOHN R. (1975a) 'Indirect Speech Acts', in Cole and Morgan, eds, 59–82

SEARLE, JOHN R. (1975b) 'The Logical Status of Fictional Discourse', *New Literary History*, 6, 319–32

SOMMERS, FRED (1963) 'Types and Ontology', *Philosophical Review*, 72, 327–63

SGALL, PETR, HAJIČOVÁ, EVA, and BENEŠOVÁ, EVA (1973) *Topic, Focus and Generative Semantics*. Kronberg: Scriptor

SOSA, ERNEST, ed (1975) *Causation and Conditionals*. London: Oxford UP

STALNAKER, ROBERT C., and THOMASON, RICHMOND H. (1970) 'A Semantic Analysis of Conditional Logic', *Theoria*, 36, 23–42

STANZEL, FRANZ K. (1964) *Typische Formen des Romans*. Göttingen: Vandenhoeck & Ruprecht

STEINBERG, DANNY, and JAKOBOVITS, LEON, eds (1971) *Semantics*. London: Cambridge UP

STRAWSON, P. F. (1952) *Introduction to Logical Theory*. London: Methuen

STRAWSON, P. F. (1971) *Logico-linguistic Papers*. London: Methuen

STRAWSON, P. F. (1974) *Subject and Predicate in Logic and Grammar*. London: Methuen

SUDNOW, DAVID, ed (1972) *Studies in Social Interaction*. New York: Free Press

THOMASON, RICHMOND H. (1970) *Symbolic Logic*. New York: Macmillan

THOMASON, RICHMOND H. (1972) 'A Semantic Theory of Sortal Incorrectness', *Journal of Philosophical Logic*, 1, 209–58

THOMASON, RICHMOND H. (1973*a*) 'Philosophy and Formal Semantics', in Hughes Leblanc, ed *Truth, Syntax and Modality*. Amsterdam: North Holland

THOMASON, RICHMOND H. (1973*b*) 'Semantics, Pragmatics, Conversation and Presupposition', University of Pittsburgh, mimeo

THORNDYKE, PERRY W. (1975) *Cognitive Structures in Human Story Comprehension and Memory*. PHD Diss, Stanford

TULVING, ENDEL, and DONALDSON, WAYNE, eds (1972) *Organization of Memory*. New York: Academic Press

URQUHART, ALASDAIR (1972) 'Semantics for Relevance Logics', *The Journal of Symbolic Logic*, 37, 159–69

WHITE, ALAN R, ed (1968) *The Philosophy of Action*. London: Oxford UP

WILSON, DEIRDRE (1975) *Presuppositions and non-truth conditional Semantics*. New York – London: Academic Press

WINOGRAD, TERRY (1975) 'Frame Representations and the Declarative-Procedural Controversy', in Bobrow and Collins, eds 185–210

VON WRIGHT, GEORG-HENRIK (1957) 'On Conditionals', in G. H. von Wright, *Logical Studies*. London: Routledge & Kegan Paul, 127–65

VON WRIGHT, GEORG-HENRIK (1963) *Norm and Action*. London: Routledge & Kegan Paul

VON WRIGHT, GEORG-HENRIK (1967) 'The Logic of Action: A Sketch', in Rescher, ed 121–36

WUNDERLICH, DIETER (1976) *Studien zur Sprechakttheorie*. Frankfurt: Athenaeum

WUNDERLICH, DIETER, ed (1972) *Linguistische Pragmatik*. Frankfurt: Athenaeum

Index

Purpose —
to locate what C.V.S call
the point or So What? of the
article in question. — Tells whether is
deductive or inductive ?

audience / author accomodation
defined by use & relativity of proximity class

style & method — patterns of
normalization
verification

/
lexicon, both
sentence & both
sentence cognitively

pragmatics — ground
analysis/ relativity in
grammar/ syntactic symbol
the uses to sense to
groups to understanding/ uses

①
②
③